MORAL THEOLOGY TODAY:
CERTITUDES AND DOUBTS

CONTRIBUTORS TO THIS VOLUME

His Eminence
  Joseph Cardinal Ratzinger
  Prefect of the Sacred
  Congregation for the
  Doctrine of the Faith
  Rome

The Reverend
  Benedict M. Ashley, O.P., Ph.D.
  Professor of Moral Theology
  Aquinas Institute of
  Theology
  St. Louis University
  St. Louis, Missouri

Joseph Boyle, Ph.D.
  Associate Professor of
  Philosophy
  Center for Thomistic Studies
  University of St. Thomas
  Houston, Texas

Gerard Brunelle
  Director
  Family-Action-Famille
  Ottawa, Ontario, Canada

Lisa Sowle Cahill, Ph.D.
  Associate Professor of
  Theology
  Boston College
  Chestnut Hill, Massachusetts

The Reverend John R. Connery,
S.J., S.T.D.
  Cody Professor of Theology
  Loyola University of Chicago
  Chicago, Illinois

The Reverend Thomas J. Deidun,
I.D., D.S.S.
  Lecturer in New Testament
  Studies
  Heythrop College
  University of London
  London, England

The Reverend Monsignor
  Francis X. DiLorenzo, S.T.D.
  Associate Professor of Moral
  Theology
  St. Charles Borromeo
  Seminary
  Philadelphia, Pennsylvania

The Reverend Thomas P. Doyle,
O.P., J.C.D.
  Secretary
  The Apostolic Pronunciature
  Washington, D.C.

The Reverend John Gallagher,
C.S.B., S.T.D.
  Associate Professor of
  Theology
  St. Michael College
  Toronto, Ontario, Canada

The Reverend Karl Kertelge,
Dr. Theol.
  Professor of New Testament
  Exegesis
  University of Munster
  Munster, West Germany

The Rev. Monsignor James
McHugh, S.T.D.
  Director of the Diocesan
  Development
  Program for Natural Family
  Planning
  Washington, D.C.

Gene Outka, Ph.D.
  Dwight Professor of
  Philosophy and
  Christian Ethics
  Yale University
  New Haven, Connecticut

The Reverend Val J. Peter, S.T.D.,
J.C.D.
  Professor of Theology
  Creighton University
  Omaha, Nebraska

MORAL THEOLOGY TODAY:
CERTITUDES AND DOUBTS

The Pope John Center
Saint Louis, Missouri

Nihil Obstat:
   Rev. Robert F. Coerver, C.M., S.T.D.
   Censor Deputatus

Imprimatur:
   The Most Rev. Edward J. O'Donnell, D.D., V.G.
   Archdiocese of St. Louis

                                        May 1, 1984

The Nihil Obstat and Imprimatur are a declaration that a book or pamphlet is considered to be free from doctrinal or moral error. It is not implied that those who have granted the Nihil Obstat and Imprimatur agree with the contents, opinions, or statements expressed.

Library of Congress Cataloging in Publication Data
Main entry under title:

Moral theology today.

      Includes bibliographies and index.
      1. Christian ethics — Catholic authors — Addresses, essays, lectures. 2. Catholic Church — Doctrines — Addresses, essays, lectures. I. Pope John XXIII Medical-Moral Research and Education Center.
BJ1249.M67   1984   241'.042   84-11714
ISBN 0-935372-14-8

Contents

PREFACE

This book presents the content of the workshop conducted for 240 bishops of North and Central America and the Caribbean by the Pope John Center in Dallas, TX, Feb. 6-10, 1984. The Knights of Columbus generously funded this workshop as well as the three previous ones in Dallas in 1980, 1981, and 1983. We congratulate the Knights and their Supreme Knight, Mr. Virgil Dechant, for their vision and magnanimity in underwriting these programs which permit Catholic bishops, not only from the United States but from other nations and cultures, to study together the profound issues facing the Church today.

The Pope John XXIII Medical-Moral Research and Education Center was founded in St. Louis, MO, in 1973. The Center's staff has developed it as a research and education center responding to emerging ethical issues in health care from the perspective of the Judeo-Christian tradition and Catholic teaching. The many publications of the Center, listed at the back of this volume, and its monthly newsletter, *Ethics and Medics,* indicate the wide range of research and education the Center has undertaken in its first decade.

This fourth workshop the Center conducted for bishops developed almost spontaneously from the considerations in the previous three. Each of these had examined specific issues as the published proceedings indicate: *New Technologies of Birth and Death,* (1980), *Human Sexuality and Personhood,* (1981), and *Technological Powers and the Person,* (1983). Important discussions in each of these workshops pointed to an essential underlying question — the exceptionless character of certain basic moral norms in Catholic teaching.

Hence the planning committee for this workshop undertook to examine fundamental moral theology within the Church today. They designed the workshop to deal on three successive days with certitudes in moral theology (Part II of this volume), doubts in moral theology (Part III), and applied moral theology (Part IV).

Under the heading of "doubts," the workshop addressed the controversy about exceptionless moral norms which has been simmering within Catholic moral theology for the past 15 years. This controversy arose in the context of Pope Paul VI's 1968 encyclical, *Humanae Vitae (Of Human Life)*, which reaffirmed the traditional Catholic teaching that a deliberate and direct contraceptive intervention in conjugal relations is morally wrong without exceptions. Part III of this volume sheds considerable light on this controversy which has broadened to challenge the Church's understanding of human acts and morality itself. The discussion in chapter 10 which concludes Part III indicates that the core Catholic teaching on contraception has not been changed even though some theologians have used the new moral methodology called proportionalism or teleologism in a way which would dissent from Church teaching.

The planning committee for the workshop invited His Eminence Joseph Cardinal Ratzinger, who is both an internationally acclaimed theologian and the Prefect of the Sacred Congregation for the Doctrine of the Faith, to keynote this workshop and to summarize its deliberations at the end. Despite his demanding schedule, Cardinal Ratzinger graciously accepted the invitation and prepared the profound and challenging keynote address which appears as Part I of this volume. Cardinal Ratzinger diligently attended all the sessions of the workshop and presented a masterfully succinct summary at the end which appears here as the Epilogue. We are most grateful to him for the magnificent role he played in this dynamic theological enterprise.

The 13 other speakers at the workshop who are listed at the beginning of this volume each contributed particular expertise and, without exception, made brilliant presentations to the bishop participants. We are pleased to present the final, footnoted versions of their lectures plus their responses in the discussion chapters which they kindly reviewed and edited for publication.

This workshop was designed to assist the bishops in clarifying for their priests and people the certitudes and doubts in contemporary moral theology. We believe that this published account of the workshop will not only assist the bishops themselves but will serve a much larger audience of theologians, seminary students, parish priests and lay women and men who are struggling with the controversial issues within Catholic moral teaching.

Hence we repeat our gratitude to the Knights of Columbus for their indispensable financial assistance. We are grateful to His Holiness, Pope John Paul II, for the message which he sent to the bishops at the workshop, and to Most Reverend Daniel E. Pilarczyk, Archbishop of Cincinnati and Chairman of the Board of the Pope John Center, for his wise assistance and guidance. We wish to thank all the members of the Board of the Pope John Center for their continuing encouragement, especially the bishop members of the Board, The Most Reverend Daniel A. Cronin and The Most Reverend John S. Cummins, and Mr. Frank J. Schneider who served on the planning committee along with our former Board Chairman, The Most Reverend Bernard F. Law, Archbishop of Boston. We are likewise grateful to the Catholic Health Association staff for their cooperation with our work, and to the President, Mr. John E. Curley, Jr., who joined in welcoming the bishops to Dallas.

This volume would not have appeared without the cooperation of the entire Center staff which joined in conducting the workshop. For this publication we are also grateful to Father Thomas J. Herron of the Sacred Congregation for the Doctrine of the Faith who assisted in the English translations of Cardinal Ratzinger's manuscripts. Father Larry D. Lossing, the Director of Communications for the Pope John Center, designed the cover and assisted with the page layout of this book. Mr. Timothy Cooper of the Pope John Center did copyreading for the entire volume. Miss Tina Sgroi typed the several versions of chapters 5, 10, and 15, while Mrs. Jo Anne Probst and Mrs. Charlene Renda, also of the staff, assisted with other phases of the book's preparation.

We are pleased to dedicate this Volume to the happy memory of the late Pope John XXIII (1958-1963) whose inspiration guides our endeavors at the Center to bring the rich theological tradition of the Roman Catholic Church to bear on emerging medical-moral issues.

June 15, 1984   The Reverend Donald G. McCarthy, Editor

To my brother Bishops
from North and Central America
and the Caribbean

It is a particular joy for me to greet you as you gather to reflect once again on the mystery of life in Christ Jesus. I know that the great generosity of the Knights of Columbus has made it possible for so many of you to come together to listen, to share, and to ponder the riches of life lived in the grace of God. This opportunity, provided by the Pope John XXIII Center, is very rare, not only because you all have such demanding schedules, but also because you are separated by such great distances from one another. My hope is that you will value this time you have together for the special occasion it is. What you are doing here will not be time taken away from your ministry, but time spent to strengthen it, since as Bishops you have been called to teach, to sanctify and to govern. You can do no better than to give of your time and energy this week to discern more clearly what the Spirit of Jesus is teaching in the Church. Your understanding of that teaching will directly affect your leadership in the community of faith: that leadership, by the Lord's own will and strength, will bring his people closer to him, thus making them the holy people they have been called to be.

In the course of the next few days, you will study various issues in the wide field of moral theology. The multiple problems of today's world, seen with ever greater urgency through modern means of communication, will surely receive the attention they deserve, and I shall not try to list them here. Nevertheless, I would like to offer you a context within which, and by means of which, you will be able to penetrate the sometimes dark cloud which has from time to time obscured the Church's teachings in the area of morality and Christian living. That context is none other than the person of the Lord Jesus himself, who said, "I am the way, the truth and the life" (Jn 14:6). His words are both a fact and a promise: not only does he represent the sole path to eternal life, but he pledges us his own grace, the fruit of the Redemption, that perennial power released into the world by his Cross and Resurrection. We should never fail to consider this grace of his: it is the only hope we have. Jesus is also the truth: not a dry, sterile sort of truth, but a *person*, present just as truly in our world as he was in the world of two thousand years ago. When we study moral theology, we ask: "What difference does Jesus make in our lives?"

And Jesus is life. The facts of his own historical existence make more and more clear this central fact: life in Christ Jesus is life directed by and toward holiness, because God, the source and goal of all life, is holy. In a deep sense, then, it can be said, it *must* be said: the Church is for life! Her Magisterium is a living and active reality. In the members of the Church, joined by one faith, sustained by hope, and living in love, it is the Lord Jesus himself who is alive in the world. Through the Gospel the Church preaches life and in the sacraments she celebrates life: the Church is alive in the Lord!

It is no wonder, then, that human life, in all the richness of its existence, is cherished by the Church as the sacred reality it is. Your study of moral theology will deepen your appreciation of life. When, by your ministry in the local churches entrusted to your pastoral care, you lead your people to honor, to defend, to choose life in all its dimensions, you will be bringing them to an ever closer relationship with the triune God, who is the eternal community of life and love. In doing this for your people, be assured that you can serve them in no better way. Through your pastoral ministry you can communicate nothing more precious than a sharing in the life of the Most Holy Trinity: Father, Son and Holy Spirit, to whom be glory and honor for ever and ever.

From the Vatican, January 25, 1984

Joannes Paulus PP. II

Part I:
Moral Theology Today

Bishops, Theologians, and Morality

His Eminence Joseph Cardinal Ratzinger

The word "moral" is slowly beginning to regain a place of honor. For it is becoming ever more clear that we should not do everything we can do. It is becoming ever more evident that the peculiar sickness of the modern world is its failings in morality.

Recently a Russian author has said:

Mankind today, with his dread of missiles, is like a man who lives in continual fear that his house will be burned down. He can think of nothing else but how to prevent the arson. In so doing, he does not notice that he has cancer. He will not die of arson, but by the inner decomposition of his body brought on by the alien organism of the cancer.

So mankind today, says this author, is in danger of being ruined from within, by his own moral decay. But instead of strug-

3

gling against this life-threatening disease, he stares as though hypnotized at the external danger, which is only a byproduct of his own inner moral disease.

Still, it has become a rather common observation that the value placed upon technical expertise is out of all proportion when compared to the scant attention paid to moral development. Today we seem to know more about how to *build* bombs than how to judge whether it is moral to *use* them. This lack of proportion paid to morality is the key question of our day. Therefore, the renewal of morality is not just some rearguard action of a zealot opposed to progress, but *the* critical question upon which any real progress will depend.

Thus, in this volume we will not be dealing with disputed points of interest only to the Church, but rather we are standing at the very point where the Church goes beyond herself. It is precisely when we look at her moral message that we can see that the Church is not some kind of club for the satisfaction of social or even personal ideal needs. Rather, we see that she performs an essential service right in the midst of the turmoil which society is going through. She is not, in the first place, some kind of "moral institution." That is how they tried to describe her and to justify her existence in the period of the Enlightenment. Nevertheless, she *does* have something to *do* with the moral resources of humanity. We could call these moral resources the most important raw material we have for human existence *now* and for making possible a *future* in which it will still be worthwhile to be a person.

The question which is posed by my theme might be formulated like this: What contribution can the Church make toward forging a balance between external progress and morality? What can she do, not just to keep herself in existence, but to open up once again the moral resources of humanity? One might go so far as to say the Church will survive only if she is in a position to help mankind overcome this hour of trial. In order to do this she must show herself as a moral power. And she must do this in two ways: She must set standards, and she must awaken both the will and the power of people to respond to these standards. In this context the question takes on a particular shape, namely, how can bishops work together with theologians, the bishops being charged with the transmission of the faith and the theologians being charged with the dialogue between the world of faith and the mind-set of the world at large?

It would be too facile to answer these questions with a few tactical formulas to produce a satisfactory agreement between those who are responsible for the decisions and the experts, even though it is so important to work out and make use of such practical rules. But it is not at *all* so easy to reproduce mechanically the general structural relationship between the competence to make decisions and expert knowledge. Each maintains its own form through the particular character of the matter involved. So it is necessary before searching for rules for collaboration between bishops and moral theologians, first of all, to reflect — at least in very general outline — on the question of the sources and the method of moral knowledge. How can we arrive at moral knowledge at all? How do we arrive at correct moral judgments?

I. The Four Sources of Moral Knowledge and Their Problems

1. Reduction to "Objectivity"

When we come now to the question we have posed for ourselves concerning the method of moral knowledge, we see very clearly the poverty of the modern world about which we have already spoken: its lack of ideas when faced with the moral problem, the underdevelopment of moral reason as compared with calculating reason. A mark of modern society is specialization, which also includes a division of labor. This results in competence to acquire knowledge: In the individual fields of human knowledge and action the particular specialist is competent who, in the process of our ever-expanding and precise knowledge, manages to get an overview and an experience of a specific sector. But are there specialists in the field of morality, which does not admit of division of labor, when they all proceed each in his own way?

A division of labor in the area of knowledge presumes a quantification of the object of knowledge. One might think here of Henry Ford's famous assembly line. Every worker performs a specific task in the overall construction of the Model T. No one worker can build a whole car, much less design one, or even know how the mechanism functions.

One can divide and distribute only that which has become quantity. The success of modern science is based on the translation of the reality we encounter into quantitative measures. In this way the world becomes measurable and technologically exploitable. But could we not say that the crisis of humanity in our times finds its roots in this method and in its increasing domination in all aspects of human life? Calculation, which in turn is subject to what is quantitative, is the method of what is not free. It works when we are dealing with what can be calculated, ordered and necessary. It is good for building cars.

If morality, however, is the area of freedom and if its norms are laws of freedom, then inevitably these laws will not be sufficient for us: They must leave us perplexed in the face of that which is truly human. A simple answer suggests itself here. Perhaps freedom is only an illusion, the remains of an old dream of humanity from which, for better or for worse, we must separate ourselves. Does not everything point to the fact that man, caught up in the physical and biological net of reality, is thoroughly determined? Must not a complete enlightenment lead to a situation in which even in mankind morality will be replaced by technique, that is, by a correct ordering and combination of predetermined elements which will then yield the desired result?

And so there emerges the thought of calculating human behavior to analyze the predetermined state which is proper and fundamental to man and so to discover a formula for happiness and survival. Statistics and planning together provide the new "morality" with which man prepares his way into the future. All moral rules, which man could then calculate, would thus be directed to those ends which man himself has in mind for humanity. Just as man designs technical tools for his own purposes, so in the area of morality he imposes his own goals on the laws of nature.

But here the decisive question remains open: Who determines the goals? Who plans the future of man? Granted there are many who are powerful who would gladly arrogate this right to themselves, no one of us has the right to do so. Who then could have the right to oblige all men to pursue one particular goal or another? At this point we must postpone attempts to answer the question of the sources of morality, but this is not to imply that it is either resolved or unessential.

A second question now emerges: If there are ends which man must pursue, how does he know them? It should be clear that we cannot reduce moral knowledge to some model of knowledge in general, understood as the calculation and combination of known measures which are demonstrable because of their repetition.

Obviously, it cannot be disputed that a good amount of useful data about mankind and the world can, nevertheless, be gathered in this way. But since human behavior is not at all so easy to repeat or reproduce identically in others, any attempt to subject human behavior to a purely scientific analysis encounters sooner or later an insurmountable limitation: namely, the limitations of humanity itself, which is after all what we are discussing.

Only at the price of ignoring what is precisely human could the question of morality be analyzed in the ordinary way of human knowing. The fact that this is actually being attempted in various quarters today is the great inner threat to mankind today. The tree of knowledge, from which man eats in this case, does not give the knowledge of good and evil, but rather blinds man to discerning the difference between them. Man will not return to paradise through such blindness, because it is not based on a purer humanity, but on the rejection of humanity.[1]

2. Subjectivity and Conscience

We see then that in the question of morality there cannot be experts in the same way as there can be in microelectronics or computer science. Plato realized that when he said that a person cannot express "with scholastic words" what the word "good" means.[2] But in what other way can we learn it?

There are a number of suggestions here which must be examined in order, but briefly. It is only in the convergence of the various ways that we can find the way itself.

To begin with, there is today a broadly accepted alternative to the complete objectification of moral knowledge, whose shortcomings we have just seen. In one sector of modern thinking we have the strange situation where man, faced with both the greatness and the limitations of quantitative analysis, tries to overcome the distinction between the subject and object. We can calculate the world since and to the extent that we make it an "object." Opposed to this "objective," which is what can be studied by science, there remains the "subjective," the world of the incalculable and the free. In this division of the world, religion and morality are relegated to the world of the subjective. They are subjective in the sense that they cannot be analyzed by science nor placed within the generally valid criteria of ordinary knowledge. In this view the subjective really does exist, though the ultimate analysis of it is up to the individual's imagination to decide.

Obviously, in such a reduction of morality to the subjective it becomes impossible to address the objective concerns of our day which demand a moral answer.[3] To that extent, this approach to the problem is losing favor today. Still, in practical life and especially in the discussion within the Church itself, it still plays an important role, insofar as here the subjection of morality to the area of the subjective has become linked with the long Christian tradition of the teaching on conscience.

Conscience is understood by many as a sort of deification of subjectivity, a rock of bronze on which even the Magisterium is shattered. It is said that in light of the conscience, no other cases apply. Conscience appears finally as subjectivity raised to the ultimate standard.

We will have to examine this question in closer detail, as it already touches directly the precise theme of my essay. For the moment, however, I note that conscience is presented as one source of moral knowledge, that is to say, a personal, primitive knowledge of good and evil which appears in the individual man as a source of his ability to make moral judgments.

3. The Will of God and His Revelation

If we follow a little further the pathway of *conscience* as we find it in the tradition, then we encounter another fundamental element in the moral area. The idea of conscience cannot be separated in its history from the idea of the responsibility of man before God.

To a great extent, it expresses the thought of a kind of co-knowledge of man with God, and precisely from here there emerges the absoluteness with which conscience asserts its superiority over any and all authorities. The history of morality is inseparably linked with the history of thought about God. As far as the fixed character of the natural laws is concerned, morality means the free "yes" given by one will to another, in this case, the conformity of man to the will of God and the consequent correct perception of things as they really are. As an ultimate source of morality, then, we have to take into consideration the process of how God makes His desires for mankind known, how one acquires knowledge of the divine commandments in which the special ends of man and the world become clear. If such objective morality is based on revelation, then immediately the next question arises: How can one know revelation as revelation? How can revelation be identified as such?

4. The Community as a Source of Morality

Here we meet with another factor which has played and still plays an extremely important role in the working out of various moral theories. The Latin word *mores* without any distinction contains meanings which we have learned to distinguish carefully: Mores are the habits, customs and lifestyle of a people, practically what we would call today "the American way of life" or the "California style." At the same time, alongside the totality of life habits, the word also has a specifically moral meaning.

When St. Augustine, for example, wrote *De Moribus Ecclesiae et de Moribus Manichaeorum*, it was not a question of comparative morality in today's sense. Rather, in making a comparison between the form of life of the Catholic Church, her total lifestyle, and that of the Manicheans, he goes on to distinguish two distinct types of morality within the broader context of lifestyle. Likewise, in the language of the Council of Trent the formula *fides et mores* does not simply mean faith and morals in today's sense of the terms, but rather in the broader sense in which the customs of the life of the Church, including moral order in the strict sense, are understood.

In this use of language something very important appears: "Morality" is not an abstract code of norms for behavior, but it presupposes a community way of life within which morality itself is clarified and is able to be observed. Historically considered, morality does not belong to the area of subjectivity, but is guaranteed by the community and has a reference to the community. In the lifestyle of a community the experience of generations is stored up: experiences of things which can build up a society or tear it down, how the happiness of an individual and the continuity of the community as a whole can be brought together in a balanced way and how that equilibrium can be maintained.

Every morality needs its "we," with its prerational and suprarational experiences, in which not only the analysis of the present moment speaks, but rather in which the wisdom of the generations converges.

A crisis in morality occurs in a community when new areas of knowledge emerge which the current life patterns cannot cope with, to the point that what up until then appeared as supportive and proven appears now as insufficient, or indeed as contradictory or as an obstacle to the new knowledge and reality. Then the question arises, how can the community find a new way of life which will once more make possible a common moral existence for life and for the world itself? It remains true that morality needs a "we" and that it requires a link with the experience of past generations and with the primitive wisdom of humanity.

And so we return to the question from which we began, namely, the problem of revelation. We can make this assertion: The various concrete community experiences of different races and peoples are valuable as signposts for human behavior, but by themselves cannot be considered sources for morality. It is impossible in the long run to have a society which lives, as it were, only as a reaction from what is negative and evil. If a society wishes to survive, it must to a certain extent return to the primitive virtues, to the basic standard models of humanity.

Still, it is certainly possible for important areas of life in a society to become corrupt, so that the predominant custom of men and women does not guide but seduces as in a society with the custom of cannibalism, slavery or dependence on drugs. An individual can rely on his own experience and on the common historical experiences only to a limited degree. In history, therefore, morality was never based exclusively on experience and custom. Its unconditional character could not be understood except in reference to the unconditional character of God's will:

In the last analysis, morality was founded on a divine revelation of will, out of which alone a community could emerge and in accord with which the survival of the community as such was guaranteed.

I must leave aside at this point a series of questions which really ought to be asked, so that I can return to my particular theme. Despite the fragmentary nature of these reflections so far, we can nevertheless see that the faith of the Church is in agreement with the fundamental traditions of humanity on several points. Christian faith is also convinced that God alone can be the measure of man and that only the divine will can unconditionally oblige man. Christian faith is further convinced that revelation situates us in the community life model of a "we" whose nature and direction cannot be explained simply in terms of the human will alone.

Clearly the Christian looks at this "we" whose customs constitute the proximate source of moral knowledge, not simply in terms of his own local society, but in terms of a new society which can be explained only through revelation and which transcends all local societies (it is "catholic") and which subordinates them to the dictates of the divine will which are addressed to them all.

With this as a context, one can experience what morality is by seeking in the first place the *mores ecclesiae*: Thus the person who is by virtue of his office responsible for the form of life of the Church — the bishop — in Catholic tradition bears the principal responsibility for teaching Christians morals as well as faith. It also means that in the area of morality those who have the greatest right to speak are those who live according to the deepest essence of the Church to the most profound degree — the saints. But with these remarks I have moved on too quickly. I simply wanted to note the fact that we are still working toward our theme, even though it may seem that our aim has disappeared in the individual points of this reflection. Perhaps it would be good at this point to sum up what we have seen, so that then, as far as we can, we can move on to the concrete implications of all of this.

We have located four sources of morality. If taken in isolation from each other, each leaves several questions unanswered.

But when they are taken in combination, then the path of moral knowledge opens up before us. If on one hand we have to conclude that authentic morality cannot be constructed on the basis of an examination of the concrete world alone, still morality must be concerned with objective morality since moral behavior must do justice to truth. It is in this way that reality — and reason which knows and explains reality — is without a doubt an irreplaceable source of morality.

As a second source, we spoke of conscience.

The wisdom of tradition is a third source, embodied in a living "we," an active community which for the Christian is concretely realized in the new community of the Church.

Finally we saw that all these sources lead to true morality when the will of God is present. For in the final analysis, only the will of God can establish the boundary between good and evil, which is something different from the boundary between what is useful or not or what is proven and what is unknown. The Catholic Church sees an important confirmation of her teaching in the fact that within her these elements interpenetrate and illumine each other. Her teaching brings conscience to expression. Conscience is seen to be valid precisely because it incorporates the inner truth of things in accord with reality, which is after all the voice of the Creator.

These three things, objectivity, tradition and conscience, in turn point to the divine commandments.

These commandments on one hand constitute the basis of the Church's teaching, they form consciences and make reality intelligible. On the other hand, because they correspond to reality as perceived by conscience, they are for their part able to be confirmed as true revelations of the divine will.

II. Second Principal Problem: Conscience and Objectivity

No doubt it might be observed that what I have just said is an idealization of a reality which in fact is not all that harmonious. A number of nuances would have to be added in order to be more realistic. Two main objections, related to the first two of the four sources of morality, tend now to arise.

There is the rather common impression that the Church is not in a position to respond in a correct manner to reality in today's world. Instead of listening to the language of reality, she is immovably chained to antiquated points of view which she tries to impose on men. Right here a conflict arises between the bishop and the expert. In many ways this conflict appears to be a conflict between a doctrine which is distant from reality and an exact understanding of current reality.

The second objection comes from the area of conscience: The consciences of many Christians are by no means in harmony with many expressions of the Church's Magisterium. Indeed it often seems that the conscience is that which gives dissent some legitimacy.

So then if we wish to arrive at a clear position as regards the function of the bishop as teacher of morality and his relationship to the experts in moral theology, then it is necessary, if only in rough outline, to look into the two questions which have arisen: What is conscience? And how can one learn which form of behavior corresponds to things as they really are, to reality, and is thus moral behavior in the meaningful sense of the term?

1. What Is Conscience and How Does It Speak?

When one speaks of conscience today, three principal streams of thought come to mind.[4] We have already touched on the first of these. For conscience asserts the right of subjectivity which can in no way be measured objectively. But in response there immediately arises the objection: Who establishes such an absolute right of subjectivity? It may indeed have a relative right, but in really important cases must not that right be sacrificed to an objective common good of the highest level?

It is strange that some theologians have difficulty accepting the precise and limited doctrine of papal infallibility, but see no problem in granting *de facto* infallibility to everyone who has a conscience.

In fact it is not possible to assert an absolute right for subjectivity as such.

Conscience also signifies in some way the voice of God within us.

With this notion the completely inviolable character of the conscience is established: In conscience we have a case which would be above any human law. The fact of such a direct bond between God and man gives man an absolute dignity. But then the question arises, does God speak to men in a contradictory manner? Does He contradict Himself? Does He forbid one person, even to the point of martyrdom, to do something which He allows or even requires from another?

It is clear that it is not possible to justify the equation of the individual judgments of conscience with the voice of God. Conscience is not an oracle, as Robert Spaemann rightly noted.

We now encounter a third meaning: Conscience is the superego, the internalization of the will and the convictions of others who have formed us and have so impressed their will on us that it no longer speaks to us externally, but rather from deep within our inner self. In this situation conscience would not be a real source of morality at all, but only the reflection of the will of another, an alien guide within ourselves. Conscience would not then be an organ of freedom, but an internalized slavery from which man would logically have to free himself in order to discover the breadth of his real freedom.

Even though one might explain many individual expressions of conscience in this way, this theory cannot stand completely.

On one hand we find children, before they are formally educated, who react spontaneously against injustice. They give a spontaneous "yes" to what is good and true which precedes any educational interventions, which often enough only darken them or crush them rather than let them grow. On the other hand, there are mature men and women in whom one finds a freedom and an alertness of conscience which sets itself against what has been learned or what is commonly done. Such a conscience has become an inner sense of what is good, a kind of remote control to guide man through what he has been taught.

What is the real position of conscience? I wish to make my own what Robert Spaemann has said about it: Conscience is an organ, not an oracle.[5] It is an organ because it is something which for us is a given, which belongs to our essence and not something which has been made outside of us. But because it is an organ, it requires growth, training and practice. I find the comparison which Spaemann makes with speech is very fitting in this case. Why do we speak? We speak because we have learned to speak from our parents. We speak the language which they taught us,

14

though we realize there are other languages which we cannot speak or understand. The person who has never learned to speak is mute. And yet language is not an external conditioning which we have internalized, but rather something which is properly internal to us.

It is formed from outside, but this formation responds to the given of our own nature, that we can express ourselves in language. Man is as such a speaking essence, but he becomes so only insofar as he learns speech from others. In this way we encounter the fundamental notion of what it means to be a man: Man is "a being who needs the help of others to become what he is in himself."[6]

We see this fundamental anthropological structure once again in conscience. Man is in himself a being who has an organ of internal knowledge about good and evil. But for it to become what it is, it needs the help of others. Conscience requires formation and education. It can become stunted, it can be stamped out, it can be falsified so that it can only speak in a stunted or distorted way. The silence of conscience can become a deadly sickness for an entire civilization.

In the Psalms we meet from time to time the prayer that God should free man from his hidden sins. The Psalmist sees as his greatest danger the fact that he no longer recognizes them as sins and thus falls into them in apparently good conscience. Not being able to have a guilty conscience is a sickness, just as not being able to experience pain is a sickness, again as Spaemann says.[7] And thus one cannot approve the maxim that everyone may always do what his conscience allows him to do: In that case the person without a conscience would be permitted to do anything.[8] In truth it is his fault that his conscience is so broken that he no longer sees what he as a man should see.

In other words, included in the concept of conscience is an obligation, namely, the obligation to care for it, to form it and educate it. Conscience has a right to respect and obedience in the measure in which the person himself respects it and gives it the care which its dignity deserves. The right of conscience is the obligation of the formation of conscience. Just as we try to develop our use of language and we try to rule our use of rules, so must we also seek the true measure of conscience so that

15

finally the inner word of conscience can arrive at its validity.

For us this means that the Church's Magisterium bears the responsibility for correct formation. It makes an appeal, one can say, to the inner vibrations its word causes in the process of the maturing of conscience. It is thus an oversimplification to put a statement of the Magisterium in opposition to conscience. In such a case I must ask myself much more. What is it in me which contradicts this word of the Magisterium? Is it perhaps only my comfort? My obstinacy? Or is it an estrangement through some way of life which allows me something which the Magisterium forbids and which appears to me to be better motivated or more suitable simply because society considers it reasonable? It is only in the context of this kind of struggle that the conscience can be trained and the Magisterium has the right to expect that the conscience will be open to it in a manner befitting the seriousness of the matter.

If I believe that the Church has its origins in the Lord, then the teaching office in the Church has a right to expect that it, as it authentically develops, will be accepted as a priority factor in the formation of conscience. There corresponds to this then an obligation of the Magisterium to speak its word in such a way that it will be understood in the midst of conflicts of values and orientations. It must express itself in such a way that an inner resonance of its word may be possible within the conscience, and this means more than just an occasional declaration of the highest level. Here we need what Plato was referring to when he said the good cannot be known scholastically, but only after regular familial discussion can the notion of the good spring into the soul like light springing from a small spark.[9] This constant "familial discussion" within the Church must build up the community conscience — those who try to express their word in the teaching office, as well as those who wish to learn that word from within themselves.

2. Nature, Reason and Objectivity

Thus we have already arrived at the other point which I want to touch on: The word of the Magisterium is for many Christians today no longer plausible because its reasonableness and objectivity are no longer transparent. The Magisterium is accused of setting out from an outdated understanding of reality. Like the old Stoics, the Magisterium argues from "nature." But this expression "nature" has been completely surpassed with the entire metaphysical age.

At first, this so-called naturalism of the Magisterial tradition was seen in opposition to the personalism of the Bible. The opposition of nature and person as a basic pattern for argumentation was at the same time seen as an opposition between philosophical and biblical tradition. Still it has now long been recognized that there is no such thing as a pure "biblicism" and that even "personalism" has its own philosophical aspects. Today we see almost the direct opposite movement: The Bible has to a great extent vanished from the modern works in moral theology. In its place a tendency toward a particularly strong rational analysis has become dominant, together with the assertion of the autonomy of morals, which is based neither on nature nor on the person, but on historicity and future-oriented models of social behavior.

One must try to discover what is socially compatible and what serves the building of a future human society. The "reality" on which "objectivity" is based is seen no longer as a nature which precedes man, but rather in the world which he himself has structured, which one may now simply analyze and from which one may extrapolate what the future will bring.[10] Here we come up against the real reason why Christianity today, not only in the area of the moral, to a great extent lacks direct plausibility. As we have already seen, as a result of the philosophical change introduced by Kant, the division of reality into subjective and objective has become dominant.

The objective is not simply reality in itself, but reality only inasmuch as it is the object of our thought and is thus measurable and can be calculated. The subjective, for its part, eludes "objective" explanation. This means, however, that the reality we encounter speaks only the language of human calculation, but has within itself no moral expression. The constantly expanding radical forms of the theory of evolution lead to the same conclusion, though from a different starting point: The world presupposes no reason; what is reasonable in it is the result of a combination of accidents whose ongoing accumulation then developed a kind of necessity.

According to such a viewpoint, the world contains no meaning, but only goals, which are posited by evolution itself. [11] If the world is thus a montage of static appearances, then the highest moral directive it can then give to man is that he himself should be engaged in some kind of montage of the future, and that he himself should direct everything according to what he reckons is useful. The norm thus lies always in the future: In this view the greatest possible betterment of the world is the only moral commandment.

In contrast, the Church believes that in the beginning was the *Logos* and that therefore being itself bears the language of the *Logos,* not just mathematical, but also aesthetical and moral reason. This is what is meant when the Church insists that "nature" has a moral expression. No one is saying that biologism should become the standard of man. That viewpoint has been recommended only by some behavioral scientists.

The Church professes herself the advocate of the reason of creation and practices what she means when she says: I believe in God, the Creator of Heaven and Earth. There is a reason for being, and when man separates himself from it totally and recognizes the reason only of what he himself has made, then he abandons what is precisely moral in the strict sense. In some way or another we are beginning to realize that materiality contains a spiritual expression and that it is not simply for calculation and use. In some way we see that there is a reason which precedes us which alone can keep our reason in balance and can keep us from falling into external unreason.

In the last analysis, the language of being, the language of nature, is identical with the language of conscience. [12] But in order to hear that language it is necessary, as with all language, to practice it. The organ for this, however, has become deadened in our technical world. This is why there is a lack of plausibility here. The Church would betray, not only her own message, but the destiny of humanity if she were to renounce being the guardian of being and its moral message. In this sense she may be opposed to what is "plausible," but at the same time she stands for the most profound claims of reason. It becomes obvious here that reason also is an organ and not an oracle. And reason too requires training and community.

Whether a person is able to attribute reason to being and to decipher his own moral dimension depends on whether he answers the question about God. If the *Logos* of the beginning does not exist, neither can there by any *Logos* in things. What Kolakowski recently discovered then becomes emphatically true: When there is no God, there is no morality and in fact no mankind either.[13] In this sense, in the deeper analysis, everything depends on God, on a God who is Creator and on a God who has revealed Himself. For this reason, once again, we need the community which can guarantee God, Whom no one on his own could dare bring into his life.

Even Abraham, our father in faith, was not being completely innovative when he introduced monotheism 2,000 years before Christ. Even that primitive society already cherished its belief in the divine.

The question of God, which is the central point, is not a question for specialists. The perception of God is precisely that simplicity which the specialists can never monopolize, but rather which can be perceived only by maintaining a simplicity of vision. Perhaps we find it so difficult today to deal with the essence of humanity because we have ceased being capable of simplicity.[14]

Therefore, morality requires not the specialist, but the witness. The position of the bishop as teacher rests on this: He teaches not what he himself has discovered. But he witnesses to the life wisdom of faith in which the primitive wisdom of humanity is cleansed, maintained, deepened. Through contact with God, depending on how perceptive the conscience is, this primitive human knowledge becomes a real vehicle of communication with truth by means of the communion it shares with the conscience of the saints and with the knowledge of Jesus Christ.

Naturally it does not follow from this that scientific work regarding the criteria of morality and specialized knowledge in this area have become unnecessary. Since conscience requires training, since tradition must be lived and must develop in times of change and since moral behavior is a response to reality and therefore requires a knowledge of reality, for all these reasons the observation and study of reality as well as the traditions of moral thought are important. To put it another way, to seek a thorough

19

knowledge of reality is a fundamental commandment of morality. It was not without reason that the ancients placed *prudence* as the first cardinal virtue: They understood it to mean the willingness and the capacity to perceive reality and respond to it in an objective manner.[15]

III. Applications

Now that we have considered all of this, we can formulate the essential tasks of both bishop and specialized theologian in moral questions and from this will automatically emerge the rules for their working together in a correct manner.

1. The Bishop as Teacher of Morality

a) The bishop is a witness to the *mores Ecclesiae Catholicae*, to those rules of life which have grown up in the common experience of the believing conscience in the struggle with God and with historical reality. As a witness the bishop must in the first place know this tradition in its foundations, its content and its various stages. One can only bear witness to what one knows. The knowledge of the essential moral tradition of the faith is therefore a fundamental demand of the episcopal office.

b) Since it is a question of a tradition which comes from conscience and speaks to conscience, the bishop himself must be a man of a seeing and listening conscience. He must strive, in living the *mores Ecclesiae Catholicae*, to see that his own personal conscience is sharpened. He must know morality not second-, but firsthand. He must not simply pass on a tradition, but bear witness to what has become for himself a credible and proven lifestyle.

c) Setting out from such a personal knowledge of the moral word of the Church, he must attempt to remain in discussion with those experts who seek the correct application of the simple words of faith to the complicated reality of a particular time. He must therefore be prepared to become a learner and a critical partner of the experts. He must learn to see where it is a question of the knowledge of new realities, new problems, new possibilities for understanding and so for maturing and cleansing the moral heritage. He must be critical when expert science forgets its own boundaries or reduces morality to a simple specialization.

2. The Tasks of the Moral Theologian

On the basis of our reflections so far, we might define the tasks of the moral theologian in the following manner:

a) As a theologian, the moral theologian also finds his starting point in the *mores Ecclesiae Catholicae* which he researches and which, in their essential link with what is Catholic, he distinguishes. And so he also tries to recognize in the *mores* that which is specifically moral and constant and to understand them in a unified way in the total context of the faith. He seeks the *ratio fidei.*

b) He then brings this reason of faith in a critical way into dialogue with the reason and the plausibility of the particular time. He helps toward the understanding of the moral demands of the Gospel in the particular conditions of his day and so serves the formation of conscience. In this way he serves also the development, purification and deepening of the moral message of the Church.

c) Above all, the moral theologian will also take up the new questions which new developments and relationships pose for the traditional norms. He will attempt to know precisely the objective components of such discussions (for example, the technology of armaments, economic problems, medical developments, etc.) in order to work out the best way to pose the questions and so to arrive at the relationship with the constants of the moral tradition of the faith. In this sense he stands in critical dialogue with the moral evaluations of society and in all this he helps the teaching office of the Church to present its moral message in the particular time.

3. The Relationship Between Bishop and Theologian

From our reflections on the individual tasks it is now possible to derive the fundamental rules for the relationship between teaching office and expert.

a)The teaching office depends on the specialized knowledge of the experts and must let itself be thoroughly informed by them about the content of the matter in question before making an utterance regarding new problems. The teaching office must therefore not be too hasty in taking up a position regarding questions that are not yet clarified nor must it apply its binding statements beyond what the principles of tradition permit.

On the other hand, the teaching office of the Church must defend man against himself to prevent his destruction even if this means opposing the philosophy of an entire epoch. For example, in a period in which the world thinks of itself only as a product and as an end, the teaching office of the Church must continually try to get nature to be recognized as creation in its defense of the unborn. There is an obligation to information, an obligation to respect the boundaries of universally binding moral statements and an obligation to witness. The moral catechesis must go beyond that which can be determined with certainty and should offer models of behavior in concrete circumstances (casuistry).

But it seems important to me clearly to distinguish between these cases and the specific moral teaching. I have the impression that the regular and unnuanced introduction of cases into the specific moral statement or likewise the failure to distinguish between them has contributed to discrediting the moral teaching of the Church in our century in a substantial way.

b) But the task of the moral theologian is not simply to be in service to the teaching office. It also stands in dialogue with the ethical questions of the time and contributes, through the development of models of behavior, to the process of the formation of conscience. As regards the Magisterium, his task is to precede it: He goes before it, noticing new questions, gathering knowledge of their objective content and preparing answers. The moral theologian likewise accompanies the Magisterium and follows it, bringing its pronouncements into the dialogue of his time and relating the basic lines of the discussion to concrete situations.

4. *Criticism of the Magisterium: Its Rules and Limits*

Today interest in the relationship between the episcopal magisterium and scientific theology is concentrated above all on the question: Can the moral theologian criticize the teaching office?

After what we have said about the structure of moral expression and about its relationship to specialized science, we must distinguish:

a) First of all, we must apply here what the Second Vatican

22

Council said about the steps of assent and in like manner the stages of criticism with regard to Church teaching. Criticism may be framed according to the level and demands of the Magisterial teaching. It will be all the more helpful when it fills in a lack of information, clarifies shortcomings of the linguistic or conceptual presentation and at the same time deepens the insight into the limits and range of the particular teaching.

b) In the light of our reflection, on the other hand, we see that it is not for the expert himself to draw up norms or to annul the norms, perhaps by setting up factions or pressure groups. As we have seen, norms can only be witnessed to, but not produced or annulled by some calculated analysis. When this happens, the peculiar nature of morality itself is misunderstood. Therefore, dissent can only have meaning in the area of casuistry, not in the specific area of norms. The most important thing in the relationship between the Magisterium and moral theology appears to me, in the last analysis, to lie in what Plato recommends as the path to moral knowledge, in "regular familial discussion," a discussion in which we must all learn to become more and more hearers of the biblical word, vitally addressed and directed to the *mores Ecclesiae Catholicae.*

Notes

1. For the problems addressed here, cf. F.H. Tenbruck, *Die unbewältigten Socialwissenschaften oder Die Abschaffung des Menschen,* (Graz, 1984).

2. Letter 7, 341c; cf. R. Spaemann, *Moralische Grundbegriffe,* (München, 1982).

3. This issue is very nicely set forth by W. Heisenberg, *Der Teil und das Ganze* (München, 1969), 116-30 and 279-95.

4. Cf. for the following, R. Spaemann, *Moralische Grundbegriffe,* 73-84; also helpful is A. Laun, *Das Gewissen. Oberste Norm sittlichen Handelns,* (Innsbruck, 1984).

5. *op. cit.,* 81.

6. Spaemann, *op. cit.,* 79.

7. *op. cit.,* 80.

8. *ibid.,* 83.

9. Letter 7, 341c.

10. For these issues, cf. the painstaking presentation by J. Finnis, *Fundamentals of Ethics,* (Washington: Georgetown University Press, 1983); also enlightening is, F. Ricken, "Kann die Moralphilosophie auf die Frage nach dem 'Ethischen' Verzichten?" in *Theol. Phil.* 59 (1984), 161-77.

11. For a treatment of this problem area, cf. R. Spaemann and R. Löw, *Die Frage Wozu? Geschichte und Wiederentdeckung des teleologischen Denkens,* (München, 1981).

12. We learn much about the idea of Nature in its relation to morality in, H. Ratner, "Nature, Mother and Teacher: Her Norms," in *Listening,* Journal of Religion and Culture, 18 (1983), 185-219.

13. L. Kolakowski, *Falls es keinen Gott gibt,* (München, 1982), 173-91; see also 82; it would be profitable in this connection to reflect again upon Ludwig Wittengenstein's, *Aussagen zu den ethischen Sätzen* in his *Tractatus logico-philosophicus* (deutsch-englisch, London-New York, 1961), especially 6.41: Der Sinn der Welt muss ausserhalb ihrer liegen . . . 6.42: Darum kann es auch keine Sätze der Ethik geben . . . 6.422 . . . Also muss diese Frage nach den Folgen einer Handlung belanglos sein.

14. Kolakowski, *op. cit.,* p. 157, has formulated the gist of this issue from a unique perspective, saying, "One must take this opportunity to repeat the question posed by Erasmus and his colleagues: Why is the Gospel so understandable for everyone except those spirits who are ruined by theological speculation? This pertains to all sacred texts, whether they were written or orally handed on. Believers understand the language of the Saints in their proper role, i.e., as an aspect of adoration."

15. Cf. J. Pieper, *Das Viergespann,* (München, 1964), 15-64.

Part II:
Certitudes In Moral Theology

OVERVIEW
of PART II

Catholic moral theology has been developing over a two thousand year span of reflection upon the Scriptures and the way of life that Jesus taught. Part II of this volume begins in Chapter 1 with the scriptural teaching about sin, conversion, and the following of Christ. Chapter 2 offers a survey of the theological development of these themes. Chapters 3 and 4 examine the living Magisterium of the Church teaching morality today and the pastoral approach to that teaching, encompassing religious assent and the problem of dissent. In Chapter 5 the authors of the previous four chapters dialogue with the bishops at the workshop who raised questions that surfaced in the table discussions after each of the authors of these chapters had spoken.

Father Karl Kertelge, author of *Chapter 1*, holds the title of Professor of New Testament Exegesis at the University of Munster, Germany, and serves on the Doctrinal Committee of the German Bishops' Conference. He points out that modern society has lost its sense of sin as a theological concept, whereas both the Old Testament covenant and the New Testament doctrine of redemption dealt honestly with sin as turning away from God.

Father Kertelge insists that conversion from sin occurs, according to the Scriptures, as a response to God's turning to His sinful creatures. Conversion means reconciliation with God and with other human persons. The Sermon on the Mount outlines the following of Christ as demanding this key ingredient of reconciliation. Jesus did not abolish the Ten Commandments but enriched His followers with their full and true meaning.

Thus the moral teaching of the Bible calls for a renewal of the human community by the power of God's kingdom and human persons cannot do what is good by their own efforts alone, but only by experiencing the love of God. Hence morality has a religious basis and the Bible teaches us the will of God, though expressed in the language of the time.

Father Benedict Ashley, O.P., author of *Chapter 2*, is a Professor of Moral Theology at the Aquinas Institute of St. Louis, MO, and a frequent lecturer at workshops of the Pope John Center. His chapter studies the development of moral thinking in the Church since biblical times. He outlines three periods preceding the present post-Vatican II period. In the first, the Fathers of the Church emphasized the image of God theme in moral teaching; in the second, the scholastics systematized ethics on the Greek model of the ultimate end; in the third, the post-Tridentine manualists systematized ethics as a legal code based on the Ten Commandments.

The present period of moral theology, Father Ashley suggests, has returned to the patristic emphasis on the image of God in a strongly Christological form: the following of Christ. He analyzes sin in this context, defending the necessity of distinguishing mortal from venial sin as a radical difference in the kind of harm that sin does rather than as a difference in sanction or kind of punishment. A mortal sin "makes impossible an essential conformity to the New Adam, Jesus Christ." Father Ashley concludes that, "the Commandments of God for us are manifested only in Jesus Christ

Who calls us to follow Him to the Father in the power of His Holy Spirit."

In *Chapter 3*, Monsignor Francis X. DiLorenzo, Vice-Rector of St. Charles Borromeo Seminary in Philadelphia and Associate Professor of Moral Theology there, moves the discussion to the moral teaching of the Magisterium, the authentic teaching agency within the Church. He traces the role of the Magisterium to the Pauline doctrine of the Mystical Body of Jesus wherein the Body's unity includes unity with those who have the authentic and authoritative teaching ministry. He pictures in broad brushstrokes the Church's competency in both infallible and non-infallible teaching. The former calls for an internal assent of faith and the latter calls for an internal, religious assent of mind and will.

In his chapter Monsignor DiLorenzo then presents a series of challenges to her competency in moral matters which the Church is experiencing today. Three come from within the Church: the reductionism of religious experience to mere psychological phenomena, a distorted ecclesiology based, for example, in exaggerated feminism or in self-righteous elitism, and the relativizing of the Church's moral teaching by public dissent. Four other major challenges arise from outside the church: 1) fundamentalism which prefers personal religious experience to authoritative teaching, 2) secular humanism which rejects religious truth, 3) excessive rationalism which prefers empirical reasoning to revealed truth, and 4) Marxist-Communism which rejects faith and spiritual reality. The author concludes with a call for Catholic education and evangelization and continued dialogue between theologians and the Magisterium.

Father Val J. Peter, a Professor of Theology at Creighton University of Omaha, begins *Chapter 4* with the internal religious assent to authentic Church teaching mentioned in Chapter 3. He analyzes this assent according to the approved authors prior to Vatican II as the doctrinal commission of that Council had recommended. This assent meant a real acceptance of the teaching and the authors insisted that dissent remain private.

Developments since Vatican II included widespread public dissent, not authorized by the Council but attributed to it by some liberal and radical commentators. Father Peter then singles out four mainly secular factors which have fostered this public dissent within the Church. He concludes with an appeal for the virtue of *pietas* toward Holy Mother Church as indicating "when and where and how dissent can appropriately take place."

In *Chapter 5* the previous four authors respond to a variety of questions. Father Ashley answers queries about sin and rejects the new threefold category of mortal, serious, and venial sin. Father Kertelge speaks of social justice and the sin against the Holy Spirit. Father Ashley and Father Kertelge delineate the different roles of bishop, theologian, and confessor.

Monsignor DiLorenzo describes dissent as appropriately a matter of private conscience rather than institutional policy. He clarifies his views on exaggerated feminism, Catholic fundamentalism, and on rapport with secular cultures and Marxist governments. Father Peter offers pastoral advice for deciding when a person who errs in good faith should not be disturbed, speaks about the range of theological speculation, and reflects on the Magisterial authority of individual bishops and of national conferences of bishops.

Throughout Part II the Church's moral teaching is seen in the context of the Magisterium and the assent of those who are taught. Parts III and IV of this volume will address the content of Church teaching, first in terms of moral norms, and then of key principles for applied moral theology.

Chapter 1

Biblical Revelation about Sin, Conversion, and the Following of Christ

The Reverend Karl Kertelge, Dr. Theol.

Introduction

In the Apostles' Creed the Church confesses its faith in the remission of sins: *"Credo in . . . remissionem peccatorum"*. In the Nicene Creed the remission of sins is directly connected with baptism: *"Confiteor unum baptisma in remissionem peccatorum"*. This makes it clear that there is an interrelation between the remission of sins and the beginning of a new life that is made in baptism. Man is born as a sinner, he is enmeshed in a net of evil through no fault of his own. Left to himself, he cannot free himself from this net. On the contrary, it is God who saves him from sin and evil. This is what happens in baptism. Baptism enables man to follow Christ. Only in community with Christ can a man be sure that his sins are forgiven and that he has been born anew.

This is, in short, what the Creed tells us about "sin and conversion". The questions and problems, however, that are connected with this subject in the context and view of the present time are too manifold to be covered merely by this quotation of the Creed. The Creed only states the fundamental importance of the remission of sins for the life of a Christian. But pastoral experience has shown that there is a far-reaching lack of knowledge about sin.[1] What does "sin" mean to people today? How can they really comprehend what is called sin in the Bible and in Christian tradition? This is not only a problem for non-Christians but also for Christians who, although baptized, have great difficulty in relating the reality of their faith to the obligation to fight sin. At best they identify the evil against which the Christian has to fight with the social grievances and the physical needs of mankind. This accounts for the view that the removal of social evil should be the *essential* duty of a Christian following Jesus. From this view follows the belief that improvements in economic and social structures will improve man too, enabling him to do what is morally good.

This optimism pervades much theological and pastoral thought today. Those who propose such views too easily forget that it is *God* who saves man and "liberates" him. Man is integrated in the work of God not merely as an instrument but as a free agent.

These introductory remarks already indicate the basic elements of the "biblical revelation about sin, conversion and the following of Christ". In what follows we shall try to treat the basic elements of the biblical teaching about sin and conversion in a way that will be fruitful for the Church's present-day moral teaching.

I. Man and His Sin

The biblical tradition mentions sin already in the very beginning and in close connection with the creation-story. The creation-story makes clear that man was not created as a sinner. He is not originally a sinner by nature, but he *becomes* a sinner through seduction and the transgression of a commandment. Two elements constitute the sin in which man becomes entangled:

consent to temptation and disobedience to God's command. In the letter to the Romans St. Paul rightly interprets man's evil deed as an act of disobedience (5,19). This means that man, as a being created by God, has to submit to the claim of his creator. If he acts according to what he essentially is, a creature, then he will have life. His existence is a creaturely existence. His freedom to do what is good and to abstain from evil is based on his status as God's creature. To use freedom in this way is his task. If a man evades this task imposed on him by his creator and misuses his freedom, then he becomes a sinner. He becomes a prisoner to the power of sin and, in consequence, to his own concupiscence. Sin, then, is nothing else but the refusal of the created being to give his creator what is due to him.

Sin is intimately connected with man's relationship to God. This does not exclude the possibility that a concrete sinful deed may occur in social intercourse, in man's dealings with his fellows. There are many forms of sin in the life of the individual and of the human community. They are recognized as sins corresponding to the respective duties that a man is faced with in his actual environment. It remains true, nonetheless, that all individual sins embody the fundamental sin of disobedience to the Creator.

Thus man's relationship to God is presupposed as the basis of our idea of sin. "Sin" is essentially a theological concept. Though one can submit an actual sin, in so far as it is the "misbehavior" of a person, to a sociological and psychological examination, one can never overlook the theological basis of those special sins.[2]

This theological basis can be further illuminated by the biblical traditions of the Old and New Testaments. We shall do this in two ways:

a) by examining the Old Testament concept of God's covenant with Israel;

b) by examining the New Testament concept of redemption through Christ.

a) God made a covenant with Israel. Its basis is God's free choice of Israel, experienced by that people in its national history, especially in the Exodus. God grants "his people" space to live in and gives them a fixed order, according to which they can settle their internal and external affairs. Israel will find life if it adheres to the order that God has given (cf. Dt 30,19). But God convicts

Israel again and again of disloyalty. Forgetting God, Israel goes its own way. Just this is the sin of God's people: their unfaithfulness and that they forget God's guidance. The prophet Jeremiah deplores Israel's violation of the covenant and accuses the people of adultery: 3,8f (and in other places). This view of disloyalty characterizes the concept of sin throughout the Old Testament, whether it is the unfaithfulness of the whole people or that of a single individual. The remission of sins which is offered by God means the renewal of the covenant. In the announcement of the "New Covenant" in Jer 31,31, finally, the remission of sins reaches its ultimate and eschatological intensity. The New Testament kerygma proclaims Jesus Christ as the fulfillment of the prophetic announcement of the "New Covenant".[3]

This view of sin in the Old Testament remains fundamental for Christianity. Sin is not only a wrong deed, but first and foremost a wrong attitude of man, the perversion of the true divine worship to the adoration of the creature. St. Paul has distinctly brought out this view of sin in Rom 1,18-32, especially verses 21-23: "Although they knew God they did not honor him as God or give thanks to him, but they became futile in their thinking . . . and exchanged the glory of the immortal God for images resembling mortal man or birds or animals or reptiles."[4] The distinctness of this characterization is based on the fact that the Apostle preaches Jesus Christ, by whom illuminating light has been shed on the situation of all men. In the light of the Gospel the sins of all men and their need for redemption are revealed.

b) We Christians speak of sin regularly in the context of redemption and forgiveness.[5] According to St. Paul man is indeed a sinner, but not a hopeless one. Man hopes for redemption from sin, which holds him prisoner. Indeed, in Jesus Christ this redemption has already been offered. Believing in Christ, man can attain this redemption and realize it even now. As a believer he "has been freed from sin" (Rom 6,7). He recognizes sin as a reality that belongs to the past. Even though he is still surrounded by the reality of sin, it now no longer holds him prisoner. He is no longer the "slave of sin" (Rom 6,20). Thanks to his redemption he is now in "the service of righteousness" (Rom 6,19).

This is the fundamental Christian point of view concerning sin. It is not a minimizing of sin as a fact of human history, but a new view that takes seriously the reality of sin both in the life of the individual and of mankind, yet prevents the believer from surrendering to it. The believer perceives the reality of sin more distinctly. Though he knows of the certainty of redemption, he takes sin into account in self-critical sobriety.

The increased awareness of man's responsibility also belongs to this view of sin in the New Testament. We are taught by faith not only to avoid sin but also to act responsibly and to do what is good. We are urged by faith to act from love, and by this the "new creation" (Gal 6,15), the true sense of God's creation, is realized even now. God is honored in that a man realizes what he can do with the help of the Holy Spirit, if only little by little.[6] Yet it is not our good works, which we like to be proud of, that are decisive here, but the fundamental direction of our lives as believers in Christ. This fundamental direction is no longer dominated by sin but by love.

Behind the numerous passages in the New Testament that mention sin we thus find a comprehensive conception of salvation history. This says that God has overcome man's sin, and that we are called to faith by Jesus Christ so as to attain redemption from sin. We are called upon to assent to God's work and to maintain this assent. If a man refuses or rejects it he commits a "sin unto death" (1 Jn 5,16), thus negating a life in community with God, Christ and the brethren.[7] The biblical concept of sin, thus, should not primarily be understood in terms of ethics and anthropology but in terms of soteriology and theology.[8] This forms the basis from which all moral acts of man must be judged.[9]

II. The Conversion of Man

If sin means that man has failed, then conversion corresponds to it as his self-correction, his metanoia, through which he becomes a believer. In conversion, man turns to God. This is not his own religious achievement, however, but only an answer to God's call. Conversion is a response. It is preceded by God's turning towards man. God himself encourages his people according to the prophet Isaiah: "Turn to me and be saved . . ., for I am God, and there is no other". (45,22) God's prior offer makes conversion possible for us. Thus, conversion can only be dealt with in connection with the theology of grace.

The call to conversion reaches us in the Gospel. The programmatic statement in Mk 1,15 shows us that it is Jesus himself who proclaims the Gospel and calls to metanoia and faith. Here metanoia "is something more than mere repentance for past sins. It means a radical change of conduct"[10]. What Jesus understands by metanoia is shown in his life and deeds. He preaches the prior goodness of God and realizes that goodness by turning towards sinners. Jesus' intercourse with the outcasts of society, with publicans and sinners, becomes an outstanding characteristic of his whole life. This is also shown by the fact that his behavior towards sinners gave offense. It seemed to be morally unjustified and brought Jesus the reputation of being "a glutton and a drinker, a friend of tax-gatherers and sinners" (Mt 11,19). Jesus, then, did not merely *talk* about man's conversion to God; he has also made it possible by showing sinners that God had not forgotten them. He demonstrated, indeed, that God's love reveals to man his sin and that God is ready to forgive man's sin and thus he enables human beings to live in community with him and with each other. Jesus' deeds and preaching, indeed his whole life, are a clearly visible sign of the fact that God turns towards man and offers him reconciliation. In the parable of the Prodigal Son this aspect is represented by the father: he had compassion, ran to meet his son and welcomed him home (Lk 15,20).

This marks the difference between Jesus' preaching of conversion and that of John the Baptist.[11] John proclaimed that judgement on the sinful world was imminent. Only a short time was left to repent, to confess one's sins and to receive the baptism of metanoia. Both preach metanoia. But John stresses the judgement on sin; Jesus, by contrast, emphasizes more strongly that the kingdom of God is at hand, and that all men are invited to enter it. Both things must be distinguished, but cannot be separated from one another. There is no doubt that Jesus understood his invitation to metanoia to be urgent. The parable of the marriage feast shows us that those who refused the invitation were excluded by their own choice. Thus, the idea of judgement is not lacking in the preaching of Jesus. The Gospel sees conversion as the only way open to man, who is a sinner, to attain fellowship with God. There is no alternative to the conversion demanded by

36

Jesus save that of excluding oneself.

Conversion, preached and made possible by Jesus, is realized in various forms. First of all, we are to listen readily to the call of God that has reached us in the Gospel. Listening, we are left to the right estimation of "time". Jesus tells us: "The time has come" (Mk 1,15), that is, time is ripe, God's mercy is being offered now. Now is the time for man to come to a new estimation of himself. Faced with the imminent kingdom of God, man realizes his true state. Before God he is "poor", needy. This is how we hear and understand the promise of Jesus: "Blessed are the poor in spirit; the kingdom of Heaven is theirs" (Mt 5,3). Metanoia thus is a personal act in which man assumes a new position towards God. God accepts him, God shows himself to be man's father. Sinful man learns to accept himself as God's child, as his new creature.

This conversion is continually necessary for Jesus' followers. Again and again the Christian turns to Jesus and finds in him his own beginning. And, throughout all the progress he will make by the grace of God, the decisive thing remains his lasting community with Christ.

Conversion also becomes the substance of the missionary work to which the risen Lord sends his disciples: "In his name repentance and forgiveness of sins should be preached to all nations . . . You are witnesses of these things" (Lk 24,47f). To preach the Gospel and to call to metanoia is and will remain the Church's essential missionary task.[12]

In all this, metanoia is something that concerns an individual person and leads him to the community with God. But conversion has a *social* element, too, which cannot be separated from the religious and theological one. Turning towards God corresponds to turning towards our fellow men. This social aspect is already expressed in Jesus' conduct and bearing towards those whom he approaches, or who approach him. Jesus enables people to form a community by liberating them and inspiring them to act in a new way, to act from love. This accounts for what Jesus says when instructing his disciples: they are to take the first step, namely reconciliation with others. The essential thing is to gain the other person as a brother and to serve God in community with him. This is what Jesus means when he says in the Sermon on the Mount: "When you are offering your gift at the altar, and there remember that your brother has something against you, leave your gift where it is before the altar. First go and be reconciled with your brother, and then come and offer your gift" (Mt 5,23f).

The readiness for reconciliation, which Jesus demands of the Christian, even includes abandoning retaliation when enduring wrongs and thus becoming a messenger of peace. "If someone strikes you on the right cheek, turn to him the other also" (Mt 5,39). Such conduct is dominated by the spirit of love. At the same time the reconciliation that we offer and that we are trying to attain must not be seen in isolation. It is based on the reconciliation effected by Christ. Reconciliation with our brother may be very successful from a human point of view; and regarded in itself it is a morally good act. But its true value before God comes, not from itself, but only from the fact that it makes effective Christ's selfless deed of reconciliation. The Christian ethic of turning towards our fellow man presupposes belief in our salvation through Christ and follows from it as it consequence. This is how St. Paul understands the ministry of reconciliation, with which he himself has been entrusted: "So we are ambassadors for Christ, God making his appeal through us. We beseech you on behalf of Christ, be reconciled to God!" (2 Cor 5,20).

III. The Ethics of Following Christ

The new life that man receives from God through faith and baptism needs to be preserved and proved. God's grace must bear fruit in the life of a Christian. For this purpose he is guided and instructed by the Gospel.

The basic rule, given by the Gospel to the believer, says that he is to remain in union with Christ. In the third chapter of his Gospel Mark narrates the election of the Twelve Apostles, and we can read there: "He appointed twelve to be with him and to be sent out to preach the Gospel . . ." (3,14). Thus these two things belong together: remaining in union with Christ, and preaching the Gospel. Together they constitute what we call the following of Christ. They are interrelated. The disciples staying with Jesus live in community with him, in his "field of force" as it were. From him they receive the power they need for their mission, especially for the proclamation of the Gospel. On the other hand, the disciples can preach only what Jesus has told and taught them. The Church has to prove itself as the body of Christ, as the community of his disciples through all the different epochs of its history. For this reason, the assistance of the Holy Spirit was given it. According to John 16,13f, he is "the Spirit of truth", who "will guide you into all the truth . . ."

Of course, the "guiding" work of the Holy Spirit is concerned with the *whole* truth of the Gospel, with the revelation of the dogmatic truths necessary to salvation and with the instructions that order the moral life of a Christian. As we are dealing here with the following of Christ, it is the latter that we are most interested in.

It is especially the *Sermon on the Mount* that supplies the guidelines for the life of a Christian. It has been transmitted to us in the New Testament in two versions, a shorter one in Luke (6,20-49) and a longer one in Matthew (chaps. 5-7). Both versions agree in their basic message: first, the promise of salvation is given to the disciples (and this promise proves its validity even in the situation of persecution, cf. Mt 5,10-12: God's power shows itself in his creatures just when they suffer persecution). And secondly, the disciples are commanded to be perfect as God is perfect (Mt 5,48). Therefore they are to love even their enemies, that is, those who persecute them and do them wrong (v. 43f). This is what makes them like Christ.

But, again and again, nowadays, we hear the humanly understandable objection: is this demand not excessive? Even if man receives God's grace to enable him to fulfill God's demand, man can never reach the perfection of God. Indeed, it is characteristic of *God* to love his enemies and to reconcile with himself those that have forgotten him. St. Paul has emphasized this strongly in his preaching (cf. esp. Rom 4,5; 5,6-11; 2 Cor 5,18-21).[13] But just because God's love came to us undeservedly, when we had forgotten him, we are called upon to put it into effect in dealing with others. This accounts for the Pauline exhortation: "Repay no one evil for evil . . . Do not be overcome by evil, but overcome evil with good." (Rom 12,17-21). This passage can be read as a comment on the command to love one's enemies. Thus, Jesus' instruction must be understood as follows: what God has done sets the standard for what a Christian must do. From a soteriological point of view what God has done can be defined as reconciliation. Jesus Christ has demonstrated and realized God's offer of reconciliation till death. The offer of reconciliation and the decision to stand up for it, then, becomes the main characteristic of the life of a Christian following Jesus.[14]

Viewing the Sermon on the Mount we must say that the different instructions of Jesus it contains can be reduced to that *one* key idea of reconciliation. On the other hand, we can also say that the several special instructions of the Sermon on the Mount (Mt 5,21-48) explain and articulate the obligation to strive for reconciliation in new and different situations. The command to reconciliation with one's enemy does not make an excessive demand on a Christian, so long as one remembers what *God* has done already and the connection between the fulfillment of the command of Jesus and God's act of reconciliation. On the contrary, reconciliation with enemies offers the Christian a new possibility, which he can and should realize in an incipient but authentic manner at least. Thus, following Christ does not lead either to passing enthusiasm or to moral rigorism but rather to confident action and to a new and really Christian view of man as a "brother" (cf. Mt 5,23f; 18,15). So we take the idea of brotherhood seriously. Seen in this light, the Sermon on the Mount reveals a new sphere for the moral life of a Christian, which is therefore no longer led by the letter of the law only, but by the spirit of Jesus' love of God and men.

Of course, not everything has been said concerning morally responsible action. There is a saying of Martin Luther that "the world cannot be governed with the Gospel". It is connected with his doctrine "of the two kingdoms". Luther went his own way in overcoming this dilemma that a Christian has to face when confronted with political action.[15] That is why Reformation theology makes a distinction between "Gesinnungsethik" (attitudinal ethics) and "Verantwortungsethik" (ethics of responsibility).

This implies for the politician that his primary guide is not the ethics of the Sermon on the Mount (Gesinnungsethik). Rather he must act according to the responsibility he bears for the public welfare and must decide with the help of his political reason. Though such a distinction may be justified in principle, it must not lead to a dual morality. Fundamentally, the instruction of the

40

Sermon on the Mount holds good for the whole sphere of human action, including that of social and political responsibility. However, the ethics of the Sermon on the Mount does not eliminate the Christian's rational thought and action. It acts rather to inspire rational thought and action. The Christian, following the principles of the ethics of Jesus, does not act irrationally but with a morally illuminated reason; that is, he respects human dignity and tries to leave nothing undone that may lead to reconciliation and concord even with persons of different opinions.

It can easily be seen that Jesus' ethics, understood in this way, do not abolish God's commandments. They lead us to fulfill the commandments' true meaning. This accounts for the ethics of early Christianity[16], which did not direct men to effect revolutionary changes in society and in the state but called upon them to fulfill God's will, as especially St. Paul often stresses.[17] This world, which "lies in the power of the evil one" (1 Jn 5,19) and whose "form is passing away" (1 Cor 7,31), cannot set the standard for Christian action. That is why St. Paul exhorts his readers: "Do not be conformed to this world but be transformed by the renewal of your mind, that you may prove what is the will of God, what is good and acceptable and perfect" (Rom 12,2). To turn away from the world continually does not mean to leave the organization of human life and society to others. Rather, the Christian must keep in mind his distance from the world and give effect to it in his dealings with the things of the world. This is exactly what the ὡζ μή (hōs mē), "as if not", in 1 Cor 7,29-31 stands for: "From now on, let those who have wives live as though they had none". This does not mean that a Christian must absolutely renounce the privileges of married life. It does mean that Christians must remember that married life and all the troubles and duties of the world are related to the reality of God who wants to prevail in and through the things of this world.

Conclusion: Christian Ethics in Our Time

If we transfer these New Testament trains of thought to the present time we can find some important principles for modern Christian ethics. They can be fruitfully applied to our modern problems and questions.

(1) The aim of the ethical instruction in the Bible, especially in the New Testament, is not any "moral society" or "moral rearmament", but the renewal of man and of the human community by the power of God's kingdom, which was preached by Jesus and has been brought to us by him. [18] Though the ethical imperative is duly emphasized, it must not be overlooked that it is embedded in the soteriological indicative, that is, in Jesus' offer of salvation. We can say therefore that man cannot do what is good by his own efforts but only by experiencing the love of God in his life. This is the first message to be proclaimed by the Church. God loves his creation — in spite of its sin, and Jesus stands up for the love of God and risks his life for it.

(2) The Bible does not offer us a manual of moral directives that can be used without further reflection in modern moral theology. But it testifies to the fact that man's morality has and must have a religious basis. These two things cannot be separated from one another. That is why the moral laws contained in the Bible are not merely special forms of the natural moral law, conditioned by cultural history, but express in terms of revelation history what God has done for man. Being based on the history of revelation, these commands receive their ultimate obligation and man's action its strongest motivation. Obviously it is this that is expected by the fathers of the Second Vatican Council when they say that the scientific endeavor of moral theology should be "more richly nurtured by the teaching of the Holy Scripture" ("*doctrina S. Scripturae magis nutrita*") (*Optatam Totius* 16).

(3) As the basis of the ethical instruction which the Church owes Christians, the Holy Scriptures offer the testimony of revelation concerning the right estimation of man: he is both made in God's image and a sinner who needs redemption. In its commands and instructions, especially in the teachings of Jesus, Scripture shows us the will of God, though expressed in the language of the time. God's will can also be perceived in the changed circumstances of our own time. Here, however, the commands and instructions of the Bible offer indispensable hermeneutical assistance. That means: the criteria of

Christian morality (as well as of moral theology) cannot be taken solely from human experience and from human reason, neither can they be taken solely from the Bible as the document of divine revelation, but biblical insights and knowledge from human reason and experience must encounter each other.[19]

(4) The biblical tradition presents man as being responsible for his deeds. God has given man freedom to exercise this responsibility. The individual is a member of the community he lives in, to be sure, and dependent on its rules and customs. But it is nevertheless up to him to choose between good and evil. The individual is responsible for the consequences of his acts, as are also those many individuals that form a community and live together in it. The acts of the individual Christian, who belongs to the people of God, are influenced by the set of common values and by the hierarchy of values accepted in the community. Whoever separates himself from it does so to his own disadvantage and to that of the whole community.[20]

(5) The practical life of a Christian consists in perceiving the possibilities of doing good and realizing them to the best of his ability. It is not enough, however, to be enthusiastic for a moment. Sobriety and perseverance are needed to stick to what one has seen to be good. "Soberness and vigilance" (cf. 1 Pt 5,8) keep us from overlooking that sin is still present and that we are in continual danger of getting entangled in this sin. But soberness and vigilance increase our ability to "distinguish true spirits from false" (1 Cor 12,10). The Christian's moral conduct depends on this ability more than ever today.

Notes

1. Cf. K.A. Menninger, *Whatever Became of Sin?*, New York 1973; S. Fagan, *Has Sin Changed?*, Dublin 1978. Cf. also the document of the International Commission of Theologians "Über Versöhnung und Buße", in: *Internationale Katholische Zeitschrift*, 13 (1984), pp. 44-64, esp. 45: "In weiten Teilen der heutigen Welt ist es zu einem Verlust des Sinns für die Sünde und folglich auch für die Buße gekommen. Diese Situation hat vielfältige Ursachen."

2. Cf. A. Gëlin and A. Descamps, *Sin in the Bible*, New York 1965, passim; B.J. Malina, "Some Observations on the Origin of Sin in Judaism and St. Paul," *Cath. Bibl. Quarterly*, 31 (1969), pp. 18-34; S. Lyonnet and L. Sabourin, *Sin, Redemption, and Sacrifice, A Biblical and Patristic Study (Analecta Biblica* 48), Rome 1970, pp. 3-11; P. Schonenberg and K. Rahner, art. "Sin", *Sacramentum Mundi*, vol. 6, New York, 1970, pp. 87-94.

3. Cf. H. Leroy "Zur Vergebung der Sünden, Die Botschaft der Evangelien," *(Stuttgarter Bibelstudien* 73), Stuttgart 1974, pp. 18-22.

4. For the exegesis of this passage see C.E.B. Cranfield, "The Epistle to the Romans," (JCC), vol. I, Edingburgh 1975, pp. 104-125, and K. Kertelge, "The Epistle to the Romans," *(New Testament for Spiritual Reading*, ed. by J.L. McKenzie), London 1972, pp. 23-30.

5. Cf. S. Lyonnet, *op.cit.*, p. 3: "The notion of redemption is intimately connected with that of sin."

6. Cf. S. Lyonnet, *op.cit.*, p. 57: "Man cannot be liberated from the tyranny of sin except by receiving a new dynamism, the life-giving Spirit, the Spirit of God, the only source of life."

7. Cf. R. Schnackenburg, *The Moral Teaching of the New Testament*, Freiburg, London, 1965, pp. 344f. With this expression we have to compare the other one, "sin against the Holy Spirit" (Mk 3,29 parallels), though the distinction between them must not be overlooked, as Schnackenburg emphasizes.

8. P. Ricoeur, "Guilt, Ethics and Religion," *Concilium*, vol. 56, New York 1970, pp. 11-27, has expressed especially the difference between the ethical (in Kantian terms) and the religious significance of evil: "It seems to me that religion is distinguished from ethics in the fact that it requires that we think of freedom under the sign of hope" (*ibid.* 23).

9. T.J. Deidun, "New Covenant Morality in Paul," *(Analecta Biblica*, vol. 89), Rome 1981, p. 50, understands the idea of the "fulfilment of the New Covenant through God's salvation deed in Christ" as the main "theological context of christian morality" according to Paul.

10. A. Feuillet, "Metanoia," *Sacramentum Mundi*, vol. 4, New York 1969, pp. 16-23, here 20. Cf. also R. Schnackenburg, *op.cit.*, pp. 25-33: "The Demand for Repentance".

11. Cf. A. Feuillet, *op.cit.*, p. 20, and G. Bornkamm, *Jesus von Nazareth*, 12th ed., Stuttgart, 1980, p. 73-75: Metanoia in the preaching of Jesus means: "das schon gegenwärtige Heil ergreifen und dafür alles darangeben. . . Heil und Buße. . . haben jetzt ihren Platz vertauscht."

12. Cf. K. Kertelge (ed.), "Mission im Neuen Testament," (*Quaestiones Disputatae* 93), Freiburg 1982, passim.

13. Cf. K. Kertelge, "The Epistle to the Romans," pp. 65ff.

14. Cf. V.P. Furnish, *The Love Command in the New Testament*, Nashville, New York, 1972, p. 211: "The New Testament word. . . which best describes love's work in calling a community of love into being is *reconciliation*. It describes the meaning of God's gift of love and of the commandment to love inherent in the gift."

15. Cf. E. Iserloh, "Mit dem Evangelium läßt sich die Welt nicht regieren," — *Luthers Lehre von den beiden Regimenten im Widerstreit*, Düsseldorf: Westdeutscher Verlag, 1983.

16. Cf. R. Schnackenburg, *loc.cit.*, p. 168-260.

17. Cf. V.P. Furnish, *Theology and Ethics in Paul*, Nashville, New York, 1968, pp. 227-241.

18. This is also the starting point in the development of the ethics of Jesus and in laying the foundation for an encounter between the New Testament and moral theology in the profound book of H. Merklein, *Die Gottesherrschaft als Handlungsprinzip, Untersuchung zur Ethik Jesu (Forschung zur Bibel.* vol. 34), Würzburg, 1978.

19. In this way we understand the suggestion of H. Schürmann, "Die Frage nach der Verbindlichkeit neutestamentlicher Wertungen und Weisungen," in: J. Ratzinger, *Prinzipien Christlicher Moral*, Einsiedeln 1975, pp. 9-39, esp. 39: "Modern critical knowledge and the ethical knowledge of the Holy Scriptures must be confronted with each other again and again. . . The exegete cannot decide the questions of ethical hermeneutics single-handed." Schürmann has oftentimes been engaged in this question of ethical

hermeneutics on the basis of Scripture. See also his contribution, "Die Verbindlichkeit konkreter sittlicher Normen nach dem Neuen Testament, bedacht am Beispiel des Ehescheidungsverbotes und im Lichte des Liebesgebotes," in: W. Kerber (ed.), *Sittliche Normen, Zum Problem ihrer allgemeinen und unwandelbaren Geltung,* Düsseldorf, 1982, pp. 107-123. The question of ethical hermeneutics on the basis of biblical revelation and Christian faith is nowadays recognized to be a major problem in moral theology, treated and solved in different ways, as can be seen in the publications cited above and in the following papers: B. Schüller, "Zur Diskussion über das Proprium einer Christlichen Ethik," *Theologie und Philosophie,* 1976, pp. 321-343; J. Fuchs, "Bischöfe und Moraltheologen, Eine innerkirchliche Spannung," *Stimmen der Zeit,* 1983, pp. 601-619. A position of "balance" seems to be taken by F. Böckle, "Weisung aus dem Wort, Moraltheologie und Exegese heute," in: K. Kertelge (ed.), *Ethik im Neuen Testament (Quaestiones Disputatae),* Freiburg, 1984 (in print).

20. Cf. esp. H. Schürmann, "Die Gemeinde des Neuen Bundes als der Quellort des sittlichen Erkennens nach Paulus," *Catholica,* vol. 26, Münster 1972, p. 15-37.

Chapter 2

The Development of Doctrine
about Sin, Conversion
and the Following of Christ

The Reverend Benedict M. Ashley, O.P., Ph.D., S.T.M.

Development of Doctrine

Everyone admits that moral theology, like all of theology, ought to be securely grounded in the Sacred Scriptures. Yet the traditional manuals contented themselves with a few, scattered proof-texts, and post-Vatican II moralists tend to construct their analyses on purely philosophical lines, christening them with occasional references to the Great Commandment of love of God and neighbor.[1] No wonder, when the only help they receive from so many biblical specialists is the assurance that the Bible contains many different strands of ethical tradition, often at odds with each other, each of which is so profoundly colored by changing historical situations that it has little or no relevance to our current problems![2] The result is that some moral theologians today argue that Christian ethics is not specifically distinct from philosophical ethics, and that the Scriptures cannot provide us today with concrete moral norms, but only with *paranesis*, that is, inspiration to follow our own consciences.[3]

Historically Catholic efforts to use the Scriptures as the foundation of a pastorally effective moral instruction have gone through four major phases. For the first thousand years, the patristic period and early middle ages, the chief concern was the moral instruction of catechumens and the homiletic instruction of the faithful, along with works of spiritual guidance for ascetics. During this long time little attention was given to developing a systematic moral theology. The rich heritage of moral thought took the form of commentary on various scriptural themes and their application to current problems of Christian life.[4] The most fruitful of these themes seems to have been the wisdom theme taken from *Deuteronomy* and the wisdom literature of the Two Ways, "the way of death and the way of life"[5] and the theme of Christ as the New Adam, the true Image of God.[6]

In the second phase, from the founding of the universities at the end of the twelfth century to the Reformation, the scholastic doctors developed a systematic Christian ethics as an integral part of a total systematic theology. Their treatises aimed to resolve the apparent contradictions in biblical teaching and to unify it around some fundamental principle.[7] They modeled their ethical systems on Greek philosophy, principally the Platonic "ascent of the mind to God," or the Aristotelian pursuit of happiness by rational choices of appropriate means to that end. Both models stressed the perfecting of human nature ("character") by the cardinal virtues of temperance, fortitude, justice and prudence elevated by grace through the specifically Christian theological virtues of faith, hope, and charity, with charity as the unifying principle.[8]

In this Scholastic theology the themes of wisdom (*sapientia*) and of the New Adam or Image of God still predominated, and we may well speak of this as a "sapiential" Christian ethic. At the end of the Middle Ages, however, especially through the influence of the great doctors, Duns Scotus and William of Ockham, a radical shift began from this sapiential model to a *voluntaristic* one in which the stress was no longer on Christian character but on obedience to the sovereign will of God expressed in the biblical commandments.[9] The causes of this shift are complex, but it can be seen as a reflection of the rapid social changes produced by urbanization and the formation of strong national states. People lost faith in the possibility of achieving order in social and personal life through a wisdom achieved by reasonable discourse and placed their hope in inculcating obedience to legitimate, indisputable authority. [10]

This late medieval shift emerged full force in the Reformation and Counter-Reformation period after Trent. The Reformers took their point of departure from a voluntaristic conception of the Law of God in His absolute sovereignty before which sinful man is driven to despair and then saved by the mercy of God in the Gospel to which the only significant response is trusting faith. From this the Lutheran tradition tended to view Christian ethical reflection as a dangerous reversion to Pharasaic self-righteousness. The Calvinist tradition, on the other hand, insisted on the so-called "third use of the Law" as necessary moral guidance for the elect and dutiful believer. [11] In the Catholic camp after Trent the same voluntaristic emphasis on the Law, on a Divine Command ethics, also predominated, having one of its best formulations in the work of Francis Suarez, [12] from which it shaped the great treatises and manuals on what came to be called "Moral Theology".

This Moral Theology tended to be separated from Dogmatic Theology and from Ascetic or Spiritual Theology, and it was systematized around the Ten Commandments of God and the commandments of the Church. Rooted as it was in the Ten Commandments and concerned to be literally consistent with all biblical norms, applied with a casuistic scrupulosity reminiscent of the rabbis, this "manual theology" cannot fairly be described as ignorant of Scripture. Moreover, it was needed pastorally in a period when the Church, severely criticized by the Reformers for moral laxity, and suffering from the growing religious division and secularization in Europe, was striving through the more frequent use of the confessional to instruct Christians in a clear, concrete knowledge of their moral obligations. Its great weakness was its negativism and minimalism which made it appear a reversion to an Old Testament level of morality. [13]

Clearly Vatican II called theologians to recover the more broadly scriptural and pastoral approach of the early church and the sapiential emphasis of the Scholastics, without losing the practical pastoral and disciplinary gains achieved in the post-Tridentine period. The way to such a renewal had already been prepared in the hundred years previous to the Council by the great progress in biblical and patristic studies, on the one hand, and the revival of an historically accurate appreciation of scholastic theology on the other.[14]

The Following of Christ

To return to the Bible as the foundation of Christian ethics requires us — this much the medieval scholastics have taught us — to look for a unifying principle amidst the various and even apparently contradictory strands of tradition revealed by current critical scholarship. One obvious candidate for this unifying principle (as the post-Tridentine moralists trying to meet Protestant criticisms realized) is the Ten Commandments. These "Ten Words" are the core of the Old Law, the Torah, and Jesus in the Sermon on the Mount clearly reaffirms them:[15]

Do not think that I have come to abolish the law and the prophets. I have come, not to abolish them, but to fulfill them. Of this much I assure you: until heaven and earth pass away, not the smallest letter of the law, not the smallest part of a letter, shall be done away with until it all comes true (Mt 5:17-18).

Jesus was a Jew "born under the law" (Gal 4:4) and carefully observant of its precepts.[16] His holiness, therefore, reflects the holiness of the Law: "the law is holy and the commandment is holy and just and good" (Rom 7:12). To the rich young man who asked "What must I do to share in everlasting life," Jesus answered, "Why do you call me good? No one is good but God alone. You know the commandments: You shall not kill, etc." (Mk 10:18-19). Thus any valid Christian ethics must be founded in the Ten Commandments, but is this its *ultimate* foundation?

Certainly not, for two basic reasons. First, it is obvious from the Old Testament itself that God's will for us is not merely *negative*, while all but two of the Ten Commandments are "Thou shall not's".[17] The term "Torah," which applies not only to this brief code but to the whole of the Pentateuch, is not correctly translated "Law" but "Instruction," and it is identified with "Wisdom" in the broad sense in which the Bible speaks of God's creative and providential care for His creatures, and in which we, as created in His "image and likeness" (Gn 1:27) are called to share. Thus it includes all those 613 commandments (of which 248 are positive) which the rabbis have ennumerated. [18] Moreover, the prophetic and wisdom literature of the Old Testament, as well as its historic narratives which have a moral exemplary meaning, show us that in the course of time, guided by the Holy Spirit, the Jews came to understand the commandments of the Torah in an ever deeper and broader way, thus penetrating to more ultimate principles. When Jesus said, "Treat others the way you would have them treat you: this sums up the law and the prophets" (Mt 7:11), he would have found agreement among many of the rabbis. [19]

Second, although Jesus confirmed and fulfilled the Torah, he also exercised the plenary authority given Him by His Father (Mt 28:18; Mk 11:27-33) to re-interpret the Mosaic Law so as to restore the original intentions of the Creator, freed from the limitations placed on it by the historical particularism of the Jewish people, chosen by God as His witness in a fallen world (Mt 5:21-48, and 19:3-9). Guided by this, St. Paul (and St. Peter, Acts 10:18 and 15:6-12) took the bold step of declaring that the Gentiles are not bound by the Old Law, because salvation comes from faith in Jesus Christ:

We are Jews by birth, not sinners of Gentile origin. Nevertheless, knowing that a man is not justified by legal observance but by faith in Jesus Christ, we too have believed in him in order to be justified by faith in Christ, not by observance of the law: for by works of the law no one will be justified. (Gal 2:16)

This teaching of Paul was, of course, accepted by the Catholic Church from the beginning, [20] but, as the Reformers were to point out, its implications have not always been fully implemented. Even among the Fathers of the Church St. Augustine had to battle to have it recognized, [21] and the earlier Scholastics did not always appreciate it. [22] In reaction to the Reformers the post-Tridentine moralists, while strictly adhering to its dogmatic truth, seldom allowed it to shape their moral treatises. [23]

In the light of Vatican II we should be able to surmount these inhibitions and fully recover the Pauline and patristic awareness that the supreme principle of Christian morality is not the Law, not any law, even the Great Commandment of love of God and neighbor (Mk 12:28-34) but faith in Jesus Christ, who thus Himself is that supreme principle, the New Law itself. Thus the New Law (if it is permissible to speak of it as a "law" at all[24]) is not a code written on tablets of stone, but on the hearts of believers as the prophets have foretold it would be by the Holy Spirit of God resting on the Messiah and shared by His followers (Is 11:1-3; Ez 36:26-27; Jl 2:17-18). This certainly does not mean, as some would misinterpret Paul, that faith in the holiness of Jesus as the One who has fulfilled the Law, absolves us of any responsibility to God's commands. Rather it means that the Christian way of life is the following of Christ, the *imitatio Christi* by the power of His Spirit, and as members incorporated by faith and baptism into His Body, the Church.[25]

Thus the unity of biblical teaching on the Christian way of life is to be found, not in the Law, nor in any abstract norms, nor even, as the Scholastics thought, in our ultimate end conceived as the beatific vision which is beyond our present experience, *but* in the supreme principle who is a person, in the Word of God made visible in human nature, Jesus Christ. Since He is the Second Person of the Trinity whose very existence is in His *relation* to the Father in the Spirit,[26] to live in Him and as He lives, is to live in this relation of living faith, hope, and love unto the Father which will be consummated only in the beatific vision but which is already really begun here and now in baptism, confirmation and Eucharistic Communion. In Him and only in Him we return to the image of God in which we were created, fulfill the Law, and become perfect as our heavenly Father is perfect (Mt 5:48). Thus we are enabled to fulfill that greatest commandment of love of God and neighbor in which all other commandments are included (Mk 12:28-34).

Sin

Since the fundamental principle of a specifically Christian morality is not a commandment but a relation to God the Father through the Person of the incarnate Son in the love which is the

Holy Spirit, it is clear that sin is the disruption of this relation and the forgiveness of sin is its restoration by the conversion of the sinner's will through the grace of the Spirit gained for us from the Father by the self-offering of the incarnate Son. This relation is often spoken of in the Scriptures as "the Covenant," the Old and New Testament.[27] This Covenant was initiated by the gracious act of God who will never fail us, but it can be broken by our freely chosen acts of sin, not only of commission but of omission.[28]

Some theologians today seem to think that the only kind of act which can break this relation based on a "fundamental option for God" is a direct act of hatred of God (or one against the other theological virtues).[29] They forget that Jesus linked the words of *Leviticus* (19:18; Mt 22:38-39) "You shall love your neighbor as yourself" to the *Deuteronomic* (6:5) command to love God above all things, including oneself; and that the *First Epistle of John* (4:20-21) interprets this Great Commandment:

We, for our part, love because he first loved us. If anyone says, "My love is fixed on God," yet hates his brother, he is a liar. One who has no love for the brother he has seen cannot love the God he has not seen. The commandment we have from him is this: whoever loves God must also love his brother.

Morever, this "hatred" includes even omissions, for the same epistle says, "I ask you, how can God's love survive in a man who has enough of this world's goods yet closes his heart to his brother when he sees him in need?" (3:17). The reason is that our love of God can only be a share in God's creative love for us ("We love . . . because he first loved us") and that divine love extends to all God's creatures. The only way we can "harm" God or do good to God out of love is by harming his creatures (ourselves included) or doing them good out of love.[30]

To break the covenant of love between God, ourselves, and our neighbors is to sin in the strict and proper sense of the term, that is, to commit a "mortal sin."[31] The Bible uses the term "sin" and its synonyms[32] in a variety of senses which it became the task of theologians to distinguish with technical precision, but the *primum analogatum* is "mortal sin." It should be noted, contrary to the opinion of some, that we can commit mortal sins against ourselves, as well as against our neighbors, because God's covenant is with us all. In fact every mortal sin does fatal harm to the sinner and is first of all an offense against one's authentic self as a person created in the divine image.[33]

Catholic tradition has always maintained that not all sins are mortal.[34] The Reformers, finding no explicit grounds for the notion of "venial" sin in the Bible, accused Catholic moralists of inventing it as an excuse for moral laxity.[35] On the contrary, the function of the distinction between mortal and venial sin is to take sin seriously by not reducing mortal sin which breaks our relation to God and neighbor to the kinds of sin which do not break that relation, although they do tend to erode it, and will, if unrepented, eventually lead to such a break.[36] Equally unacceptable as this Protestant contention that no sins are venial is the recent theory of some Catholic moralists that sins can be "serious" without being mortal.[37] As we have seen, the Bible clearly teaches that to do serious harm to our neighbor is absolutely incompatible with loving God. Both errors betray a fundamentally legalistic understanding of sin according to which what makes it mortal or venial is nothing more than the kind of punishment which God has decreed for its sanction, rather than its effect on our relation to God and neighbor.

The real question, therefore, is how do we determine whether a certain kind of act does serious harm, either by commission or omission, to ourselves or our neighbor? On this determination and on it alone depends whether a sin is objectively mortal. The classical manualists used various criteria but these seem to reduce to two: (1) those sins are mortal which seem to be labeled as very grave by the Scriptures, especially when the Old Law decrees capital punishment for them; (2) they are mortal if they seem to be have been treated as such in the Church's penitential discipline, e.g. if they led to excommunication, public penance, etc.[37b] It should be obvious that such criteria are no more than useful *signs* that a sin does serious harm, but they are not infallible signs. The sanctions for sin fixed in the Old Law are sometimes too heavy, sometimes too light, if judged by the later practice of the Church, and the Church's own disciplinary practice has varied greatly in different times and places.[38] One of the most urgent tasks of moral theology today is to develop a better set of criteria for the harm and benefit of human actions, taking into account all that we have learned from the experiences of history and from the behavioral sciences. The wise St. Augustine said that "What sins are trivial (*levia*) and what grave (*gravia*) it is for divine judgement, not human judgement to decide",[39] but in all humility the theologian must try.

Certainly the problem cannot be solved simply by urging people "to do what is most loving," since to act lovingly is to do good and not harm, and how are we to know what really benefits and what really harms?[40] Nor is it enough to say with moralists of the proportionalist school, "Always do more good than harm," which is a mere truism.[41] Instead it is necessary to measure harms and benefits against a model of what it is to be truly human. An action is seriously harmful, and therefore a mortal sin, if either by commission or omission it makes impossible an essential conformity to the New Adam, Jesus Christ.

In Jesus' life and teaching we find respect for the four basic goods without which a truly human life is impossible.[42] First, by His practice of non-violence and His work of physical and mental healing and feeding the hungry, He taught us respect for life.[43] Second, by His own manly chastity and His blessing of marriage and children, He taught us our sexuality can be exercised genitally only in wedded love.[44] Third, by His acceptance of the outcast and respect for civil authority, He taught us how to live together in peace and justice. Fourth, by His teaching and prayer and His witness to the wisdom of God on the Cross, He demonstrated the supreme value of truth, especially that loving truth which is fidelity to the Father.[45] Acts which are directly contrary to these fundamental goods which must be harmoniously integrated to form human life are intrinsically evil, and, if they concern what is *essential* to these goods, are mortal. Thus lying is always wrong because it is contradictory to the truth of communication necessary for human social life, but it can be only venial if the truth in question concern matters not essential to that life.[46] On the other hand, the direct killing of non-aggressors is intrinsically wrong and always mortal because it deprives the victim of the good of life itself.

Some today argue that a single act cannot be a mortal sin, because the fundamental option for God and neighbor cannot be so easily changed.[47]. It can be conceded that ordinarily it requires

54

many sinful acts to change one's fundamental option, but these are venial sins which prepare the way for the decisive act which is a mortal sin. It may also be granted that in the case of someone struggling to overcome a habit of objectively mortal sin occasional failures may not be mortal for subjective reasons.

Conversion

The recognition of this gap between subjective and objective morality raises the question of *conversion* which first of all concerns the conscience and the inner act of choice. Jesus' whole Sermon on the Mount stresses the significance of a right intention (Mt 5-7), and, against the Pharasaic emphasis on the exterior act, He said "What emerges from within a man, that and nothing else is what makes him impure."[48] Certainly that is not to say the intention alone counts, since Jesus goes on to enumerate evil intentions as "acts of fornication, theft, murder, adulterous conduct, greed, maliciousness, deceit, sensuality, envy, blasphemy, arrogance, an obtuse spirit" (Mk 7:22). What is meant is that the morality of an act proceeds from its conformity to the actor's personal conscience, or judgement as to whether what he or she is doing will cooperate with God's love for His creatures.

Nevertheless this subjective rectitude of conscience, although it excuses the agent from personal sin, does not fulfill God's loving purpose unless it is also objectively right. The soldier who kills an "enemy"in good conscience, still destroys the life of a brother who may be as innocent in God's eyes as himself. How is it possible that we live in a world where even subjectively moral actions contribute to increase human misery? Surely the devil's work is less evident in the evil done by evil men, than in the harm done by good men.[49] In the sad prophecy of Jesus, "The time will come when anyone who puts you to death will claim to be serving God." (Jn 16:2).

This tragic gap between subjective and objective morality is the principal theme of modern moral theology. In the past, although moralists were perfectly acquainted with the distinction, they tended to assume that, generally speaking, men and women of good will would know the difference of right and wrong.[50] Especially if they were Catholics, if they were in doubt, they had only to ask their confessors. The modern world, however, is characterized by its plurality of value systems, by its confusion of ideologies, and by a distrust of institutions, traditional standards, and authorities. Consequently it is possible even for Catholics of good will to live by false moral norms in what they suppose is a conscientious dissent from the moral teachings of the Church.

This situation (so prominent today, but not without historic parallels[51]) makes very meaningful the doctrine of original sin. Current theology has done a good deal to rehabilitate this doctrine and to show that it was not merely the creation of St. Augustine, as is sometimes asserted, but has secure roots in Scripture.[52] Original sin (although it is, as Trent said,[53] truly sin) is only analogous to actual sin, just as venial sin is only analogous to mortal sin. Moreover, it is best understood not merely as the isolated sin of the first human beings, but as the actual human condition which has resulted from the historic accumulation of all the sins of human society.[54] God intends that each human soul He creates in a body produced by its parents should come to exist in a world and a human society in which everything would be directed to endowing that human person with the natural and supernatural gifts that would enable him or her to grow up in a covenant relation with God and neighbor. In fact, however, because that world has been distorted by the history of human sin, each of us comes into existence alienated from God, our neighbor, and our true selves. Not only are we deprived of many of the helps God intended for us, but we are perverted into ways that lead from Him and divide us from our fellow humans. No wonder then that even when grace has converted us again to God and neighbor, we walk in profound confusion, only dimly seeing the path of objective moral truth!

This sensitivity to the gap between the subjectively good conscience and objective moral truth gives us the clue to the pastoral strategy of the Church appropriate to our times.[55] The Church must continue to present the objective moral truth without compromise because ultimately only such norms can lead to the Kingdom of God on earth as in heaven. At the same time, however, the Church must see that its task is not merely "to lay down the law," but to educate consciences, necessarily a very delicate and gradual task, by first teaching our world to see Jesus

Christ as He really is in all His beauty. Only if He is first loved will our age be drawn to follow His way of life. If men and women are to be converted to God, and not only converted in will, but enlightened in conscience to see what is truly of benefit to themselves and to human society, they must come to know not a moral code, but a Person in whom the law and the prophets are fulfilled.

In summary, it can be said that the trajectory of the development of moral theology from the New Testament to the present has been a dialectical process in which we have come to see more clearly that the Commandments of God for us are manifested only in Jesus Christ who calls us to follow Him to the Father in the power of His Holy Spirit.

Notes

1. The issues relating to the use of the Bible in ethics are well discussed by Protestant authors. See James M. Gustafson, "Place of Scripture in Christain Ethics: A Methodological Study," in his *Theology and Christian Ethics* (Philadelphia; United Church Press, 1974), pp. 121-146, and Bruce C. Birch and Larry Rasmussen, *Bible and Ethics in Christian Life,* (Minneapolis: Augsburg Press, 1976). The most useful Catholic efforts to provide a biblical moral theology are Ceslaus Spicq, O.P., *Théologie Morale du Nouveau Testament*, 2 vols. (Paris: J. Gabalda, 1965) and Rudolf Schackenburg, *The Moral Teaching of the New Testament* (New York: Seabury, 1973). See also Pierre Grelot, *Problèmes de Moral Fondamentale: Une éclairage biblique* (Paris: Cerf. 1982).

2. See, for example, the conclusion of the chapter on "The Bible and Human Sexuality" in A. Kosnik et al. *Human Sexuality: New Directions in American Catholic Thought*, A Study Commissioned by the Catholic Theological Society of America (Garden City, N.Y., Doubleday, 1979), p. 49, "Looking at the plurality of the statements and attitudes on human sexuality in the Bible, the inconsistencies among them, and the historical circumstances that gave rise to them, critical biblical scholarship finds it impossible on the basis of the empirical data to approve or reject categorically any particular sexual act outside of its contextual circumstances and intention. In view of the weight of contrary historical evidence, anyone who maintains that the Bible absolutely forbids certain forms of sexual behavior, regardles of circumstances, must likewise bear the burden of the proof.

This is not to say, however, that the Bible leaves us without ideals or any guidance whatever. Scripture provides us with certain fundamental themes as a basis on which to construct a modern theology of human sexuality. Despite changing historical circumstances and perspective, the biblical authors consistently give common witness to the nature of God as gracious and loving, and to the ideal of fidelity as a foremost expression of our loving response. While the Bible does not provide absolute dictates about specific sexual practices, it declares that sexual intercourse is good, always to be seen, however, within the larger context of personhood and community."

3. See for example Edward Schillebeeckx, *Christ: The Experience of Jesus as Lord* (New York: Seabury, 1980), pp. 585-600, who reduces such norms as those pronounced by Jesus and Paul either to customs of the time or to ideals. Schillebeeckx is correct in insisting that the literary form of the Sermon on the Mount and other pronouncements be carefully analyzed before interpreting its sayings as either legal precepts or moral norms; but his own interpretations seem to me to be an anachronistic reading of modern ethical relativism into the biblical text.

4. Unfortunately there exists no up-to-date history of Christian moral thinking. Useful is the outline by G. Angelini and A. Valsecchi, *Disegno Storico della Teologia Morale* (Bologna: Edizione Dehoniane Bologna, 1972).

5. Thus the "Two Ways" section of the *Didache* used for the instruction of Christian candidates for baptism in the first century seems to be a revision of a short moral catechism for Jewish proselytes. See B. Altaner, *Patrology* (New York: Herder and Herder, 1960), pp. 51-53; See also Francis X. Murphy, *Moral Teaching in the Primitive Church* (Glen Rock, N. J. Paulist, 1968).

6. See Vladimir Lossky, *In the Image and Likeness of God* (New York: St. Vladimir's Seminary Press, 1974), and George Maloney, S.J., *Man the Divine Icon* (Pecos, NM, Dove Press, 1973).

7. See Yves M.-J. Congar, O.P., *A History of Theology* (Garden City, N.Y., Doubleday, 1968), pp. 85-143 for the different notions of "systematization" among the Scholastics, and Thomas Deman, O.P., *Aux origines de la théologie morale* (Conference Albert le Gran, 1951): (Montreal/Paris: J. Vrin, 1951) on the significance of the application of such systematization to Christian ethics.

8. The only biblical basis for the adoption of the four cardinal virtues into Christian ethics from Stoic (and hence from Platonic and Aristotelian) influences is one text, *Wisdom* 8:7. The theological virtues are, of course, derived from *1 Cor* 13:13.

9. See Robert Prentice O.F.M., "The Voluntarity of Duns Scotus Seen in His Comparison of the Intellect and Will," *Franciscan Studies* 28 (1968): 63-104 and David W. Clark, "Voluntarism and Rationalism in the Ethics of Ockham", *Franciscan Studies* 31 (1971): 72-87. Clark defends Ockham on the grounds that Ockham admits a natural law, but Clark grants that the principles of the natural law for Ockham are grounded in the will of God which is free to change concrete moral norms, and that Ockham goes so far as to teach that God by his *potentia absoluta* could command us to hate Him and then to do so would be an act of charity!

10. See Gordon Leff, *The Dissolution of the Medieval Outlook* (New York: Harper and Row, 1976) for a discussion of the cultural and intellectual influences on theology in the late Middle Ages and for bibliography.

11. See N.H.Søe, "The Three 'Uses' of the Law" in G.H. Outka and P. Ramsey, *Norm and Context in Christian Ethics* (New York: Scribner's, 1968), pp. 297-324. For Lutherans the Law has the function for the non-believer of maintaining public order, and for the believer of "terrifying the conscience" which only the announcement of God's mercy in the Gospel can pacify. On the third use of the Law to instruct the conscience of the believer, Lutherans are divided, but Calvin defended this third use. See Werner Elert, *Law and Gospel* (Philadelphia: Fortress Press, 1967), and Paul Althaus, *The Ethics of Martin Luther* (Philadelphia: Fortress Press, 1972), Ronald S. Wallace, *Calvin's Doctrine of the Christian Life,* (Grand Rapids: Eerdmans, 1959).

12. On the history of post-Tridentine moral theology, see Louis Vereecke, "Preface à l'histoire de la théologie morale moderne" in *Studia Moralia* (Rome: Academia Alfonsiana Institutum Theologiae Moralis, 1962, I), pp. 87-120. On the period of "Orthodox" Lutheranism see Robert D. Preuss, *The Theology of Post-Reformation Lutheranism* (St. Louis: Concordia Publishing House, 1970), and on Calvinist developments see Brian G. Armstrong, *Calvinism and the Amyraut Heresy* (Madison: University of Wisconsin Press, 1969), Appendix I, pp. 273-275.

13. See Bernard Häring, C.S.S.R., *The Law of Christ* (Philadelphia: Westminister Press, 1961), vol. 1, Chapter 1, for a history and criticism of the manualists.

14. For example, the well known work of Gerard Gilleman, S.J., *The Primacy of*

Charity in Moral Theology (Westminster, MD: Newman Press, 1961).

15. See Johann J. Stamm and Maurice E. Andrew, *The Commandments in Recent Research*, Studies in Biblical Theology, Second Series (Naperville, IL: Allenson, 1962), and Warren S. Kissinger, *The Sermon on the Mount: A History of Interpretation and Bibliography* (Metuchen, NJ: Scarecrow Press, 1975).

16. For an argument from a Jewish point of view showing that although Jesus gave His own interpretation of the Torah, He was careful not to violate it, see M. Lowe and David Flusser, "Evidence corroborating a modified Proto-Matthean Synoptic Theory," *New Testament Studies* 29 (Jan., 1983): 25-47.

17. See Grelot, *op. cit.* , pp. 19-24; and 103-146.

18. See Maimonides, *The Commandments (Sefer Ha-Mitzvoth)* trans. by Rabbi Dr. Charles B. Chavel, (London/New York: Soncino Press, 1967), vol. 1: the positive commandments; vol. 2: the negative; and Herbert S. Goldstein, *Between the Lines of the Bible: A Modern Commentary on the 613 Commandments* (New York: Crown Publishers, 1959).

19. See Schnackenburg, *op. cit.* pp. 90-98.

20. Even the Nominalist theologians of the fourteenth and fifteenth century never denied that without the gift of saving faith no human work is profitable to salvation. See Francis Clark, "A New Appraisal of Late Medieval Theology," *Gregorianum* 46 (1965): 733-65.

21. See Charles Boyer, S.J., "Le système de Saint Augustin sur la grace" in his *Essais anciens et nouveaux sur la doctrine de Saint Augustin* (Milan: Marzorati, 1970), pp. 269-294.

22. The decrees of the Council of Orange were unknown to the earlier Scholastics and even to the younger Aquinas so that their language could sometimes be accused of Semi-Pelagianism, yet this is a lack of theological rigor rather than a tendency of their thought.

24. The manualists, of course, were never Pelagians but they failed to give *grace* the central position it must have in a sound moral theology. For example, even so Thomistic a manualist as Dominicus M. Prümmer, O.P., in his well known *Manuale Theologiae Moralis* (Fribourg: Herder, 1958), deals with grace only in his third volume while treating of the sacraments.

25. The concept of the *imitatio Christi* must not be interpreted in such a way as to negate the necessity for moral theology to deal both with an analysis of the virtues and of the commandments, but must be treated as the principle from which these are derived. For an able refutation of false understandings of the *imitatio* see Louis B. Gillon, O.P., *Christ and Moral Theology* (Staten Island, NY: Alba House, 1967). See also Rudolf Schnackenburg, "The Imitation of Christ" in his *Christian Existence in the New Testament* (Notre Dame, IN.: University of Notre Dame Press, 1968), pp. 1-128 and Joseph Fuchs, S.J., "The Law of Christ" in Enda McDonagh, *Moral Theology Renewed* (Dublin: Gill and Son, 1964), pp. 75-84.

26. St. Thomas Aquinas, *Summa Theologiae* I, q. 40, a.1, ad lm. "For the personal properties are identical with the persons for the same reason that the abstract is identical with the concrete; for these properties are the subsistent Persons, so that Paternity is the Father Himself, and Sonship is the Son Himself, and Procession is the Holy Spirit Himself."

27. On the importance of the concept of "Covenant" for Christian ethics, see Grelot, *op. cit.* pp. 77-85; 93-94.

28. *Ibid.* pp. 142-143.

29. On the fundamental option, see Eugene J. Cooper, "Notes and Comments: Fundamental Option," *Irish Theological Quarterly*, 39 (1972):383-392; Felix Podmatten, O.F.M. Cap., "What is Mortal Sin," *Clergy Monthly*, 36 (Feb., 1972): 57-67, and J.A. O'Donahoe, "Sin (Theology)," *New Catholic Encyclopedia*, vol. 17, pp. 610-11. Authors critical of the concept are Theodore Hall, O.P., "That Mysterious Fundamental Option," *Homiletic and Pastoral Review*, 78 (Jan., 1978): 12-20 and Joseph Boyle Jr. "Freedom, the Human Person, and Human Action," in William E. May, *Principles of Catholic Moral Life* (Chicago: Franciscan Herald Press, 1980), pp. 237-266. The Congregation for the Doctrine of the Faith in its *Declaration on Certain Questions Concerning Sexual Ethics*,

1976, says: "There are those who go as far as to affirm that mortal sin, which causes separation from God, only exists in the formal refusal directly opposed to God's call, or in that selfishness which completely and deliberately closes itself to the love of neighbor. They say that it is only then that there comes into play the fundamental option, that is to say, the decision which totally commits the person and which is necessary if mortal sin is to exist; by this option the person, from the depths of the personality, takes up or ratifies a fundamental attitude towards God or people. On the contrary, so-called "peripheral" actions (which, it is said, usually do not involve decisive choice), do not go so far as to change the fundamental option, the less so since they often come, as is observed, from habit. Thus such actions can weaken the fundamental option, but not to such a degree as to change it completely. Now according to these authors, a change of the fundamental option towards God less easily comes about in the field of sexual activity . . . In reality, it is precisely the fundamental option which in the last resort defines a person's moral disposition. But it can be completely changed by particular acts, especially when, as often happens, these have been prepared for by previous more superficial acts. Whatever the case, it is wrong to say that particular acts are not enough to constitute mortal sin."

30. St. Catherine of Siena was told by God the Father that, "I would have you know that every virtue of yours and every vice is put into action by means of your neighbors. If you hate me, you harm your neighbor and yourself as well (for you are your chief neighbor) and the harm is both general and particular." *The Dialogue*, Chapter 6; trans. by Suzanne Noffke, O.P. (Classics of Western Spirituality) (New York: Paulist Press, 1980), p. 33.

31. St. Thomas Aquinas, *Summa Theologiae* I-II, q. 72, a. 5.

32. Synonyms for sin are discussed in the article "*hamartánō*" by G. Quell, G. Bertram, G. Stählin, W. Grundmann, and K. Rengstorf in: Gerhard Kittel, *Theological Dictionary of the New Testament* (Grand Rapids, Mich.: Eerdmans, 1964), vol. 1, pp. 267-335.

33. See note 30 above. Every sin is an action contrary to reason and, therefore, contrary to the nature of the rational person who performs it. Those acts whose objects are *intrinsically* evil are directly contradictory to one of the basic needs or goals of human nature, as, for example, lying directly contradicts the basic human need to communicate the truth.

34. On the history of the development of the distinction between mortal and venial sin, see Th. Deman, article "Péché" in DTC, 12:1, col. 140-275. Also, Hubert L. Motry, *The Concept of Sin in Early Christianity* (diss.) (Washington, D.C.: Catholic University of America, 1920), and the excellent collection, *Théologie du Péché* (Bibliothèque de Théologie, Serie II, Théologie Moral, vol. VII), (Tournai: Desclee, 1960), especially M. Huftier, "Péché mortel et péché véniel", p. 633-451. Another helpful discussion is Henri Rondet, S.J., *The Theology of Sin*, (Notre Dame, IN, Fides: 1960). A useful collection of patristic texts is to be found in Hubert Gerigk, *Wesen und Voraussetzungen der Todsunde*, Breslau, 1903. Motry argues that the distinction is *implicitly* in the *Didaché* and early Fathers and certainly in Tertullian. Huftier credits Augustine with its earliest clear formulation. It must be admitted, however, that it was not until the Scholastics that theologians got beyond the consideration of the kinds of *punishments* due to mortal and venial sins, to the *essences* of these sins themselves. It may be a shock to realize that Christians got along for 1300 years without a clear distinction between mortal and venial sin! The truth is that there was never any doubt that certain kinds of acts exclude from the Eucharist and merit eternal damnation, but that not all sins do so. What was not clearly formulated was *why* not all sins are mortal. To Augustine and Aquinas is chiefly due the solution of this problem.

35. According to C. Vogel, *(Théologie du Péché*, preceding note pp. 522-523), Luther's position is that all sins are of themselves mortal because they flow from man's corrupted nature, but that in the believer they become venial by reason of the imputation of justice through faith. Calvin's position was that all sins are mortal, since all involve a rebellion against the Divine Sovereignty. See the work of Wallace, note 11 above.

60

36. The Thomist view is that venial sin is impossible for an angel because the angel's spiritual intelligence cannot deceive itself as to the inconsistency between willing the good and choosing a means inappropriate to attain it. Nor could Adam and Eve sin venially in their first sin because they were free of concupiscence, i.e., a conflict between their reason and their appetites, due to the special graces in which they were created. Nor can a child in its *first free* choice, because in that choice it must also make a fundamental option according to or against its conscience. After this first choice human beings are, in their fallen condition, able to commit venial sins, because while continuing to adhere to their fundamental option (good or evil), they are able by reason of the weakness of their intelligence and the concupiscence of their appetites, to deceive themselves about the consistency of the means they choose with the good end they have chosen (if their fundamental option was good) or know they should have chosen (if their option was bad).

37. For speculations on this subject see M. Sánchez, "Por un división tripartita del Pecado", *Studium* (Madrid), 10 (1970): 347-358, and Thomas N. Hart, S.J., "Sin in the Context of the Fundamental Option," *Homiletic and Pastoral Review* 71 (1970-71): 47-49.

37b. Thus, Prümmer, *op. cit.* (note 24 above, vol. I, pp. 247-8) says that a sin is to be judged mortal (1) *on the basis of authority* (a) if the Scriptures attach the death penalty, say that it condemns to hell, or characterize it as detestable; (b) if the decrees of the Councils or the Pope have so declared; (c) if so declared by the common teaching of theologians; (2) *or the basis of reason*, if from the object and the circumstances it involves a grave deordination from the eternal law of God, i.e. against God, human society, the neighbor, or oneself, *according to a prudent judgement* concerning the precept and the end which the act impedes. Certainly this is correct, but Prümmer then gives as an example of a mortal sin the omission by the priest of a few drops of water in the chalice at Mass because "the reason for this, e.g. the effusion of the water and blood from the side of Christ is very grave"! Is it really a prudent judgement that the neglect of a single (and secondary) symbolic act in the Eucharist which contains so many is "very grave"? I fear that such "traditional" opinions resemble the attempts of the Pharisees to "fence in the Law." Irreverent negligence in celebration of the liturgy is hardly to be remedied by creating scruples, yet this seems to have been the good purpose of the manualists in many of their "prudent judgements."

38. See the article of E. Amann, A. Michel and M. Jugie, "Pénitence-Sacrament," *Dictionnaire de Théologie Catholique*, tom. 12:1, col. 747-1138.

39. St. Augustine, *Enchiridion*, PL 40: 78, col. 269. Translation by B. Peebles, *Writings of St. Augustine*, vol. 4, (Ludwig Schopp, ed., *Fathers of the Church*, Cima Publishers, 1947), p. 433.

40. The "situation ethics" controversy was started by Joseph Fletcher in his *Situation Ethics* (Philadelphia: Westminister Press, 1966). For a critique, see Paul Ramsey, *Deeds and Rules in Christian Ethics* (Edinburgh: Oliver and Boyd, 1965), pp. 144 ff. The view was never defended by Catholic moralists and is best understood as a reaction to Protestant legalism. The same problems, however, have arisen in the Catholic proportionalist controversy.

41. For a bibliography on proportionalism and a critique see Benedict M. Ashley, O.P. and Kevin D. O'Rourke, O.P., *Health Care Ethics*, 2nd ed. (St. Louis: Catholic Health Association, 1982), pp. 160-171.

42. These four basic ends of human life are derived from Aquinas, *Summa Theologiae* I-II. q. 94, a. 2. Germain Grisez in *The Way of the Lord Jesus: A Summary of Catholic Moral Theology* (Chicago: Franciscan Herald Press, 1984) has developed a refinement of this list, according to which basic goods can be divided into two classes (a) "reflexive" (because they imply choice), namely (1) self-integration; (2) authenticity; (3) justice and friendship; (4) religion; and (b) "substantive", namely, (5) life; (6) knowledge or truth and appreciation of beauty; (7) activities of skillful work and play.

43. Jesus accepted the Old Testament commandment "Thou shalt not kill," and in the Sermon on the Mount added to it precepts against anger and violence. He accepted the Old Testament regulations, some of which had a hygenic purpose, and others which

aimed at providing the poor with proper food, clothing, and housing. He was the advocate of children and other weak persons whose bodily needs are often neglected. Finally He was miraculously the "Divine Physician" in lieu of medical care which was then unavailable. At the same time He advocated a spirit of simplicity and reliance on God for bodily needs. Christian ascetics, sometimes too much influenced by Platonic dualism, have sometimes given the impression that the Gospel is negligent of the body, but the doctrine of the Resurrection is evidence that proper bodily discipline does not imply contempt for the body.

44. That Jesus approved marriage is evident from His strengthening of the Old Testament regulation of divorce and His blessing of children. His own example of celibacy, followed by St. Paul against the usual rabbinical interpretation of the Law, did not arise from dualism but from the need to witness to the fact that the Kingdom of God transcends the historical cycle of birth and death to bestow eternal life.

45. Jesus' teaching centered on the Kingdom of God, which, according to the Old Testament prophets, includes the reign of justice to the oppressed, whose realization on "earth as in heaven", Jesus taught us to pray for. This Kingdom, moreover, is above all the Kingdom of Truth, not in the sense of abstract knowledge, but in the sense of knowing and loving God.

46. St. Augustine, in his treatise *De Mendacio* PL 40:517-548, took a firm stand that lying is intrinsically wrong. Proportionalists today tend to defend lying to achieve a greater good or avoid a greater evil and accuse those who consider it as intrinsically wrong as dishonest in defending "mental reservations" and "equivocations" as a way of escaping tight situations where it seems obviously immoral to tell the truth at the expense of other important values. Most difficult cases, however, are easily solved if we remember two things: (1) truthfulness does not require us to give information to those who have no right to it; (2) the meaning of any statement depends on the context in which it is spoken. Consequently, it is no lie to answer illegitimate questions under unjust coercion by statements whose meaning in the context is ambiguous, in order to maintain confidentiality. It should also be noted that the reason lying, although intrinsically always wrong, is sometimes only a venial sin, is because not all information is *essential* to human fulfillment. On the contrary, killing the innocent can never be a venial sin, because life *is* essential to human fulfillment. As for sexual sins, these can be venial if they do not involve consent to orgasm (e.g. immodest touches *may* be venial); but if they involve consent to orgasm, they are analogous to a lie about a serious matter essential to human fulfillment, since the genital act is by its very nature designed to express the permanent *commitment* of married love.

48. The theme which runs throughout the Sermon on the Mount (Mt 5-7) is expressed in the verse, "When you are praying do not behave like the hypocrites, etc." (5:5).

49. The tragedy of the New Testament is that it is not the harlots and publicans who reject Jesus, but the most religious and zealous of the Jews, who were blinded to His truth by their own love of the Holy Law. It is difficult not to see in this opposition of the good to the Good the work of a superhumanly intelligent Deceiver.

50. Thus Aquinas, *Summa Theologiae* II-II, q. 11, a. 3, taught that heretics should not only be excommunicated but put to death, without taking into consideration that most "heretics" are probably only so *materially* and not formally, and therefore, by his own principles, not guilty of sins against faith.

51. Even in the so-called "Age of Faith", the High Middle Ages, the gap between the objective moral standards developed by the Scholastic doctors and the level of subjective moral understanding of the common faithful was very great indeed, as evidenced by the relative infrequency of their reception of the sacraments.

52. For reviews of these opinions see Henri Rondet, S.J., *Original Sin* (Staten Island, NY: Alba House, 1972); James L. O'Connor, S.J., "Original Sin: Contemporary Approaches," *Theological Studies*, 29 (1968): 215-240; Maurizio Flick and Zoltan Alzeghy, S.J., *Il peccato originale*, 2nd ed. (Brescia: Queriniana, 1974); G. Vandervelde, *Original Sin: Two Major Trends in Contemporary Roman Catholic Interpretation* (Amsterdam: Rodopi N.V., 1975). On the exegetical problems, see A.M. Dubarle, *The Biblical Doctrine of Original Sin* (New York: Herder and Herder, 1964).

53. The Council of Trent, Session 5, (Denziger 787-792), declared that original sin is transmitted to all "not by imitation but by propagation" and that the grace of baptism removes whatever has "the true and proper nature of sin." Consequently the concupiscence which remains after baptism is the effect of sin, but is not properly speaking sin. Original sin, on the other hand, has "the true and proper nature of sin" not in the manner of actual sin, but in the sense that it deprives the unbaptized child of that life of grace in which God intended the child to come into existence. Thus original sin is truly and properly sin but only by *analogy* to actual sin.

54. See note 52 for references.

55. See the commentary of Cardinal Ratzinger on the 43 propositions of the Synod of Bishops of 1980, *La Documentation Catholique*, no. 1806, (1981), pp. 393 ff. and Pope John Paul II, *Familiaris Consortio* (1981) n. 34. The Pope insists that the *lex gradualitatis* is not to be confused with a *gradualitas legis*. The moral law as founded in objective relations is always and universally binding, not as a mere ideal, but as a true law and the Church as witness must not conceal or water-down its demands. Yet there remains the pastoral and pedagogical problem of helping people to come to understand that law, not merely as an imposition, but as a wise and kindly guide, and to know how to implement it in their lives, not in a grudging, external manner, but with the proper internal motivation without which it does not have full ethical value. The compassion of the Church is to be found in the way in which she remains true to *both* these aspects of her pastoral task. This would be impossible without the guidance of the Holy Spirit who "reaches from end to end mightily and governs all things well" (Wis 8:1).

Chapter 3

The Competency of the Church's Living Magisterium in Moral Matters.

The Reverend Monsignor Francis X. DiLorenzo, S.T.D.

The outline of this chapter will be as follows: First, I will present a brief exposition of what it is we as a Church actually believe from an historical perspective about the Magisterium. Secondly, I will highlight what this means in terms of natural law. The intricacies of subjective and objective morality, as well as conscience formation, will be treated in the next chapter. Thirdly, I will review the contemporary challenges to this particular gift that the Church has. There are many sectors in society both within and without the Church that are challenging this general belief that the Church does have competency in moral matters. The effects of these challenges are reflected in the minds, hearts, and lives of most Catholics today. Finally, I will propose a program of evangelization in this area.

Historical Perspective

In terms of a brief exposition of where we are as a Church, it suffices to say that an investigation of the New Testament suggests the following picture: there seems to be found within the New Testament a clear formulation of Paul's doctrine of the Mystical Body of Jesus.[1] This imagery suggests to us the fact that as in the body there happen to be many members which form one body, so also within the Body of Christ there are a diversity of members, ministries and functions. The Holy Spirit gives his gifts according to the requirements of the Body of Christ. And, finally, in this imagery Paul suggests that the Apostles and their head St. Peter are charged with the real responsibility for the whole Church. In short, Paul is portraying to us the experience and reality of unity that is found in the early Church.[2] At this particular time in the life of the early Church we are talking about three kinds of unity: the unity of faith, the unity among one another, and the unity with those who have the authentic and authoritative ministry of teaching.

When we talk about the unity of faith, we highlight the fact that the members of the Church should inwardly believe and outwardly confess what they believe. Furthermore, there ought to be a unity among one another. Paul suggested that this unity be rooted in their common baptism in Christ, their participation in the sacraments and their participation at worship. For our purposes here though, the unity that I would like to suggest and which many of the New Testament studies point out is the unity all must have with those that have the authentic and authoritative ministry of teaching in the Church.[3] We are talking here about Peter, the Apostles, and clearly by implication, their successors, the Pope and the College of Bishops. The many members of the Church are invited, persuaded and exhorted to completely respond to the hierarchical ministry of Peter and the Apostles or, if you will, of their successors, the Pope and the Bishops. This becomes clear from the very beginning. As one scholar pointed out, the early Apostolic experience initiated by Jesus Himself became normative for and within the college of the early Apostles with Peter as its head. This particular group which was set aside especially by Jesus becomes the benchmark for other faith experiences. It is this particular benchmark that will act as the guide, if you will, for all the other experiences within the Church itself.[4]

As time goes on, this authority of authentically and authoritatively teaching is more fully reflected upon and developed during the patristic era.[5] For example, the confession of the whole Church with the concurrence of Rome now becomes the ultimate benchmark of faith and morals within the early church. It is interesting to note that the early Bishops of this time happen to be doubly gifted. They not only possess the charism of authentically and authoritatively formulating matters of faith and morals, but also possess the competency of explaining them as well.

This general belief continued throughout the Middle Ages. Apparently from the patristic era to the era of the Scholastic period there is a separation of the role of bishop and theologian. But in the following era, especially at the time of Trent,[6] one sees a marvelous unity, interaction, and proper balance between the two. By the 18th and 19th century it is still the general belief of the Church that she definitely has competency in the areas of faith and morals. There may well have been a greater centralization at this particular period of time. Many of the studies in ecclesiology explain why this emerged. As we know, the First Vatican Council was completed at the Second Vatican Council. As a result some of the notions of papal responsibility for teaching may not have been completely fleshed out to the degree that would have been the desire of the many Fathers of Vatican Council I. Nevertheless, the essential teaching was present in Vatican I[7] and was completed in Vatican II.

There emerges at this particular period in history a rather complete doctrine of the Church's competency in faith and morals. It is the role of the Pope and the College of Bishops to serve the people of God by authentically and authoritatively teaching. Vatican II talks about the collegiality of Pope and Bishops. We envision the structure of the collegiality in this way: the Pope is head of the College of Bishops. He is the head of the Church of Christ in fact and in authority. When we talk about this notion of collegiality, we affirm that the Bishops when in union with their brother Bishops and the Pope do teach authentically and authoritatively especially in the context of an ecumenical council.

Infallible and Non-Infallible Teaching

We know that this Church can teach infallibly. It is this very issue of infallibility that I would like to briefly discuss. When we talk about the notion of infallibility, at least within the contemporary context, we would like to talk about the faithful's shared infallibility with the hierarchy in union with the Pope, and the Pope himself. That gives us a fuller notion of the idea of infallibility. The common and general estimate today is the following: When the whole people of God unhesitatingly hold a point of doctrine or morals under the direction of the Holy Spirit and in union with the Pope and the collectivity of Bishops, then they are sharing in the Church's living Magisterium and in the gift of infallibility. Here we are talking about the hierarchy in union with the Pope. This we call the *Magisterium proper* — the hierarchy in union with the Pope have a decisive authority to pass judgement on what has been revealed. It is not merely ratifying the assent already expressed by the faithful, it can intervene and assist when internal disagreements arise and cause disunity in the one Body of Christ. We have talked about the faithful's shared infallibility and secondly, the Magisterium proper.

We now turn our attention to the Pope himself and his role in this whole experience within the Church which we call infallibility. It is the gift of the Pope himself, not as a private theologian, but only as a public person, that is, the head of the Church in his relation to the Church universal. He is not infallible simply as Pope, but as Pope subject to the divine assistance guiding him. He is infallible only in the context of the Church as teacher of all Christians and intending to speak for the whole Church. He judges and defines what is to be believed or rejected by all. The Pope is bound to ascertain the truth. Ascertaining the belief of the faithful is had when he is involved in an Ecumenical Council, Episcopal Synods, and Councils of Bishops and Cardinals and Theologians. Need the Pope necessarily use these means? He need not, but ordinarily they are provided for his assistance in arriving at an infallible judgement.

Another issue that comes up today and one that we must discuss is the notion of the authentic non-infallible teaching of the Church. When comparing the characteristics of infallible teaching with authentic non-infallible teaching the following picture emerges. The characteristics of infallibility are as follows: It is real authority, it has the special assistance of the Holy Spirit, it is guaranteed free from error, it is irreversible, it can be deepened, and one must rely on it and give internal assent of faith. The characteristics of authentic non-infallible teachings are as follows: it has real authority, special assistance of the Holy Spirit, and it gives a deeper insight into the Gospel and Will of Christ which guards it in a special way. It is not infallible, but one may rely on it and must give religious assent of mind and will. One scholar in his reflections has defined religious assent as follows: "Religious assent means that the motive for our assent is a religious one, namely, the authority given by God to the Pope in fulfillment of his duties." Even if the arguments are unclear or unconvincing, we are called to assent to the core truth of the issue involved. Clearly, in this business of internal assent, even though persons have problems with some of the arguments that are involved, the presumption is in favor of the Church.[8].

We have established now, at least in general the broad brushstrokes, the outline of the Church's competency in faith and moral issues. As far as we understand, it has been the collective belief of the Roman Catholic Church for nearly 2000 years that she does (in very specified and defined areas) have a competency in moral matters to point out authentically and authoritatively in the midst of a situation where God's loving will can be found and what values are to be accepted and what values are to be rejected. This overall general understanding has been there both in theory and as well as in the practice of the Church.

Having discussed the general topic of the Church's competency in moral matters, we turn our attention to how this relates to natural law. As one Catholic scholar puts it:

> To the present author, it seems tenable that the Church has the competence to pronounce with doctrinal certitude about the existence of natural law, its basic knowability in its essential outlines, and whether specific natural law theses are reconcilable with revelation. . . . All Catholic authors agree, it would seem, that the Church has authoritative (authentic), non-infallible teaching power in natural law matters. The proper response due this teaching

office, however, continues to be an intense subject of Catholic theological disagreement, particularly in the light of *Humanae Vitae*. Two main trends are discernible. One position, actually contained in the *Dogmatic Constitution on the Church,* n. 25, stresses obedience or "religious submission of mind and will" as the proper response of the believer to the authentic teachings of the popes and bishops. "It must be shown in such a way that his supreme Magisterium is acknowledged with reverence, the judgments made by him are sincerely adhered to, according to his mind and will." Intellectual assent to and acceptance of the authentic teaching, then, are the ordinary obligatory responses of the faithful Catholic. In matters of public conduct one must always act according to the opinion proposed; dissent becomes possible only in rare, extraordinary cases of private conduct. . .[9]

I would suggest that this particular competency and gift of the Church is coming under fire. Of course there are probably many reasons why this is taking place. I will discuss some of these reasons because I am especially concerned as to how they impact on the Church at large.

Challenges To Magisterium

From my perspective there are at least two general divisions that we can discuss in terms of challenges to the Church's competency in moral matters. The first would be challenges from persons within the Church, and the second would be challenges from sources outside the Church.

Reductionism

Regarding challenges from persons within the Church, the first serious consideration I would like to address is a tendency in the literature today, and in practice, to reduce religious experience to mere psychological phenomena. In an attempt to have an interdisciplinary and a more holistic approach to spiritual direction, many religious counselors attempted to try to make an integration between psychology and spirituality or the theology of Christian living. Their attempts spring from a real desire to integrate the behavioral sciences and moral theology.

Unfortunately, certain problems emerged. Perhaps the greatest was the problem of what is called today "reductionism," namely, the assumption that religious experience and the movements of grace are one and the same. In short, the various stages and levels of personality development and the anxieties associated with going through each and every stage are identified almost completely with the movements of conversion, metanoia, and justification. There is no distinction made between the movements of grace in the life of a person and the natural developmental progress or process of developing into a wholesome and whole human being. There seems to be little or no room for the movement of grace in this kind of an explanation. So spiritual direction is simply identified with psychological counseling and they appear to be, for all purposes, one and the same.

Now the specific challenge of this approach to the Church's living Magisterium is as follows: the ultimate goal of living would be trying to live up to God's loving will, but with little emphasis on the traditional means, or help, of His grace in the sacramental liturgical life. Rather, one is challenged to go through levels and stages of personality development as articulated by particular psychologists or personality theorists. In effect, when the Church teaches in the area of sexual ethics, for example, she is rather firm in pointing out that a particular attitude or behavior is either considered to be a vice or a virtue. This is not necessarily so in a psychological context, for herein it would be considered neither vice nor virtue, but rather a step towards human maturity or a step backwards from human maturity.[10] In other words, the value assigned to the particular statement by the Church's living Magisterium is seen more in the context of a suggested guideline, rather than a religious insight that can and does make a claim on us totally, both intellectually and volitionally. In that sense, "reductionism" is probably a sincere and honest attempt to address some pastoral problems; but the implications of such happen to result in a challenge to the Church's living Magisterium itself.

70

Distorted Ecclesiology

The next area that poses a challenge to the Church's living Magisterium is what I call a distorted sense of ecclesiology. We believe the Church's living Magisterium in structure and function is hierarchial and collegial within specified limits as defined in *Lumen Gentium.* When we speak of a distorted notion of ecclesiology, we are not referring to specific scholarly works which have systematically set out to undermine the Church's living Magisterium, rather we are referring to currents of thinking that are popular today in some of the religious newspapers and journals, and in some of the lecturing. These currents are ill defined. Nevertheless, I wish to clarify what I perceive them to be with the kinds of clarity I believe they ought to have.

These currents of thought are associated with two problematic areas, namely, an exaggerated feminism and self-righteousness of the elitist variety. Many of our past sins of discrimination do catch up to us. As a result of trying to correct a bad situation, we have an exaggerated form of feminism that may be speaking from an interior posture of hurt, severe disappointment, identity searching, and anger. Certainly we have experienced this impact in the lives and institutions of Catholics. The general impression given is that the position of the Church has been bound up in sexual politics; and now the general imperative arising from this perspective will be: There is to be no more sexual politics in the Church.

This specific mindset articulates itself in the following way: The existing moral insights are the product of an extremely sexist power clique. Hence, because of their sexism, the validity of these moral insights is really questionable. Their claim on us and on our allegiance is little or negligible. In other words, this exaggerated notion of feminism suggests that somehow or other the validity of truth is very much undermined by sexist language and values. Somehow or other this sexist language and value system has so distorted our capacity to get at the truth as a Church that now we must rediscover the truth all over again devoid of our sexist perspective.

There is probably some validity to the fact that sexism is found in some of the language patterns and value formations of theology.[11] But this does not prove that the truth to which we are asked to assent by the Church's living Magisterium, the essential core truth, is totally distorted beyond recognition. Hence, it is a real exaggeration to suggest that we have to rediscover the truth devoid of sexist language and sexist thought-patterns. The implications of this suggest that we may come up with a truly revolutionary value system regarding the meaning and significance of God's loving will for us. Even though the Church's living Magisterium expresses herself in words and concepts that are found in culturally conditioned language patterns, nevertheless the core truth of what God wanted communicated to His people in the Church remains essentially free from error.

Another notion that tends to flow from a distorted sense of ecclesiology is an elitist vision of who are "real" members of the Church. It is a very self-righteous form of thought. Persons of this rather self-righteous bent of mind basically have the idea that God works within and is present in the lives of *"we good persons."* Their thoughts along these lines are as follows: God couldn't possibly endorse those stuffy institutional persons with all their political machinations and ambitions. Institutional persons may be defined as clergy, specifically bishops and cardinals, persons who are heads of Roman Congregations, or persons who are in charge of chancery offices in the various dioceses throughout the United States. Somehow or other the simple lifestyle of the average Catholic seems to be better than the quality of life lived by somebody who is a diocesan official or an official of the Roman Curia. Persons who work in one of these offices have their credibility impugned because their personal worthiness is questioned by the self-righteous.

This translates into the following unspoken assumption: The correctness of the truth and the allegiance I owe it is in direct proportion to your worthy lifestyle as a cleric and/or religious. Hence, if the lifestyle of the Pope, bishops, cardinals, or other persons charged with the responsibility of teaching in the Church is such that it is not in conformity with the vision that these self-righteous people possess, then the capacity of those who are charged with the responsibility of exercising the Church's living Magisterium is not only impugned, but in many cases ignored. The authority associated with alleged unworthy authority figures is so devalued that their religious statements make little or no impact on the minds and hearts of these self-righteous people.

Dissent and Relativity

Another area that presents challenges to the Church's living Magisterium especially today is the *relativity* introduced by moral theologians who publicly dissent. This dissent is found in literature, public media presentations, and in classrooms on college campuses and in graduate schools. Taking the signal from a variety of sources, the suggestion is advanced that persons have a right to dissent. Even though there are legitimate guidelines for licit theological dissent, the implication which insinuates itself in popular parlance is that, if one objects, that is all right. The proper nuances associated with licit theological dissent are neglected for a much broader doubtful interpretation. Persons who observe this current swirling around them become cautious and skeptical that they can attain the truth. They can become discouraged and start to relativize all that comes forth from the Church's living Magisterium. This is a delicate problem that I must confess is not easily resolved if one attempts to preserve the values in the situation that must be preserved.

Another area which I perceive as a challenge to the Church's living Magisterium is not necessarily from sources within the Church, but from sources outside the Church life. Here I would like to mention first the growing reality of fundamentalism that is found especially here in North America. It has been revived also in many Latin American countries.

Fundamentalism

Many fundamentalist Protestant groups, well meaning as they are, come to the whole process of evangelization with a very definite theological structure.[12] Generally speaking, there is in this form of Protestantism a tremendous tendency towards subjectivism. These Christians place a heavy emphasis on personal religious experience. Classical Protestantism tended to hold that the rule for a person's life is Scripture only. I do believe that classical Protestant theology suggested that the Holy Spirit speaks through the Scriptures to the individual person. The particular religious response that is evoked by the Spirit is considered to be

73

a genuine religious communication from the Spirit. It is normative to this particular individual. Consequently, the Magisterium, properly so called, is *a priori* effectively wiped out.

Fundamentalism suggests that the Holy Spirit speaking through Scripture and the person's response to the Holy Spirit is sufficient for developing a rule for life. Of course the Roman Catholic tradition has been at complete variance with this. Certainly we believe that the Holy Spirit speaks to the hearts of each believer, and certainly we believe that the individual's heart is genuinely touched. God makes the first initiative, touching our hearts, as it were. Through God's Word the Holy Spirit speaks, and we believe that although personal religious experience is good and worthwhile, it nevertheless cannot be raised to the level of a universal religious principle within the Church itself, but it must be tested and validated by the Church's living Magisterium. In effect, Jesus Christ provided that a rule of life be shared with the whole Church. It is to be proclaimed, continually tested, and validated by the whole Church in solidarity with one another and in union with the Pope and the College of Bishops. Therefore, the teaching authority (the Church's living Magisterium) is the ultimate benchmark which can validate personal religious experience. For that matter, it can declare some *"personal religious experiences"* as not authentic, authoritatively. It is only by looking at this benchmark of the Church's living Magisterium that we can determine whether or not a particular religious experience happens to be coming from the promptings of the Spirit or from the promptings of the flesh.

Secular Humanism

Another area which challenges the Church's living Magisterium originating from a source outside the Church is the philosophy of secular humanism.[13] In many cases it has insinuated itself into North American culture. It is found as a basis for some laws that govern our various countries. I see its presence in the academic world, the media, politics, scientific research, and sometimes in certain religious denominations. It is a philosophy that probably emerged in the late 19th century. Secular humanism, as an ideology, is really nothing more than the beatification of man, excluding any real acknowledgement, or recognition of supernatural experience and reality. Secular humanism treats all religious concepts and values as devoid of any significance whatsoever. Many forms of secular humanism happen to be atheistic in their concrete historical manifestation.[14]

Our purpose here is to highlight the fact that secular humanism is encouraged in the public forum. When considering religious realities, secular humanism asks the public to acknowledge and recognize a studied neutrality. When attempting to discover the answer to significant questions, secular humanism tries to root out any religious explanation underlying these questions. Such questions would be: What are the origins of man or the origins of the universe? What is the meaning of life? What is the ultimate source of values? What is the answer to the problem of evil or the source of guilt? Or, what is the meaning of death? These traditional questions that have perplexed inquirers for centuries have traditionally been answered by some religious response. In secular humanism the religious elements associated with the traditional responses have been stripped away. Therefore, in secular humanism it becomes clear to us that the Church's living Magisterium, couched in a religious context, would be viewed as having no claim on the minds and hearts of persons. Secular humanism suggests that persons ought not to have their lives cluttered with the insights of religion and morality.

Excessive Rationalism

Another challenge to the Church's living Magisterium originating from a source outside the Church is the improper application of scientific methodology to theological research and investigation.[15] A clarification was presented above of what is meant by the religious assent of mind and will which is due to the Church's ordinary Magisterium. We said the ordinary Magisterium of the Church is due proper and respectful religious assent. Further, we stated that the motive for one's assent is a religious one, namely, the authority given by God to the Pope in fulfillment of his duty. Even if the arguments are unclear or unconvincing, nevertheless, we are called to assent to the core truth of the issues at hand. In other words, there is to be (generally speaking), on our parts, a presumption in favor of the Church's living Magisterium. This having been said, we note there is present today a lingering on of a 19th century rationalism that is associated with the scientific method. This 19th century rationalism, though out of vogue today, is nonetheless present. This form of rationalism exaggerates the power of human reason and sets human reason up as the ultimate guide/arbiter of reality.

Coming forth from this rationalism, of course, is a value stance. This value stance tends to underlie modern scientific investigation. Philosophically speaking, there seems to be a greater worthwhileness assigned to knowledge which comes from scientific observation and experimentation than from supernatural revelation. The only worthwhile information is that which springs from an exaggerated sense of independence and freedom from any religious presuppositions whatsoever. There flows from this philosophy of inquiry an attitude which challenges in the following way: My assent can be compelled only if you show me with overwhelmingly convincing evidence. This so-called "show me" attitude starts off with a certain universal methodological doubt applied to all of reality. This philosophy seems to suggest that a certain indignity is imposed on the human mind by asking it to assent to something that isn't subjected to the laws of rigorous proof, especially that of an empirical variety. It is precisely this "show me" attitude that has subtly made itself felt in the process of theological investigations in some quarters. We are not opting for superficial scholarship. But in the "show me" attitude there is great reluctance, if not downright resistance, to the propositon that the Church's ordinary Magisterium ought to be given the presumption of truth.

Therefore, if the arguments which are set forth to support the Church's position in a particular area are not convincing, if they don't compel human reason, the person can withhold assent until some very convincing evidence is brought forth to support the position. In my estimation this is a very serious challenge.

Marxist-Communism

The final challenge to the Church's living Magisterium that I would like to review centers on Marxist-Communism.[16] We in

North America may not have as direct experience of this as do our neighbors in Mexico, Central or South America, or the Antilles area. The Bishops from these regions have a very difficult job proposing the Church's moral values to a group so ideologically opposed to Christianity. It is clear that, philosophically speaking, Marxist-Communism is clearly rooted in matter, and this impersonal matter is seen as the ultimate "stuff" from which we came, and to which we are ultimately destined to return. There is a complete incompatibility between Marxist-Communism with its underlying presuppositions of materialism, and the Roman Catholic Church with its underlying presuppositions of spiritual reality. It is clear that Marxist-Communism, not only in principle, but also in the concrete historical reality, will try continually to undermine the authority that the Roman Catholic Church attempts to exercise.

In my estimation it is very questionable whether there can be any real meaningful, ongoing, *lasting* rapport struck by Catholics with persons who sincerely and honestly subscribe to Marxist-Communism in its current form. The point I wish to highlight here is the fact that many well meaning Christians, in an attempt to right an unjust social order believe they can strike an accord with this ideology. My cautiousness is rooted in the very incompatibilities of the ideologies. Ultimately, the underpinnings or foundations of all of our social justice theology are rooted in Christian justice and Christian charity. In the final analysis a grace-inspired love has God as its ultimate initiator. Our vision of the human person, his dignity and eternal destiny, and the quality of the motivation underlying social and economic change is substantially different in Christianity from Marxist-Communism which in principle and in practice cannot acknowledge or recognize it. Since this is the case, Marxist-Communism must of its very nature deny the Church's living Magisterium and the authority it holds.

Response: Evangelization

In the second part of this chapter we talked about the contemporary challenges to the traditional belief that the Church's living Magisterium does have competency in moral areas. I would like to complete this discussion by offering some responses to the various challenges to the Church's living Magisterium. I think we need a very assertive program of evangelization — I happen to be a very firm proponent of Catholic education, specifically Catholic schools. I understand that there are many financial problems involved with the whole business of Catholic schools, nevertheless, I do believe that there is probably no substitute for the worthwhileness of a good Catholic education in a Catholic school. Even understanding that we have very meager resources, and that it is a terribly difficult sacrifice to ask from persons, given the various challenges that are found in our society today, I support Catholic education. I am not calling for "ghetto schools," as it were, or a "Catholic ghetto." I am talking about a genuine worthwhile pursuit of human and religious information in an atmosphere that is willing to acknowledge and recognize, in principle, the fact that there are not only human but also supernatural realities. In principle, this will not be found in many educational systems throughout the world today. Therefore, I believe that we can have a better and worthwhile assertive program of evangelization if we commit ourselves to a quality Catholic education.

I support and affirm also the Confraternity of Christian Doctrine classes in which we have programs of evangelization and also I think it is essential for non-Catholic college campuses to have Newman Centers, or whatever the equivalent is in other countries throughout the world. The Catholic Church should be clearly made visible and present on campus by this ministry in academia. The intellectual challenges that are found in campus life should be acknowledged and recognized by trained and competent personnel. Students in these non-Catholic settings should be able to see and be made to understand that Catholic theology continually invites new intellectual challenges. At the same time they should see that our value placed on the person's dignity can enrich the area of human knowledge rather than stifle its development.

I also think that an assertive program of evangelization has to take place among clergy and religious. Many times we tend to forget them as persons who need evangelization. This evangelization must have an intellectual component. Furthermore, I believe that many clergy and religious today are very deficient in the area of moral theology. In their training there may be a strong emphasis on speculative theology and pastoral theology. When one considers religious life and the formation programs associated with such, one may observe emphasis on personal religious experience and formation of the individual within community. But how many technical courses in moral theology are people exposed to in religious life today? Therefore, I think that the faithful, religious, and clergy ought to have ongoing education as part of an assertive program of evangelization.

Finally, I think it is absolutely necessary that the ongoing rapport and dialogue between theologians and the Church's living Magisterium should continue. For the most part, it is characterized by respect, honesty and professionalism. At the same time, too, many of the Bishops who are part of the Church's living Magisterium should continually educate themselves.

Notes

1. G. Friedrich, *Theological Dictionary of the New Testament* Vol. VII (Grand Rapids: W.B. E. Erdmans Publishing Co., 1971), pp. 1068-1081; Colin Brown (Ed.), *Dictionary of New Testament Theology,* Vol. I (Grand Rapids: Zondervan Publishing House, 1975), pp. 232 ff; John McKenzie, S.J. *Dictionary of the Bible* (Milwaukee: The Bruce Publishing Company, 1965), pp. 100-102; and R. Jewett, "Body" in *The Interpreter's Dictionary of the Bible,* Supplementary Volume (Nashville: Abingdon Press, 1976), pp. 177 ff.

2. Eugene La Verdiere, "The Teaching Authority of the Church: Origins in the New Testament Period," *Chicago Studies* (Summer '78), pp. 172ff; G. Thils, "Unity of the Church" *New Catholic Encyclopedia,* Vol. 14, (New York: McGraw-Hill Book Co., 1967), pp. 450-451; P.F. Chirico "Unity of Faith" *New Catholic Encyclopedia,* Vol. 14, p. 450; P.F. Chirico "Unity of the Church" *New Catholic Encyclopedia,* Vol. 14, pp. 395 ff.

3. Klaus Berger, "Apostolic Church," in *Sacramentum Mundi,* Vol. I (New York: Herder and Herder, 1969), pp. 79-82, and Jean Danielou, "Apostolic Church" in *Sacramentum Mundi* Vol. I, pp. 84-85; W. Brenning, "Apostolic Succession," *Sacramentum Mundi* Vol. I, pp. 86-90; F. Klostermann, "Apostle," *New Catholic Encyclopedia* Vol. I, pp. 679 ff; F.A. Sullivan, "Apostolic Succession," *New Catholic Encyclopedia* Vol. I, pp. 695 ff; S.E. Donlon "Authority, Ecclesiastical" *New Catholic Encyclopedia* Vol. I, pp. 1115 ff.

4. Rudolf Schnakenburg, *The Moral Teaching of the New Testament* (New York: Herder and Herder, 1965), pp. 15-167; Joseph Fitzmyer, "Pauline Theology," in *The Jerome Biblical Commentary* Ed. by Raymond Brown, (New Jersey: Prentice-Hall, Inc. 1968), pp. 862 ff.

5. F.X. Murphy "Moral Teaching, History of (to 700 A.D.)," in *New Catholic Encyclopedia,* Vol. 9, pp. 1117-1119. F.X. Murphy *Moral Teaching in the Primitive Church,* (New York: Paulist Press, 1968); Louis Vereecke "Moral Theology, History of (700 A.D. to Vatican Council I)" in *New Catholic Encyclopedia,* Vol. 9, pp. 1119-1122.

6. Michael Place, "Theologians and Magisterium from the Council of Trent to the First Vatican Council," *Chicago Studies* (Summer '78) pp. 225 ff.

7. For an excellent summary of Catholic thought regarding the whole question of authority, infallibility, and conscience in this time framework cf: John Henry Cardinal

Newman, *A Letter Addressed to His Grace the Duke of Norfolk on Occasion of Mr. Gladstone's Recent Expostulation* (New York: The Catholic Publication Society, 1875), and James Kaiser, *The Concept of Conscience According to John Henry Newman,* (Washington, D.C.: Catholic University of America Press, 1958).

8. *Sacrosanctum Oecumenicum Concilium Vaticanium II, Constitutiones, Decreta, Declarationes* Vol. I "Const. Dogm. De Ecclesia" #25; confer also: H. Vortgrimler, *Commentary on the Documents of Vatican II* (New York: Herder and Herder, 1967) pp. 208-216. For background material, cf. J. Salaverni *Patres Societatis Jesu Facultatum Theologicarum in Hispania Professores, Sacrae Theologiae Summa* Vol. I, pp. 704-37, 790-805.

9. George Regan, *New Trends in Moral Theology* (New York: Newman Press, 1971), pp. 115-144; cf. also W. May, "Natural Law," in *New Catholic Encyclopedia,* Vol. 17, pp. 460-461. *What follows herein is a fair sample of the ongoing debate in Fundamental Moral Theology:* Richard Gula, "Shifts in Catholic Moral Theology: A Primer for the Perplexed Personalist," *The Living Light,* (Winter, 1981), pp. 296 ff; Kevin Mc Donald, "Moral Theology: Retrospect and Prospect," *The Clergy Review,* (February, 1982) pp. 41-48; Norbert Rigali, S.J. "After The Moral Catechism," *Chicago Studies* (1981) pp. 151-162; John Connery S.J. "Catholic Ethics: Has the Norm for Rule Making Changed?" *Theological Studies,* (June, 1981), pp. 232 ff; Richard McCormick, S.J. "Notes on Moral Theology: 1981" *Theological Studies* (March, 1982); Philip Keane, S.S. "The Objective Moral Order: Reflection on Recent Research," *Theological Studies,* (June, 1982), pp. 260 ff.

The reader of this section may well be perplexed as to what practical moral guidance is given by the Church concerning negative moral absolutes. Even though theologians may speculate as to this or that position regarding moral absolutes, nonetheless the Roman Catholic Church has continuously endorsed the existence of moral absolutes. To support this contention confer: *Declaration on Religious Liberty, #3* (II Vatican Council), *Declaration on Certain Questions Concerning Sexual Ethics (1975),* from the Sacred Congregation for the Doctrine of the Faith; *To Live in Christ Jesus,* N.C.C.B. (1976), and *Sacred Congregation for the Doctrine of the Faith* (1979) RE: "Human Sexuality" Prot. Number 553/55. pp. 3-4.

10. For some theological background concerning the integration of the social sciences into Catholic Theology, cf. the following Documents of Vatican II: Decree on Priestly Formation, *(Optatam Totius), #2; 3; 11; 20;* Pastoral Constitution on the Church in the Modern World *(Gaudium et Spes), #62;* Decree on Bishop's Pastoral Office in the Church *(Christus Dominus), #14;* Decree on the Apostolate of the Laity *(Apostolicam Actuositatem), #32,* and Declaration on Christian Education *(Gravissimum Educationis)* #1;2.

For an exposition of the role of psychology and moral theology cf. the following: Robert Springer, "Concience, Behavioral Science and Absolutes," in *Absolutes in Moral Theology,* Charles E. Curran (Ed.) (Washington D.C. Corpus Books, 1968), pp. 19-56; James Gustafson, "The Relationship of Empirical Science to Moral Thought," in *The Catholic Theological Society of America Proceedings* (June, 1971) pp. 122-137. John Loftus, S.J., "The Integration of Psychology and Religion: An Uneasy Alliance" *National Guild of Catholic Psychiatrists Bulletin,* Vol. 27 (1981), pp. 88 ff. James Jones, "The Delicate Dialect: Religion and Psychology in the Modern World," *Cross Currents,* (Summer 1982), pp. 143 ff.

11. For an in-depth study of this whole question cf. the following: L. Quinonez, "Women's Liberation Movement," *New Catholic Encyclopedia,* Vol. 17, pp. 719-720. M.A. Getty, "Women's Rights of" in *New Catholic Encyclopedia,* Vol. 17, pp. 708-709. C. Safilior-Rothschild. "Women in Society," *New Catholic Encyclopedia,* Vol. 17, pp. 714-715. John McKenzie. *Dictionary of the Bible,* (Bruce Publishing Co., 1965), pp. 935 ff; W. B. Flaherty. "Women (Catholic Teaching On)" *New Catholic Encyclopedia,* Vol. 14, pp. 998-1000. Must be read in conjunction with N. Foley, "Women in the Church," *New Catholic Encyclopedia* Vol. 17, pp. 715-719. Rev. Vincent Mainelli (ed.), *Official Catholic Teaching: Social Justice* (Wilmington, N.C.: A Consortium Book, 1978), paragraphs #280; 306; 534; 655; 975; 980; 1079; 1291; 1429; 1646 to 1655 AND Pope Paul VI, "The Role of Women in Contemporary Society," *The Pope Speaks* Vol. 19, #4 (1975) pp. 314 ff; Pope

80

Paul VI "Importance of Women in Society and the Church" *The Pope Speaks,* Vol. 21 #2 (1976); Pope Paul VI, "Women in the Life of Society," *The Pope Speaks,* Vol. 22, #1 (1977), pp. 22. Pope John Paul II, *On The Family,* (Washington, D.C.: U.S. Catholic Conference, 1982).

12. For a study of this whole question on the ecumenical dimensions of Moral Theology cf. the following: "Graymore Papers III," *Journal of Ecumenical Studies,* (Fall, 1978) pp. 614-683, and C. Kossel, *"The Moral Majority and Christian Politics,"* *Communio* (Winter, 1982), pp. 339 ff.

13. W.P. Haas "Humanism, Secular" *New Catholic Encyclopedia,* Vol. 7, pp. 226-229.

14. John Brinkley, *Conflict of Ideals: Changing Values in Western Society* (New York: Van Nostrand, 1969) pp. 84-281. Donald Hodges, *Socialist Humanism,* (St. Louis, MO: W.H. Green, 1974): All of this work. S. Gerson, (Ed.), *Marxist Humanism and Praxis* (Buffalo: Prometheus Books, 1978): All of this work. M. Store, (Ed.) *Humanistic Ethics,* (Buffalo: Prometheus Books, 1980): All of this work.

15. P. Durbin "Probability" *New Catholic Encyclopedia* Vol. II, pp. 815-16. AND D. Shapere "Scientific Revolutions" in *New Catholic Encyclopedia* Vol. 16, p. 402ff.

16. For an entire exploration of this issue cf. the following: Pope Pius XI, *On Atheistic Communism* (1937); P. Hebblethwaite, *Christian Marxist Dialogue,* (Paulist Press, 1977); A.F. McGovern, "Marxism and Christianity" *New Catholic Encyclopedia* Vol. 17, pp. 391-393; P. Peachy. "Church in Communist Countries," *New Catholic Encyclopedia* Vol. 17, pp. 126-128; E. Duff. "Private Property" *New Catholic Encyclopedia,* Vol. 17, pp. 543-544; P. Higginson "The Vatican and Communism from *Divini Redemptoris* to Pope Paul VI," *New Blackfriars,* (April, 1980) pp. 158-171 and (May, 1980) pp. 234-244; J. Kramer "The Vatican Ostpolitik," *Review of Politics* (July, 1980) pp. 283-308; "Karl Marx: Symposium," *Review of Social Economy* (December, 1979) pp. 261-387; U.S.C.B. "Pastoral Letter on Marxist Communism," *Origins,* (December, 1980), pp. 433 ff. R. Louis, "Why are Most Christians on the Defensive with Respect to Marxism," *New Blackfriars,* (Jan. 1983), pp. 29-34. M. Spieker, "Eurocommunism and Christianity," *Review of Politics* (January, 1983) pp. 3-19.

Chapter 4

The Pastoral Approach to Magisterial Teaching

The Reverend Val J. Peter, S.T.D., J.C.D.

This chapter provides a brief overview of certain pastoral aspects of the assent due to the ordinary non-infallible Magisterium in three steps. First I will review the Church's teaching, especially at Vatican II. Then we will take a look at developments since that time. Finally, I will suggest a possibly helpful way to view the appropriateness of dissent in the Church today.

The Teaching of Vatican II

The question of the assent due to the ordinary non-infallible Magisterium attracts widespread attention today. More often than not, the question is formulated negatively — in terms of dissent. There is no better place to begin our study than with Vatican II's central statement on this issue:

In matters of faith and morals, the bishops speak in the name of Christ and the faithful are to accept their teaching and adhere to it with a religious assent of soul. This religious submission of will and of mind must be shown in a special way to the authentic teaching of the Roman Pontiff, even when he is not speaking *ex cathedra*. That is, it must be shown in such a way that his supreme Magisterium is acknowledged with reverence, the judgements made by him are sincerely adhered to, according to his manifest mind and will. His mind and will in the matter may be known chiefly either from the character of the documents, from his frequent repetition of the same doctrine, or from his manner of speaking.[1]

Recall that episcopal ordination confers the fullness of priesthood as well as the functions (*munera*) of governing and teaching.[2] So the pope and the bishops in union with him are by God's gracious purposes endowed with a "charism of truth" and constitute the "authentic Magisterium."[3]

The assent properly called for in response to ordinary non-infallible teaching (e.g. in papal encyclicals) is described by the Council in traditional terms. It is *internal* assent, not just keeping quiet, but really accepting the teaching as true. It is *religious* assent, not based on the authority of God revealing, but on the authority of the teaching office given by Christ to His Church in the person of the pope and bishops. This is different from the assent of divine faith which is absolutely certain and *super omnia firma*. Internal religious assent is rather only "morally certain," excluding not the possibility of error but only the probability of error. In addition such ordinary non-infallible teaching enjoys the presumption of truth, even if the arguments are unclear and unconvincing.

Some further points help to highlight this central text. In the document on the Church sent out to all bishops before the Council are found several principles regarding dissent.[4] Subjects in accord with their competence — one finds here — have the obligation at times to point out what they see as evils in the Church. In so doing they are to avoid giving scandal and are to follow the procedures for fraternal correction set down by the

Lord in the gospel. (Mt. 18: 15-17) These formulations did not find their way into the final text.

In the same preconciliar document, one reads: "if the sovereign pontiffs (in the ordinary Magisterium) deliberately pass judgement on a matter heretofore controversial, it should be clear to all that, according to the mind and will of the popes, the matter may not be further discussed publicly by theologians."[5] This statement, taken from Pius XII's *Humani Generis,* was dropped from further drafts of the *schema de ecclesia* — for reasons not clear.

It is this *"religiosum voluntatis et intellectus obsequim"* that Paul VI calls attention to in *Humanae Vitae* when, in addressing priests, he says:

> Be the first to give, in the exercise of your ministry, the example of loyal internal and external obedience to the teaching authority of the Church. That obedience, as you know well, obliges not only because of the reasons adduced, but rather because of the light of the Holy Spirit, which is given in a particular way to pastors of the Church, in order that they may illustrate the truth.[6]

In the third session of Vatican II (1964) the doctrinal commission of the Council was presented with some interesting amendments (*modi*) which help explain the Council's teaching on assent and dissent. *Modus* 159 was submitted by three bishops who ask what is to be done in "the case, at least theoretically possible, of an educated person who when faced with doctrine not infallibly proposed cannot give internal assent for good reasons."[7] The response of the commission is: "Approved theological explanations should be consulted in such a case."

Similarly, *modus* 160 recommends that a clear distinction be made in the text (*Lumen Gentium,* 25) between this kind of internal assent and the kind of response due to infallible teaching, since the former is clearly not "absolute and irreformable assent."[8] Again the doctrinal commission says it is better simply to refer to approved authors (*"auctores probati"*).

So to correctly understand Vatican II on this point, let us consult the *"auctores probati."*[9] The Scholastic manuals written by approved authors and surveyed here date from 1891 to 1963. They all affirm that the proper response to the ordinary non-infallible magisterium is the internal and religious assent which is a real acceptance of the teaching as true and not a mere reverent silence. They agree that this assent is different from the assent of divine faith; for it is only morally certain. Most of the authors say this assent (accepting the teaching as true, not just keeping quiet) is *conditional.*

— You accept the teaching as true "unless by an equal or superior authority the Church should decree otherwise." (Salaverri)[10]

— You accept the teaching as true "unless the Church should at some time decide otherwise or unless the contrary should become evident." (Sullivan)[11]

— You accept it as true until and "unless a grave suspicion should arise that the presumption is not verified." (Lercher)[12]

— Assent is prudently suspended when there first appear sufficient motives for doubting. (Pesch)[13]

— Assent can be conditioned "insofar as a son of the Church knowing the decree is not preemptory is so disposed that he would by no means wish to retain his assent if there came a time when the Church would judge otherwise through an infallible decision or if he himself were to discover its divergence from the truth." (Straub)[14]

— What we have said about the decisions of the Roman Congregations applies also to the teaching and decrees of the pope himself whenever he does not intend to render an *ex cathedra* definition . . . The decrees of the Sacred Congregations must be received with respect and obedience, so long as there is no positive evidence that they are erroneous. (Brunsmann-Preuss)[15]

— If the Supreme Pontiff, exercising his authority, but not at its highest level, obliges all to assent to a thing as true (because revealed or coherent with revelation), he does not seem to be infallible *de jure*; nor is it necessary to say that the Holy Spirit would never permit such a decree to be issued, if it should be erroneous . . . It is true that the Holy Spirit will never allow the Church to be led into error by such a decree. The way in which error would be excluded would more probably consist in the assistance of the Holy Spirit given to the head of the Church, by which such an erroneous decree would be prevented. But it is not entirely out of the question that the error might be excluded by the Holy Spirit in this way, namely, by the subjects of the decree detecting its error and ceasing to give it their internal assent. (Lercher)[16]

When the presumption of truth is overturned by prevailing evidence, then abstention from internal assent is called for. However this abstention — as the *auctores probati* point out — should be private. What is called for, they say, is an *obsequium silentii*. Many authors recommend that the reasons should be privately given to the proper authorities so that they can correct the error. Palmieri says the pope might authorize public discussion on the issue.[17]

Finally Straub gives this earnest warning to dissenters: "Each person should beware lest, being preoccupied by the love of his own opinion, he easily deceive himself, having shortly to render an exacting account to the Lord who scrutinizes hearts."[18]

Developments since Vatican II

a) **Public dissent**

As is well known, Vatican II's treatment of assent, seen above, soon became a focal point of debate especially in the controversy over *Humanae Vitae* (1968). The collective pastoral letter of the U.S. Hierarchy issued on November 15, 1968, in response to *Humanae Vitae* posits three clear conditions for legitimate (private) dissent:

When conclusions reached by such professional theological work prompt a scholar to dissent from non-infallible received teaching, the norms of licit dissent come into play . . . The expression of theological dissent from the magisterium is in order only if the reasons are serious and well-founded, if the manner of dissent does not question or impugn the teaching authority of the Church and is such as not to give scandal.[19]

Yet it was precisely at this point that some theologians and others, arguing from the Council's statements on religious freedom,[20] from the need to correct inadequacies in doctrinal formulations,[21] and from the Council's procedures themselves,[22] went against *Humani Generis* and beyond the Council's teaching (*Lumen Gentium*, 25) to hold public dissent from encyclicals justifiable.

Since some were loudly supporting the legitimacy of public dissent on the basis of the Council and its procedures while others were denying this, the question naturally arises: how are these and other divergent interpretations of Vatican II to be explained? Here are three answers each offering an *unjustified* and *unwarranted* interpretation of the Council's teaching on authority and obedience:[23]

1.) Some liberal commentators held that the normative teaching of Vatican II is found in its departures from traditional views. What is important is the Council's neglect of *Humani Generis* and its insistence on continual reform of the Church, including a purification of doctrinal formulations of inadequacies. The point here is that the Council's repetition of prior Catholic doctrine can be practically disregarded. It was only a sop to placate the conservative minority.

2.) Some conservative commentators found just the opposite to be true. The focal point of the Council's teaching is found in its repetition of the constant teaching of the Church. While disciplinary and liturgical matters underwent profound changes and modifications, the same was not true for the authentic teaching of the Council.

It should be clear that many people are using the words of Vatican II without scholarly regard for its authentic meaning. However difficult it may be to accurately describe the disparate threads in the fabric of Vatican II teaching, such glaring oversimplifications, whether by liberals or conservatives, are highly unprofessional and totally unwarranted.

3.) A more radical view rejects both as quibbling over the Council's words. This view abandons the letter of the Council and embraces its "spirit". Here the pope and the bishops in union with him are not blessed with a special "charism of truth." They do not comprise the "authentic Magisterium". The main thrust or spirit of Vatican II was to do away with authoritarianism and clericalism. A free and open church encourages and even demands disagreements among members.

The problems besetting this more radical view cannot be adequately explained by recourse to the categories of ideology or lack of scholarship or mental confusion. Rather we are here face to face with a lack of faith. Holders of this radical view simply do not believe pope and bishops are gifted by God with a charism of truth comprising an authentic Magisterium. Cardinal Newman's comment comes quickly to mind: "I may love by halves, I may obey by halves; I cannot believe by halves; either I have faith, or I have it not."[24]

b) The new concept

There are other significant factors, mainly secular currents, which themselves comprise a new context, so different from that in which and for which the *auctores probati* wrote. They wrote in a context of trust and confidence among Catholics in the teaching authority of pope and bishops. In other words, they wrote in a context of stability and certainty about traditional truths of faith and morals. The basic conditions they give for withholding assent (centering around "solid reasons" for doubting the specific teaching) are still valid in our day. But they are so context dependent that simple transposition of them without further qualification to our own very different anti-authoritarian context would be unscholarly and unjustified.

As examples, let us point to four such currents comprising a new context in which assent to non-infallible teaching finds itself today. The *first* is what Hans Urs von Balthasar calls "the anti-Roman Complex."[25] It is, of course, not new in itself, having an ancient lineage. But it does arise in a new form today within the Church. Appearing in every age, it must be transcended anew in every age by the community of faith, while at the same time resisting the temptation to romanticize the Church's leadership. This anti-Roman attitude finds its most powerful expression on the level of symbol where most people live and work out their salvation. On this level Rome is like the Kremlin, a symbol of autocracy, or, to put it more vividly, a symbol of Antichrist.

The *second* is the widespread breakdown, peculiar to modern life, of many traditional certitudes. In classical Western civilization institutional arrangements for marriage, family, church and other elements of society were experienced in about the same way as the laws of gravity.[26] Their objectivity was a fact of life. Their truth was unquestioned by and large. You could not, for example, disregard the permanence of marriage or reduce it to an optional choice. But this matter-of-factness is precisely what has broken down in modern life. In our day doubt is the rule, and certitude the exception. This context of the breakdown of many traditional certitudes does raise strong questions about the origin and authenticity of much dissent in the Church today. It also disallows widespread use of the traditional moral adage: *in dubiis libertas.*

Thirdly, there is the modern phenomenon of the privatization of religion and morality.[27] Most opinion polls show the great majority of Americans hold firmly to many of our traditional religious and moral values. But something has changed. Religion and morality are now privatized. They are not matters for public, reasoned discourse. This involves a denial of the possibility of making normative, objective distinctions between truth and falsehood, good and evil. It means that truth is more and more thought of as a matter of personal preference, individual taste, and prevalent mood or sentiment. Dissent is thought about precisely in these terms: The Pope may like chocolate ice cream. God bless him. But I like vanilla. It is a matter of private tastes which persons of good will should be civil and tolerant about.

Fourthly, there is the information explosion. There is so much that is so different in so many philosophies and theologies that no single person can possibly master them all. There is such complexity in so many epochs of history that no one person can master all ages. Once moral theology opens itself to viewing life in terms of dynamic processes, a hugh flood of developmental data and hypotheses deluges the moralist. He has so many more

89

questions than answers.[29] The same is true in every branch of learning.

It is factors such as these four that help form the present context in which authority and obedience interact today. We have to find ways to utilize the blessings of modernity in such a way that these shortcomings of the age do not diminish, much less destroy, the *communio* of faith and worship that is authentically Roman Catholic. Precisely because the modern context of dissent from ordinary non-infallible Magisterium includes a massive attack on many traditional values, more care, not less, is called for if dissent is not to be destructive of *communio*. It is with this in mind that Y. Congar reminds us that "a right to dissent exists, but within the limits of a *jus communionis.*"[30]

Dissent and the Virtue of *Pietas*

Many thoughtful and serious Catholics, including bishops and theologians today are asking themselves this question: Is there a model or set of coordinates that can help us and guide us in understanding the proper place for dissent in the Church today?[31] And how would you know it?

Let us begin with the realization that the notion of dissent today is more often than not described in dependence on a political model. Only totalitarian states dictatorially crush all dissent. More democratic states recognize dissent as an inalienable right of persons and groups. In our time political dissent often assumes the strident form of confrontation. (In the Church it is called "prophetic denunciation.") Some find its attractiveness in the splendid opportunity confrontation provides to overcome social conformism and institutional pathology. But there are other forms. For example, the "loyal opposition" within a political party which has substantial unity on principles.

There is, I believe, an unconscious transfer that takes place whereby we think of religious assent and dissent in legal or political terms. Such a transfer obscures rather than renders transparent the real mystery of the Church. It misguides the unwary and in so doing renders a disservice to the community of faith, which is the People of God. We will not know or understand when and where and how dissent is appropriate by acting like politicians, by thinking like lawyers.

As a remedy for this unwarranted transfer of religious assent/dissent into the political realm, Aquinas' notion of *pietas* can, I believe, be helpful — if we expand it and apply it to the Church. If we look at the *Summa,* II-II, q. 101, all four articles, I do believe we will find a model that may help us understand when and where and how both assent and dissent are appropriate in the Body of Christ. For Aquinas, *pietas* is what we owe our parents and country, those from whom we have come. "*Pietas* consists in a profession of charity for parents and country as joint principles of our existence." (Art. 3)

Aquinas insists that *pietas* is a matter of justice owed by all, not merely an optional devotional practice. We all owe our parents so much — our lives, our homes, our sense of being loved and cared for, our sense of self worth and destiny. So devotion to parents is not an optional practice for the pious. It is what we all owe them in justice.

Similarly we all owe Holy Mother Church this much: it is from her that any hope we may have of eternal life has been mediated to us. No matter how ill-mannered or shabby or inadequate the Church's ministers might have on occasion been in our youth, yet it was from this Church and none other that we received the hope of eternal life that burns brightly in our hearts today. *Pietas* toward Holy Mother Church is not an optional devotional practice good for pious old ladies. It is a matter of justice, something we all owe.

But *pietas* is more. For, as Aquinas points out, our obligation or debt to our parents can never be fully repaid or adequately discharged. We owe them more than we can say. So we discharge the *debitum,* knowing in our hearts we will never succeed in full measure. As we go through life, there are special and precious moments when in discharging our *debitum* to Holy Mother Church we get fleeting glimpses of how impossible it is for us to succeed in full measure.

Aquinas also deals realistically with conflicts between *pietas* and *religio.* (Art. 4) Here too there is much food for thought about apparent conflicts in our duties to parents and religion, to Church authorities and God.

As contemporary philosophy reminds us, all our actions take

place within a field of affectivity which influences the nature and character of the actions themselves. In the Christian family (the Church) our actions should take place within the field of affectivity Aquinas calls *pietas*. It is a fundamental disposition toward Holy Mother Church which may provide us the sense of when and where and how dissent can appropriately take place.

It can give us a special sensitivity to the harm dissent may cause the Christian family — by the way the dissent is manifested or orchestrated, by the position the one who dissents occupies in the community as a private or public person. It is by *pietas* that we pick up the nuances implicit in these shapes and forms of dissent and understand their implications for ourselves and the community. In other words, it is *pietas* that may help us locate dissent within the *jus communionis*.

There is always the danger of collapsing *pietas* into pure sentimentality. But that would be a gross misunderstanding of Aquinas. When it is combined by the theologian with solid scholarship, with the presumption of the truth of Magisterial teaching, with modesty of presentation of one's own position, with openness to revision of one's position in the light of papal teaching, then there is a diminished likelihood of mistakenly identifying all conformity with loyalty, all differences with dissent, and all dissent with disloyalty.

The idea of *pietas* as a field of affectivity seems to me vital today in the lives of theologians. It seems equally necessary for those who constitute the ordinary Magisterium. It cuts both ways. The degree to which members of the hierarchy fulfill their covenant of loyalty with theologians, pastors, and the whole Christian family is the degree to which they help create an atmosphere where *pietas, veritas,* and *caritas* can flourish.

It is not easy to sort out all the affective elements that come together to form *pietas* — faith, love, gratitude, a sense of belonging, a sense of being home, a sense of being well off, identity, etc. It is something that we have all experienced from our most elementary loyalties of blood and soil to the loyalty to our favorite football team.

We conclude with a story from the life of St. Nicholas of Flue.[32] At age 50 he retired to a hermitage where people used to come for advice. One day representatives of two Cantons came.

92

They were on the brink of war with each other and wanted some advice. St. Nicholas tied a knot in his cincture and said: "Untie this knot." When they said this would not be difficult, he replied: "But you would not have been able to do it if each of you had pulled in his own direction."

Notes

1. *Lumen Gentium*, 25. Walter Abbot ed., *The Documents of Vatican II* (New York: America Press, 1966). See the commentary by Karl Rahner on articles 18-27 in *Commentary on the Documents of Vatican II, Vol. I*, H. Vorgrimler, gen'l ed., (New York: Herder and Herder, 1967), pp. 186-220.

2. *Lumen Gentium* 21.

3. *Dei Verbum* 8, 10.

4. *Aeternus Unigeniti Pater* 38.

5. *Humani Generis. AAS* 42(1950) 568. For a discussion of this, see John Ford and Gerald Kelly, *Contemporary Moral Theology*, vol. 1 (Westminster, Maryland: Newman, 1958), chaps. 2 and 3.

6. *Humanae Vitae* 28.

7. *Schema Constitutionis Dogmaticae De Ecclesia: Modi a Patribus conciliaribus propositi a commissione doctrinali examinati*, III: Caput III, *De Constitutione hierarchica Ecclesiae et in specie de Episcopatu* (Vatican Press, 1964), p. 42.

8. *Ibid.*

9. I am here following closely the excellent study by Joseph Komonchak, "Ordinary Papal Magisterium and Religious Assent" in *Readings in Moral Theology No. 3*, eds. C. Curran and R. McCormick (New York: Paulist Press, 1982), pp. 67-90.

10. J. Salaverri, "De Ecclesia Christi" in *Sacrae Theologiae Summa*, vol. 1 (Madrid: BAC, 1955), pp. 716, 720. Cited in Komonchak.

11. F. A. Sullivan, *De Ecclesia*, vol. I: *Questiones Theologiae Fundamentalis* (Rome, 1963), pp. 348, 354. Cited in Komonchak.

12. L. Lercher, *Institutiones Theologiae Dogmaticae*. 5th edition by F. Schlangenhaufen, vol. 1 (Barcelona, 1951), p. 297. Cited in Komonchak.

13. C. Pesch, *Praelectiones Dogmaticae*, vol. 1: *Institutiones Propaedeuticae ad Sacram Theologiam* (Freiburg, 1915), p. 370. Cited in Komonchak.

14. A. Straub, *De Ecclesia*, (1912) quoted by Salaverri, *op. cit.*, p. 702.

15. J. Burnsmann, A. Preuss, *A Handbook of Fundamental Theology* (London: B. Herder, 1932), pp. 98, 100.

16. L. Lercher, *op. cit.* p. 297. Cited in Komonchak.

17. D. Palmieri, *De Romano Pontifice cum prolegomeno De Ecclesia*. 2nd ed. (Prato, 1891), p. 719. Cited in Komonchak.

18. A. Straub, *De Ecclesia*, (1912) quoted by Salaverri, *op. cit.*, p. 703.

19. *Human Life in Our Day*. (Washington: United States Catholic Conference, 1968), p. 18.

20. *Dignitatis Humanae* 3.; *Gaudium et Spes* 16.

21. *Unitatis Redintegratio* 4, 11.

22. Its allowing open debate on the Council floor, its press office holding briefings, its members reporting debates in the media, etc.

23. See Avery Dulles, "Authority and Obedience," in *The Tablet* (Dec. 18, 1982), p. 1252. I have applied here a threefold distinction of Dulles, but in a way that is different from his own use.

24. Cardinal Newman, *Discourses: Addresses to Mixed Congregations*. (London: Longmans, 1909), p. 216.

25. Hans Urs von Balthasar, *Le Complexe Antiromain*. (Paris: Editions Paulines, 1976).

26. We are here dependent upon Peter Berger's descriptions in *The Heretical Imperative* (Garden City: Anchor, 1980) chapter one.

27. See the treatment of this topic by David Tracy, *The Analogical Imagination: Christian Theology and the Culture of Pluralism* (New York: Crossroad, 1981), chapter one.

28. For a discussion of the relationship between the information explosion and theology, see Karl Rahner, "Pluralism in Theology," in *Theological Investigations* vol. 11 (New York: Seabury, 1974), pp. 3-23.

29. As an example see the current discussions about the meaning of the objective moral order. Cf. Josef Fuchs, "The Sin of the World and Normative Morality" in *Gregorianum* 61 (1980) 51-76; Norbert Rigali, "The Moral Act" in *Horizons* 10 (1983) 252-266; Bernard Haring, *Free and Faithful in Christ,* vol. 2 (New York: Seabury, 1979), chapter 10, esp. part 6 (sins against chastity), pp. 551-564. Even the interpretation of basic texts of Vatican II (*Dignitatis Humanae* 3 and *Gaudium et Spes* 16) is disputed. See Josef Fuchs, *Personal Responsibility and Christian Morality.* (Washington: Georgetown University Press, 1983) chapter 11.

30. Yves Congar, "Le droit au desaccord" in *Annee Canonique* 1981, pp. 277-286.

31. We are focusing our discussion on dissent from ordinary non-infallible magisterium. There are other objects of dissent ranging from the denial of the truths of faith to resistance to abuses of office by Church authority to differences over practical matters such as fast days, feasts of saints, concordats, the appointment of bishops, etc.

32. Story told by Congar, *op. cit.,* p. 286.

94

Chapter 5

Pastoral Concerns Regarding the Moral Magisterium

Part I — Discussion With Fathers Ashley And Kertelge

Bishop: Father Ashley said, "Mortal sin takes place in critical acts." We are wondering what "critical acts" might mean?

Father Ashley: I only meant by critical acts that venial sins ordinarily precede a mortal sin. In other words, if you think of a mortal sin of anger, ordinarily we get a little bit mad at somebody before we get ready to wish that they were dead. It's at the point at which we finally break through and wish serious harm or do serious harm that a mortal sin is committed. That would then be the critical act.

Bishop: In the traditional presentation of moral theology the authors followed the system of explaining the ten commandments. In the explanation of all the commandments, we were told that there is serious matter and lighter matter, even in the commandments pertaining to God. Then when we came to the sixth commandment, governing the whole area of chastity and sexuality, the authors said that in this area there is no parvity of matter. When somebody with sufficient will and reflection did something against the sixth commandment, it was always a mortal sin, it could not be a venial sin. To many of us it seemed strange that in all the other commandments, even in the ones pertaining directly to God, there is parvity of matter, but in this one commandment the authors asserted there is no parvity of matter. What is the current teaching of theologians on this point, and, even more importantly, what is the teaching of the Church on this point?

Father Ashley: If you actually look at precisely what the classical moralists said, they said there is no parvity of matter with regard to the will to take complete satisfaction in sexual act. But they admitted that there could be acts of immodesty, glances, words, or touches which do not necessarily involve the will to have full satisfaction, and those could be venial. So it's only with regard to the willingness to take full satisfaction that there is no parvity of matter. The reason that that was said to be serious is because such a will as that, in the case of a married person, is contrary to their fidelity to their spouse, and, in the case of a non-married person, is a use of sex which does not involve life-long commitment. This would be parallel to the matter of perjury. In perjury you lie about a serious matter, but there could be venial lies as well. I think that sometimes people thought that everything that is a sin against purity is a mortal sin, and that's not true. Immodesty, for example, or telling a dirty joke might be a sin against purity, but a venial sin.

If a person wills to take sexual satisfaction in thoughts as a substitute for orgasm, that would be certainly mortal. But if it was a thought about something immodest, it would not necessarily be mortal. That was the teaching of the classical moralists. Now at present I don't think there's been any change of teaching in the Church about this. If you read the instruction on sexual ethics from the Sacred Congregation for the Doctrine of the Faith, it seems to be clear there that they regard sins against the sixth commandment which involve consent or the will to complete satisfaction as serious and, therefore, mortal sins.

Father Kertelge: One would say from the biblical tradition that sexual acts also are obliged to be dominated or governed by love. Love is the main commandment and the sin in sexuality is the offense as a refusal to love. Man has the obligation to use his sexuality as a medium of love, of love for other human beings and, too, of love of God at the same time. So sins in the field of human relationships, also in sexuality, participate in the quality of offenses against love. One should not isolate sins in sexuality from the principle of the love commandment, which Jesus Christ testifies is the chief commandment.

Bishop: But the problem is this: Why is it that moral theologians never use that expression *nulla parvitas materiae* (no parvity of matter) in relation to any of the other commandments, only to the sixth?

Father Ashley: Let me add an historical explanation. The reason may be the fear that in the area of sexuality, if you give people an inch, they'll take a mile!

I think the principles were clear that there can be sins against the sixth commandment which are only venial. There can be such sins, but the authors were very cautious about saying that, because in this particular area people are very inclined to take advantage of an excuse.

Bishop: It appears that some theologians are making a threefold distinction of sin: mortal sin, grave sin, and venial sin. We always thought and were taught that grave sin and mortal sin were one and the same thing. Do you have any explanation for that?

Father Ashley: That distinction seems to me to make no sense. What makes a sin a mortal sin is not that you hurt God, you can't hurt God, it's that you break your relation to God. That relation could either be broken by a direct sin against the theological virtues (which is probably not so common) or by a sin against your neighbor, which is the much more common situation. If the sin against your neighbor is serious, if you knowingly and willingly do *serious* harm to your neighbor, you can't at the same time love God. So it's a mortal sin. That is my argument in Chapter 2.

Bishop: You would stand by the traditional distinctions?

Father Ashley: Yes, I think that there is something legalistic about that distinction between mortal and serious sin because it implies that mortal sin differs from venial sin only in degree. But, as Saint Thomas teaches, there's a *toto caelo* difference between a mortal sin and a venial sin. They are only analogously the same thing because mortal sin is the willingness to do something seriously wrong, and that's utterly different than what we do in venial sins. As bad and as dangerous as venial sins are, they do not involve this will to do serious harm to other people (or oneself) and therefore to break off one's relation to God.

Bishop: Could you elaborate on the difference between an act of sin and an attitude of sin?

Father Ashley: I was trying to emphasize, and Father Kertelge also emphasized very much, that the New Testament begins with the idea of sin as coming from the heart, from an interior attitude. But our attitudes are not only expressed by acts, they are formed by acts. You don't just have an attitude without acts. You get the attitude by doing something, and it usually results in doing something.

Father Kertelge: In the New Testament teaching, especially in Saint Paul, there is the meaning that sin is a power, and the power of sin will overcome man. Then all personal sins are concretions of this being under the power of the sin. The main statement of redemption and of salvation history is that Christ has redeemed us from this power of sin. Therefore there's an obligation to fight against all actual acts of sin in which the power of sin seems still to be alive.

Bishop: How do you deal effectively in a pastoral way with the good Christians who in their confusion follow a guidance and a morality other than that of the Magisterium and show a loss of a sense of sin, a sense of guilt, and are not guided by the objective, moral principles that we preach? Sociological surveys show an alarming number of people who adopt contraceptive measures as a way of life, regardless of what the Church teaches, and, of course, the media highlight this all the time. We have also an increasing number of young people who marry, divorce, and then enter noncanonical marriages with the concept that God understands. And in the United States particularly, we have sociological studies on Mass attendance, which has gone from

75% to 80% down to 60% to 50% and in some places even below 50%. How do you in a pastoral way get across the ideas that were so brilliantly presented?

The second question is whether we ourselves as a Church, as Bishops, are in some way responsible for this relaxation of the observance of the laws? The American Bishops brought out a document on penance, emphasizing the need for it and insisting that the best way to do penance is fast and abstinence. We recommend very highly that what had been prescribed by law should now be done voluntarily by abstaining on Friday. And yet among the clergy and the religious, as well as the laity, all of the fine distinctions of such documents seem to have been lost. In the relaxation of some of the laws following the Second Vatican Council, have we contributed to a general concept that laws after all aren't all that important?

Father Ashley: It seems to me that the Church has three main ways by which it raises the conscience of people. One of them is in catechesis and religious education, one is in the confessional and one is in preaching. Those are the three means that are the traditional, and perhaps the most powerful, weapons that we have to form Christian conscience. It seems to me that in some respects we neglect all three. I don't hear preaching in our parishes very often these days, but the preaching that I do hear as regards moral instruction often tends to be very vague. We are told to love God and neighbor — which we need to hear, of course. But this Great Commandment is not made practical by a discussion of how we should actively show love and how we must actively avoid harming our neighbor and ourself. The preaching is not sufficiently concrete. I think a lot of priests are afraid to deal with some of these moral questions and so they prefer to pass over them. I think preaching, not only preaching at Mass, but also the use of the public media is one of the things we have to work at.

Another concern is religious education. I needn't belabor that. As we know, there was recently a period in which that got very confused and our students were not very clearly instructed in Christian morality.

Then, thirdly, as regards the confessional, I think this is hooked to the preaching problem because I very seldom hear sermons about going to confession. It used to be that this was a regular part of preaching, encouraging people to use the sacrament of penance. Nowadays it's not very often mentioned in preaching. Of course, we have to find an approach which is not merely legalistic, but, as Father Kertelge has shown, it must be truly biblical. We must start from fundamental principles, but instruction must also be made very concrete so that people will understand what these principles mean in practical life.

Bishop: Father Kertelge made a very important distinction concerning Luther's conception of morality. He made a distinction between the personal and the public expression of morality. May that have had an influence on the culture of our society as we live it today, if our people don't comprehend the meaning of sin in its reality? Do you think that it comes from that far back in the history of our modern culture?

Father Kertelge: The distinction was between "Gesinnungsethik", an ethics of attitude, and "Verantwortungsethik", an ethics of responsibility. This is a Lutheran tradition which is not so convincing to us that we can see here the solution of all problems. I think it poses the danger of dualism between private Christian life and life in society with its political challenges. The politician is also a man with a personal life, the father of a family, and so on. He must discover the intention of the divine commandments for his personal life and for the field of public affairs for which he bears responsibility. He has to translate them in the actual demands of various situations and there is no direct appeal, no direct advice from the Gospel for these special concrete situations, but only the command to follow Christ. In politics, also in the family and in the various professions, little by little, it is possible to overcome the duality of these two kinds of ethical approaches.

Bishop: We would like Father Kertelge to elaborate further on the sin against the Holy Spirit. For example, would the unjust structures that exist in society today on different levels that create the exploitation of people be considered as sins against the Holy Spirit?

Father Kertelge: Social sins will always be sins against love, sins against God, sins against the Holy Spirit, in so far as you can never isolate the sin against the Holy Spirit from other sins.

100

The sin against the Holy Spirit is a lack of faith in the saving work of God and this goes closely together with a lack of love for one's fellow-men. There is a tension drawing us to love God in all situations and in all demands of our human being. The main task is to maintain readiness to hear again and again the voice of God also through the voice of social conscience.

Father Ashley: I think Father Kertelge made the point in his paper that the principal moral theme to be found in the New Testament is the notion of reconciliation. But social injustice is always a breach in the social order, it's a negligence or injury to one's fellow man, to the social bond. The Holy Spirit is always working against that, the Holy Spirit is trying to bring people together, to get people to act in a spirit of forgiveness and consideration and care for each other. Therefore, we sin directly against the Holy Spirit when we forget that.

Bishop: I would like to ask about two issues. The first is revisionism in moral theology. This seems to be a problem that is especially difficult for the young, and for those who are studying theology today. They seem to have a revisionist mentality. For example, revisionists consider that homosexuality is a new problematic today, a different situation from that which the New Testament authors confronted, particularly Paul who speaks about this. How ought we be guided in an effort to cope with this issue?

A second question concerns the problem of *auctores probati*, approved authors. We have always been schooled in the idea that one way of determining a sound moral stance is to consult *auctores probati*. Now how do we gauge today who are the *auctores probati*?

Father Ashley: With regard to revision, there's no question that there has to be some revision of manualist moral theology for the reasons I gave in my chapter. There certainly has been and must be a historical development here. We need to purify moral theology of its legalism and its voluntarism and return to a more biblical and patristic and — yes — even a scholastic point of view. This would mean revisions about some of our particular judgments. But I think what is actually the problem in the United States is the dispute over a basic theoretical issue. There is polarization in American moral theology between the people who believe in proportionalism as a system of moral theology and those who oppose it. I think that probably what you are talking about as revisionism is really proportionalism.

Now there have always been different systems of moral theology in the Catholic Church and I would not advocate some kind of monolithic situation. But I do think it is important for the hierarchy to study this particular controversy and to make up their mind which system they think is correct and which one they are following, at least as individual bishops. Because that is what is at issue here and I think the bishops need to know whether, for example, proportionalism is being presented as the preferred method of moral theology in their seminaries.

I don't think there are any approved authors, (*auctores probati*), any longer in the old sense that prevailed in post-Tridentine moral theology because that was essentially a legalistic system of precedents. Authors copied previous authors and one counted these up to determine whether an opinion was solidly probable or more probable. That is a system that was falling into disfavor even before Vatican II, and I doubt that it is going to return again. Looking at the people who are writing in moral theology today, one can determine whether they conform to the Magisterium and one can find out what sort of moral system they themselves follow. You can use that to determine whether their opinions are trustworthy or not.

Bishop: Many people are proposing the teaching of Christ in various areas, such as family and marriage, as ideals. The question is, when are we placing a burden on our people?

Father Kertelge: Throughout the Old and the New Testament we are obliged to give God thanks and to fulfill His will. But, on the other hand, we find we are too weak, without God's help, to fulfill His commandments. Therefore, we have the help of Christ in hearing His Word and in the Sacraments, and thus we realize our being as new creatures. That is the point of reconciliation. Jesus did enough for us and we are told to do as Jesus did, to be reconciled with our brothers and sisters. This is not an unattainable ideal, but a promise that we *can* do what we should do. I think this is a tension which should go through the whole of moral theology.

Father Ashley: The very notion of "ideal" is not particularly biblical, it's a Platonic notion. I agree that it is rather dangerous to talk about morality as simply trying to achieve some kind of ideal, because the Christian has concrete obligations. It's not simply an ideal that I should tell the truth, I've got to try to be honest with people. It's not simply an ideal that I should pay money back that I borrowed. It's not an ideal, it's an obligation. I don't think that we should dissolve obligations into ideals. Now it's very true that none of us achieve perfection, but with the help of grace it is really possible for us to perform our limited obligations. For example, in marriage it is possible for people to remain faithful to each other through life. That's not an ideal, it's an obligation that they undertake.

Bishop: As pastors, we are concerned about the great pain that a lot of people are suffering because of the multiplicity of theological positions taken rather dogmatically, very often by those who are teaching in seminaries or Catholic universities or writing in periodicals. These theologians sometimes admit that the Holy Father has spoken of this or that issue, or the bishop has spoken of this issue, but they suggest that they're really not that well informed so it is not necessary to follow them. People will say, to whom do I go to for the truth because I've gone to three different confessors giving me three different solutions?

Father Ashley: One thing that we could do would be more frequently to explain to people what the role of the bishop is in moral guidance, what the role of the theologian is, and what the role of the confessor is. I think people twenty years ago thought that these were all the same and that all would agree. Even then it really was not all that true, but that's the impression people had. Nowadays theological controversy has become of interest to the public. I don't think it used to be this way twenty years ago, but now theology appears in *Time* magazine. So people know all of these opinions of theologians that they never heard before. They need to be instructed just what the theologian is supposed to do and what the limits of his task are. They should be told that the theologian has no authority to speak for the Church. He is a scholar who presents his hypotheses. The bishop speaks and teaches for the Church.

The person who administers the Sacraments, the confessor, must act in the name of the Church so he has to give advice in keeping with the teaching of the Church. I do think the faithful of the Church need to be told that sometimes there are disputes about how to apply the teaching of the Church to individual cases. In these instances confessors are going to differ and people shouldn't be shocked at that. They should be instructed not to go "shopping" for a confessor who will be nice, but rather to find a confessor they respect, one they consider a faithful and well-instructed priest.

But the real source of the confusion today is the tendency of people to think that if a theologian says something, because he is a learned man, he has the same authority as the bishop. People are not making the distinction between two different kinds of authority: the authority of the theologian and the authority of the Church.

Father Kertelge: I would like to underline what Father Ashley has said. There are two kinds of teaching and there is a bridge between them. A theologian has his own authority. You know, I'm sure, of our experiences and problems in Germany in this regard. But the theologian is also a living member of the Church. As such he has a responsibility for what he is teaching in scriptural exegesis or moral theology and he must take this responsibility seriously. He will both listen to what the Magisterium is saying and to what his competence as a scholar tells him.

Part II — Discussion With Monsignor DiLorenzo And Father Peter

Bishop: I have heard people ask this question. How is it possible to give assent to something when the reasons for it are not convincing to the person? How would you answer?

Father Peter: There are many situations in my life and yours where we accept things, even in a non-religious area, that we have not been intellectually convinced of and I don't think that we do that in any dishonest way or inauthentic way. There are very, very many things I accept because I trust the people who know something about that area. Let me give you some examples.

104

The ones that come immediately to my mind are medical ones. If my doctor says XYZ is the case, I don't normally dissent. So I am saying that I can assent to things in circumstances where I am not myself possessed of expertise and cannot say anything more than that this is a trustworthy person. If someone has the charism of truth, assent is the normal response.

Bishop: I'm asking if there's an obligation to do that? The obvious situation would be *Humanae Vitae.* I can see that there are people who don't accept the reasoning of the conclusions. They think their reasons are better and therefore, they just have to say that. And I have no problem about anyone saying that. What must such a person do in practice, however? Can he as an individual and a married person practice contraception because he thinks his reasons are better? I'm asking this because of the added dimension of who has spoken, the organ of articulation of the Mystical Body placed there by Christ, presenting, therefore, the authentic official teaching.

Father Peter: The answer of traditional moral theology is that there are situations where dissent is called for or obligatory — even in cases where the conscience is invincibly in error. We must surely follow an invincibly erroneous conscience.

Bishop: But we must presume good faith in all of this. The verb "to be in good faith" is a defective verb, it has no first person singular or plural. We can say, "you are in good faith" or "they are in good faith". By very definition to be in good faith is to be in error, and if one says "I am in error", he has to correct the error. I am just describing a person who knows how the Church has spoken officially and by its authentic teaching. What is his obligation, in the mind of the Church at least?

Father Peter: That person must follow his conscience.

Monsignor DiLorenzo: Several years ago one of the Bishops talked about this when the *Ethical and Religious Directives for Catholic Health Facilities* were published. He made a distinction between the institution, whether a school or health care facility, and an individual person whose private problems could be handled in the confessional or in moral counselling. As far as the school or the institution were concerned, he believed it was the role of the institution to proclaim, to give witness, to conserve and to enforce Ecclesial values. One ought not to make incarnate in institutional policy his/her dissent, or personal religious moral problems. In effect it appears that anyone who is officially associated with a school or an institution must give clear witness to the Church's teaching, even though he/she may personally and privately not agree with it.

Bishop: Monsignor DiLorenzo stated that there is complete incompatibility between Marxist Communism and Christianity. If these two are diametrically opposed, what formula or model would you propose for the Church, when it happens to find itself suddenly under Marxist government?

Monsignor DiLorenzo: In my estimation it is very questionable whether there can be any real meaningful, ongoing, and *lasting rapport* with persons who sincerely and honestly subscribe to Marxist Communism in its current form. The reason I said that in Chapter 3 is I do believe that periodically we can buy time. I think there can be a temporary rapprochement on occasion. But I do not believe this rapport can be long lasting or that a Catholic Christian Bishop can be really secure with it. I think that concrete, historical events have shown it is an extremely risky business to put long term trust in this kind of agreement. I have no immediate formula to give, that is something that would take a lot of time and hammering out.

Bishop: One of the main problems of the living Magisterium of the Church is the opposition from other magisteria both inside the Church and also outside the Church. Is it possible to build a bridge in this field between the living Magisterium of the Church and the science, the culture, the secular wisdom of the world?

Mosnignor DiLorenzo: I would like to address the challenge of ongoing dialogue of the Magisterium and the newer insights into human knowledge. I think that our tradition has always supported a truly liberal arts education. From the time of the ancients throughout the ages we have always been interested in a rapport between revelation and the humanities. Christianity's philosophy of education, understood properly, has always invited new and creative efforts centering on the synthesis of human and religious knowledge. Therefore, I think the whole background of the Church has been cautiously optimistic that there can be a rapport struck between science and technology and revelation. I think we do have the kind of resources to engage the modern world. I know an easy or facile synthesis is very elusive. We have an international theological commission that tries, despite many divergent perspectives centering around theology, to address many modern problems. I'm optimistic that there can be dialogue. It certainly requires very creative and very resourceful leadership, but I'm hopeful.

Bishop: Father Peter, you described faith, love, gratitude, a sense of belonging, a sense of being home, a sense of being well off and of identity. Those are very difficult categories for the person angry with the Church to identify with. It really puts a very heavy burden on those of us who find all those things in the Church to translate that experience to the person who does not.

Father Peter: My experience has been that an angry person wants somebody to listen, and I think our listening is the first step towards this kind of *pietas* that I'm talking about. I honestly think they want us to listen. In many cases it's the hardest thing to do, to listen. On the other hand, it's very therapeutic to listen because some of these people have anger that has welled up for 10, 20, 30, or 40 years.

When (after much listening) we have reached the point that they are ready to hear something, I tell them a story about a Jewish lady from Cologne in Germany whose father was a dentist. He was destroyed by the Nazi Holocaust, as were her mother, her three brothers, and another sister. Ruth lives in my town; I said to her one day, "Why don't you hate?" She said to me, "If I opened the door of my house to hatred just a little way, I wouldn't have room for anything else in my house or my life."

A person can be totally enveloped and destroyed if hatred begins to control his or her life. Anger turns off affectivity towards any other human being, and is the source of violence. Somehow or other individuals who are angry have to come to grips with the wrath that is in their lives, lest it destroy them. This is a very painful process, but this is the way I would try to bring people home, very slowly.

Monsignor DiLorenzo: I would like to clarify that my discussion of feminism was not dealing specifically with the immediate concerns of persons in the Church who feel they have been mistreated. I was discussing it from a philosophical viewpoint. The philosophical roots of the feminist movement of the 19th Century designed by Elizabeth Katie Stanton are found in the intellectual trends of the day. These were rationalism, the Quaker notion of inner light, transcendentalism, and individualism. These intellectual trends formulated the underpinnings, the metaphysic, as it were, of the feminist movement of that time. That metaphysic is at variance with the belief and witness of the Christian community. I would say that the movement has been updated quite a bit especially by those who form the National Organization of Women. Nonetheless the philosophical basis is generally the same. Thus feminism in this specific sense would tend to reject in principle what we mean by Magisterium.

Bishop: We had a question about whether or not you could have a solidly probable opinion in contradiction to clear-cut current teaching of the authentic Magisterium. I think that the response of the Sacred Congregation for the Doctrine of the Faith on sterilization in 1975 was specifically addressing that question.

Father Peter: Here is the text: "The Congregation, while it confirms this traditional doctrine of the Church, is not unaware of the dissent against this teaching from many theologians. The Congregation, however, denies that doctrinal significance can be attributed to this fact as such, so as to constitute a 'theological source' which the faithful might invoke and thereby abandon the authentic Magisterium and follow the opinions of private theologians which dissent from it."

I think they are saying that you can't have a solidly probable opinion in contradiction to current, clear, direct teaching of the Magisterium.

Bishop: But within the realm of legitimate dissent could a person who is a spiritual director, for instance, tell people that they could practice artificial contraception, or could a person who clearly understood the official Church's teaching but thought it was wrong go ahead and practice it? Are not the answers to both of those questions, no?

108

Father Peter: However qualified, the answer is yes to both questions. Dissent can be legitimate in these cases. Recall also the teaching of St. Alphonsus Liguori on good faith: is a confessor obliged to warn a penitent about grave material sin when he foresees the warning will not benefit the penitent? Alphonsus Liguori's response is no, one is not obliged, but there is an exception when the common good may be at stake. Secondly, I refer to Father Zalba's statement about Fraternal Correction in reference to superiors and people who are acting specifically in the external forum. Father Zalba says: "Material sin should also *per se* be corrected by the superior, and likewise by others where there could be scandal or danger of a bad habit leading to formal sins. For these are also harmful to the neighbor, although less demanding of correction than formal sins. If, however, correction or warning would be foreseen to be non-beneficial but rather harmful, it should be omitted unless the common good demands otherwise."

Bishop: Suppose someone says I cannot accept this teaching because I have really serious problems with it and I have studied the matter?

Father Peter: I think in all honesty that what you and I have to do is to explain to this person (as best they're able to accept it) the common teaching of the Church about this. We should not impose a private opinion on them. We are bound to give them the common teaching of the Church precisely about the matter. The teaching of the Church on this is normative and binding but it also admits of occasions when dissent is permissible. The teaching on dissent must also be explained to them.

Monsignor DiLorenzo: The clarification mentioned earlier may be of help here. The individual who is part of an institution or a school, in point of fact, really does have the obligation to proclaim, to give witness, to conserve and to enforce those values which are the teaching of the Church. I don't think that someone can raise his personal dissent to the level of an institutional policy. He must teach what the Church wants taught. Nor can he encourage or persuade or do anything to invite people away from embracing and interiorizing such values. I really believe that he must be very firm in proclaiming that teaching even though he has personal problems with it. The priest should not introduce his personal problems in any dialogue between himself and the penitent or the person he is religiously counselling.

Bishop: This first question is for Monsignor DiLorenzo. There is obviously some validity to a holistic approach to the human person. So we would ask you to comment on the line of demarcation between grace and nature, between psychology and religion.

The second question is for Father Peter. Would you comment on this proposition that, assuming, of course, that a bishop is in communion with the Holy Father and the college of bishops, he does teach with Magisterial authority when he teaches in his own diocese?

Monsignor DiLorenzo: What is the relation of the behavioral sciences to moral theology? Can there be a rapport struck? I am of the definite opinion that there can be a rapport struck. One must develop a basic metaphysic or description of reality to begin with. That's the first thing. Once one has provided adequately a basic description of what reality is, then it wouldn't be incompatible to find that the behavioral sciences could be integrated well into Catholic moral theology. The difference would be primarily that the behavioral sciences are empirical in their orientation. Hence they can never really adequately reach the realm of the supernatural. Psychology, for example, can help describe the inner world of the moral agent, it can help the moralist in understanding the stages and levels of moral development. If there are dynamics associated with moral development, it may be able to describe them from an empirical point of view. It may also be of help in understanding the environment the subject lives in, the kinds of pressures he or she is under. This also may help us to a great degree to understand the issue of diminished responsibility. But to say that psychology has all the answers, I would find that to be a mistaken notion.

There have been some descriptions of how this rapport can be struck, but they tend to come and go depending on the strength or the weakness of a particular psychological theory as criticized by persons in the field themselves. Some psychologists may disagree with the pychological theory that has been synthesized with theology, and the beautiful rapport between psychology and theology is fragmented. Then one has to start the synthesis all over again with a newer approach.

Father Peter: Does a bishop in union with the Holy Father teach with Magisterial authority in his own diocese? The answer is affirmative and the reason is this. By ordination and mission, a bishop just isn't a part of a choir, or part of a whole, he is the pastor of that flock. But furthermore, what he teaches he teaches in two senses, one as a witness to the saving Mysteries of faith, but the other, in the most profound sense, like a martyr.

Bishop: What about good people who do not grasp the ordinary Magisterium?

Father Peter: If theologians, priests, and bishops have a hard time understanding certain questions, what about very good Catholics who just don't understand? We're very sympathetic, and in many cases we say we have to leave such people in good faith. But then, on the other hand, we are torn by a dialectic because of the degree to which there is social justice involved. What do you tell these rightist groups, these assassination squads in Central America, do you say, "your conscience is just fine"? You surely don't. You cannot leave them in "good faith". Cardinal Ratzinger put this very well. He said that on one hand there isn't any absolute right of conscience, but, on the other hand, the persons who have the greatest right to speak in the Church are the Saints. The charism of sanctity extends to many folks who are not bishops.

I hear teachers saying that the greatest thing you can do is to be pastoral and leave people in good faith. That may be true in some situations, but in all the situations where people are being exploited you must say just the opposite. They are not to be left in "good faith". Where there are, for example, problems of sexual abuse in families, or where children and families are being destroyed or peoples exploited, you would not leave people in "good faith".

Bishop: Would you comment on Catholic fundamentalism which is something to deal with as we think about the Magisterial pronouncements?

Monsignor DiLorenzo: What is dubbed "Catholic fundamentalism" is difficult to define, so therefore I should define it for our purposes of discussion. The individual person somehow or other has been turned on or feels turned on, particularly with the use of Scripture alone. Somehow or other there's a general perception that God speaks to one through the Scriptures in a highly individualized way. The role of the Church as a source of knowledge and values remains vague in this framework. One's religious and moral insights may or may not correspond to the endorsed religious insights of the whole Christian community.

This process tends almost automatically to exclude Church teaching. There doesn't seem to be a reference to the Church's position. Worse, there is no reflection on whether or not this Church of ours does have the capacity to test out authentically and authoritatively for an individual this personal, religious experience. Now when this happens, we have a problem with "Catholic fundmentalism".

Bishop: We wonder whether theologians have unlimited range to speculate?

Father Peter: I'll answer like St. Thomas does. First, they clearly don't have unlimited range because their minds are limited. Secondly, they do have unlimited range in the sense that no human being can ever penetrate the truth fully. There's an unlimited range with regard to truth and with regard to law. Thirdly, is there unlimited range with regard to the faith? If by unlimited range with regard to the faith, you mean, can a theologian study the best arguments against any position that the Roman Catholic Church has, the answer is yes, he can. He not only can, but he ought to. The next question is can he do it with regard to faith in a way that is destructive of his faith or anybody else's faith? Here the answer is obviously no; spiritual suicide is forbidden. This is the same question that we ask in science in an analogous way. May a scientist blow up the world to figure out how it was made? The answer is no. We owe that much to ourselves and to those who have gone before us, to the community and others.

Bishop: We would like to ask your reflections, in the light of the Second Vatican Council's teaching on collegiality, about the possible teaching authority of the Episcopal conference and of the auxiliary bishop.

Father Peter: I'll be very careful, but I'll start with auxiliary bishops. There is an opinion about auxiliaries — I don't hold it, of course — which says auxiliary bishops are "mule bishops". They are without pride of origin and without hope of progeny. This opinion is mainly held — so I am told — by the Ordinary of the place. The Second Vatican Council clearly says a bishop's teaching authority does not come solely from the canonical powers of jurisdiction. Many of you have read articles on the proper role of a national conference of bishops. There are two divergent schools of thought about this. One of them says that collegiality is the individual bishop in his own diocese in union with other bishops and in union with the Pope, and that the national conference of itself doesn't add any specific weight, power, or authority; that is the more traditional position. The second position says, to the contrary, that, as collegiality develops more and more, bishops will themselves see their role precisely as being part of the voice of the larger Church by being a conference of bishops. This position says the bishops of a conference together have both the *munus* and the *mandatum* of teaching.

Bishop: We have a comment from the Spanish-speaking Bishops at our table who are very conscious of Marxism in their apostolate and their work of evangelization. The comment is that in the process of evangelization the Church must consider the social, educational and economic dimensions of human experience along with the spiritual values we teach. Our question is this: how do we best resolve the tension between subjective and objective considerations in the formation of conscience?

Monsignor DiLoreno: I have made a distinction between what goes on in confession or moral counseling and what goes on in institutional policy. In your dioceses you have Catholic institutions of higher education, secondary schools, grammar schools, and health care facilities. I suggest that we must not raise to the level of institutional policy these exceptional, rare, and disputed case solutions that take place in an academic setting. The institution should very clearly proclaim, witness, con-

113

serve, and enforce the values which the Church teaches. This may not be the most pleasant task but I do not know of any other way to remain faithful to the goals of a Catholic institution than what I have just suggested.

I would like to add immediately that we do have resources available in Catholic social services, compassionate confessors, and good religious counselors who can resolve individual dilemmas on a private level. Hence when institutions in a diocese come to the bishop with a difficult pastoral problem, it seems to me that raising the resolution of that pastoral problem to the level of institutional policy can be a mistake.

Father Peter: I like to use examples that are familiar to people — examples of how good intentions are not enough. For example, no matter how well-intentioned a member of a family may be, setting fire to his bedroom every night will sooner or later be disruptive of the whole family. Or, if a physician told you he diagnosed your having pneumonia and then three months later said the real diagnosis was cancer, his good intentions would not warm your heart. So the demands of conscience are great precisely because conscience calls out to us to realize goods which are really real. That is the source of our obligation to act in a particular way. In the last analysis it is the harmony of true values that makes life worthwhile and makes the teaching of the Church eminently successful.

Part III:
Doubts In Moral Theology

OVERVIEW
of PART III

Contemporary Catholic moral theology has entered a period of critical doubt and controversy about the exceptionless character of certain key moral norms traditionally considered absolute. This part of our volume surveys that situation with Chapter 6 presenting the challenge to these norms and Chapter 9 responding to it. Chapters 7 and 8 offer insights from the Protestant tradition and biblical exegesis. Chapter 10 presents a dialogue between three of the authors and the bishops.

Lisa Sowle Cahill, Associate Professor of Theology at Boston College, suggests in *Chapter 6* that proportionalism accepts the absoluteness of moral norms prohibiting a physical act in specific circumstances. In his later chapter Father Connery raises the issue which proportionalism advances, that some circumstances may outweigh other circumstances in moral evaluation.

In her discussion Dr. Cahill focusses on physical human acts like contraception and masturbation which have traditionally been fobidden. Proportionalism would designate these acts as ontic or premoral evil, rather than moral evil, with the result that they can be justified by sufficient reason. Dr. Cahill responds to four basic objections to this theory and concludes by suggesting that proportionalism has arisen from the objective reality of moral dilemmas. She suggests that this method can be used cautiously with Magisterial guidance on the objective relations and priorities of values which the theory uses to permit exceptions to traditional norms.

In *Chapter 7*, Dr. Gene Outka, the Dwight Professor of Philosophy and Christian Ethics at Yale University, presents a wide-ranging survey of the Protestant tradition and exceptionless moral norms. He begins with four questions about key moral norms: 1) Does the violation of them always negatively affect one's relation to God? 2) Does such a violation always conflict with the normative content of neighbor-love? 3) Are the grounds for commending such norms natural, objectivist, and generally negotiable? 4) Are such grounds revealed ones, depending on the Bible in some way?

Dr. Outka first explores the Reformation legacy in which the affirmative answer to question 1) is challenged and the verdict about exceptionless moral norms depends more centrally on question 2). He then explores the work of a dozen twentieth century Protestant ethicists who ground their verdicts about exceptionless moral norms more or less exclusively on revelation, i.e. question 4). Finally, in the second half of his chapter, Dr. Outka presents a careful analysis of the work of Reinhold Niebuhr and Paul Ramsey, two giants of Protestant ethics in this century. He concludes with three characteristically Protestant themes about exceptionless moral norms.

In *Chapter 8*, Father Thomas J. Deidun, I.C., a Lecturer in New Testament Studies at Heythrop College at the University of London, focusses on the New Testament Epistles of St. Paul for biblical insights into moral norms. He presents a careful analysis of seven arguments and presuppositions according to which St. Paul saw no place at all for norms in Christian living. As a result of these analyses, Father Deidun argues for St. Paul's affirmation of moral norms in his teaching.

118

In conclusion, Father Deidun clarifies three senses in which St. Paul supposes his injunctions are "absolute." They are absolute in the sense that they have an objective validity, in the sense that St. Paul nowhere envisages the possibility of their being "relativized in the light of higher claims," and in the sense that St. Paul intends at least some norms to express the ethical implications of the Christian's relationship with Christ. On the other hand, the norms are not "absolute" in the sense that they are "hypostasized," or contain within themselves their own *raison d'être*. A norm is decisive, "not because it is a norm, but because it is understood to confront the Christian with the inescapable implications of some aspect of his relationship with Christ." Father Deidun does not believe that this biblical absoluteness definitively includes a universal and timeless validity of moral norms which might rule out ethical proportionalism.

Father Connery responds in *Chapter 9* to the challenge of proportionalism. He uses the term "teleologists" for those upholding this method rather than "proportionalists." He argues that the basis for certain key exceptionless moral norms in contemporary Catholic thought lies in the unalterable *moral* evil, rather than "premoral" or "ontic" evil of certain kinds of human acts. He cites the actions of killing human beings and of sexual intercourse. These human acts cannot be considered abstractly but only in a concrete context. If the acts, for example, involve killing the innocent or sexual intercourse between unmarried persons, these acts constitute *moral* evil. Father Connery argues that to designate them as merely ontic evil which can be justified by proportionate reasons or values is to depart from "the basis for moral teaching and preaching in the whole Christian era."

Father Connery does not hold that the physical act of contraception is an absolute evil; he would admit the justification of contraception as a defense against rape. But he holds that contraception apart from such circumstances is moral evil in itself and not merely ontic or premoral evil. He points out that various metaethical norms may be used (a natural law norm, or personalist, or right reason norm, for example,) to decide that such acts *are* moral evil. In any case, he finds no basis for the reductionism involved in shifting certain kinds of human acts from the category of "moral evil" to that of "ontic evil."

The dialogue in *Chapter 10* includes responses from Dr. Cahill and Fathers Connery and Deidun. Dr. Cahill restates her position that a circumstance *can* constitute a given human act as intrinsic, and, presumably, moral evil. She affirms the moral evil of killing innocent non-combatants in warfare, not excusing it because it will save more lives in the long run, but upholding the value of life itself. She cites polygamy and capital punishment as actions which might be justifiable in given cultures and circumstances.

In the second half of Chapter 10, Father Deidun reaffirms his position that Scripture itself does not provide a hermeneutic to determine if any of its moral norms are not culturebound and hence timeless and absolutely universal. Father Connery points to the use of proportionalism by some ethicists to dissent from some Church teaching. However, he also notes that one *could* embrace proportionalism and yet hold that in questions where there is specific Church teaching there are no proportionate reasons to permit exceptions in practice to that teaching. He states that, unlike traditional theologians, teleologists tend to admit the probability of sufficient reasons for an opinion even opposing Church teaching. These key issues of proportionalism and dissent will continue to hover in the background throughout the discussion of applied moral theology in Part IV.

Chapter 6

Contemporary Challenges
To Exceptionless
Moral Norms

Lisa Sowle Cahill, Ph.D.

Introduction

The nature and function of moral norms has been a hot topic in Christian ethics at least since the "situation ethics" debates of the 1950's and 1960's. The Episcopalian Joseph Fletcher created a stir with a book *(Situation Ethics¹)* which virtually equated Christian love with finding the most efficient means to the best immediate consequences of any particular act. While few agreed with his conclusion that rules are at best unreliable summaries of past experience, many did appreciate his insistence that human moral experience is not captured adequately by codes of laws, whether derived from the Bible or natural law. To correlate with moral reality, guidelines must reflect the unique aspects of moral situations, personal responsibility, and moral ambiguity.

In Catholicism, the discussion of moral norms has proceeded

on the basis of dissatisfaction with the deductive and rather rigid methods of the neo-Scholastic manualists and of encouragement by the "personalism" implied by the Documents of Vatican II, especially the Pastoral Constitution on the Church in the Modern World (*Gaudium et Spes*). Most moral theologians concur in this document's exhortation to scrutinize "the signs of the times," and to realize "the human race has passed from a rather static concept of reality to a more dynamic, evolutionary one."[2] What is less clear than the general validity of these mandates is how their fulfillment may be successfully integrated with the more traditional and no less important commitments of Catholicism to an objective moral order and reliable guidance in concrete moral decision-making.

It is at this point that there emerges the controversy we are here addressing. What does it mean today to speak of "human nature," "the natural moral law," and "moral norms"? Are traditional formulations of these concepts adequate to such insights into the historicity of human persons and communities as those endorsed by *Gaudium et Spes*? If not, how can they be reformulated in a way which retains continuity with the tradition while refreshing its vitality for contemporary moral theology? It seems that Catholic moral theology or ethics is caught in a "time between the times," a time of change, of necessary revisions, and of inevitable disagreements about how to accomplish that for which we all hope: an evolution of thought which is both genuinely "conservative" and genuinely "progressive."

Types Of Moral Norms

The so-called "challenges to exceptionless moral norms" amount to a proposal for furthering that evolution.[3] Unfortunately, this proposal has tended at times to generate more heat than genuine illumination. Some have interpreted it as a repudiation of all moral absolutes and even of all objectivity in ethics, or of the commitment to the non-negotiability of some human values in the face of expediency. My task will be to clarify some of the fundamental issues at stake and the exact nature of the claims made. First of all, I cannot think of any contemporary moral theologians who repudiate exceptionless moral norms entirely; what is at stake is a specific subcategory of moral norms. It is possible to distinguish at least four types of norms, the absoluteness of only the last of which is truly under challenge:

1) *Formal moral norms*, such as "Be honest," "Be just," and "Respect persons." These principles are absolute: dishonesty, injustice, and disrespect for persons are wrong without exception. However, these norms are formal in that they do not tell us exactly what is concretely to count for these wrongs. Is telling a literal untruth to save a life from an unjust aggressor an instance of "dishonesty"? Is taxing the wealthy to provide social welfare for the poor an "injustice"? Is imprisonment of a criminal a violation of the "respect" due persons? Even after general moral absolutes have been defined, their substantive meaning remains to be filled out.

2) *Analytical or tautological norms*, such as "Do not commit murder," "Do not tell a lie," and "Do not be cruel." These specify a certain sort of act, and indicate furthermore that it is carried out in circumstances which make it immoral. However, the precise nature of those circumstances is not specified. The norms prohibiting murder, lying, and cruelty deal with homicide, telling an untruth, and inflicting suffering, all of which *might* be justified in some but not all circumstances. The norms forbid (absolutely) performing these acts in wrong (but still unspecified) circumstances. The wrongness of the circumstances is conveyed by what are sometimes referred to as "value terms," e.g., murder, lying, and cruelty, But we are not told what kind of homicide counts as murder, of untruth as lying, or of infliction of pain as cruelty.

3) When some of these circumstances are specified, we arrive at still another sort of absolute norm: one which in addition to the physical *act*, includes specific *circumstances* in which it would be wrong to perform it. Examples of *norms regarding acts plus specific immoral circumstances* are: "Do not kill to gain an inheritance (but do so in self-defense)", "Do not tell a falsehood to evade due punishment (but do so to save an innocent)", and "Do not mutilate a child for sadistic pleasure (but do so as life-saving therapy)." Sometimes the "act plus circumstances" can be specified in a single word, such as "rape" or "adultery" or

"mercy-killing." Unlike an open-ended word like "murder," these terms imply some specific sort of injustice, e.g., intercourse by force, intercourse with someone other than one's spouse, and killing the sick to avoid suffering. It is important to note that ethical discussions about norms in this category will be about precisely *which* circumstances create immoral settings for which acts. For example, what are the circumstances under which homicide is *always* murder, or falsehood is *always* lying?

4) *Norms which prohibit a physical act abstracted from circumstances* (strikingly often a sexual act). Examples are: "Do not use artificial contraception," "Do not masturbate," "Do not abort a fetus." Now we are in much more controversial territory, though perhaps not so controversial as might at first appear. It is agreed, even by revisionists, both that these actions generally are to be avoided, and that not just any sort of reason can justify them. But the question of those who are inclined to revise our traditional understanding of these norms as absolute is whether there are *any* reasons which can justify such acts, e.g., artificial contraception to preserve a woman's health, abortion to save her life, or masturbation as part of medical investigation of and therapy for infertility.

Rather than taking the physical act as the equivalent of a *moral* norm, some would see it as an evil which is "premoral," "ontic," "material," or "physical."[4] Now this is not to say that a "premoral evil" is morally neutral. To the contrary, it is regarded as something generally not fulfilling for human nature, and indeed harmful to it. It always counts as a negative factor in a total moral evaluation. But taken by itself, it is not morally *decisive*. Completion of the evaluation of which it is a part depends on other factors as well. Although there is a presumption that the premoral evil will be avoided, it can be justified in exceptional cases, when there is sufficient reason in the form of an even higher good at stake than that safeguarded by the norm.

To emphasize, what is questioned is whether specification of an act apart from circumstances can constitute an exceptionless moral norm. If a specific norm (as opposed to a formal or tautological one) requires circumstances in order to be absolute, then the discussions of moral theologians should attend to the nature of those circumstances, i.e., to settings in which the generally undesirable act is really the best of the available alternatives. We are dealing with conflict situations; what is in question is not the *prima facie* obligation to avoid acts such as contraception and masturbation, but the exceptional justifiability of taking less-than-ideal routes to the resolution of less-than-ideal situations. If human moral agents were never confronted with such situations, the very notion of a "moral dilemma" would be meaningless.

Moral Norms and the Natural Law

Revisionist moral theologians such Richard McCormick, Charles Curran, Josef Fuchs, Bruno Schüller, and Louis Janssens share certain fundamental presuppositions with the tradition of Thomistic ethics, including those fellow members of the tradition who disagree with their conclusions regarding norms. All are committed to an objective moral order, to nature as the norm of human action, to the knowability of nature by reasonable reflection, and to the responsibility of the Church (the *Magisterium*) to clarify the natural law and give moral guidance. What is distinctive about the revisionist approaches (to take the liberty of generalization about theories which are not actually identical) is their recognition of the historicity of human persons and communities, and thus of the development of human nature itself; of epistemological limits and the partial and progressive character of human knowing, which has implications for the *formulation* of norms which express what nature is and demands; and of the responsibility of each person to consider how the values protected by norms best can be realized in concrete situations.

Josef Fuchs has expressed some of the consequences of these insights in a nuanced and representative way. First, he presupposes that morality should respect and represent the authentically human: *agere sequitur esse*. But the normative power of nature lies in "the *person*" whose reality is "a human nature with all its particular elements and a concrete historical condition. Otherwise, the formula 'action follows being' is not being taken seriously enough . . ."[5] The essential issue, then, is one of true objectivity, not of relativizing the objectively moral to the subjective decision. Fuchs suggests that the "absoluteness" of moral norms does "not signify primarily universality but objectivity." What is objectively (and in that sense absolutely) demanded may not be the same in every historically and culturally conditioned society,[6] or even for every individual. Thus specific behavioral norms can be both absolute and objective without being universal.

"Proportionalism"

The method of those thinkers who challenge the notion that physical acts in the abstract can be prohibited absolutely is often referred to as "proportionalism." This term comes from the relation of their challenge to the principle of double effect. This principle has been at the center of the Catholic controversy over moral norms, since much of the rethinking of norms originated in attempts to explain and apply the principle. Double effect is a principle with which to consider the morality of acts which bring about some good result at the expense of some undesirable one. It is helpful to understand the principle as an attempt to take consequences seriously into account in moral evaluation, while at the same time avoiding utilitarianism. (Utilitarianism is the theory that the morally right act is whatever is necessary to bring about "the greatest good for the greatest number.")

The principle applies four criteria to an act with a good and an evil effect. To be morally justified, the act itself must not be "intrinsically evil;" the evil effect must be tolerated rather than directly intended; the good result must not be a direct effect of the evil one; and the good must be equal to or greater than the evil, that is, "proportionate" to it. The revisionists claim that the last condition is the most important, and object in particular to the additional requirement that the act not be a member of the category "intrinsic evil."[7] The reason for this will be clear from what has been said above. First of all, there is confusion inherent in the way the notion of "intrinsic evil" traditionally has been explicated. Standard lists of examples tend to include terms which are not really all of the same sort, e.g., "blasphemy, perjury, masturbation, and murder."[8] Obviously "masturbation" denotes a specific physical action apart from accompanying circumstances, while the other three assert that the sometimes licit acts of speaking God's name, telling an untruth, and homicide are accompanied by circumstances which make them immoral. Furthermore, the terms "blasphemy" and "perjury" give us some notion of just what those circumstances might be, while "murder" does not. We are left with the question why a generally to be avoided use of sexuality is never justified, while a generally reprehensible action against human life may be. *The "proportionalists," finding no persuasive answer to this question, suggest that there is, in theory, no physical act defined simply as such which can never be justified if in a concrete situation of conflict of values and duties, the performance of the act is the "greater good" or "lesser evil," that is, if the good realized is "proportionate" to the good sacrificed.*

Critiques and Responses

It is now appropriate to consider some criticisms of this theory, possible responses to them, and some remaining problems. Keep in mind that the proponents of the proportionalist method are not always dogmatic or emphatically antagonistic toward more traditional methods. Their revised view of moral norms is still very much in the process of correction and refinement. As Richard McCormick concluded regarding recent revisions in the "Moral Notes:" "Does this clarify matters? I shall await the reactions of my kind and gracious critics."[9]

At least four types of objection emerge as important:

1) *Does this theory amount to a claim that "the end justifies the means"?*

Yes and no. Certainly any means is chosen with an end in view, which is perceived as the reason for engaging in the action at all. The real issue here is whether the proportionalists are allowing an admirable end to justify a *morally* evil means. The revisionists, of course, would not agree to this description of their method. At the same time, however, they are changing the definition of what constitutes a morally evil means. The abstractly defined physical acts which used to inhabit the old category of "intrinsic evil" (meaning intrinsic *moral* evil or sin) have been redefined as premoral evils, with their moral character awaiting some relation to circumstances, i.e., to other, perhaps greater, goods which may be at stake. The "evil means" which the proportionalists permit to be justified by a good end is only evil in a premoral, material, ontic, or physical sense (roughly equivalent terms), and to bring it about is not a sin *in se*. Thus a good end does *not* justify a morally evil means, but possibly *does* justify a means which is in some respect a departure from the ideal fulfillment of human nature (a "premorally" evil means). Examples of such means employed in pursuit of a proportionate end would be artificial contraception in service of responsible family planning, or fertilization in vitro to accomplish a pregnancy which cannot be realized through the usual and ideal means. The distinction between morally and premorally "evil" means, and the fact that the proportionalists are not taking a position of moral *neutrality* toward even the premoral evils (inasmuch as a very good reason is needed to justify causing them) appears sometimes to be lost on the proportionalists' critics.[10]

2) *Is this theory the equivalent of "utilitarianism" or "consequentialism"?*

This objection is not unrelated to the preceeding one, for both express the apprehension that important moral commitments are being sacrificed to expediency. There are differences in the contexts of the questions, however. To talk of "utilitarianism" is to raise a set of questions about how best to conceive the fundamental nature of moral experience and the ethical analysis of it.

Two basic models shape the language of current moral philosophy and theology. These are deontology (from the Greek word *deon* or "duty"), and teleology (from the Greek word *telos* or "goal"). "Utilitarianism" is a subcategory of "teleology."[11] The deontologist basically thinks of moral experience and obligation in terms of obedience to duty or laws, while the teleologist conceives moral activity as purposive, as seeking to realize goals. The theory of Immanuel Kant is deontological, in that he defined "respect for persons as ends in themselves" as an absolute duty or "categorical imperative." The theories of Aristotle and Aquinas are teleological, in that they see the moral agent as striving for "happiness" or, in Thomas's Christian transformation of

Aristotle, for the beatific vision. In a teleological system, some rules or principles may function in a "deontological" way in the sense that they define absolutely some preconditions of realization of the ultimate *telos*, and therefore cannot be set aside out of consideration of mediate goals. Examples are the norms already discussed as the noncontroversial moral absolutes of various sorts, e.g., "Do not be unjust," "Do not murder," and "Do not masturbate for solitary pleasure." (This is not to say that all violations of these "absolutes" have the same degree of seriousness, i.e., deter progress toward the *telos* in the same degree.) The fundamental justification of these norms is still teleological in that they are derived from the notion of the end and the requirements of its realization.

Utilitarianism is a form of teleology. Its distinctive characteristic is its way of specifying the "end" or *telos* to be sought. The end and criterion of all moral acts is "the greatest good for the greatest number". Now this differs from Aristotle's and Aquinas's brands of teleology in that it allows "respect for persons" to be set aside to the detriment of a minority of persons if so doing will further the welfare of the majority. ("Respect for persons" can be specified in various ways, such as truth-telling to medical patients, equal access to employment and social security, and the immunity of noncombatants in war.)

Most Roman Catholic moral theologians, including the proportionalists, find utilitarianism objectionable. In their (the proportionalists') theory, as in other Thomistic theories, the ultimate good to be sought, the *summum bonum*, is not a temporal and hence finite good, a good which is quantifiable and hence limited in its range of distribution. The ultimate end of human life is a sharing in the life of God (the universal common good) in community with other persons. For this reason the exclusion of some minority from participation in that good will be neither necessary nor moral. And since that transcendent good is the norm and criterion of all lesser goods, all moral decisions which diminish or prevent the participation of persons in it are *absolutely* wrong. But such decisions have to do with the *moral* virtue of persons, with their justice, their perseverance, their honesty, their love, their mercifulness, etc. And moral virtue is contingent on the ways persons choose to maximize or destroy the virtues of self

129

and others, and the premoral goods related to the welfare of persons. Choosing not to actualize a certain premoral good in a given situation is objectively wrong only if it is sacrificed for a lesser value; and it is furthermore a moral evil (a sin or, if habitual, a vice) if deliberate. Proportionalism does not include a "no limits" mentality to the effect that *anything* can be justified if more good will result either immediately or in the long run. The objective moral order implies an objective (though not necessarily static) hierarchy of values that present themselves to choice, however tentatively and partially it may be known.

The task of moral theology or ethics is to pursue the illumination of this objective hierarchy (the *ordo bonorum*), and to further the formulation of moral norms which describe particular value relations and evaluate the legitimacy or illegitimacy of sacrificing one of the values in a relation to another. For example, when the values of financial welfare and fetal life are in a relation of conflict, the former may not outweigh the latter, though both are undoubted goods. The function of moral norms is thus, as Joseph Fuchs has said, to form "schemes for human activity" which are true to human nature in its most concrete and hence most objective sense.[12]

All this having been said, it still is true that the exact nature of the difference between utilitarianism and proportionalism bears further study, since in both methods values are weighed on some approximate scale. However, the basic difference is that for the utilitarian, the *only* criterion of morality is the maximization of temporal good consequences for individuals or society, while the proportionalist would include both a criterion of equal respect for all persons, and an ultimate criterion of consistency with the transcendent "goal" or *summum bonum*.

3) *Does this theory make moral evaluation and decision-making too difficult, too tenuous, and too ambiguous for a "healthy" moral life?*[13]

Certainly the proportionalist method makes no claim to offer a set of clear and specific moral directives about concrete, material acts which all persons in all circumstances can follow with perfect security. But then, does our moral *experience*, an experience of the complex and rich, but often enigmatic and even tragic dimensions of personal relations, tell us that such confidence is likely to be warranted? Moral simplicity is not necessarily the equivalent of moral objectivity. Further, few proportionalists insist that the definition of Christian morality and moral education *begin* with "exceptional" moral dilemmas. The central place in the Christian self-understanding of such "traditional" values as loving and procreative marriage, the preservation of human life, and literal honesty in speech is not brought into question.

4) *Is the method in itself defined with sufficient precision?*

One legitimate criticism of the method under discussion, I think, is that sometimes the definitions of and distinctions between certain key concepts, such as "value term," "premoral evil," and "physical act" are not as clear as one might desire.[14] This confusion lends to the impression that the method is difficult to apply and, in the end, not very objective. Is the example of an "intrinsically evil act" offered by one critic of the proportionalists, "bestiality,"[15] really a physical act pure and simple, or is it an act (sexual intercourse) plus circumstances (with an animal)? How about "contraception," which has been redefined by the proportionalists as a premoral evil, rather than a moral one? Could this "physical act" be described credibly as also an act (sexual intercourse) plus circumstances (using artificial barriers to conception)? Is it possible to break "actions" down into pieces so fragmentary that they incapacitate moral analysis? Is "homicide," for instance, only a combination of circumstances surrounding an act such as "pointing the gun" or "pulling the trigger"? "Actions" often do not have clearly defined limits and accordingly can be broken down into absurdly discrete units or expanded into meaningless comprehensiveness. Another example of the former was the unconvincing argument made by some during World War II (and more recently) that killing noncombatants is only a circumstantial part of actions intended to uphold justice, freedom, and even human life.[16]

An area genuinely in need of refinement is that of the distinction and relation between act and circumstance, and of the way the intention of the agent relates to both, especially when the "act" represents something usually to be avoided, and the "cir-

131

cumstance" a setting which determines its actual morality. I think it is fair to say, however, that over against the more traditional notion of "intrinsically evil act," the distinction between premoral and moral evil represents at least an attempt to distinguish moral norms which are fairly specific regarding circumstances from those which either: 1) commend moral values (justice, love) or 2) forbid acts without taking the concrete conditions of moral agency at all sufficiently into account (masturbation, contraception.)

Conclusion

Most advocates of some version of the "proportionalist"method invite exchanges which will clarify points such as these. The basic perspective from which they attempt to advance the discussion is that of an Aristotelian-Thomistic, non-utilitarian sort of teleology. In this ethical model, norms can be truly exceptionless if they define formal moral virtues ("justice"), indicate that some acts can be made immoral by disproportionate circumstances ("murder"), or indicate specifically what are those circumstances (homicide for monetary profit). Moral norms regarding abstract physical acts ("Do not kill"), however, are *prima facie* or presumptive duties, not absolute ones. They can be overridden if a greater good is at stake than the one generally protected by the norm (human life). The practical effect is the same as that of many so-called "pastoral solutions." Yet at the theoretical level, there is a *greater* commitment to consistency and objectivity, insofar as great importance is given to rational analysis of *why* it is that pastoral prudence or common sense commend certain flexible solutions which depart from the strict meaning of certain norms promulgated as absolute.

Proportionalism within the context of natural law morality presupposes that norms are *as* objective and *as* stable as they are *truthful* descriptions of the objective ordering of values. In this respect, the method is genuinely "conservative." It is "progressive," however, in that it recognizes that the value relations with which moral choice concerns itself are never known with perfect adequacy by the human intellect, and may even shift, change, progress, and be transformed historically as humanity realizes itself in relation to the *summum bonum* by which it is always attracted and in relation to which its actualization of mediate *boni* is judged.

In conclusion, the reiteration of three points may encourage a balanced assessment of the assets and deficits of the "challenge" of proportionalism.

1) Doubts about the absoluteness of moral norms concerning "intrinsically evil" physical acts generally have arisen from a concrete, practical appreciation of the difficulties and ambiguities of the moral life. Many Christians, including some theologians, have perceived that certain absolutes do not meet adequately the objective reality of moral dilemmas. Some traditional absolutes do not account satisfyingly for our moral experience. This gap between theory and reality prompts the moral theologian to ponder why it exists and to analyze traditional principles in an effort to discover whether they can be reinterpreted in some way which enhances their adequacy.

2) Although some see the proportionalist method as "dangerous" because it may allow too much, its implications need not be exaggerated. There have always been in the Catholic tradition certain acts requiring specific circumstances for full evaluation, e.g., killing or homicide and sexual intercourse. To these, the revisionists want to add others, such as contraception and masturbation. However not all proportionalists want to reject all those sets of circumstances which the tradition regarded as immoral settings for such acts, e.g., killing an innocent person, sexual intercourse between persons at least one of whom is married to someone else, contraception to avoid sexual responsibility, and masturbation for solitary enjoyment. The key difference is that the focus of discussion in the proportionalist approach shifts from the act in itself (the moral "object") to the act in relation to proportionate or disproportionate circumstances (object, intent, and circumstances considered together).

3) Proportionalist exception-making to traditional absolutes does not have to be subjectivist and individualist. Why should the Magisterium not continue to provide teaching about the objective relations of values about which we choose? Such teaching could be preceded by discussion in the Church of what will constitute

a legitimate exception to which norm. Open discussion in the hope of fostering consensus in the faith community will facilitate both moral education and the decision-making of the individual. I suspect that many pastors in the post-*Humanae Vitae* era have found that the only way to teach and minister flexibly while at the same time maintaining formal conformity to the "official" position has been to take the route of advising the Roman Catholic to "follow your own conscience," even though it may be "objectively mistaken." But as a matter of fact, it may be the case that such a "pastoral " solution, which endorses an absolutely "exceptionless" norm and then encourages the individual to act upon "subjective" convictions, may have contributed to subjectivist and relativist strains in Christian ethics. Such a solution effectively precludes any discussion of legitimate or objectively justifiable exceptions, and thus makes it appear that the evaluation of special circumstances devolves completely to the individual's judgment.

One must conclude with the question whether more orderly and public discourse in the Church about acceptable and unacceptable exceptions to traditional norms would promote, rather than detract from, the Catholic sense of faithful community, a broader appreciation of the legitimate functions of moral absolutes, and the credibility of the Magisterium.

Notes

1. Joseph Fletcher, *Situation Ethics* (Philadelphia: Westminster Press, 1966).

2. *Gaudium et Spes,* 4. and 5., respectively. In *The Documents of Vatican II,* ed. Walter M. Abbott, S.J. (New York: The America Press, 1966), pp. 201 and 204, respectively.

3. Some of the important names in this discussion are, in the U.S., Charles Curran and Richard McCormick; and, on the Continent, Josef Fuchs, Bruno Schüller, Louis Janssens, and Peter Knauer. Much of the debate in this country has followed upon McCormick's *Ambiguity in Moral Choice* (Milwaukee: Marquette University Theology Department, 1973). A collection of responses to this monograph, which includes both *Ambiguity* and McCormick's response to his critics, is *Doing Evil to Achieve Good,* ed. Richard McCormick and Paul Ramsey (Chicago: Loyola University Press, 1978). Other articles important to the discussion are made available to an English-speaking audience in *Readings in Moral Theology No. 1: Moral Norms and Catholic Tradition,* ed. Charles Curran and Richard McCormick (New York: Paulist Press, 1979). The latter contains contributions both by proponents of proportionalism and its critics.

4. See Louis Janssens, "Ontic Evil and Moral Evil," *Louvain Studies* 4 (1972), pp. 115-56 (also in *Readings No. 1*), and *Ambiguity,* p. 54. A helpful recent contribution is Josef Fuchs, " 'Intrinsece malum': Uberlegungen zu einem umstrittenen Begriff," in Walter Kerber, ed., *Sittliche Normen: Zum Problem ihrer allgemeinen un unwandelbaren*

Geltung (Dusseldorf: Patmos, 1982), pp. 74-91. Fuchs's basic proposal is summarized by Richard McCormick, "Notes on Moral Theology, 1982," *Theological Studies* 44 (1983), pp. 73-76.

5. Josef Fuchs, *Personal Responsibility and Christian Morality* (Washington, D.C.: Georgetown University Press, 1983), p. 213. This is a collection of previously published essays, recently made available in English.

6. *Ibid.*, p. 120.

7. See McCormick's *Ambiguity*, pp. 69, 78-9, 82, where he develops the method of "proportionate reason." Peter Knauer refers to "commensurate reason" in "The Hermeneutic Function of the Principle of Double Effect," *Natural Law Forum* 12 (1967), pp. 132-162; and "Fundamentalethik: Teleologische als deontologische Normenbegründung," *Theologie und Philosophie* 55 (1980), pp. 321-60. See also Fuchs, *Personal Responsibility*, 140-142.

8. Gerald Kelly, *Medico-Moral Problems* (St. Louis: Catholic Hospital Association, 1958), p. 13.

9. "Notes: 1982," p. 86.

10. See, for instance, William E. May, "The Moral Meaning of Human Acts," *Homiletic and Pastoral Review* 79, no. 1 (1978), 17 (also in *Readings No. 1*); and Paul Ramsey, "Incommensurability and Indeterminacy in Moral Choice," in *Doing Evil*, p. 82. Also note McCormick's response in "Notes: 1982", pp. 77-78, to Servais Pinckaers, "La question de actes intrinsequement mauvais et le 'proportionalisme,'" *Revue thomiste* 82 (1982), pp. 181-212.

11. For a discussion of the philosophical background of these categories, see my "Teleology, Utilitarianism, and Christian Ethics," *Theological Studies* 42 (1981), pp. 601-629.

12. Fuchs, *Personal Responsibility*, p. 177.

13. This is the objection of John Connery, "Catholic Ethics: Has the Rule for Norm-Making Changed?," *Theological Studies* 42 (1981), pp. 232-50. See also his "The Teleology of Proportionate Reason," *Theological Studies* 44 (1983), especially pp. 495-6.

14. See Connery, "Teleology," pp. 489-494.

15. May, "Moral Meaning."

16. See John C. Ford, "The Morality of Obliteration Bombing," *Theological Studies* 5/3 (1944), pp. 261-309, for a refutation of this argument.

Chapter 7

The Protestant Tradition And Exceptionless Moral Norms

Gene Outka, Ph.D.

The vast historical and conceptual terrain covered by this subject requires a decisively selective approach. For "the Protestant tradition" embraces staggering diversity on doctrinal and moral matters. And the very meaning of the phrase "exceptionless moral norms" is sometimes controversial, as modern discussions in both Roman Catholic and Protestant theological circles attest.

The most illuminating class of possible exceptionless moral norms at issue includes, quintessentially, the parts of the second table of the Decalogue which forbid killing, stealing, adultery and lying. Although the norms in the class differ significantly among themselves, they share two features.

First, these norms are comparatively *specific*. They locate action-kinds which are delimited, spatially and temporally. We typically contrast these more specific norms with terms of wide extension. The latter terms are often uncontroversially exceptionless, partly because they refer to many possible actions. They allow reasonable dispute about which actions exemplify them without thereby calling into question their bindingness as such. For example, we praise courage and censure cowardice whenever we believe we encounter them as perduring traits of character; to cite contemporary cases, we unhesitatingly approve personal authenticity and consciousness-raising and condemn sexism and racism. While such terms of wide extension have indispensible moral work to do, my concern here is with norms which identify a more particular action-kind.

Second, these norms are *basic* in the context of interaction between human beings.[1] That is, they refer to certain actions perceived as irreducibly significant. The actions must be taken into account in all situations in which they occur because they remain always relevant considerations in characterizing a situation, whatever we judge their decisiveness to be in our final evaluation. As characterizations, they cannot be "elided" into terms which describe their consequences.[2] Their perceived significance derives from the depth of their impingement on fundamental human interests. For instance, it matters basically to you if I threaten your physical survival; I violate your autonomy if I lie to you; I treat you unjustly if I rob you of the rightful benefits of your labors.

My primary concern here will be with the religious reasons for endorsing or challenging the verdict that selected specific and basic moral norms ought to be judged exceptionless. To address this concern I shall focus on representative and distinctively Protestant answers to four questions: (1) Does the violation of certain moral norms always negatively affect *one's own* relation to God? Does it necessarily influence, for example, one's prospects for salvation, or define in part the content of one's disobedience to God? (2) Does such violation always conflict with the normative content of *neighbor-love*? Are there certain actions one must never do to others if one genuinely loves them? (3) Are the grounds for commending exceptionless moral norms *natural*, objectivist, generally negotiable ones, i.e., not requiring explicit appeals to revelation? (4) Or are such grounds *revealed* ones, i.e., appeals to immediate divine commands, the Bible, or the person and work of Jesus Christ?

137

These questions are distinguished in order to help us see where shifts occur and generally to make comparisons between complex theological schemes more easily. After a brief excursus on the Reformation legacy, I shall refer to modern Protestant writers, namely, Kierkegaard, Barth, Brunner, Bonhoeffer, Henry, H. Richard Niebuhr, Lehmann, George F. Thomas, Yoder, Hauerwas, Cone, Evans, and in greater detail, Reinhold Niebuhr and Paul Ramsey.

Three qualifications should be appended. First, these four questions certainly do not exhaust the possibilities. For example, we can alter or supplement question (1) by asking: does the violation of certain moral norms define in part, by way perhaps of a permitted *de facto* communal lifestyle, the content of the *Church's* disobedience to God? Second, answers to these questions are not exclusive. We are not compelled to choose (say) either a positive answer to (1) or (2), rather than a positive answer to both. In fact many versions of a positive answer to both questions exist. Indeed, positive and/or negative answers are linked in various combinations among all four questions. Third, while twentieth century writers will occupy much of my attention, I stop short of explicit reference to the revisionist debates which preoccupy many Roman Catholic moralists at present, despite the fact that Protestants like Paul Ramsey and certain moral philosophers take a serious interest in these debates.[3] This interest in an exceedingly important discussion is welcome and promising, but I cannot examine it if I am to order the inquiry in a manageable way. I hope that the aim of ecumenical conversation will be served nonetheless by an attempt to locate some of the most instructive angles of vision which distinguish parts of the Protestant tradition.

I. A Note On The Reformation Legacy

I shall argue here that an affirmative answer to question (1) is challenged during the Reformation period, at least on the matter of *soteriological* significance, and that a verdict about exceptionless moral norms depends more centrally on the answer given to question (2). Agent-performance loses some of its religious urgency and force; recipient-benefit becomes the primary criterion for making moral judgements. Such a shift removes one incentive for the development of casuistry.

One's *de facto* moral performance affects one's own fundamental relation to God: this teaching Luther and Calvin resist. According to this teaching, I am so constituted that an internal or necessary connection obtains between my actual moral performance and my relation to God. Faithlessness to God, treachery toward neighbors, and self-destructive behavior all unavoidably affect my relation to God. This claim is certainly compatible with a strong doctrine of grace in which my faithlessness or treachery collapse under God's implacable pressure, and the *telos* of such pressure is forgiveness and restoration rather than doom. Yet the claim seems also compatible with my taking a powerful religious interest in asking whether certain kinds of faithlessness or treachery affect my relation to God more negatively than others, and whether there are definite action-kinds the performance of which jeopardize my relation altogether. To affirm the latter possibility assuredly disposes me to regard the prohibitions of such actions as exceptionless. And to affirm that actions may be assessed as more and less grave means, unsurprisingly, that a distinction such as the one between mortal sin and venial sin emerges.

Whether my account of this teaching accurately reflects Roman Catholic doctrine I shall not presume to judge. I am concerned now only with Luther's and Calvin's resistance, and not with the question whether the objects of their attacks were often straw persons. They identify a "proper" or "spiritual" or "theological" use of the moral law: to drive persons to an awareness that they are sinners. "For among Christians," Luther writes, "we must use the law spiritually . . . to reveal sin."[4] Discrimination among specific sins tends to be swamped by an awareness of sin in the generic sense. Thus Calvin repudiates as invalid the distinction between mortal and venial sin. Venial sin he rejects as a diversion which serves only to soothe sluggish consciences.

> Let the children of God hold that all sin is mortal. For it is rebellion against the will of God, which of necessity provokes God's wrath, and it is a violation of the law, upon which God's judgment is pronounced without exception. The sins of the saints are pardonable, not because of their nature as saints, but because they obtain pardon from God's mercy.[5]

The law in its spiritual use has a systematically ambiguous status. On the one hand, it cannot be given up, for it is invoked at the first stage to render a common verdict of equality of sin. In this it plays an essential role. And we cannot ask which of the law's parts are exceptionless and which are not, for it condemns in all of its parts without exception (though transgressing the first table of the Decalogue discloses most clearly that sin consists above all in distrust of God). On the other hand, the law cannot be incorporated at the second stage, where the gospel proclaims that pardon comes only by God's mercy. Our endeavors to adhere to the law possess no justificatory significance and cannot have the status of a warrant for salvation. This latter stage is intended as adoration of the mercy of a judging God. The judgment is natural and expected. The mercy is miraculous.

The great religious question now becomes whether I will trust and accept such mercy, or whether I will inwardly prefer my defiant, despairing willfulness. One form my willfulness can take is to focus on my own moral performance. I presumptuously aspire to adhere to the law. At bottom, my moral earnestness is a trap for my own self-preoccupation and a desire to justify myself at all costs. By this point we have traveled far from the teaching that a necessary connection obtains between my actual moral performance and my relation to God.

James M. Gustafson's conclusion seems correct:

> If salvation, the principal concern, comes through God's imputation of righteousness to persons, then the moral life no longer has the same *religious* seriousness. It is serious, but is set in a different religious and theological context. Ethics and moral theology no longer have the same theological significance.[6]

The altered religious and theological context produces in Luther's case, especially, this sort of appraisal: "These are the most important three parts of the Christian life: faith, hope, and love. The first two look to God and belong above, the third looks to the neighbor and belongs down here."[7] And in the following statement Luther turns from question (1) to (2): "If you find a work in you by which you benefit God or His saints or yourself and not your neighbor, know that such a work is not good."[8] Neighbor-love serves as the

140

effective criterion of the good. The content of this good often consists in benefits actually conferred in terms of the ordinary life of human interaction. "A good work is good for the reason that it is useful and benefits and helps the one for whom it is done; why else should it be called good?"[9]

To concentrate one's moral energies on what will, in fact, benefit another peson does not negate the possibility that certain actions always conflict with any conceivable benefit and accordingly should never be performed. This judgment is certainly not gainsaid. Yet it receives little rigorous discussion, partly because Luther is rather random in the actions he cites as instances of neighbor-love.

> Thus it is not your good work that you give alms or that you pray, but that you offer yourself to your neighbor and serve him, wherever he needs you and every way you can, be it with alms, prayer, work, fasting, counsel, comfort, insruction, admonition, punishment, apologizing, clothing, food, and lastly with suffering and dying for him.[10]

Even when Luther treats the second table of the Decalogue in his *Large Catechism*, he transmutes each commandment from a negative prohibition to a positive injunction as well. Certainly he does not deny the force of the negative prohibition. Yet he concentrates on traits of character and relatively definite policies of conduct rather than on the activity associated with casuistry, namely, the subsumption of cases.[11]

Gustafson calls striking attention to the contrast between the role of the Roman Catholic priest (with an instructive affinity to the office of the rabbi in Judaism) and the Protestant pastor. The latter

> has not needed the refined case-oriented literature that Catholic moral theology provides because he has not been the examiner of conscience and the judge of conduct in the same way . . . He has not had to assign penitential acts (there are exceptions, for example, the use of "shunning" in Anabaptist communities and the denial of a person's right to take communion in Puritan congregations) but has read to the penitent congregation "the comforting words" of forgiveness.[12]

The theological or spiritual use of the law accounts in significant measure for the elimination of the need for such case-oriented literature. Apart from certain segments of the Anglican community and Puritan writings on cases of conscience, there is little concern for refined criteria to determine the degree of seriousness which various acts possess, whether specifiable sins are mortal or venial, and what penance is appropriate. Writings in ethics and moral theology within Roman Catholicism acquired much of their rationale as they served the priestly role in the sacrament of penance. One powerful incentive for the development of nuanced judgments was present in Roman Catholicism but not in Protestantism. And this entire process arguably contributed to the conviction that certain delimited actions are exceptionless. Writings in ethics and moral theology within Protestantism have had more of a pedagogical than a juridical role to play.

The circumscribed conclusion that the Reformers shift from question (1) to question (2) does not mean either that moral seriousness as such dissolves or that any turn to neighbor-love renders religious belief redundant. Let me underscore such seriousness and the absence of redundancy before I end this section.

(a) Gustafson's observation that the moral life remains a serious matter during the Reformation and its aftermath deserves emphasis, however altered the religious and theological context proves to be. For instance, two other uses of the law are distinguished and defended. Luther and Calvin acknowledge the permanent legitimacy of a civic use. Societal viability requires that civil justice be administered in an ongoing way, that social roles be honored, the duties of various offices be conscientiously filled, and so on. Both believers and nonbelievers remain capable of such activities. While extreme cases of Protestant attacks on the powers of the practical reason are readily found,[13] even Luther contends that the commandments of the second table of the Decalogue "are not Mosaic laws only, but also the natural law written in each man's heart."[14] We may appeal to such law when we adjudicate disputes which arise inevitably in the civil community. And when we consider the moral life under the governance of Christian faith, we find that Calvin especially extols a "third use of the law." Believers continue to need the law as a positive source of instruction and exhortation, and not only insofar as they still labor under the promptings of the "old

142

Adam."[15] Indeed, later in the *Institutes* Calvin is sufficiently stringent to banish the "Schoolmen's" distinction between precepts and evangelical counsels. "Let them . . . recognize that the Lord was Lawgiver, and . . . not falsely represent him as a mere giver of counsel."[16]

(b) The injunction to love the neighbor is itself warranted and informed by religious belief. For example, Calvin justifies the claim that the term "neighbor" embraces "the whole human race without exception in a single feeling of love" by urging the reader to contemplate everyone "in God, not in themselves."

> . . . If we rightly direct our love, we must first turn our eyes not to man, the sight of whom would more often engender hate than love, but to God, who bids us extend to all men the love we bear to him, that this may be an unchanging principle: whatever the character of the man, we must yet love him because we love God.[17]

Furthermore, the turn to neighbor-love need not exhaust the considerations to be urged on behalf of exceptionless moral norms. Certain actions are prohibited because they fail to display Christian convictions taken as a whole. These convictions constitute a complete "web of belief" surrounding appraisals of what is permitted and forbidden in human interaction. Helmut Thielicke, a modern ethicist who tries to retain distinctively Lutheran insights, offers this verdict on torture:

> In face of this possibility that a man is "capable of anything," the Christian is summoned to adopt a confessional stance. For the Christian owes to the world the public confession that he is one who is committed, "bound," and hence not "capable of anything." If we make ourselves fundamentally unpredictable, i.e., if as Christians we think that torture is at least conceivable — perhaps under the exigencies of an extreme situation — we thereby reduce man to the worth of a convertible means, divest him of the *imago Dei*, and so deny the first commandment. This denial can never be a possible alternative.[18]

More than neighbor-love is at stake in this judgment. It weaves such love together with a confessional stance and an appeal to the first commandment.

II. Some Twentieth Century Appeals To Revelation

Before turning to two twentieth century figures — Reinhold Niebuhr and Paul Ramsey — who in important respects carry forward "centrist" Protestant theological schemes, in rather close relation to Roman Catholic ones, certain figures who proceed more radically should be examined. These figures ground their verdicts about exceptionless moral norms more or less exclusively in revelation, i.e., by appeals to direct divine commands, the Bible, or the person and work of Jesus Christ. Attention centers therefore on certain answers to question (4) and what these answers imply.

Let us begin with figures who vindicate direct divine commands. The position typically viewed as most radical is espoused by Soren Kierkegaard's pseudonym, Johannes *de silentio*, in the book *Fear and Trembling* (written in the nineteenth century, but massively influential only in the twentieth).[19] Johannes examines the Biblical story of Abraham's near sacrifice of Isaac in obedience to a direct divine command, calling Abraham's action "a teleological suspension of the ethical." The "ethical" in this instance is crystallized in the prohibition against murder as the direct killing of innocent life, a prohibition that heads the class of norms described earlier as both specific and basic. What seems implied is an extremely troubling answer to question (1). For Johannes, the violation of a certain moral norm defines in part the content of Abraham's *obedience* to God, not his disobedience. *Fear and Trembling* proves to lend influential support to four claims: (a) we should not commit ourselves in principle to a necessary link between antecendently known moral prohibitions and God's will, but instead should remain dispositionally open to God's self-disclosures here and now; (b) the distinctive and irreducible importance of the individual's relation to God requires that it remain direct and unmediated; (c) such a relation is constituted only by a personal encounter with God; (d) given God's nature, this encounter takes the form of a divine command and a primal response of obedience.[20]

These claims are appropriated in part by a group of twentieth century figures who all strive to retain some element of personal encounter in which God's command is immediate, concrete, and requisitely self-interpreting. Something unmistakably dialogical occurs: God can entrust a certain distinctive task to me, and I know what I have to do. Such writers can be grouped under the common heading of "theological contextualists." [21] They include Karl Barth and Emil Brunner most clearly, and also with qualifications Dietrich Bonhoeffer, H. Richard Niebuhr, and Paul Lehmann. [22] Certainly none of these writers dwell as Johannes does on the possible in-principled collision between obedience to God and physical harm to another person. Several rule out certain actions in the confidence that God can never command them. Bonhoeffer, for example, provides a compelling theological case against suicide. [23] Moreover, their views must not be conflated with the rational, consequentialist calculation which marks Joseph Fletcher's empirical situationism. [24] One note, however, is repeatedly sounded: they share a wariness of legalism. Brunner summarizes the position well:

> The fact that the holiness of God must be remembered when we dwell on His love means that we cannot have His love at our disposal, that it cannot ever be perceived as a universal principle, but only in the act in which He speaks to us Himself. [25]

For Brunner, even the biblical injunctions such as those found in the Decalogue and the Sermon on the Mount are "unsystematic" and "casual" examples of the infinitely varied life of love. They are not generalized "cases" or "instances" which anticipate particular decisions.

Such a free attitude toward biblical precepts offends many conservative or evangelical Protestant writers. For example, Carl F. H. Henry argues that modern Protestant works in Christian ethics (he has the theological contextualists principally in mind) share in a "revolt against an authoritative biblical criterion . . . " [26] The heart of Henry's charge is that the appeal to love alone cannot yield the determinate content, which the Sermon on the Mount and the Decalogue precisely afford. This content is not casual and unsystematic, but rather is constitutive. According to Henry, the alternative to such content proves to be an eclecticism both arbitrary and unpredictable. The final result is often conformity with prevailing cultural standards, whatever these happen to be.

Standing behind Henry's view and those he attacks are contrasting accounts of revelation and the authority of scripture. Henry contends that Brunner and other so-called "neo-orthodox" theologians espouse a notion of revelation as a "mystical supracognitive encounter" which sets the divine will over against specific biblical commandments. For such theologians, specific commandments always contain features which are historically contingent. Revealed ethical propositions or commandments are debarred. Even the Decalogue is "simply a fallible human witness to a single command," "a verbal symbol pointing to the Divine summons to personal obedience."[27] Those Henry opposes refuse, in his judgment, to identify the content of the law of love with biblical precepts because they endorse a critical view of the Bible. For example, although George F. Thomas endorses biblical laws as furnishing guidance for the believer, and acknowledges that the pre-critical attitude toward the Bible is shared by Aquinas and Calvin, he nevertheless opts in the end for a critical view himself, and so disjoins the law of love from the moral laws of the Bible. These laws represent for Thomas "differing levels of 'insight.'"[28] Some possess little ongoing value. Conversely, Henry defends a notion of revelation which has a "conceptual and propositional form" and this includes both "a revealed world-view" and "a revealed life-view." Unlike Schleiermacher, for whom "God communicates redemption," Henry affirms that God communicates doctrine.

Henry's position confronts well-known difficulties with which he must struggle. For instance, he opposes the Mennonite endorsement of pacifism on the grounds that Jesus does not explicitly reject war and capital punishment, for if Jesus did he would contradict the Old Testament record. Biblical ethics for Henry retains an "essential continuity" between Old and New Testaments.[29] He must therefore combat the sobering legacy of the Radical Reformation in which varying and sometimes incompatible exceptionless moral norms are held to receive biblical endorsement, e.g., pacifism, violent revolution, refusal to take oaths, dissolution of mixed marriages, communist property values, etc.

While this legacy may be sobering, it also receives formidable restatement at present by John Howard Yoder and Stanley Hauerwas. Both commend nonviolence, but not because it will necessarily prove politically or socially effective in the world at large. They write Christian ethics for the Church, for those who have conscious-

146

ly accepted the obligations of the Messianic community, and not for all persons of good will. Yet they refuse to adopt a traditional strategy of sectarian withdrawal. They insist that it is impossible to live apolitically. Yoder wants "not the avoidance of political options, but one particular social-political-ethical option."[30] Jesus calls persons to participate in the nonresistant community. The option one finds there makes no appeal to natural law. It is a new social order in which suffering rather than "brute power" is accepted as the meaning of history. Hauerwas is "quite content to assume that the Jesus we have in Scripture is the Jesus of the early church"[31] and he departs from Henry's reading of the Bible. But he believes the Sermon on the Mount is more than an unrealizable ideal. "To be sure, Jesus' demand that we forgive our enemies challenges our normal assumptions about what is possible, but that is exactly what it is meant to do."[32] Such forgiveness must assume a thoroughgoing institutional form; nonviolence must be practiced without exception as a communal way of life. The claims of Yoder and Hauerwas not only call for assessment on exegetical and other grounds, but also for comparisons with, e.g., James H. Cone's very different account from the vantage point of Black Theology of "ethics, violence, and Jesus Christ" in *God of the Oppressed*, and also with Paul Lehmann's biblically grounded case in *The Transfiguration of Politics* for violence as both unavoidable and never justifiable.[33]

III. Twentieth Century Christian Realism: Reinhold Niebuhr

The "Christian realism" of Reinhold Niebuhr paradigmatically expresses another influential strand of Protestant thought in this century. Let me first place him in relation to the views canvassed so far. Niebuhr certainly assumes a critical view of the Bible. He regards various "allegedly absolute" scriptural norms, more specific than the "law of love" itself, as marked by historically contingent elements which render their authority questionable (his example is Paul's attitude toward women in the Church).[34] Niebuhr also declines to treat immediate divine commands as possibilities to be taken routinely into account. Such commands form no necessary part of the depiction of Christian thought and life he commends.

His response to question (1) noted at the outset is to stress divine mercy and forgiveness as humanity's only hope for overcoming the imperfect moral performance to which every person inevitably succumbs. He thereby perpetuates a version of the doctrine of justification by faith alone beyond all moral striving. Consider this typical mixture of affirmation and denial:

> I do not believe that the incarnation is "redemption" from history as conflict. Since I believe that sinful egoism expresses itself on every level of moral and spiritual achievement and is not absent from the highest levels of Christian life, I cannot regard redemption as freedom from sin. The redemption in Christ is rather the revelation of a divine mercy that alone is able to overcome the contradictions of human history from which even the best of us cannot extricate ourselves.[35]

When Niebuhr turns to neighbor-love in question (2), he extols an absolute and perfectionist ideal which condemns all self-assertion. Everything we manage to accomplish falls short of "more ultimate possibilities of love." Yet this ideal remains relevant in the approximations it encourages and the judgments it influences. We neglect it at our peril, even if the only rational formula we can devise to encapsulate it is simply this: "a complete love" is one "in which each life affirms the interests of the other."[36] Still, we must settle for compromises with its dictates, or else acquiesce to evil forces which eviscerate neighbor-love altogether. The often brutal realities of power and corruption require that responsible decision-making in history consists in the "nicely calculated more and less."

In the case of questions (3) and (4), Niebuhr resists any strict either/or between natural and revealed grounds for moral norms. Here he proceeds "dialectically," as his treatment both of natural law and of Jesus' love ethic demonstrates.

Niebuhr reiterates two general theses about the tradition of natural law, usually in the form of two kinds of repudiation: he thinks both pessimistic detractors and sanguine defenders of the tradition go wrong. "Secular and Reformation relativists" err when they dismiss all moral codes and principles of justice as possessing only limited spatio-temporal validity. (The prohibition of murder, for example he finds to be binding cross-culturally.) He resists those Protestant pessimists who conclude that sin has destroyed any natural sense of justice whatsoever. Augustine is correct that sin "cannot tear up nature by the roots." Thus he grants the following:

> Even if we do not accept the Catholic theory of a highly specific "natural law" we all do accept principles of justice which transcend the positive enactments of historic states and which are less specific and not so sharply defined as positive law, and yet more specific than the law of love. These are generated in the customs and mores of communities; and they may rise to universal norms which seem to have their source not in particular communities but in the common experience of mankind.[37]

Yet Niebuhr also opposes those defenders of natural law who, as he sees the matter, suffer from unsubstantiated optimism about how many specific applications of natural justice in a given social order perdure as universally valid and acceptable. Far fewer instances of ongoing acceptability survive scrutiny than such defenders acknowledge. (Here his example is the prohibition of usury.)[38] For Niebuhr, two factors intrude, and intrude ceaselessly: sin and human freedom. Sin is reflected in the intrusion of self-interest that corrupts numerous rational attempts to define the implications of justice in concrete situations. Marxism, for all the ways it has proven pernicious — ways Niebuhr takes continuous pains to identify — is right in its awareness of an "ideological taint" which haunts our efforts at disinterested adjudication.[39] Moreover, human freedom introduces variable factors which no given scheme of justice can fully foresee or accommodate. We must always reckon with the "endlessly unique social configurations which human beings, in their freedom over natural necessity, construct," and so reject "the idea of fixed forms of human behavior and of social organization."[40]

In his account of Jesus' love ethic, Niebuhr contends that the character of God is offered as the only motive for forgiving enemies. Such forgiveness affords no guarantees of social or prudential benefits to the forgiver. The universal scope of this love ethic is likewise justified by reference to God, not to the disparate and morally inconclusive facts about human nature. On the other hand, love is not an ideal "magically superimposed upon life by a revelation which has no relation to total human experience."[41] Rather, it reflects and summarizes all of our own highest goals and deepest

149

needs. Though it can never be an historical "success story" in terms of the material benefits it brings or responses in kind it elicits, it remains the finally authoritative norm of human existence.

For our inquiry, the key question about Christian realism is this: how much determinate guidance in specific situations of moral choice can such a complex dialectical scheme provide or does it aim to provide? To see how matters stand, let us focus on a single moral problem, the morality of warfare.

In 1934, Niebuhr formally left the Fellowship of Reconciliation, an organization of pacifists. From that time onwards, he emerged as one of the most formidable critics of the pacifist tradition, engaging in extensive debates with various pacifists prior to the United States' entry into the Second World War. In 1940, he wrote this open letter:

> Your difficulty is that you want to try to live in history without sinning. There is no such possibility in history. The danger of admitting this is, of course, that we make sin normative when we declare it to be inevitable. We must see the sinfulness of war but we must also see the sin of egoism in which all life is involved and of which war is the final expression. Furthermore, we must be able to see the difference between the relative virtue of a decent scheme of justice and the real peril of tyranny. [42]

One interpreter of the just war tradition, James Turner Johnson, argues that it is Niebuhr's turn from pacifism which marks the beginning in this century of the recovery of this tradition (in the United States at any rate). Niebuhr revives the notion "that within sinful history, where perfection could not be reached by human moral and social evolution, violent coercion including war should be recognized as a moral possibility." [43]

To be sure, Niebuhr's concerns were chiefly *jus ad bellum* ones (criteria for resorting *to* war) and according to Johnson it remained for others, most notably Paul Ramsey among Protestants, to clarify *jus in bello* concerns (criteria for just conduct *in* war). Niebuhr is seen merely to have left undeveloped the criteria of appropriate limits in the use of force. Faced with the effective task of re-inventing the just war tradition from scratch, Niebuhr progressed no further on the *jus in bello* side than to urge as much moderation of coercion as it was politically and militarily viable to attain. Such an in-

150

terpretation maximizes the points of continuity between Niebuhr's Christian realism and Ramsey's subsequent explicit defense of the just war tradition. While Niebuhr makes a moral place in principle for violent coercion, he assuredly views it as a last resort and always counsels restraint in the conduct of war. Yet certain aspects of his scheme cast doubts on the conclusion that he could subscribe to the principle of non-combatant immunity from direct attack as an exceptionless moral norm.

A comparison will help to locate these aspects. The Roman Catholic philosopher G. E. M. Anscombe vigorously defends the principle of non-combatant immunity as exceptionless. Anscombe criticizes absolute pacifism for its failure to distinguish "between the shedding of innocent blood and the shedding of any human blood." [44] Pacifism makes certain evangelical counsels such as turning the other cheek and non-resistance to evil into precepts. When they are judged to be strictly obligatory and yet prove hopelessly non-realizable by all, they encourage those who fall short to compromise without limits. For her on the other hand, "the truth about Christianity is that it is a severe and practicable religion, not a beautifully ideal but impracticable one." [45] Its ethic includes absolute prohibitions which are bedrock: "without them the Christian ethic goes to pieces." [46] And one of these is "that the shedding of innocent blood is forbidden by divine law." [47] To justify exceptions to this prohibition is to evacuate all substance from the "Pauline principle" that we may not do evil that good may come. The prohibition continues practically to apply to non-combatants in circumstances of modern war. In the present age too, for all the technological changes, non-combatants may still be reasonably identified, and they must not be directly and intentionally killed for any reason. Anscombe denounces as blasphemous, for example, the stance that "we must fear Russian domination more than the destruction of people's bodies by obliteration bombing." [48] Any such stance reflects the absence both of fear of God and of trust in God's promises to the Church that it cannot fail. She enjoins the faithful instead

> to fear God and keep his commandments, and calculate what is for the best only within the limits of that obedience, knowing that the future is in God's power and that no one can snatch away those whom the Father has given to Christ. [49]

151

Niebuhr would draw back from this defense of an exceptionless moral norm at two points. First, he thinks we cannot fix a line of demarcation between the guilty and the innocent on the collective level with the exactness available to us on the personal level, and that once we face the larger, more indiscriminately destructive capabilities present in group relations, we frequently lack the practical means to avoid harming the innocent. He writes in 1932:

> Gandhi's boycott of British cotton results in the undernourishment of children in Manchester, and the blockade of the Allies in wartime caused the death of German children. It is impossible to coerce a group without damaging both life and property and without imperilling the interests of the innocent with those of the guilty. Those are factors which are involved in the intricacies of group relations; and they make it impossible to transfer an ethic of personal relations uncritically to the field of inter-group relations.[50]

And the more a given social process achieves interdependency, the less moral room for maneuver we have.

Niebuhr's account of the features which distinguish group relations, and the peculiar difficulties these features pose for moral reflection, has occasioned much debate and criticism.[51] Sin seems to him parasitic on collective life in a special way. Descriptively, effective coercion of a group often jeopardizes unavoidably the interests of the innocent as well as the guilty. Normatively, anguished choices sometimes arise in situations where the morally preferable options are all unrealizable, and only a lesser-of-evils verdict stands as a realistic alternative to abandonment of large numbers of persons to those who are totally unscrupulous. So in 1940, Niebuhr wrote that he would support an American war effort if it were undertaken because he believed Nazism embodied a collective force whose aspirations clashed systematically with the directives of natural justice and Christian love.

> We have allowed ourselves to forget as much as possible that this resurgent Germany not only shares imperial ambitions with all strong nations, but that its fury is fed by a pagan religion of tribal self-glorification; that it intends to root out the Christian religion; that it defies all the univer-

sal standards of justice that ages of a Christian and humanistic culture have woven into the fabric of our civilization; that it threatens the Jewish race with annihilation and visits a maniacal fury upon these unhappy people that goes far beyond the ordinary race prejudice that is the common sin of all nations and races; that it explicitly declares its intention of subjecting the other races of Europe into slavery to the "master" race; that it intends to keep them in subjection by establishing a monopoly of military violence and of technical skill so that they will be subordinated in peace and in war. . .[52]

Against such ambitions, Niebuhr is prepared to say that the issue of a declaration of war as such is a strategic rather than a moral matter, and that "we ought to do whatever has to be done to prevent the triumph of this intolerable tyranny."[53]

To do whatever has to be done? Suppose the choice is analogous to the one envisaged by Anscombe. Should we fear Nazi domination more than the destruction of people's bodies by obliteration bombing? I think Niebuhr would say that we should fear both, without benefit of a lexical ordering between them. That is, he could agree that the prohibition of murder is cogently applied *via* the principle of discrimination to the protection of non-combatants from direct attack. And he could accept that such protection is always binding *prima facie*. Any departure from it has, at a minimum, the independent burden of proof. Yet Niebuhr not only praises the tradition of just war for calling "attention to the importance of means appropriate to ends sought, to the danger of excessive violence;" he also criticizes it when its "detailed elaborations . . . result in a rigid and highly artificial structure, more likely to confuse than illumine the conscience."[54] Moreover, too many statements appear in his corpus to the effect that it is impossible to adhere to any single moral absolute[55] to conclude that he would accept the view that the principle of non-combatant immunity from direct attack can never be overridden for any reason whatever. I think he would find congenial Michael Walzer's highly cautious defense of "supreme emergency" (Churchill's phrase in 1939).[56] Yet because for Niebuhr self-righteousness is such an ubiquitous human failing , which group relations only intensify, he would immediately look for corruptions of an appeal to supreme emergency. In his view they would be bound to arise.

The second point at which Niebuhr would draw back from Anscombe's defense concerns the content of the Christian ethic itself. For him its essential component does not consist in bedrock prohibitions, the removal of which shatters Christian ethics to pieces. He proceeds mainly at a different level of generality. Beyond the law of love itself, what remains permanent, is a view of the human condition. Sin and human freedom intrude endlessly, as I noted earlier, amidst continuous interaction between the ideals of love and justice and the egoistic realities of personal and collective existence. The ongoing relevance of the ideals means that obedience has no fixed limits. We ought to endeavor to *prevent* evil in an imperfect world, and not only to *avoid* it. Niebuhr's view here is reminiscent of negative utilitarianism. We ought to concern ourselves with what will *happen* and not only with what we are *doing*. In this sense consequences loom prominently in our moral deliberations. Yet Niebuhr's vision is closer to absolutism than to utilitarianism in his insistence that when we must compromise by doing less than love requires we cannot claim full moral justification for our deeds. They never become *all right*. Forced choices and lesser-of-evils policies are never on balance positively loving. And while the mere statement of ideals never suffices to guarantee their realization, it matters enormously that we realize them as far as we can. The only thing that matters more is the assurance of divine mercy which it is the special calling of the Church to proclaim.

IV. Twentieth Century Debates about Deeds and Rules: Paul Ramsey

Paul Ramsey articulates the final strand of Protestant thought in this century that I shall consider. He allies himself with Christian realism at important junctures, yet he departs from it in critical respects as well. The influence of Roman Catholic moral theology, particularly in his later writings, is pronounced. Any "ecumenical convergence" among Roman Catholic and Protestant ethicists we find at present owes him an incalculable debt.

He shares with Niebuhr a critical view of the Bible. As he summarizes, the Scriptures are not the only or "a *sufficient* rule for practice."[57] He also objects to a focus on immediate divine commands which he observes in "certain so-called Barthian circles" and in the treatment of the Abraham-Isaac story by Kierkegaard in *Fear and Trembling*.[58] In brief, "an ethic of Christian love, in contrast to an ethic of immediate moral impressions, shows abundant content for determining what should be done."[59]

Considering question (1), Ramsey likewise affirms a version of the doctrine of justification by faith beyond all moral striving. But he dwells less than Niebuhr does on the contrast between divine mercy and imperfect, human performance. Rather, he takes up the distinction "between trust in works out of concern for one's own eternal welfare and trust in works out of concern for the needs of another."[60] The concern of faith working through love is that the agent display what *love* is by actually meeting the needs of others, not by displaying that the agent is *him/herself* thereby actually faithful.[61] Ramsey wants to negate "the general religious desire for salvation as the supreme personal value to be gained . . ."[62]

Ramsey's depiction of neighbor-love in question (2) concentrates on other-regard as such. This passage captures his view decisively:

> Love is simply love, the genuine article; and it intends the good of the beloved one and not the response of mutuality; it intends the good of the other and not its own actual self-sacrifice or sufferings. It is the *neighbor*, and not mutuality or heedlessness or sacrifice or suffering, who stands ever before the eyes of love.[63]

Such concentration on the neighbor, rather than on qualities such as self-sacrifice, disposes Ramsey more readily than Niebuhr to consider the possibility that love may generate or otherwise justify exceptionless moral norms. Ramsey is not preoccupied with the subject of compromise "lest worse befall"; he avoids from the start stepping onto dialectical ground where the interaction between the "ideal and the real" holds sway. Absolutely every action is permitted or commanded, without exception, he says, if and when love permits or commands it.[64]

As for questions (3) and (4), Ramsey joins with Niebuhr in resisting any strict either/or between natural and revealed grounds for moral norms. Yet again Ramsey's procedure is not similarly dialectical. He breaks with those Protestant pessimists who indiscriminately repudiate the tradition of natural law. Worldly wisdom is not merely to be despised; instead, continous though always *ad hoc* use must be made of it. *Agape*-love reigns in Christian ethics to be sure, but it is not so fully equipped that it can ignore serious moral reflection from any quarter. Ramsey never stresses, however, Niebuhr's recurrent critical claims that natural law betrays an unsubstantiated optimism about how many specific moral judgments retain their validity over time, and that sin and human freedom intrude to make various status quo arrangements either suspect or dated. On the other hand, Ramsey never affirms that there are a great many such exceptionless moral judgements. He simply holds that there are such, and that the search should be held open. He takes pains not to allow the positive role he ascribes to moral reason to naturalize his depiction of *agape*, to identify it only as an immanent principle. For while *agape* does not confront a structureless natural world, its own "primary dimension stems from revelation."[65] And this revealed source keeps it "dominant and free," without necessary and permanent coalition with any scheme of natural morality.[66] *Agape* proves to have transformative force and effect *in* the world, but not by virtue *of* it.

Ramsey brings these several claims together in *War and the Christian Conscience*, a book published in 1961.[67] Here he agrees with Anscombe that the immunity of noncombatants from direct attack remains a fitting application of prohibition against murder in modern, thermonuclear circumstances. As such it is exceptionless. Yet his own case relies more expressly on an appeal to *agape*. He attempts to show that it is "love transforming natural justice" which governs the reflection of Augustine and Aquinas as they develop a preferential ethics of protection for innocent third parties, a "defense of the defenseless." In a subsequent book, *The Just War*, he attends principally to *jus in bello* questions, and wrestles with the issue of whether the principle of discrimination can be viably applied in counterinsurgency campaigns.[68] He concludes that it can; insurgents bear the onus of responsibility for enlarging the area of morally acceptable collateral damage to civilian populations. Johnson sees this increased attention to *jus in bello* questions and the erosion of *jus ad bellum* ones to be the most recent stage of a long-term trend in just war thought.[69] In any case, Ramsey's commitment to noncombatant immunity means in the end that he agrees with Anscombe: no appeal either to different political systems or to different long-term consequences in the conduct of war (e.g., the calculations preceding the decision to drop atomic bombs on Hiroshima and Nagasaki) can ever justify the direct, intentional killing of noncombatants.

Later Ramsey confronts widespread challenges to *any* exceptionless moral norm. He criticizes in particular Joseph Fletcher, the best-known defender of situation ethics. Fletcher construes *agape* as materially equivalent to utilitarianism. He denies that beyond love itself there are any exceptionless moral norms. The authority he ascribes to specific norms wavers between treating them as illuminative maxims and *prima facie* rules. An illuminative maxim may be *disregarded* if it appears to conflict with a direct application of love in a particular situation. A *prima facie* rule may never be disregarded because it carries with it in any situation to which it applies a presumption in its favor. But it may be *overridden* if in so doing the best consequences of all the things considered are realized.[70] Ramsey's case against Fletcher is widely perceived to succeed."[71] Yet on one point, usually overlooked, Ramsey agrees with Fletcher.

> I take it . . . as the question whether the "lesser evil" is not the same as the "greatest good" possible, and therefore better characterized as the good or the right thing to do. Well do I remember D.C. Macintosh making this same logically compelling point at the onset of Niebuhrian Christian realism. This is still the mood: going about responsibly doing the greatest good possible, and gaining a general sense of guiltiness by calling it the lesser evil . . . It can only confuse ethics if in order to aggravate our sense of sinfulness we *insist* on calling the greatest possible good the lesser evil (which, of course, it is tragically, but not immorally).[72]

The debate about exceptionless moral norms should proceed on its own merits without continuous recourse to a doctrine of sin; certain actions may be right even when they are also tragic.

A most illuminating exchange in the debate is between Ramsey and Donald Evans.[73] Ramsey and Evans both debar *singular* exceptions, i.e., purely random or unique cases which violate the requirement of universalizability (in a particular situation of moral choice one logically commits oneself and anyone else to making the same judgment in any similar situation); and both concur that it is *logically* possible for there to be exceptionless moral norms. The remaining issue between them is whether there *ought* to be moral norms judged to be exceptionless: the issue is *normative* rather logical or empirical.[74] The point at which Ramsey and Evans nearly agree concerns certain species of action which "have an inherent moral relevance, weight, and significance, quite apart from their consequences." Ramsey offers these examples:

(a) Never experiment medically on a human being without his/her informed consent.
(b) Never punish a person whom one knows to be innocent of that for which he/she would be punished.
(c) Never rape (i.e., force sexual intercourse on someone who is totally unwilling).[75]

Evans is prepared to grant that the role of individual moral autonomy in such cases is so minimal and so limited in scope that the rules should be regarded as *virtually* exceptionless: "the theoretically possible exceptional cases are virtually zero in their practical probability."[76] Evans continues to differ from Ramsey, however, on other rules, e.g., "no pre-marital intercourse." In short, for Evans "moral rules form a continuum: some are open to very extensive revision, some are much less open, and some are in varying degrees exceptionless."[77] Evans worries that sometimes Ramsey errs in the direction of a creeping legalism but that Ramsey nonetheless identifies the genuine dangers of a creeping exceptionism.

V. Conclusion

No one claim about exceptionless moral norms unifies the Protestant tradition *qua* tradition. Rather, I have located different and sometimes rival verdicts in complex theological schemes. Characteristically Protestant themes merge, however, and I conclude by commenting on three of the most important.

(a) *Stringency*. Attacks during the Reformation period on the distinction between mortal and venial sin pointed to a heightened stringency respecting both judgment and obligation. In terms of judgment, this stringency brings together honesty and interiorization: we continually break the commandments anyway and our desires prove as wrong as our deeds *vis-à-vis* God. In terms of obligation, this stringency mixes positive injunctions and negative prohibitions, and often gives primacy to the criterion of recipient-benefits. Indeed, sometimes the gravest sins were of omission.

Such stringency forms part of the structure of the Protestant conscience. This conscience arguably finds a modern secular home in the phenomenon of "liberal guilt." Some inchoate sense of responsibility attaches to higher possibilities still unrealized and perhaps unrealizable, as well as possibilities one is free to realize. Its "timbre" is one of infinite liability. Such a conscience opposes the complacent, the stingy, and the callous in human interaction. In this it is doubtless right. And insofar as Christian beliefs continue to govern its preoccupations and aims, it helps to keep alive radical claims endemic to the gospel. Yet this heightened stringency faces two closely related objections. The first objection applies in part to utilitarianism as well. Can a heightened zeal to do good specify any clear cut-off point, or is it prepared to employ any means for the sake of benefits overall? If so much is demanded, is anything ever strictly prohibited? The second objection appeals to longstanding assumptions about degrees of stringency: avoidance of evil is a naturally more determinate and realizable demand than the promotion of good. We can refrain from the grossest kinds of action which harm others, but we lack "world enough and time" to do everything that serves the needs of others. Recent work by moral philosophers supports these assumptions, illuminating the difference between not doing harm, "nonmaleficence," and doing good, "beneficence," and the reasons why the former is, *ceteris paribus*, more stringent. Can this difference be cogently ignored?

These objections deserve a response. Perhaps we should bracket the question of soteriological significance for a time, and look again at a cluster of allied distinctions: between nonmaleficence and beneficence, first and second mile demands, precepts and counsels, duties and works supererogation. They have more to commend them than the Reformers acknowledged.

(b) *Sin and moral norms.* Reinhold Niebuhr utilizes the doctrine of original sin to oppose complete certainty in the moral life. A sinful world defies any tidy classification of unambiguous rights and wrongs. The weight of this vision goes against exceptionless

159

moral norms. Yet we should ask more energetically than Niebuhr does whether a stress on sinfulness also furnishes one kind of powerful moral support for prohibitions precisely because attention is called to a familiar, intractable pattern in human interaction: persons are disposed to take advantage of one another. Prohibitions like the second table of the Decalogue reckon with this pattern and identify certain action-kinds as particularly egregious cases of advantage-taking. They protect us from harms which cut deeply into our physical and psychical well-being. The prohibitions make sense only in a world where such effects of sin continually threaten. This negative case for exceptionless moral norms proves most persuasive of all perhaps for numerous Roman Catholics and Protestants alike.

Though Niebuhr accepts a high degree of uncertainty and imperfection — and often transitoriness — in our specific attempts to apply love and justice to cases corrupted by sinful striving on all sides, he insists nonetheless that sin cannot tear up nature by the roots. Jesus' love ethic is not just superimposed upon us, but connects deeply with our natural hopes and needs. The effects of the Fall are not so profound that no sense of natural justice is in place, even if we cannot know it adequately or apply it clearly. The Protestant pessimism he exemplifies does not then inevitably lead to moral relativism. To talk, as he does, of a Marxist-informed "ideological taint" in our specific moral and political judgments makes sense only because we can conceive of a love which is not thus tainted. Without such a conception, we have a world in which rival ideological claimants merely strive to persuade a majority of persons to accept a particular interpretation of events and a particular evaluative scheme, or fight to the death to seize the mechanisms of social and political control and impose their particular interpretation and scheme. Either by persuasion or imposition, the winner takes all. By contrast Niebuhr's world contains moral bedrock. Its prominent features are not Anscombe's prohibitions. But it is there, despite our sinfulness and the contingent facts about who happens now to control social and political life. Nazism is opposed in its name. Ethicists in the Protestant tradition are obliged to say whether and in what sense they agree with him.

(c) *Love and law.* Thinkers in the Protestant tradition often concern themselves with Paul's insistence that love is the fulfilling of the law (Rom 13:10). Those such as Henry construe love as a compendium of specific biblical commandments which are themselves exceptionless; while those like Fletcher construe love as the one exceptionless standard to be applied extemporaneously in varying situations. Ramsey and Evans disagree with these construals and seek some genuine interplay between love and law-as-specific-moral-norms. The interplay they envisage however seems formally closer to Fletcher. For they accord to love an independent and finally authoritative status. They appeal directly to it in debating about possibly exceptionless moral norms, regarding it as more than a compendium of biblical commandments. It is also more than a summary of action-kinds forbidden by nature. Greater controversy surrounds this last point, because Ramsey shows more sympathy than Evans for arguments in Roman Catholic moral theology that certain actions are wrong by their very nature — in themselves, intrinsically — apart from consequences. Yet the debate with Evans suggests that in the end Ramsey's case on behalf of exceptionless moral norms does not require that such arguments succeed. Ramsey is willing to assume the empirical possibility that in a given case following the rule (e.g., not lying, not committing adultery) may produce worse consequences than breaking it, or at least revising it. He contends simply that this empirical possibility is less likely than the possibility of making a moral mistake if one regards the rule as breakable. For self-deception and special pleading can easily corrupt us. The loving person concludes that human well-being is best served by holding certain actions closed to future possible exceptions. This contention would be irrelevant if the action-kinds in question were regarded as wrong by nature, whatever the consequences. Ramsey disagrees with Fletcher therefore, not because the latter appeals to love as such, but because Fletcher thinks the loving person should allow all specific moral norms to be breakable.

This appeal to love by all the disputants has a distinctively Protestant character. Ramsey and Evans nevertheless prize critical reflection and reasoned argument in reaching their verdicts. In this at least they show common cause with much that is best in Roman Catholic moral theology.

Notes

1. For elaboration, see my discussion of basic moral rules and how they differ from relational norms in "Character, Conduct, and the Love Commandment," *Norm and Context in Christian Ethics*, eds. Gene Outka and Paul Ramsey (New York: Scribner's, 1968), esp. pp. 44-48.

2. For an illuminating account, see Eric D'Arcy, *Human Acts* (Oxford: Clarendon, 1963), esp. pp. 2-39.

3. See especially the essays in Richard McCormick, and Paul Ramsey, eds., *Doing Evil to Achieve Good* (Chicago: Loyola University Press, 1978). For a collection of influential essays by Roman Catholic moralists on the revisionist task, see Charles E. Curran and Richard A. McCormick, S.J., eds., *Readings on Moral Theology No. 1: Moral Norms and Catholic Tradition* (New York: Paulist Press, 1979).

4. Martin Luther, "Against the Heavenly Prophets in the Matter of Images and Sacraments," *Luther's Works*, Vol. 40, trans. Bernhard Erling (Philadelphia; Muhlenberg Press, 1958), p. 83.

5. John Calvin, *Institutes of the Christian Religion*, Vol. 1, trans. Ford Lewis Battles (Philadelphia: The Westminster Press, 1960), p. 423.

6. James M. Gustafson, *Protestant and Roman Catholic Ethics: Prospects for Rapprochement* (Chicago: University of Chicago Press, 1978), p. 10.

7. Quoted in George W. Forell, *Faith Active in Love: An Investigation of the Principles Underlying Luther's Social Ethics*, (Minneapolis: Augsburg Publishing House, 1954), p. 101.

8. *Ibid.*, p. 103.

9. *Ibid.*, p. 102.

10. *Ibid.*, p. 101.

11. Outka, "Character, Conduct, and the Love Commandment," pp. 60-65. See Martin Luther, "The Large Catechism," *The Book of Concord*, ed. and trans. Theodore G. Tappert (Philadelphia: Fortress Press, 1959), pp. 379-407. See also John Calvin, "Geneva Catechism," *The School of Faith*, ed. and trans. Thomas F. Torrance (London: James Clarke and Cot., 1959), esp. pp. 30-37.

12. Gustafson, *Protestant and Roman Catholic Ethics*, p. 3.

13. For one such attack, see Jacques Ellul, *To Will and To Do*, trans. C. Edward Hopkin (Philadelphia: Pilgrim, 1969). For an assessment of Ellul, including comparisons with the Roman Catholic tradition, see Gene Outka, "Discontinuity in the Ethics of Jacques Ellul," *Jacques Ellul: Interpretive Essays*, eds. C. G. Christians and J. M. Van Hook (Urbana: University of Illinois Press, 1981), pp. 177-228.

14. Luther, "Against the Heavenly Prophets," p. 97. This document is especially useful in acquiring an understanding of Luther's views on natural law.

15. Calvin, *Institutes*, vol. 1, pp. 360-366.

16. *Ibid.* p. 419.

17. *Ibid.*

18. Helmut Thielicke, *Theological Ethics*, vol. 1, trans. John W. Doberstein (Philadelphia: Fortress Press, 1966), pp. 646-647.

19. Søren Kierkegaard, *Fear and Trembling*, trans. Howard V. Hong and Edna H. Hong (Princeton: Princeton University Press, 1983).

20. Gene Outka, "Religious and Moral Duty: Notes on Fear and Trembling," *Religion and Morality*, eds. Gene Outka and John P. Reeder, Jr. (Garden City: Doubleday Anchor, 1973), pp. 204-254.

21. Gene Outka, *Agape: An Ethical Analysis* (New Haven: Yale University Press, 1972), esp. pp. 229-233.

22. See Karl Barth, *Church Dogmatics*, II/2. trans. G. W. Bromiley, *et. al.* (Edinburgh: T. & T. Clark, 1957), *Church Dogmatics*, III/4, trans. A. T. MacKay, *et. al.* (Edinburgh: T. & T. Clark, 1961); Emil Brunner, *The Divine Imperative*, trans. Olive Wyon (Philadelphia: The Westminster Press, 1947); Dietrich Bonhoeffer, *Ethics*, ed. Eberhard Bethge (New York: Macmillan, 1965); H. Richard Niebuhr, *The Responsible Self* (New York: Harper, 1963); Paul Lehmann, *Ethics in a Christian Context* (New York: Harper, 1963).

23. Bonhoeffer, *Ethics*, pp. 166-172.

24. Joseph Fletcher, *Situation Ethics* (Philadelphia: The Westminster Press, 1966).

25. Brunner, *Divine Imperative*, pp. 117-118.

26. Carl F. H. Henry, *Christian Personal Ethics* (Grand Rapids: Eerdmans, 1965), p. 236.

27. *Ibid.*, p. 257.

28. George F. Thomas, *Christian Ethics and Moral Philosophy* (New York: Scribner's, 1955), p. 133.

29. Henry, *Christian Personal Ethics*, pp. 304-308.

30. John Howard Yoder, *The Politics of Jesus* (Grand Rapids: Eerdmans, 1983), p. 23.

31. Stanley Hauerwas, *The Peaceable Kingdom: A Primer in Christian Ethics* (Notre Dame: University of Notre Dame Press, 1983), p. 73.

32. *Ibid.*, p. 85.

33. James H. Cone, *God of the Oppressed* (New York: Seabury, 1975), esp. pp. 217-225; Paul Lehmann, *The Transfiguration of Politics* (New York: Harper, 1975) esp. pp. 259-290.

34. Reinhold Niehbur, *Christian Realism and Political Problems* (New York: Scribner's, 1958), p. 172.

35. Reinhold Niebuhr, *Love and Justice*, ed. D. B. Robertson (Philadelphia: The Westminster Press, 1957), pp. 268-269.

36. *Ibid.*, p. 50.

37. *Reinhold Niebuhr on Politics*, eds. H. R. Davis and R. C. Good (New York: Scribner's 1960), p. 167.

38. Reinhold Niebuhr, *Love and Justice*, p. 48. For a more sympathetic account of the religious and moral concerns which surrounded the prohibition against usury, see R. H. Tawney, *Religion and the Rise of Capitalism* (New York: Penguin, 1947), esp. pp. 11-163.

39. Reinhold Niebuhr, *Love and Justice*, p. 48.

40. Reinhold Niebuhr, *Christian Realism and Political Problems*, pp. 132-133.

41. Reinhold Niebuhr, *An Interpretation of Christian Ethics* (New York: Meridian, 1958), p. 98.

42. Reinhold Niebuhr, *Love and Justice*, p. 270. For a detailed examination of Niebuhr's critique of pacifism, see James F. Childress, *Moral Responsibility in Conflicts* (Baton Rouge: Louisiana State University Press, 1982), pp. 29-61.

43. James Turner Johnson, *Just War Tradition and the Restraint of War* (Princeton: Princeton University Press, 1981), pp. 336-337.

44. G. E. M. Anscombe, *Ethics, Religion and Politics* (Minneapolis: University of Minnesota Press, 1981), p. 57.

45. *Ibid.*, p. 56.

46. *Ibid.*, p. 58.

47. *Ibid.*, p. 57.

48. *Ibid.*, p. 60.

49. *Ibid.*, p. 61.

50. Reinhold Niebuhr, *Moral Man and Immoral Society* (New York: Scribner's, 1932), pp. 172-173.

51. For Roman Catholic criticism, see John Courtney Murray, *We Hold These Truths: Catholic Reflections on the American Proposition* (Garden City: Doubleday Image, 1964), pp. 262-279. For feminist criticism, see Rosemary Radford Ruether, *New Woman New Earth* (New York: Seabury, 1975), e.g. pp. 199-204.

52. Reinhold Niebuhr, *Love and Justice*, p. 274.

53. *Ibid.*, p. 275.

54. Angus Dun and Reinhold Niebuhr, "God Wills Both Justice and Peace," *Christianity and Crisis* 15 (June 13, 1955), p. 77.

55. Reinhold Niebuhr, *An Interpretation of Christian Ethics*, e.g., p. 175.

56. Michael Walzer, *Just and Unjust Wars* (New York: Basic Books, 1977), pp. 251-268.

57. Paul Ramsey, *Nine Modern Moralists* (Englewood Cliffs: Prentice-Hall, 1962), p. 7.

58. Paul Ramsey, *Basic Christian Ethics* (New York: Scribner's, 1950), p. 338. He calls this view "theological intuitionism." Yet his cryptic remarks on this page should not lead us to ignore his own general indebtedness to both Kierkegaard and Barth. For a defense

against the charge that Barth is an intuitionist, see especially William Werpehowski, "Command and History in the Ethics of Karl Barth," *Journal of Religious Ethics* 9:2 (Fall, 1981), pp. 298-320.

59. Ramsey, *Basic Christian Ethics*, p. 339.

60. *Ibid.*, p. 138.

61. *Ibid.*, p. 136.

62. *Ibid.*, p. 151.

63. Ramsey, *Nine Modern Moralists*, p. 146.

64. Ramsey, *Basic Christian Ethics.*, p. 89.

65. Ramsey, *Nine Modern Moralists*, p. 7.

66. Ramsey, *Basic Christian Ethics*, pp. 242-244.

67. Paul Ramsey, *War and the Christian Conscience* (Durham: Duke University Press, 1961).

68. Paul Ramsey, *The Just War: Force and Political Responsibility* (New York: Scribner's, 1968).

69. James Turner Johnson, "Morality and Force in Statecraft: Paul Ramsey and the Just War Tradition," *Love and Society: Essays in the Ethics of Paul Ramsey*, eds. James Johnson and David Smith (Missoula: Scholars Press, 1974), pp. 93-114.

70. For elaboration of this interpretation of Fletcher, see my *Agape: An Ethical Analysis*, pp. 93-122.

71. E.g., Alan Donagan, *The Theory of Morality* (Chicago: University of Chicago Press, 1977), pp. 62-63.

72. Paul Ramsey, *Deeds and Rules in Christian Ethics* (New York: Scribner's 1967), p. 187.

73. Paul Ramsey, "The Case of the Curious Exception," *Norm and Context in Christian Ethics*, pp. 67-135; Donald Evans, *Faith, Authenticity and Morality* (Toronto: University of Toronto Press, 1980), pp. 160-196.

74. Evans, p. 169.

75. *Ibid.*, p. 182.

76. *Ibid.*, p. 183.

77. *Ibid.*, p. 185.

Chapter 8

Exceptionless Norms In New Testament Morality: A Biblical-Theological Approach

The Reverend Thomas J. Deidun, I.C., D.S.S.

Some Caveats

This title calls for some caveats. First, the expression "New Testament morality" must not lead us to suppose that there is a single ethical approach common to all or most of the New Testament writers. The New Testament is not so much a book as a collection of writings, each of whose authors has his own distinctive theological and ethical view-point. This means that they sometimes differ significantly, not only in their answers to particular questions of conduct (e.g., whether the Mosaic Law is still to be observed), but also in their understanding of such basic matters as the ground of obligation and the nature of sin.[1]

Second, the term "morality" in the expression "New Testament morality" must not be taken to imply system or scientific reflection. The New Testament writers were not systematic theologians but evangelists, pastors and missionaries. If there is a unifying factor which presides over their ethical teaching and gives it a semblance of coherence, it is not ethical theory, but the mystery of Christ and its repercussions in Christian experience.[2]

Third, we should not assume from the outset that any given New Testament writer recognizes that norms *have* a function in Christian living. We may certainly not suppose that any New Testament writer gives anything like the same prominence to norms as they have come to assume in Roman Catholic tradition, where they have often been virtually "hypostasized," and thought of in isolation from the mystery of Christ and the imperative of personal commitment in faith.[3]

Fourth, regarding the concept *"exceptionless* norms": this obviously presupposes a level of reflection which we should not expect to find in any New Testament writer, any more than we should expect to find developed reflection on concepts like "conscience" and "natural law."[4] The New Testament is not, as has sometimes been supposed, a heavenly preview of the history of moral theology, but God's word incarnate in time.

Finally, I doubt whether this paper will represent a "biblical theological approach." A biblical theologian would not start with the specialized concerns of a modern discipline on the assumption that the New Testament writers must share these concerns. He would seek rather to discover the concerns of the New Testament writers themselves, and leave it to his colleagues in other disciplines to decide whether some of his findings contribute to their own discussion. To adopt this approach here would be sure to take us far afield without a single mention of norms, "exceptionless" or otherwise; and that would not be a very tangible contribution to this book. So, rather than a "biblical-theological approach," I should prefer to say that this chapter presents some reflections of a student of New Testament theology who is eager to contribute to at least a preliminary discussion of this theme, and yet fully aware that in doing so he runs the risk of distorting the true perspective of the New Testament writers themselves (perhaps more by what he does not say than by what he does).

I have chosen to speak not of all New Testament writings in general, but of one group of writings only — the Letters of Paul

— so as to concentrate the discussion and avoid unhelpful generalizations.

Norms in Paul's View of Christian Living

It will be useful to start with the view (strenuously defended by some New Testament scholars) that Paul saw no place at all for norms in Christian living: indeed, he considered them inimical to Christian freedom and maturity, and to authentic human existence. While he acknowledged the usefulness of guidelines for the semi-converted, he had no time for norms which claimed a decisive function in Christian choice and conduct. It is a sign of inauthentic existence to allow a norm to bear the burden of moral decision. The mature Christian is governed not by norms but by the demands of Christ's love, which the Holy Spirit and the general moral insights of the community enable him to discern in the complexities of Christian living.[5]

This understanding of Paul's thought is based on a variety of arguments and presuppositions. I shall examine each of them in turn.

Not norms, but the person of Christ, is the basis of Christian obligation.

The argument which is perhaps most commonly used in support of this understanding goes something like this: in Paul's view of Christianity, the basis of obligation is no longer a code of law but the person of Christ, present and active through the Spirit. This is undoubtedly true, and it must, I think, be conceded that we Roman Catholics have not always emphasized it sufficiently. But however that may be, the crucial question here is, whether the obligation which arises from the Christian's personal relationship with Christ is capable of being articulated, in however limited a fashion, in norms which can be used by the Christian as unambiguous indicators of what he must or must not do in a given situation.

Paul, I think, would have less difficulty in giving this question an affirmative answer than many of his interpreters. Precisely because the Christian is related to Christ and the Spirit in a particular way, he may not, for example, "take the members of Christ and make them members of a prostitute" (1 Cor 6:15). That appears to me to be a fairly clear and "operative" norm. It is true that I am left with the problem of deciding who is, and who is not, a prostitute. I am already into an elementary form of casuistry. But that's Paul's fault, for insisting that my relationship with Christ confronts me with certain obligations in the nitty-gritty of my sexual behavior. And if he continues in that vein, sooner or later he will present me with the beginnings of a "code" of sexual conduct.

There is nothing in Paul, as far as I can see, to suggest that such a "code" would be incompatible with a personal allegiance to Christ — though, of course, Paul would consider any attempt to put the "code" in the place of Christ to be contrary to the Gospel. But the *antithesis* between a personalized and a normative ethic, such as it is conceived by some moderns, is foreign to Paul.[6]

Paul, the Mosaic Law, and norms in Christian living.

A related argument, often stated but even more often assumed, is that Paul's strictures on the Mosaic Law apply to *all* law, and to any kind of norm. Underlying this argument is the assumption that Paul rejected the Mosaic Law precisely because it was *law*, i.e. it contained injunctions which exerted an absolute claim and therefore deprived the individual of a free and authentically human response to the unforeseeable requirements of any given moral situation.

This interpretation appears to me to be mistaken. Doubtless, Paul associated the Mosaic Law with a Christless and, therefore, an inauthentic existence. What exactly Paul had against the Mosaic Law is still a subject of debate among Pauline scholars. But if there is any general explanation of his objection to it, it is not the fact that it was law, but the fact that (at least in his view) it threatened to take the place of Christ, in so far as it claimed to be an instrument of transformation and a pledge of salvation.[7]

For the same reason, surely, Paul would reject anything even in the Christian community which tended to replace or supplement faith in Christ *alone.* This means — and many Roman Catholics might be scandalized by this — that he would be opposed to Magisterial pronouncements which assumed such prominence that they tended to remove Christ from the center of the Gospel. But it does not mean — and many in the Protestant tradition might be scandalized by this — that he rejected any idea of a norm which functioned precisely as a norm, i.e. as the proclamation of a particular obligation claiming the individual's obedience in a given moral situation. To say that the observance of a norm cannot effect or guarantee salvation is not to say that a norm cannot be a norm.[8] It seems to me that the uncritical application of Paul's strictures on the Mosaic Law to *any* kind of law fails to distinguish between his opposition to the Mosaic Law as a (putative) means of justification and salvation, and a contemporary trend which tends to see all law as an intrinsic evil.[9]

"Global" obedience and the observance of norms.

Another argument goes something like this: for Paul, Christian obedience is not a piecemeal compliance with particular norms but a "global" submission of mind and heart to the claim of the Gospel. Now this, in my view, contains such an important, and so frequently neglected, element of truth, that it is worth pausing to consider it for its own sake.

Undoubtedly, for Paul the only adequate response to the Gospel is faith — a faith which becomes operative in love (cf. Gal 5:6). This means a radical and decisive orientation of the whole person away from self and towards God and neighbor. No amount of compliance with norms, however zealous and well motivated, can take the place of this "global" surrender to the person of Jesus Christ. On this point, it is worth observing, in parenthesis, that we in the Roman Catholic tradition, at least in the past, may have given such emphasis to the observance of norms (I mean, by sheer quantity of talk on the subject) as to have left vast numbers of the faithful with the impression that the obedience required of them as Christians involves little more than an observable and measurable compliance with particular norms.[10] Of course, on reflection we recognize that such a mentality can be contrary to the Gospel, for compliance with norms is notoriously compatible with a profound refusal of real obedience. This point is made with a degree of urgency by Jesus in the Gospels (e.g., Lk 18:14) and by Paul on several occasions, as for example when he says that the Jews, precisely while seeking to establish their own righteousness (by Law observance), did not submit to the righteousness of God, i.e. did not respond to the claim of the Gospel (cf. Rom 10:3).

But the question here is not whether compliance with norms can co-exist with a refusal of real obedience, but whether real obe-

169

dience necessarily precludes compliance with norms. Here again, we must avoid being one-sided, where Paul is not. In Rom 8:1-15, the Christian "pleases God" only through a complete re-orientation of mind and heart in the power of the Holy Spirit, in other words, through a filial obedience which engages the whole person. But in 1 Thes 4:1ff. "pleasing God" entails not only a recognizable pattern of behavior ("how you ought to live", v. 1), but also compliance with particular injunctions (v. 2) which Paul now urges on the Thessalonians "in the Lord Jesus," that is, as part of the normal exercise of his apostolic ministry.[11]

The fact is that in Paul there is no polarization between "global obedience" and compliance with particular norms, for the latter, though never exhausting the implications of the former, can be an authentic expression of them, and is frequently required by them (cf. also 1 Cor 7:19; 2 Thes 3:10-15).[12]

Precepts or guidelines?

The flip-side of the argument that for Paul authentic obedience precludes a normative ethic is that *as a matter of fact* he never urges concrete injunctions on his communities, but offers only general guidelines, and this only to those who are not yet sufficiently mature to take the burden of moral decision on themselves.[13]

There is an important element of truth in this. Paul is in general far more concerned with what Josef Fuchs calls "transcendental" imperatives (e.g., "put on the Lord Jesus Christ," "walk by the Spirit," "let your manner of life be worthy of the Gospel") than he is with their crystallization in operative norms. Moreover, large parts of his exhortation consist of recommendations which are too general to function as operative norms (e.g. Rom ch. 12; 13:8-14; Gal 5:13-6:10).

But this is not the whole truth. For sometimes he does urge upon his communities, and expects them to comply with, some fairly well defined imperatives, which he at least considers to be sufficiently concrete to function as norms.

A good illustration of this is 1 Thes 4:1-12.[14] Here Paul is urging upon the community certain ethical directives (keeping away from fornication and doing a good day's work) which he had already insisted upon at the time of evangelization. Since, at the beginning of the letter (1:3), he praises their remarkable faith, hope and love, and in this present passage expressly acknowledges that they are

170

already complying with his instructions (cf. vv. 1 & 10), it must be that he repeats them here as a matter of course and as a matter of principle — that is, as part of the normal exercise of his ministry, and in recognition of the continuing needs of Christians who are already strong in faith, and no longer "babes in Christ."

Paul refers to his directives in this passage with the Greek word *parangeliai*. This word has a variety of connotations, ranging from "command" to "counsel." It has been argued that it is the latter connotation which is appropriate here: they are not precepts or binding norms, but practical guidelines, which Paul on no account intends to be taken as obligatory or decisive criteria for the Christian's choice and conduct. On this interpretation, Paul does not here relax his unqualified opposition to any formulation which might be interpreted as expressing an unconditional moral claim in a given situation.

Now the word *parangelia* can mean "counsel" or "advice," but elsewhere in the New Testament it means "command," and the context of this passage shows that it does so here as well. Paul's *parangeliai* are intended to crystallize certain implications of God's will (v. 3); their non-observance incurs God's eschatological punishment (v. 6), contradicts the meaning of the Christian vocation (v. 7) and constitutes resistance to the activity of God's Spirit (v. 8). All this suggests to me that Paul's *parangeliai* are intended not simply as guidelines but as decisive criteria of moral conduct. If Paul is all the time tacitly conceding that it is up to each individual to decide in the light of other factors whether or not he will observe these criteria, this passage must surely be considered something of an overkill.

Moreover, since Paul is able to refer to his *parangeliai* with the technical language of authoritative tradition (v. 1), and to recall their actual content (vv. 4ff. & 11), surely we may regard them as sufficiently concrete and particularized to deserve to be called norms. And it is perhaps significant that Paul can speak of such traditional norms in the same breath as he mentions the activity of the indwelling Spirit (v. 8) and God's immediate, inward guidance (v. 9) — the very dimension of Christian existence which, in the view of some interpreters, excludes any kind of normative ethic.[15]

171

Love — the sole absolutum?

We must now consider the view of those who do not deny that Paul recognizes at least some norms, but who claim that these are simply expressions of the single imperative of agape (Christian love of neighbor): in other words, agape is the only moral absolute, and other values and obligations have an unconditional claim only in so far as they are deducible from, or reducible to, this *unum necessarium.*

Here we catch a glimpse of the situationist view of Joseph Fletcher, who holds that "love is the only principle which always obliges in conscience," and that "anything else, including . . . the Ten Commandments, are *relatively* valid — relative to any situation in which their meaning might happen to be fitting to love's requirements." [16]

Like the views I have discussed above, this one contains a very important element of truth, which it will be useful for us to dwell upon for a moment.

There is no denying that agape is for Paul the basic imperative and the supreme criterion of choice and action. He says this expressly in several places, as for example in his "celebration of charity" in 1 Cor 13, and in Rom 13:8ff. and Gal 5:14, where he asserts that all the precepts of the Law are "recapitulated" and "fulfilled" in agape. Clearly, agape for Paul is not one ethical value among others, but the unique expression of the Christian imperative, which somehow includes all the claims of God's law and of the Gospel of Christ.

The decisive question, however, is whether all this is to be understood in the sense intended by Joseph Fletcher in the statements quoted above, i.e., is it in fact the case that Paul recognizes no particular obligations other than those which, from one situation to the next, can be more or less readily derived from the single imperative of love?

In answer to this, it must be conceded that many, certainly, of the values, counsels and injunctions which Paul presents to his communities are related, in a more or less easily recognizable fashion, to the imperative of love, since they are simply particular applications of it. But to stop there is to oversimplify to the point of falsification.

A closer look at the Letters reveals whole passages of exhortation (including precept) which contain not a single allusion to agape.

172

This is manifestly so in passages like 1 Cor 5; 6:12-20; 10:6ff., regarding aspects of sexual morality. It is particularly remarkable that in 1 Cor 6:12-20, where Paul exhorts against frequenting prostitutes, he uses almost every motivation *except* neighbor love; indeed, he shows not the slightest concern for the plight of the prostitute. Then, in 1 Cor 7:1-5, far from explaining the evil of sexual immorality in terms of an offense against a personal relationship, he seems to view the personal relationship (marriage) almost exclusively as a "protection" against the evil of sexual immorality (cf. vv. 2 & 5c; 9)!

Nor is it only sexual morality which appears to enjoy this "autonomy" in relation to the love imperative. In his directives to various categories of people in 1 Cor 7, considerations of neighbor love are not among Paul's concerns. He has a criterion of what is "good" (cf. vv. 1, 8 & 26) which has no apparent connection with what we should recognize as the claims of neighbor love.[17]

The truth of the matter is that, for Paul, Christians are liable to many particular obligations which cannot be made to coincide with "love's requirements," except perhaps by dint of some rather complex theological reasoning (which Paul himself does not embark upon). They are liable to obligations arising from, for example, their baptismal consecration, their union with Christ, their belonging to the Spirit and their membership of the Church, as well as from the dictates of conscience and the claims of justice, truth, and other "natural" values.

Now the fact that, on the one hand, Paul can "recapitulate" the Christian imperative in neighbor love, while, on the other hand, the content and motivations of many of his exhortations and injunctions are apparently unrelated to the claims of neighbor love, indicates, surely, that his assertions about neighbor love are more problematic than many seem willing to recognize. They certainly do not support the thorough-going "agapism" of Joseph Fletcher, nor, probably, can they be used as the basis of any theoretical system. For Paul, Christian morality is indeed resumed in neighbor love (for this is the reverberation of God's own love for us in Christ), but it cannot be reduced to it, if by that we mean that neighbor love can be used as the single criterion of moral action, competing with, or replacing, the particular claims which confront the Christian in virtue of his *total* situation.

173

The Spirit — an "inward monitor"?

A word must be said here about the not unrelated claim that Paul sees the Spirit — or, alternatively, love itself — as a *lex interna,* in the sense of an "inward monitor," which renders superfluous (not to say deleterious) any kind of external, formulated norm.[18]

Now it is true that for Paul Christian love brings an increase of knowledge and discernment (cf. Phil 1:9f.), and that the Spirit endows Christians with a new spiritual "instinct" and understanding (cf. Rom 8:5ff.; 1 Cor 2:14). But it is not true that Paul thought of the Spirit, or of the internal law of love, as supplying *ad hoc* guidance in the ethical complexities of daily living, or even as providing special insight into the larger ethical issues which arose in the various communities.[19]

Paul stresses the need for discernment, including prophetic and community discernment, in moral matters (here too, perhaps, we Roman Catholics ought to listen to him more),[20] but nowhere does he suggest that discernment is some sort of spiritual alchemy capable of converting precepts into optional guidelines.

Paul's handling of the commandments of Jesus.

As a final point in this part of the discussion, we need to consider the claim that in his missionary and pastoral practice Paul makes exceptions to two commandments of Jesus (the only two which he seems to know) for the sake of the Gospel and the pastoral good of the faithful.

These alleged instances are (a) Paul's disregard of Jesus' directive that those who preach the Gospel should get their living by the Gospel (1 Cor 9:14f.), and (b) his relaxation of Jesus' prohibition of divorce (1 Cor 7:10-16).[21]

With regard to the first instance — Paul's refusal to take payment from the Corinthians — in the opinion of one recent interpreter, Paul here "creates a startling impression of willful disobedience to an explicit command of the Lord," and: "The implication is dazzlingly clear: this commandment of the Lord, and no doubt many others regarding we don't know what subjects, was *relativized, i.e. obeyed or not depending on how this affected the progress of the Gospel and the unity of the Church.*"[22]

To my mind, this goes well beyond the evidence of the text. There is no clear indication that Paul ever perceived Jesus' words regarding missionaries as a command imposing an obligation on the missionaries themselves.[23] It is true that Paul understands Jesus to have made an *authoritative* disposition (*dietaxen,* v. 14). But an authoritative disposition does not have to impose an obligation on those for whose benefit it may be intended; it can equally well confer or validate a right, imposing on *others* an obligation to respect it, so long as it is not voluntarily waived. The whole drift of Paul's argument in this passage shows that this is how he perceived the intention of Jesus' words from the beginning. The impression he creates here is not one of "willful disobedience to an explicit command" (he would surely have taken the trouble to justify himself before a hostile audience, if this were the case), but one of generosity in waiving a right which he knew to have been validated by Jesus himself.[24]

With regard to Jesus' saying on divorce, Paul clearly regards it as mandatory, for he appeals to it initially as the basis of his own injunction (1 Cor 7:10f.). The question is, whether he then proceeds to relax it in the case of mixed marriages where the non-believing partner is unwilling to continue in the marriage (vv. 12f.).

The New Testament divorce texts are notoriously difficult, and have been the subject of endless debate. But the state of research among Catholic exegetes is, I think, not unfairly represented in the following quotation from a recent study: "Despite disagreement on details there is a growing consensus among Catholic exegetes that Matthew and Paul both represent an exception to the absolute prohibition of divorce and represent adaptation of Jesus' teaching to their own church situation. There is also consensus that these exegetical findings should bear on church life and practice today."[25]

The trouble is, however, that exegetes have not been able to establish what the exceptions introduced respectively by Matthew and Paul actually involve, nor, therefore, whether they do in fact represent real exceptions to the absolute prohibition.[26]

With regard to Paul's handling of the prohibition in 1 Cor 7:12ff., many exegetes (and, of course, Roman Catholic matrimonial practice, with its appeal to the *privilegium paulinum*) understand the text in the sense that, contrary to the Lord's prohibition which Paul upholds in the case of marriages between Christians (7:10f.), the Christian partner in a mixed marriage may, in certain circumstances, accept a divorce, i.e. separation, with the right to remarry. If this interpretation is correct, then Paul, in order to provide for the pastoral needs of some members of the Corinthian community, is indeed making an exception to the Lord's prohibition of divorce.[27]

But I am not convinced that this interpretation is correct. Paul says nothing about remarriage,[28] and the verb he uses for the departure of the unbelieving partner in v. 15 need not imply that the mixed marriage is "dissolved," for he has used the same verb in v. 11 of the hypothetical action of a Christian wife in a Christian marriage, to whom he expressly denies the right to remarry.[29] And when, in v. 15, he says that "in such a case the Christian husband or wife is not bound" (RSV), the verb which he actually uses in Greek (literally: "is not in a state of enslavement") would be extremely odd, if all he meant was that he or she was released from the marriage bond (with the consequent right to remarry).[30] It is more likely that by "not being in a state of enslavement," Paul means that the Christian spouse who is deserted[31] by his or her unbelieving partner must not feel constrained (by an undue sense of liability to the marriage bond) to strive to maintain the *status quo* (perhaps in the hope of "saving" the partner, cf. 7,16), since to do so would mean forfeiting the peace which the Christian is called to enjoy (cf. 7,15).

The above represents a minority position. In the context of our present discussion, it is worth pointing out that whichever interpretation we accept, we are left with something of a predicament. Because *either* we understand Paul to be conceding the right of remarriage, in which case he is making an "exception" to Jesus' "absolute" prohibition, *or* we do not read the text in this way, in which case we have to admit that the Church's matrimonial law makes an "exception" to the "absolute" prohibition (and this without any basis in Scripture).

The text is admittedly problematic. But that in itself is a good reason for not using it, as some have done, as an interpretive key to Paul's handling of moral imperatives in general.[32] Sound methodology requires us to go by the clear implications of some typical aspects of his teaching and exhortation, as we have done, rather than by one or two texts which are in fact more problematic than some interpreters seem willing to admit.

176

The "Absoluteness" of Paul's Injunctions.

Before considering the possible relevance of Paul's views to modern discussion, we must clarify the sense or senses in which he supposes that his injunctions are "absolute."

First, he regards them as "absolute" in the sense that they have an objective validity. While he recognizes the unchallengeable role of the individual's "conscience" in what we would call the "subjective" aspect of morality (cf. Rom 14:23; 1 Cor 8:7), he takes it for granted that certain ways of behaving are right or wrong, regardless of the individual's subjective evaluation (cf. e.g., 1 Cor 4:4; 10:14-22 [in contrast to ch. 8 & 10:23-33]; Rom 1,18ff.). The "intuitional" aspect of his ethics (cf. e.g., Rom 12:2; Phil 1:9f.) does not exclude the "normative," and he is able to point to commands and prohibitions which can be formulated and handed down as part of an authoritative tradition in some way analogous to that of rabbinic Judaism (cf. e.g., 1 Thes 4:1ff.), and which, moreover, claim the Christian's compliance on pain of exclusion from the goods of salvation (cf. Gal 5:21; 1 Cor 6:10).

Second, Paul regards his injunctions as "absolute" in the sense that he nowhere envisages the possibility of their being "relativized" in the light of higher claims. Though he regards agape as the sovereign and universal imperative, he never suggests that the particular moral demands which confront the Christian in virtue of his total situation might have to give way to "love's requirements," nor, *a fortiori,* to any other "contextual" consideration.

Third, Paul regards at least some of his injunctions as "absolute" in the sense that he intends them to express the ethical implications of the Christian's relationship with Christ. In his view, ethics and religion are inseparable and the former are grounded in the latter. It is true that he does not always seek to justify his injunctions theologically. But where he does seek to do so, the substance of his justification is, in the last analysis, the *incompatibility* of certain ways of behaving with the Christian's relationship with Christ. In this way, Paul's injunctions reflect the "absolute" either/or of his eschatology and soteriology (i.e. *either* Christ *or* that which is incompatible with Christ). And granted the quasi-physical nature of the Christian's relationship with Christ, as he understands it, the "absoluteness" of his injunctions is not confined to "transcendental" imperatives (e.g., "consider yourselves dead to sin and alive to God in Christ Jesus"), but extends also to whatever physical acts he deems to be incompatible with this relationship (e.g., "shall I take the members of Christ and make them members of a prostitute?", and, "you cannot drink the cup of the Lord and the cup of demons").

This leads us, however, to consider a sense in which Paul does *not* regard his injunctions as "absolute." That is, he does not consider that they contain within themselves their own *raison d'etre.* They are never "hypostasized," but always firmly anchored in the *indicative* of Christian existence. In simple language, if a norm is seen as decisive, it is not because it is a norm, but because it is understood to confront the Christian with the inescapable implications of some aspect of his relationship with Christ. That is why Paul normally takes the trouble to motivate and explain his injunctions, and is never content, as teachers of the Jewish Law would be, with appealing to the authority of the norm as such. In this sense, Paul's ethic is not nomistic, nor is it "normative," if by that we mean that it has its *basis* in norms.

Relevance to Modern Discussion?

Finally, we must ask what relevance Paul's suppositions have to a modern discussion of "absolute" norms.

The short answer to this is, I think that they have *no* immediate relevance. The fact that Paul considered his injunctions to be "absolute" does not necessarily mean that they are "absolute" in our sense. Josef Fuchs has drawn our attention to the distinction between "absolute" in the sense of "objective" (i.e. possessing an objective validity, given the presuppositions of a particular time and culture) and "absolute" in the philosophical sense of universal and timeless validity.[33] Now the fact that Paul considered his injunctions to be "absolute" need imply no more than that, in his judgement, and given the presuppositions of his time and culture, they were valid proclamations of what was right and wrong for those who shared these presuppositions.

In fact, it is easy to see that many of Paul's injunctions are culture-bound, and simply inapplicable in a culture like our own.[34] This is not surprising, when one considers that large parts of the content of his exhortations are more or less thinly Christianized importations from Jewish and Hellenistic preaching, reflecting the values, conventions and prejudices of those particular cultures.

Admittedly, the fact that some of Paul's ethical statements are culture-bound does not necessarily mean (as some seem to suppose) that they *all* are. But neither Paul nor any New Testament writer provides us with a criterion for distinguishing between those which are and those, if any, which are not. We require a hermeneutic, and this the New Testament does not provide.[35]

In other words, the New Testament scholar has nothing to offer the moral theologian on the question whether the New Testament contains "absolute" (in the sense of universally valid) norms, nor on the more basic question whether it makes sense to speak of such norms at all. On the contrary, on both of these questions, he eagerly waits to be enlightened by him.

Notes

1. Cf. e.g., the different understanding of faith in Paul, James and Hebrews; the different attitudes towards marriage in Paul and Ephesians; the prominence given to the words of the historical Jesus in the Synoptics, in contrast to Paul (and other New Testament writers); the prominence of sexual morality in Paul, in contrast to the Gospels; the absence of a Christological and sacramental dimension in the ethical teaching of James, in contrast to Paul and 1 Peter.

2. Cf. C.E. Curran, *Catholic Moral Theology in Dialogue* Notre Dame, IN, 1972, pp. 42ff.

3. Cf. J. Blank, "New Testament Morality and Modern Moral Theology," *Concilium,* May 1967, pp. 6ff.

4. No New Testament writer ever asks himself questions like, "is there such a thing as a norm which is applicable always and everywhere?", or, "is there such a thing as an intrinsically evil action?" And even if he assumes that such and such is the case, he is not thereby qualified to participate in a modern discussion of "exceptionless" norms, since this presupposes distinctions which were unknown to him.

5. Cf. e.g., J. Murphy-O'Connor, *L'existence chrétienne selon saint Paul,* Paris, 1974; C. Spicq, *Charité et liberté selon le Nouveau Testament,* Paris, 1961.

6. Cf. W. Schrage, *Die konkreten Einzelgebote in der paulinischen Paränese,* Gütersloh, 1961, ch. IV.

7. Cf. T.J. Deidun, *New Covenant Morality in Paul,* Rome, 1981, pp. 151-155; 251-258; J. Ziesler, *Pauline Christianity,* Oxford, 1983, pp. 99-103.

8. "Nichtgesetzlichkeit darf . . . nicht Unverbindlichkeit besagen wollen" — Schrage, *op. cit.,* p. 247.

9. Cf. Schrage, *ibid.,* p. 96; W.D. Davies, "Paul and the Law: Reflections on Pitfalls in Interpretation" in M.D. Hooker, S.G. Wilson, ed., *Paul and Paulinism,* London, 1982, p. 12; T.J. Deidun, "True Freedom," *The Way,* Jan. 1983.

10. A contributory factor here is the fact that the moral attitudes of Roman Catholics have to a large extent been forged in the confessional, where, by the nature of the case, one has to spell out one's disobedience *numero et specie.* This in turn has often encouraged a piecemeal approach to obedience.

11. Cf. Rom 6:17: in the middle of a chapter which is all about "global" obedience, Paul reminds the baptized (in a manner which admittedly puzzles many commentators) that they "have become obedient from the heart to the standard of teaching to which [they] were committed" — a "standard of teaching" which, in view of the whole context, must have

included traditional ethical instruction regarded as normative in the Christian communities, since it claimed the obedience of the baptized.

12. Cf. Schrage, *op. cit.*, pp. 49-70; Deidun, *New Covenant Morality,* pp. 180ff.

13. Cf. J. Murphy-O'Connor, "The Contemporary Value of Pauline Moral Imperatives," *Doctrine and Life* 21 (1971) 59-71.

14. For two contrasting interpretations of this passage, see Murphy-O'Connor, *art. cit.* and Deidun, *op. cit.,* pp. 176-183.

15. Cf. S. Lyonnet, 'St. Paul: Liberty and Law', *The Bridge* 4 (1962) 229-251; von Dobschütz on 1 Thes 4:9: "die innere, praktisch und unmittelbar wirksame Erfüllung der Herzen mit dem Geist, dem Geist der rechten Liebe . . ."

16. J. Fletcher, *Situation Ethics,* London, 1966, p. 60; p. 335 (author's italics).

17. Another example: in Rom 13:1-7 Paul urges compliance with civil authorities. It is a matter of unconditional moral obligation ("*necessary* to comply . . . also for the sake of conscience," v. 5). It has been suggested that since the context of this passage has to do with agape (cf. 12:9-21; 13:8ff.), Paul must have intended its content too to be read in this perspective. But this is by no means clear, and most interpreters remark on the fact with surprise. The motivations Paul employs here have no apparent connection with agape, nor has the language anything in common with that used elsewhere in passages expressly concerned with it.

18. See the views reported by Schrage, *op. cit.,* pp. 10f.; 74-79. Against this interpretation, see W.D. Davies, *Paul and Rabbinic Judaism,* pp. 177-226; G. Salet, 'La loi dans nos coeurs', *NRTh* 79 (1957) 449-462; 561-578; Schrage, *ibid.,* pp. 71-93.

19. In 1 Cor. 7, in his detailed answers to the Corinthians' enquiries, Paul expresses no dismay that they had referred to him, rather than consult the Spirit directly; on the contrary, in v. 40 ("I think that I too have the Spirit of God"), he appears to be discounting someone's claim to special guidance from the Spirit in the matters in question.

20. Cf. Deidun, *op. cit.,* p. 233: "The faithful are endowed in Christ with a "Christian instinct" . . . whereby each one of them is divinely qualified to collaborate within the community for an ever deeper understanding of the "things of the Spirit" and their implications for Christian living." If this is true, it has to be admitted that it is not yet adequately acknowledged by the Magisterium, at least in the formulation of its moral teaching.

21. Cf. D.L. Dungan, *The Sayings of Jesus in the Churches of Paul,* Oxford, 1971; Murphy-O'Connor, *op. cit.,* pp. 149-160 and *RB* 89 (1982) 295f.

22. Dungan, *op. cit.,* p. 33; p. 35 (author's italics).

23. It is pointless to appeal to the context of parallel sayings in the Synoptics, since it is unlikely that Paul received the saying in that context, or in any kind of context. It is generally supposed that if Jesus' sayings were already beginning to be collected together at this time, they were not yet contextualized as they were to be later in the Synoptic traditions. The question that worries Murphy-O'Connor is, "how could Paul reclassify a 'command' as a 'right'?" (*RB* 89, pp. 295f.). The real question, surely, is whether the saying was already "classified" as a command when Paul first received it.

24. Paul's handling of Jesus' saying in this passage is not to be interpreted in the light of vv. 19-23 of the same chapter, where Paul is making no policy-statement about his handling of the words of Jesus.

25. J.R. Donahue, "Divorce: New Testament Perspectives," *The Month,* April 1981, p. 119.

26. For essential bibliography, see Donahue, *art. cit.,* p. 119 notes 2 & 3; for Mt. 5:32 and 19:9, especially B. Vawter, "The Divorce Clauses in Mt 5:32 and 19:9," *CBQ* 16 (1954) 155-167 (including criticism of some rather desperate attempts by Catholic exegetes to evade the issue). As far as Matthew is concerned, it is now generally accepted that he is introducing some sort of qualification into Jesus' saying as we have it (probably) in something like its original form in Mark (*contra* Dungan), for he adds the words: "except on the ground of *porneia*". But what *porneia* means in these contexts is still debated. Possibly it refers to marital infidelity; but *porneia* is not the technical term for adultery, which Matthew would surely have used, if this is what he meant. Or it may refer to marriages contracted within the forbidden degrees — *porneia* can have this meaning, as J. Fitzmyer has shown (in *TS* 37 [1976] 197-226). But in that case, "except on the ground of *porneia*" would represent

only an apparent exception, since the marriages referred to would not have been real marriages from the start in the eyes of Matthew's community. — The "consensus" view of Catholic exegetes, as reported by Donahue in the text, appears to be over-confident about the usefulness of exegetical findings for the solution of pastoral problems today.

27. This interpretation has patristic support (Chrysostom, Ambrose) and that of the majority of Catholic exegetes. It is rejected by, e.g., P. Dulau, "The Pauline Privilege," *CBQ* 13 (1951) 146-152; Dungan, *op. cit.,* pp. 96f. (contested by Murphy-O'Connor, *op. cit.,* pp. 157f.). The view that Jesus' divorce sayings were never intended as realistic norms of conduct but as eschatological challenges or statements of the ideal for the eschatological future (e.g., Curran, *op. cit.,* p. 41; Donahue, *art. cit.,* p. 114) might explain why, on this interpretation, Paul felt free to depart from them. Against this view, however, is the fact that the New Testament itself (even Matthew and Paul) perceives Jesus' saying as pertaining to the regulation of practice in the community.

28. Cf. Dulau, *art. cit.;* Dungan, *op. cit.,* pp. 95ff. For Murphy-O'Connor, Paul does not need to mention remarriage, because the right of remarriage was "the necessary and automatic consequence of divorce" (*RB* 89, p. 295), and it would be anachronistic to suppose that Paul knew of the distinction between "separation" and "divorce," i.e. separation with the right to remarry. Many think that Paul applies this distinction in v. 11. See next note.

29. For Murphy-O'Connor, Paul's instruction for the woman to remain unmarried or be reconciled with her husband is not meant as a general rule but has to do with a specific incident at Corinth involving a wife who is in the process of being (has already been?) divorced by an over-ascetic husband for demanding her marriage rights: Paul tells her not to accept the divorce, and to remain unmarried in the hope that the misguided husband will undergo a change of heart ("The Divorced Woman in 1 Cor. 7:10-11", *JBL* 100 [1981] 601-606). This construction would explain some peculiarities in the context; but it remains pure construction, involves some difficult linguistic claims and fails to explain why Paul, who knows that it is the *husband* who is misguided, commands the *wife* to be reconciled, and has nothing to say to the husband other than that he must not do what, Paul thinks, he may have already done. All this seems a rather tortuous way of removing from the text the suggestion that Paul envisaged separation with no right to remarriage.

30. Murphy-O'Connor argues that "is not in a state of enslavement" is a natural expression for declaring the spouses free to remarry, "because in Jewish law a writ of divorce and a writ of emancipation of a bond-woman are viewed as parallel (Git. 9:3)" (*RB* 89, p. 295). The text cited suggests a parallelism between the divorce of a *wife* and the emancipation of a bond-woman. This parallelism would not extend to a *husband*, whose position in marriage could not be described as bondage. In 1 Cor 7:15 it is the husband, as well as the wife, who is said not to be in a "state of enslavement."

31. In v. 15 the verb used can have the general sense of to "depart," or "desert" (cf. Phlm 15, of a slave). Its use as a technical term for divorce is also attested (though not in the New Testament). If that is its meaning here, it is odd that Paul does not use it in vv. 12 and 13, where he tells the Christian partner not to initiate a divorce (which, on this view, is what the unbelieving partner is doing in v. 15).

32. *Contra* Murphy-O'Connor, *RB* 89, p. 296.

33. "The Absoluteness of Moral Terms," *Greg.* 52 (1971) 415-417.

34. Cf. Blank, *art. cit.,* p. 10; Curran, *op. cit.,* p. 32; pp. 37f.; Fuchs, *art. cit.,* pp. 419-422. Paul's injunctions regarding women to a large extent reflect the status and role of women in his own time and culture. He makes no ideological protest against the institution of slavery. His angry denunciation of homosexual conduct is at least partly determined by his formation in Judaism. Some of his attitudes towards marriage (1 Cor 7) are conditioned, partly by the mixed-up ideas of the community to which he was writing, and partly by his eschatological convictions, which cannot be meaningful to us except through a process of radical re-interpretation. It is this eschatological view-point of Paul (and of the New Testament writers in general) which excludes the whole area of social and political concern, which in our day has become one of the crucial areas of ethical discussion.

35. Cf. Fuchs, *art. cit.,* pp. 97ff.; J. Gustafson, *Theology and Christian Ethics,* Philadelphia, 1974, pp. 121-145; E. Hamel, "L'Ecriture âme de la théologie morale?", *Greg.* 54 (1973) 417-445.

Chapter 9

The Basis for Certain Key Exceptionless Moral Norms in Contemporary Catholic Thought

The Reverend John R. Connery, S.J., S.T.D.

No one needs to be introduced to the current controversy over absolute moral norms. Over the past fifteen or more years it has occupied the attention of moral theologians and taken a prominent place in theological journals. But before discussing the controversy itself, it will be helpful to separate what is not controversial from that which is disputed.

No one argues that it is sometimes permitted to violate a virtue such as charity, or justice, or temperance. In medieval times, particularly, moral treatises were built around the virtues, and it was considered morally wrong to violate them.[1] So injustice, intemperance and other violations of the virtues were considered morally wrong and the norms prohibiting them were exceptionless. The axiom "one may not do evil in order that good may result"

(Rom 3:8) applied to these violations and no expected good would justify them. So any norm forbidding injustice, intemperance, etc., was exceptionless or absolute.

In the first millenium the Fathers spoke of what they called capital "sins", such as pride, covetousness, lust, anger, etc., and these were also considered to be always wrong.[2] Neither pride, nor covetousness, nor lust, nor any of these inordinate movements were ever permitted. Immorality was built right into the concept of the capital sins. The Fathers indeed allowed a legitimate kind of pride, a legitimate kind of anger, etc., but as defined the capital sins involved "inordinate" pride, etc. It was because they were "inordinate" that they were sinful. And as long as they were inordinate they would continue to be sinful without exception. Again, any norm forbidding these acts would be exceptionless, and no one denied this.

In a sense these two approaches were looking at different sides of the same coin. On examination one would even find overlapping.[3] Lust was a violation of chastity. Gluttony would be identified with intemperance regarding food, etc. So, although some spoke from a structure of virtue and others from that of vice or sin, Fathers and theologians of the past were speaking of the same acts and were in agreement, at least in regard to the absolute character of the norms prohibiting these acts.

As already pointed out, Catholic theologians who deny absolutes today do not question the absoluteness of norms forbidding injustice, intemperance, lust, inordinate anger, etc. These constitute moral evil, and this is never permitted. On the other hand, they would say, and rightly so, that such norms are not very helpful. Unless one can identify a specific act as unjust, or gluttonous, these norms cannot be very helpful in judging them. The concern of these theologians is with these specific acts. Thus they are concerned about acts such as adultery, intentional killing of an innocent person, abortion, contraception, etc. And they hold that norms dealing with these acts cannot be absolute, or exceptionless, at least on the theoretical level. They are able to take this position because they hold that these acts do not constitute moral evil in themselves, but only what they call ontic or premoral evil.[4]

183

Intrinsic and Extrinsic Evil

Norms can be absolute only if the acts which they proscribe are always morally wrong. How does one arrive at such a judgment of specific acts? This judgment is often related to a distinction between intrinsic and extrinsic evil. If moral evil is intrinsic to an act, it is assumed that it is always wrong. Unfortunately, the distinction between intrinsic and extrinsic evil has been understood in different senses. In one sense an act was considered intrinsically evil if it was prohibited because it was already evil. It was extrinsically evil if it became evil because it was prohibited. The Nominalist controversy centered around this understanding of the distinction . The Nominalists held that nothing was intrinsically evil, but everything was evil only because it was prohibited by God's law. Moral theologians generally never accepted this position. While they admitted that certain things became wrong because they were forbidden, e.g., driving on the left side of the street, they always maintained that some things were morally evil prior to prohibition. It is not easy to speak of priority in relation to Divine Law, but even on this level it has meaning in the sense that evil is not the result of the will of the legislator but the reason behind it.

The other understanding of the distinction is more relevant to the present controversy. According to this understanding an act can be intrinsically evil in the moral sense by reason of its moral object. If so, no additional circumstance or good end will justify it. Thus, intentional killing of an innocent person is intrinsically evil, and no circumstance or good intention will justify it. Similarly, sexual relations outside of marriage are intrinsically evil, and no circumstance or good intention will change this.

It is moral evil which is intrinsic in the latter sense that is the basis for exceptionless moral norms. Since this kind of evil will always be in acts like killing the innocent, norms dealing with them are considered exceptionless or absolute. Teleologists who deny exceptionless moral norms regarding the acts in question, do so because they do not admit that these acts involve intrinsic *moral* evil. They do not deny that such things as adultery, killing an innocent person, etc., are intrinsically evil, but the evil is only ontic or premoral. So, although they admit intrinsic evil, it is only ontic or premoral evil. This evil becomes moral in their thinking only when it is not balanced by a proportionate good. These theologians

184

can, of course, still hold that moral evil is intrinsic in the sense that it is in the act and antecedent to law. But it is not intrinsic in the sense that it can be in the act apart from a comprehensive assessment of all the circumstances of the act as well as the intention behind it. So the term *intrinsic evil* can be ambiguous.

Also, even when the term intrinsic evil is used in the traditional sense, it may not designate absolute evil. Thus when it is said that contraception or sterilization are intrinsically evil, the statement is made within a certain context. In a sense, contraception or sterilization are analogous to killing. One cannot make a moral judgment about them. To make such a judgment, one has to know more about them. Thus, contraception as defense against rape (like killing in self-defense) may be perfectly moral. Similarly, penal sterilization is arguably permissible from a moral viewpoint. What is intrinsically evil is contraception apart from these circumstances (like killing the innocent).

The distinction between intrinsic and extrinsic evil is certainly a valid one, but considering the ambiguity pointed out above in the use of the distinction, it would be preferable to avoid it. The issue is not so much one of *intrinsic* evil as it is one of *moral* evil. As shown above, teleologists admit intrinsic evil, but do not admit that it is moral evil in the traditional sense. The key question is whether such acts as masturbation, abortion, fornication, etc., can be designated moral evil. If they can, even teleologists would admit that they are absolute, i.e., no proportionate reason will make them legitimate. It is because they do not admit that they are morally wrong (but only ontic evil) that they do not consider norms governing them exceptionless.

Teleologists could indeed set up absolute or exceptionless norms. Thus they might set up a norm like the following: killing an innocent person is morally wrong unless one has a proportionate reason. By adding the qualifying clause, they make the norm exceptionless. Since no one would want to argue that killing an innocent person could be justified without a proportionate reason, the norm would be absolute. But this is not what is meant by an exceptionless norm. It is rather a norm which is considered exceptionless apart from any consideration of proportionate reasons. Thus, the norm that prohibits deliberate killing of an innocent person is exceptionless. Regarding these norms it would seem that the basic difference between traditional moral theologians and teleologists is their stance toward what constitutes moral evil.

Basis of Moral Evil

The question then comes down to this. What is the basis for the position that killing an innocent person, or fornication, or adultery constitute moral evil, so that they are always wrong and will not allow for exception . . . or perhaps more pointedly, so that they will not yield to proportionate, and so, justifying, reason? Do we have to identify them with acts accepted as morally evil, e.g., injustice, lust, etc.? Thus do we have to identify killing an innocent person as an injustice before we can judge it morally wrong?

This might be a way of proceeding, but I do not think that we generally follow this procedure. Specific classification of this kind usually comes after we identify something as immoral. It may be difficult to discern precisely how we arrive at judgments about the morality of specific acts. Indeed there may be different approaches. Appeal may be made to some metaethical norm, e.g., a natural law (human nature) norm, or a personalist norm, or a right reason norm. But I am not sure that we have to identify any particular approach, since I do not think this is where the problem exists. Whatever the method may be, teleologists may well have recourse to the same method. The difference between them and traditional moralists will be that for them the methodology will lead only to ontic evil. Traditional moralists have claimed that it leads to judgments of moral evil, and on this basis they have judged masturbation, killing the innocent, abortion, etc., immoral acts. To teleologists these acts in themselves remain only ontic evil.

There may be other differences between individual teleologists and traditional moral theology, but this is the basic difference. What traditional theologians consider moral evil teleologists claim to be ontic evil. They admit that ontic evil will always remain such. In other words, if one wishes to use the term, they admit that ontic evil is intrinsic. Thus it can be present in an act antecedent to the will of any legislator and antecedent to any comprehensive calculus of intention and circumstances. Put briefly, teleologists will say the same thing in this respect about ontic evil that traditional moralists say about moral evil.

186

They would even concede that many of the norms dealing with these acts are exceptionless on a practical level. The acts they prohibit will always be wrong. Even though a proportionate reason would justify them, in practice no proportionate reason will be present. On the practical level, therefore, the moral judgments of the teleologist may not differ from those of the traditional moralist. Only the reason for the judgment will differ. For the traditional moralist the act will be judged immoral in itself. For the teleologist the moral judgment will be based on the presence or absence of a proportionate reason. The consequence is that since these acts cannot be judged immoral in themselves, the norms governing them cannot be considered moral norms. In other words, since to the teleologist the acts constitute only ontic evil, the norms covering them cannot even be considered morally binding in themselves. Much less can they be considered exceptionless.

As pointed out, it has been traditional to consider certain concrete acts immoral. This is reflected in our standard secondary norms. They have been accepted as moral norms because the acts they prohibit have been judged morally wrong. This was why they were prohibited. Thus, the Ten Commandments have generally been accepted throughout history as moral norms. The burden of proof, then, should be on the side of those who want to hold otherwise. So the question of concern is: How do teleologists justify the kind of reductionism their methodology involves? In other words, how do they argue that acts like adultery and killing an innocent person, which have always been considered morally evil, constitute nothing more than ontic evil?

Ontic Evil

Teleologists argue that there is and always has been ontic evil. The word may be new, but it has always been admitted that there are physical evils which may not be in themselves moral evil. So they argue, for instance, that killing and mutilation have always been considered physical (ontic) evils. One could not make a moral judgment about them unless he knew the intention behind them and all the attendant circumstances. It was only with this additional information that he could judge them right or wrong, moral or immoral.

187

It is quite true that traditional moralists have always admitted physical evil. Thus, being killed by a tornado was considered a physical evil. There was no human agency involved, so it would remain physical evil even in the concrete; it could not become moral evil. Can the same be said of the killing of one human being by another human being? Since there is human agency here, there is a difference. Such killing can be considered physical (better premoral) evil only in the abstract. One cannot make a moral judgment about killing as such. But this has been true of many abstractions in traditional morality. Thus, one could not make a moral judgment about sexual intercourse in the abstract. But in the concrete, given the human agency, these acts must become moral or immoral. Teleologists as well as traditional theologians admit this. The critical question is: How do they become moral or immoral?

In traditional morality, if the killing was in self-defense, it was judged moral; if it was killing of an innocent person, it was immoral. Similarly, sexual intercourse engaged in by spouses was moral; if it was engaged in outside of marriage, it was immoral. Even in the abstract, given this additional information, deliberate killing of the innocent was judged immoral by the traditional theologian, and so was adultery. No further information was needed, and no further information would make a difference. These acts remain morally wrong whatever the further intention of the agent or additional circumstance. Briefly, while traditional theologians admitted they could not make a moral judgment about certain insufficiently defined abstractions, even though they might be classified as physical evil, they also held that with further definition, even if not comprehensive, they could make such judgments.

Teleologists argue that all of these acts are in the same category as killing as such. One cannot judge them morally good or morally bad in themselves even with the added information. And this is true both in the abstract and the concrete. One simply cannot make a moral judgment about them unless one calculates all the good and all the evil connected with them in a concrete act. It is only after balancing all this that one can make a moral judgment. Apart from this, the most one can say is that they constitute physical or premoral or ontic evil. Even if they violate whatever basic norm one follows, whether it be natural law (human nature), the human person or right reason, they remain ontic evil. Whatever may be said about this approach, it should be clear from our discussion thus far that it is a definite departure from the morality of the past.

Elements of the Moral Act

Moral theologians have indeed always held that all the elements of an act can have a moral dimension and that the total morality of the act must include all of these elements. And they have held that for an act to be morally good in the full sense, all of the elements must be morally good. Thus even self-defense could become immoral by reason of some other circumstance of the act. This was epitomized in the axiom *"bonum ex integra causa,"* an act is good only if all its parts are good.

More relevant to our discussion is the fact that traditionally moral theologians have also held that an act can be morally evil by reason of a single dimension, e.g., an immoral object or an immoral intention, etc. This was summarized in the other part of the above axiom *"malum ex quolibet defectu,"* an act can be morally evil by reason of a single defective part. And if it is, no other good, however proportionate, will make it morally good. It might change its immorality in some way, but it would not make it moral. Thus some circumstance might mitigate the evil of adultery, but it would not justify it. Teleologists introduce a radical qualification into this part of the axiom. Although they admit that intending an evil end can make an otherwise good act immoral, they deny that intending an evil object (means) like adultery, will make an act immoral apart from the end or other circumstances of the act. In itself it is only ontic evil.

Those who argue in this way against traditional morality say that it is inconsistent to claim killing is only ontic evil but killing an innocent person is moral evil. As a result, they do not understand how one can say that a proportionate reason will justify killing but will not justify killing an innocent person. So they do not consider a norm prohibiting the latter absolute or exceptionless. The key difference between teleologists and traditionalists is that the latter have always seen a difference between killing and killing an innocent person. To them, intentional killing of an innocent person was morally wrong. This judgment was based on the innocence of the victim. Given this additional circumstance, killing was no longer just ontic evil.

The difference becomes sharper when we look at the morality of sexual intercourse. It is quite clear that one cannot make a moral judgment about sexual intercourse *sine addito*. But it seems just as clear that one can make a moral judgment about extra-marital intercourse. Although their approaches may differ, traditional theologians are in agreement that the added information makes moral judgment possible.

And since one can make a moral judgment about these acts, the axiom "the end does not justify the means," which pertains to moral evil, applies to them. This means that no good intention will justify them. And the same is true of any other circumstance. So the norms prohibiting these acts are prohibiting moral evil. They are therefore exceptionless.

This is also the assumption underlying Church moral teaching. It teaches that the acts we have been discussing are morally wrong. It follows that no further good end or other circumstance will justify these acts. So the norms reflecting this teaching, since they are moral norms, are also exceptionless. Thus, the Church teaches that adultery is morally wrong. The precept, "Thou shalt not commit adultery," is, therefore, absolute or exceptionless.

Since no one is omniscient, a traditionalist may be perfectly willing to admit that his concepts or definitions (and therefore his norms) may be open to further refinement. Such refinement might even lead to a more inclusive norm. In the question of killing, for instance, the exception made for capital punishment seems to be losing its appeal, at least in practice. Since World War II, also, it is hard to see how offensive warfare can be justified (as it was formerly). On the other hand, further refinement could possibly lead to the conclusion that some particular act should not be considered killing of an innocent person. This has happened, for instance, in regard to abortion. Knowledge of viability made it clear that removal of a fetus after a certain time could not be considered killing the innocent. Similarly, new knowledge about the pathological condition of the fallopian tube made it clear that solving the problem of an ectopic pregnancy need not involve direct abortion. Certainly, the traditional theologian will need a sufficient (proportionate) reason for making such a refinement, but I do not think one can rule out this possibility in all cases.

All this may cause one to ask what the difference is between the traditional theologian and the teleologist. The difference would seem to be this. When the traditional theologian refines his concept of some moral evil, he is saying basically that some particular act should no longer be included in the category judged immoral. The moral norm, then, does not apply to it. But it is not an exception to the norm. The theologian is not saying, e.g., that one may commit adultery with a proportionate reason. All adultery is still wrong. The norm does not apply to a particular act because there is solid reason for not considering it adultery. It is not at all being suggested that this might happen. We are merely fantasizing here to show the difference between the teleologist and the traditional theologian. Another point of difference is that the traditional theologian will still be able to make a moral judgment about the refined definition. What it condemns will be immoral, and the norm governing it will be absolute. The teleologist, no matter how he refines his definition, will have to consider the act defined as nothing more than ontic evil. He will never arrive at moral evil by redefinition.

Conclusion

In summary, then, the question of exceptionless moral norms is focused on acts like killing an innocent person, adultery, masturbation, etc. Norms prohibiting injustice, lust, gluttony, etc., are admittedly exceptionless. Sometimes the term *intrinsic evil* is used of the acts in question. Because of its ambiguity, it is preferable to avoid it. But if it is used, the precise sense in which it is being used should be made clear. What is basic is the judgment that these acts as defined are immoral. Theologians may use different metaethical norms to undergird these moral judgments. But since they do conclude that the acts in question are immoral, the axiom "the end does not justify the means" applies to them. So no good end will justify them. And this is true of any other circumstance. Norms prohibiting such acts are therefore exceptionless. This understanding has been traditional, and has been the basis for moral teaching and preaching in the whole Christian era. The burden of proof, therefore, is upon those who would deny that these acts are immoral and that the norms dealing with them are exceptionless.

Holding the traditional position does not mean a locked-in morality regarding these acts. Traditional theologians can admit that their definition of them may be open to further refinement. As redefined, they may be less inclusive. But the acts excluded cannot be reduced to exceptions. Also, the redefined acts will still be judged immoral and the norms governing them exceptionless. Put simply, traditional theologians hold that they can make moral judgments about these acts, and therefore establish exceptionless norms in their regard. Teleologists deny the possibility of such moral judgments, and hence the possibility of exceptionless norms based on them.

Notes

1. The classic model for this approach is the *Summa Theologiae,* II, II, of St. Thomas Aquinas.

2. This classification is found in the *Moralia* of St. Gregory the Great, XXXI, cap. 45, n. 87 (PL 76:620D). Although commonly referred to as capital sins, they are rather vices, or sources of sin.

3. St. Thomas takes a look at the capital vices in his *Summa,* I, II, q. 84.

4. The literature on this topic is so vast it would be impossible to name it all here. One of the basic works is that of Joseph Fuchs, "The Absoluteness of Moral Terms," *Gregorionum,* 52 (1971). Several of the more important articles are published in *Reading Moral Theology, No. 1.,* edited by Charles E. Curran and Richard A. McCormick, S. J., (New York: Paulist Press, 1979).

Chapter 10

Pastoral Concerns Regarding Exceptionless Moral Norms

Part I — Discussion With Doctor Cahill

Bishop: Do the proportionalists permit abortion in some instances?

Dr. Cahill: At whatever time the fetus has the value of an individual human being, whether from conception or from the time of implantation, then only the mother's life as a value equal to the life of the fetus would be permitted to justify an abortion. What this boils down to is allowing direct abortion if the mother's life is at stake rather than simply indirect abortion as the tradition has allowed, while maintaining the equivalence of the value of the fetus and the value of the mother, consistently with the tradition.

Bishop: Does the revisionist methodology presuppose a level of intelligence, education and maturity which makes it pastorally problematic for catechetical use with children, many adolescents, and perhaps even some adults?

Dr. Cahill: First of all, I would acknowledge that this is a difficulty and it's one that was raised by Father John Connery in *Theological Studies.* My response is that adequate morality does not necessarily equal simple morality. Even the moral situations and relationships of those who are young or not well educated or even not very intelligent are not for those reasons made simple. So I think our moral norms and our moral instruction will only be adequate if they are indeed adequate to the experience of people to whom they are promulgated. A proportionalist would say that the honest way really to deal with morality is to acknowledge what ambiguity there is, rather than trying to over-simplify it.

Now what education would come down to is not, first of all, trying to look for exceptional instances, but rather affirming the basic values which are not really changing. These are the value of human life; the value of marital intercourse in its natural setting; the value of sex as an interpersonal expression, which would avoid masturbation; and those sorts of things. One should not immediately deal with the borderline situation in moral education, but instill the fundamental values that are then the basis on which the individual can look at a more complicated situation perhaps a little bit later. So I think we should deal first of all with primary moral dispositions, not forming our morality primarily in the context of rare conflicts.

Bishop: How do you move the act from the column intrinsically evil to ontic evil? You did so, but how do you justify that move?

Dr. Cahill: Why have some of the acts traditionally described as intrinsically evil been moved to this category of ontic evil? I would say that the major reason is that it has been perceived that in the category of intrinsic evil in the tradition there are different kinds of acts included. The category includes both masturbation and acts like blasphemy or perjury or murder. So the first thing we need to do is clarify what it is that we're talking about when we say an act is intrinsically evil. The revisionists would think that, if the "intrinsically evil" act is one that is defined with circumstances, then they don't have that much problem with the description "intrinsic evil." They don't have any problem saying murder is intrinsically evil, but there is an open question on what type of killing counts as murder;

some killing does and some killing doesn't.

What they object to is including in that category of intrinsic evil an act which is defined without reference to any circumstances. An example is aborting a fetus, because they would say that that act then is precluded without any consideration whether the mother's life is at stake or not. Actually, abortion isn't that frequently given as an example, probably because it's so inflammatory and controversial and proportionalists don't want to sound like they're advocating abortion when they really are not. On abortion, most have a position very close to that of the traditional Church. But on contraception, for example, many are advocating a different position. If you just take the act of contracepting artificially, they're willing to admit that that should be avoided and that it's negative. But also they're saying there are some situations in which that act is tolerable. The reason would be another value that's even greater than the value of natural unobstructed intercourse. They're not denying the value of natural intercourse, but they're saying that there might be something even more important at stake.

So proportionalists say that, if it's conceivable that there could be something more important at stake, then you can't call that act intrinsically morally evil. Instead they call it evil in a different sense. It is evil in the sense that it is a negative factor in the evaluation of the total picture, but they won't decide whether that act is a sin until they see that total picture. So they call it ontic evil or premoral evil, meaning evil in the sense that precedes the moral evaluation. It is evil in the sense that it is not yet a sin, it is evil in the sense of something that we want to avoid, but we can't say that in the end, the "bottom line" is: "Always avoid it." That then would be the explanation of how some of these things are taken from the category of intrinsic evil to the category of ontic evil. Not everything that's always been called an intrinsically evil act is moved, because some of those things like murder, perjury, and blasphemy or even adultery include circumstances. They are not really descriptions of physical acts *per se*. Now, just as a footnote, we still have a problem with defining what is the physical act and what is the circumstance. How far do you have to break an action down before you have a pure physical act? That's where the problem area is.

Bishop: Could you explain how to distinguish between utilitarianism, situation ethics and proportionalism?

Dr. Cahill: Situation ethics and utilitarianism are generally the same thing, although there could be some people who might be called situation ethicists in a broader sense and wouldn't be utilitarians. Such ethicists may simply want to attend to the situation as important and that's not necessarily the same as utilitarianism, and it could be the same as proportionalism. But the term situation ethics generally has utilitarian overtones.

Utilitarianism is a moral theory that began with John Stuart Mill and Jeremy Bentham. They took the position that the right act is simply the act that promotes the greatest good for the greatest number. Theirs was a heavily consequence-oriented theory. But they didn't mean "consequence" in the way that Aristotle or Aquinas did when they asked whether an act contributes to the final goal of humanity or to union with God as the common good of humanity. This is also a consequence of that act in the broader sense. Bentham and Mill meant more immediate consequences. They said any act is justified as long as it has good consequences outweighing bad consequences and those good consequences are enjoyed by the majority rather than the minority. An outcome of their position was that the intrinsic dignity of the minority or the rights of a minority group could be overridden for the welfare of the majority. Now that's something that the proportionalists would not agree with.

The proportionalists come more out of the Thomistic tradition, although there's a lot of disagreement about the extent to which they really are Thomistic and about what changes they are making in the system of Thomas. Since, with Thomas, the proportionalists do share a commitment to valuing the individual person and valuing the relation of that person to God, they set limits on the way persons can be treated. The difference between the proportionalists and the tradition is that for the proportionalists those absolutely wrong violations of the dignity of the person are not tied to physical acts, they're tied to moral values or moral relationships. Proportionalists might say it's absolutely wrong to lead another person into sin or to treat a person unjustly or dishonestly or to act in an unloving way, but they aren't willing to take the next step and say that that unlovingness can be definitively and absolutely and always embodied in a certain sort of physical act. They are not utilitarians because they still are very much concerned with the ultimate destiny of the person, the nature of the person, and the inviolability of the person in a way that a utilitarian would not be. I have oversimplified utilitarianism but those are the basic differences.

Bishop: Within the proportionalist theory what weight would be given to upholding the *Communio* of the teaching Church and to avoiding public dissent?

Dr. Cahill: I realize how tough a job a bishop has! The reason that the bishop's job is so much tougher, in a way, than that of the theologian is that the bishop is a public figure and addresses a much broader audience in the Church. The theologian is a public figure among other theologians, but we discuss and examine and refine our theories in journals and at academic conferences, which is a different context. A bishop has to think twice before he makes any public statement or expresses in a public way any misgivings with regard to the Church's teaching or any openness to revisions. If he did, that would be communicated broadly and misinterpreted broadly, I'm sure. But you have raised the question of the fact that public dissent creates some friction and factionalism and lack of unity in the body of the faithful. That can be regarded as an evil to be avoided, while a greater good than dissent for the sake of dissent is the *Communio* and respect for the authentic teaching authority of the Church.

Proportionalists would reply that the *Communio* is not best served by simply squelching all dissenting opinions but that, in fact, a spirit of dialogue and discussion that is irenic and ecumenical really preserves the sense of the *Communio* and the credibility of the teaching authority of the Church. When all dissent on an issue like contraception or *Humanae Vitae* is simply squashed, then for large segments of the people in the Catholic Church, *Humanae Vitae* simply becomes incredible and is rejected and minds are closed. I have seen this with the young Catholics that I teach at Boston College in the 18 to 22 year old group. The Church becomes laughable to them when it maintains traditional teachings in an aura of exclusion of discussion. Of course, the objective is not simply to reject teachings at will or on a whim. The major obligation of the theologian is first to look for the positive insights in a teaching, and to see how far these do represent the faith and not to presume that one will immediately dissent. Hence I think open discussion really enhances the credibility of the Church and a sense of real community.

Bishop: We'd like to pose for Dr. Cahill an exceptionless moral norm not taken from the area of sexual ethics, but from the recent pastoral letter on war and peace, that is, the absolute prohibition against intending to or actually killing people indiscriminately in warfare. Do you think President Truman's decision to bomb Japanese cities for the great good of ending the war could have been a proportionalist's decision instead of a utilitarian one?

Dr. Cahill: In my opinion the bishops' pastoral letter, "The Challenge of Peace," is a good example of a teaching which allows for dissent in a very positive way, and does not categorize all dissent as simple rejection. The teaching was formulated in a collegial context which allowed for the expression of different points of view and was presented in a way which allowed for responses from different people and discussion of those conclusions. I think that that is a very helpful manner in which to teach the faithful and one which is productive. Hopefully we can look for it on other issues as well.

Now on the specific question of the absolute prohibition of indiscriminate killing in warfare, we take this as an absolute moral norm in our tradition. The inviolability of non-combatants has been seen as a moral absolute. I don't think that the proportionalists would reject that because that is not a physical act described in the abstract; killing is the physical act in the abstract. As soon as you speak of killing the innocent you've already got a circumstance. You certainly have a circumstance if you say, killing of the innocent in warfare to bring about the end of the war sooner.

The difficulty is with the kinds of reasons you're going

to give for the killing. If you are a utilitarian, you might argue either that killing non-combatants in warfare would be justified because it would save more lives in the long run, or, on the other hand, you can even make a utilitarian argument that killing non-combatants in warfare is not justified because in the long run it would lead to a disrespect for human life. However, the natural law tradition, and here I think the proportionalists would agree, would say that the lives of those individual persons are of inviolable value and would not be susceptible of violation for that reason, in as much as they're innocent and the reason for killing them is to win the war. It does not seem to me that a proportionalist would accept that decision of Truman.

Bishop: But Truman might have been a proportionalist, that is, he might have made his decision with regard to dropping bombs on Hiroshima and Nagasaki out of proportionalist concerns. He may have felt that the good to be achieved was proportionally greater than the evil to result from the dropping of the bombs.

Dr. Cahill: That's a proportionalist argument in that it uses the argument of proportion, but it's also really a utilitarian argument because it's balancing the lives of the majority against those of the minority.

Bishop: Have we adequately clarified the distinction between utilitarianism and proportionalism?

Dr. Cahill: I think that's a legitimate concern. Father Richard McCormick got himself into trouble in a lecture that he gave in 1972 at Marquette University which was then published and called *Ambiguity in Moral Choice*. He used exactly this example and said that proportionalism would not allow that bombing because the value of life would be harmed in the long run. He made a utilitarian argument which he later retracted, saying that the reason with which he supported his conclusion was not the best. But exactly why he wouldn't allow the bombing is something that he still hasn't explained as clearly as he might. But I think it has to be said that he would definitely not allow such killing.

Bishop: Dr. Cahill, what are the absolutes that are not universal and how can they be confined to cultural norms?

Dr. Cahill: First of all, if I were to make a statement that a norm might represent an absolute obligation or prohibit an act in one culture and not in another, it would be because there are objective reasons in a certain culture for that norm which don't exist in another culture. I came up with two examples. One would be the example of polygamy. We can think of polygamy in the Israelite community of Old Testament times and then today in some areas of the world where polygamy is still practiced. Certain historical situations might exist where there are more women than men and where women don't have independent means of support or independent roles in society so that, if they're not incorporated into a family, they really have no means of subsistence and almost no identity. Also, in certain communities procreation might have very high importance. This would be more important in the Israelite community than in any community in the modern world, but we can think historically of communities where procreating the race and creating as many offspring as possible is very important to the survival of that community. So among the Old Testament Jews we would consider both the fact that women needed to be married in order to have a role and also the need of the community to procreate, and we might say that there were objective reasons in that community which justified polygamy and might not justify it in modern Western Christianity.

Another example I thought of was capital punishment. There's been a lot of writing and speaking today in the Catholic Church against capital punishment and yet, if we go to the *Summa*, St. Thomas justifies capital punishment. It seems to me that what is at stake there is the social circumstance in which one would decide that killing a capital offender was a necessary means to protect the common good. Today we can question whether that's really necessary because there are other ways of dealing with offenders and removing them from their position of endangering other members of the society. In medieval times, without the prison systems that we have (granted, those have considerable problems), there were really no effective ways of permanently removing a person from the endangering role that he or she might have had in regard to others except to kill that person. So the reasons for capital punishment were more persuasive in other sorts of societies. They are more persuasive today in extreme or boundary situations, in a time of war, for example, where executions might be carried out in a situation where that's necessary, when it isn't in peace time in normal society.

Bishop: Dr. Cahill, we'd like to go back to intrinsically evil acts. If proportionalists were convinced that intrinsically evil acts were evil *ex toto genere suo*, would this prohibit them from acting in these particular cases?

Dr. Cahill: If the act considered as a whole were intrinsically evil, and that includes the circumstances of the act, yes it would. Let me give you an example. Consider masturbation simply to pursue solitary sexual pleasure. Proportionalists would see that as an intrinsically evil act because it is a physical act plus immoral circumstances. That would prohibit their justifying that.

Bishop: The Church has proclaimed certain things intrinsically evil, regardless of circumstances. Would that prohibit the proportionalist from acting? I think one example would be abortion, taught by the Church as intrinsically evil *ex toto genere suo*.

Dr. Cahill: Proportionalists would not admit that a physical act, such as direct abortion, is always intrinsically evil. They would allow it if the value sacrificed, the life of the fetus, were equal to or less than that gained, the life of the mother. What they would allow is direct abortion in the case where the mother's life is at stake. They would not agree with Church teaching that physical acts defined without any circumstances are intrinsically evil.

Bishop: In evaluating your own presentation, it would be helpful to know your own position on this basic question, namely, is there such a thing as a physical act which is intrinsically evil?

Dr. Cahill: I thought this would have been obvious, but my basic sympathies are with the proportionalists on this issue. I do not disallow that there are legitimate questions and points of this theory that need to be refined. The reason I'm in sympathy with proportionalism is that I think it does make some sense to say that you can't really evaluate an act unless you know something of the circumstances. Now, if it's possible to define a physical act without any circumstances (and this includes some of the acts traditionally called intrinsically evil, but not all of them), I would agree that one cannot say those are ab-

solutely wrong with no exceptions whatsoever. I might be willing to say that they're generally to be avoided, of course, or
even that it might be very difficult to think of justifiable
circumstances.

Part II — Discussion With
Fathers Deidun and Connery

Bishop: Do teleologists support Magisterial teaching on morality?
Father Connery: In theory teleologists, if they followed their
method, would have to say that Church teaching is not exceptionless but open to proportionate reason. In practice, in the
area of contraception, for instance, many might make such exceptions. While admitting that contraception constituted ontic evil, they would hold that the use of contraceptives would
be allowed for proportionate reasons. They never get very
specific about what would constitute a proportionate reason.
In all probability, they would settle for responsible parenthood
and go no further.

Other theologians would see other Church teaching open
to exceptions. Recently two books on sexual morality were
published by priests adopting a teleological approach. Both
make several allowances for exceptions to Church teaching on
sex, e.g., in the area of homosexuality, masturbation, pre-marital
sex, and the indissolubility of marriage. But teleologists will
differ. What one considers a proportionate reason another may
deny. Some may even say in practice almost the same thing a
traditional theologian would say. While admitting that proportionate reasons would justify certain acts, they would hold that
where there is Church teaching, there are no proportionate
reasons in practice.

Bishop: Our question would be directed to Father Deidun. We
realize that there are several catalogues of sins given in St. Paul
about which Paul concludes that these sins exclude from the
kingdom of heaven. Are they seen in Paul's mind as simply
higher norms for the Christian community, are they referring
to acts or attitudes, do they perhaps not apply to the larger
community at all, or are they intrinsically evil, to use the term
we have been hearing and talking about?

Father Deidun: I think the most instructive fact in relation to your question is that Paul uses one of those catalogues precisely in Romans, Chapter 1, where he's not speaking about Christians, but about man without Christ. In the use of that catalogue what he intends to do is to demonstrate the fact that all men have sinned and are without excuse. So the answer to your question is that he considers these catalogues to be applicable not simply to the Christian community but to the whole of mankind.

If you then ask me whether his strictures as represented in the catalogue can be translated into some kind of absolute norm for us, I have to say what I have already said, that we simply do not find within the pages of Holy Scripture a hermeneutic which will enable us to distinguish between what is culturebound and what is not culturebound. That doesn't mean to say that I myself am necessarily skeptical about such values or non-values as are reflected in Paul's list. But we have to admit soberly that we cannot find from the pages of scripture a criterion by which to assess the permanent validity or otherwise of its moral teaching. We cannot say, for example, that a moral directive is permanently valid if it is theologically grounded. St. Paul will sometimes use theological motivations for a norm of behavior or a directive which *we* know to be culturebound. For example, in First Corinthians, Chapter 11, when he speaks about the subordination of woman to man, he uses what he considers to be significant theological motivations. He claims that man is the glory of God and woman is the glory of man. I take it that that hierarchy is no longer acceptable even by those who are not particularly sympathetic to the feminist movement. We hold it as certain that there is a substantial equality of the sexes, and there is no subordination of one to the other. Now that highlights the problem of our need for a hermeneutic. You simply cannot look for those norms in Paul which he seems to take with theological seriousness, and call those absolute i.e., permanently and universally valid. We do need a hermeneutic. It is the theologian, not the Bible scholar, who must provide this hermeneutic — or perhaps both working together.

Bishop: What is the specific difference between an exceptionless moral norm and an absolute?

Father Connery: I would use the words without distinction, I think they mean the same thing. One might be able to make some theoretical distinction, but *absolute* means to me that a norm is not open to exception and that is what exceptionless means.

Bishop: Who in a given situation determines if the reasons are sufficient or proportionate to keep ontic evil from becoming moral evil, or who determines the principles for deciding? If it's the individual person, don't we have wide-open situation ethics? If it's the teleologist or a group of them, don't we have the dissolution of the Magisterium or the forming of a new one?

Father Connery: I would agree that if the judgment of proportionate reason is left to the individual we end up with the equivalent of situation ethics. Actually, teleologists do not discuss the problem very much. In practice, they seem to demand the authority we used to call for in a probable opinion. If there was sufficient agreement about a particular proportionate reason, it would be accepted. And this would be true even where there was opposing Church teaching. The difference between teleologists and traditional theologians is that the latter could not accept probability against opposing Church teaching. Since the latter is certain, it would be contradictory to hold an opposing position as probable. The teleologist, of course, would also be a dissenter in this case.

Bishop: Our group has two questions directed to Father Deidun and they're both on marriage. The first one is, concerning the problems of biblical interpretation about marriage, wouldn't it be more important or practical to study the extent of the papal power of the keys since the Church does use those powers regarding the Pauline privilege, the Petrine privilege and the *ratum, non consummatum* marriage, and also due to the fact that the Sacred Penitentiary has dissolved marriages whose nullity cannot be proven in ecclesiastical courts? The second question is, what happened to the good conscience solutions, are they still existing?

Father Deidun: The first question is the only one really which I feel competent to comment on. I don't deny that the Church has the power of the keys. I'm not suggesting that the Church

204

is being unfaithful to Christ in using the Pauline privilege. I don't deny any of that, it is simply that as an exegete I cannot find in First Corinthians, Chapter 7, a sure basis for the Pauline privilege. The majority of Catholic scholars can, though I personally cannot.

You might say, aren't you rather schizophrenic, thinking one thing when you have your exegetical hat on, and another when you have your pastoral hat on? I don't think so, because the Church has never offered an authoritative interpretation of First Corinthians, Chapter 7. It is true that in medieval times, for example, in statements about the matrimonial practice of the Church, reference was made to the Pauline text, but it is perhaps significant that in *Casti Connubii* when reference is made to the Pauline privilege, that is to say, the matrimonial practice of the Roman Catholic Church, no allusion whatsoever is made to First Corinthians, Chapter 7. It never has been therefore authoritatively stated that we must read the text in this way.

You might say, then how is it that the Church can use the "Pauline privilege"? One of the ways in which I could explain it is that there is a developing understanding of the sacraments in the Church, there is a developing understanding of the Church's own power, but this deepening perception on the part of the Church does not depend on the exegesis of any *one* scriptural text.

So I do not intend in any sense to pose a challenge to the Magisterium, as if I were saying that its practice has no scriptural basis. The practice of the Church doesn't cause me problems of conscience, and certainly it does not cause me any exegetical problems with regard to First Corinthians, Chapter 7. The other question about the good conscience solution is not within my competence. Father Connery may wish to answer it.

Father Connery: I think the good conscience solution is still valid. Provision has always been made in the internal forum for people in good conscience, that is, for people doing wrong without realizing it. Such a person cannot be guilty. The question, of course, is whether a confessor should inform him or not. St. Alphonsus' solution was that informing the penitent would be the norm, but that there were situations in which it might not be advisable to do so. It would not be advisable, e.g., if informing him would not prevent the wrongdoing, but would only change good faith into bad. In that event, unless there was some other problem such as damage to a third party, one would not have to intervene. And even if there was damage to a third party, the confessor might not have to intervene unless he could prevent it.

Now as far as marriages are concerned, if a person thinks his marriage is valid and therefore goes on with it and lives as husband or wife, then there certainly is no culpability on that person's part. That has nothing to do, however, with the external forum. The fact that the person is in good conscience doesn't necessarily mean that the Church has to recognize the marriage or go along with it. Depending upon the situation, there might be a reason to intervene. On the other hand, there are cases where intervention would be useless and do more harm than good. In that case, I suppose prudence would call for non-intervention.

The American bishops some years ago said they were willing to allow a situation where there was certainty about the invalidity of the first marriage, although it couldn't be proved. If there was less than certainty, if it was just a case of doubt, then according to the Code the presumption would be in favor of the first marriage.

Bishop: Has the Magisterium taken a favorable position regarding the teleologists' method?

Father Connery: I don't know of any Magisterial statement about proportionalism as such. Some of the practical conclusions that proportionalists come to, at least some proportionalists, go against the teaching of the Church and to that extent the Church would be opposed to their conclusions. How they came to those conclusions, though, would be something that the Church probably might not be concerned about as such. So, at least as far as I know, there hasn't been any statement for or against proportionalism, although the Church is certainly opposed to the dissent that results from it.

Bishop: Father Connery said that proportionalists like to be called teleologists but we really find that confusing because the traditional approach was a teleological approach. It assumed that

206

by human reason we could participate in eternal law and read purpose in nature generally and in certain acts. The traditional approach is truly a teleological approach and the teleologists take that good name to themselves, but they're talking about the agent's purposes in an act and not what we might see written into nature. As pastors we feel that there are very probably bad fruits to the proportionalists' system, such as irresponsible sex leading to abortion, as well as subjectivity and confusion among many people about good and evil. Do the proportionalists admit such a problem?

Father Connery: I tend to agree with you regarding the name that they seem to prefer. As you say, they call themselves teleologists chiefly because they put the emphasis on the *finis operantis* rather than the *finis operis*, and they tend to underestimate or tone down the traditional role of the *finis operis* upon the morality of the act. I would tend to agree with you also for another reason: I think that it's not just the intention that they put the emphasis on, but all the circumstances of the act, and therefore it's not teleological in that sense. Basically their norm is simply that you have to have a balance of good over evil in the whole act.

Where that good is, whether it is in the intention, or the circumstances or the object does not make much difference, as long as it outweighs the evil. However, if the evil is in the intention, they will consider the act immoral, no matter how much good there is in the rest of the act. Recently, we were interviewing a man for our faculty who presented a paper on proportionalism. In regard to this point he brought up the example of a man who made a large benefaction to some cause but did it out of vainglory. The benefaction was in the amount of several million dollars. In comparison with the goodness in what he did the vainglory seemed somewhat trivial. The proportionalist judgment in the case seemed somewhat inconsistent. If the good was in the intention and outweighed the evil in the object, the proportionalist would have allowed the act. But he would not be willing to settle for good in an object that outbalanced the evil in the intention. There seems to be inconsistency here.

I find it unsatisfying to accept the opinion that what we

always thought was moral evil really wasn't, but was only on-tic evil. It seems that this shift tends to throw everything wide open, even though teleologists might in practice seek to set definite limits. In theory, at least, it seems to open up a whole new ball game. If you can define something as morally evil as we have done, then it's easy enough to deal with it in teaching and preaching and so forth. But if you can't define anything as morally evil, it's hard to teach specific morality. There is only one moral evil, doing (ontic) evil without a proportionate reason. To me this is a little simplistic.

Bishop: Is it appropriate for us to consider the teleological method to be a legitimate moral method to be taught in schools, even if we have to take exception to some conclusions of specific theologians?

Father Connery: I think it could be taught in schools if it were taught properly. Actually, it's being taught on the seminary level, the college level, the high school level. But I am afraid that when it's taught, it is not nuanced the way it should be. It is true that some of the more reputable teleologists would say that they do not feel that teleology should open the door to dissent against Church teaching. Many will take the position that, for the most part, the Church teaching does refer to moral evil, at least in this sense . . . that even though proportionate reasons might justify going against it, practically speaking, there are no such proportionate reasons. But the difficulty is that it is open to abuse, especially when it's not handled properly and when it is coupled with a lot of misunderstanding about the role of conscience and some kind of autonomy of cons-cience. Since proportionalism can be very dangerous, I would be very cautious about recommending it.

Bishop: We are a little confused about the meaning of the word teleology as it relates to proportionalism and to traditional theology. Does the real teleology come from the *finis operis* or the *finis operantis*? Secondly, many of us are not familiar with the word "ontic" from our own studies, would you give us a definition of that word?

Father Connery: The word teleology I find a little ambiguous, at least the way it is used by teleologists. They place the em-phasis on the *finis operantis* to the disadvantage of the *finis operis.* This does not mean that they do not consider other elements of the act. Their judgment is made on a calculus of the good and evil in the whole act. In that sense I don't know why the method deserves to be called teleological.

The word "ontic" was first used by Louis Janssens, a moral theologian who teaches at Louvain. He did not wish to use the term *physical evil* because he wanted to include more than just physical evil, e.g., psychological social evil. He used the word "ontic" because he thought it would be understood from its use in the word "ontology." I'm not sure that he wanted to identify ontic evil with metaphysical evil. But he wanted it to extend to more than just physical evil.

Bishop: Should not the Magisterium integrate more positively and explicitly into moral teaching how and what it means to live in relation with the person of the Risen Christ and to respond to His call to build the communion of the Church? Should we continue in the tradition that is tempted to emphasize casuistry and brinkmanship with which Christ himself was continually confronted by the Scribes and Pharisees?

Father Deidun: I fully concur with that. I think that is one of the main tasks that faces the Church, to integrate the whole field of ethical or moral teaching with the data of revelation, correctly interpreted

Father Connery: I think all of us want to see a kind of holistic approach to the Christian life which would include more than just "minimal" moral theology. As a matter of fact, Vatican II called for this. On the other hand, while this is desirable and certainly should be on the agenda, I don't think neglecting the minimal level of moral duty would be called for either. It seems to me that a purely ascetical approach to moral theology which said nothing about obligation might be just as deficient as saying nothing about the Risen Christ.

Part IV:
Applied Moral Theology

OVERVIEW
of PART IV

In applying moral norms to specific issues, Catholic moral theology traditionally has used principles like the principle of totality, the principle of double effect, and the principle of the moral inseparability of the unitive and procreative aspects of human sexual intercourse. Part IV of this volume examines these three principles in the light of contemporary scholarship and then adds a discussion of the theological and pastoral implications of natural family planning (NFP) which preserves the two inseparable aspects of conjugal intercourse. The final chapter contains dialogue between the five authors of these chapters and the bishops who raised questions from their table discussions.

Father John C. Gallagher, C.S.B., an Associate Professor of Theology at St. Michael College in Toronto, Canada, and the Director of the Cardinal Carter Center for Bioethics there, analyzes in

Chapter 11 the principle of totality with reference to man's stewardship of his body. He begins with a careful study of the medieval teaching of St. Thomas Aquinas, followed by twentieth century interpretations of this doctrine.

Subsequently, Father Gallagher reviews the teaching of Popes Pius XI and XII on totality in which they cautioned particularly about submitting individuals to the total good of society, a real danger in political totalitarianism. The author then reviews the development of a Catholic analysis of the transplants of organs from living donors. He finds that a consensus of approval has been reached with or without the principle of totality. He concludes with suggestions for further study of this principle.

In *Chapter 12,* Dr. Joseph M. Boyle Jr., Associate Professor of Philosophy at the Center for Thomistic Studies of the University of Houston, analyzes the principle of double effect. This principle is often attributed to J.P. Gury, S.J., about the year 1850, but has its roots in the *Summa* of St. Thomas Aquinas (II,II, Q. 64, a.7). Professor Boyle states and responds to two key objections to this principle, that it is a form of moral evasion and that it is based on a distinction without moral significance between what is intended and what is accepted as a side effect. He painstakingly argues to defend the moral significance of that distinction.

In the process he also indicates his objections to the methodology of proportionalism discussed above in Part III. He finds no genuine grounds for collapsing the four indispensable conditions for applying the principle of double effect into a calculation built on the fourth condition alone, proportionate reason. He offers an interpretation of the proper use of that condition which avoids any attempt at calculating comparative values and disvalues but simply considers morally relevant outcomes.

Father Thomas P. Doyle, O.P., the Secretary of the Apostolic Pronunciature in Washington, D.C., presents in *Chapter 13* a penetrating analysis of the unitive and procreative aspects of human sexual intercourse. He readily admits that people can have sexual intercourse which is neither unitive nor procreative, but "it is quite another matter for the re-direction of the purpose of intercourse to be socially or culturally accepted."

In a lengthy description of the nature of human sexuality, Father Doyle argues that only human beings are created by God with the

214

capacity of self-giving on a spiritual level communicated through the body in sexuality. At the center of this self-giving is the power to generate human life and the responsibility to nurture it. Removing the procreative or unitive potential from sexual intercourse corrupts the language and communication of sexual intercourse. Father Doyle also outlines the destructive impact on marriage as a covenant relationship and on society when the two aspects of sexual intercourse are deliberately separated as the contraceptive mentality has now separated them.

'In *Chapter 14,* two experts on natural family planning (NFP), Monsignor James T. McHugh, Director of the Diocesan Development Program for NFP in the U.S. and Gerard Brunelle, Director of Family-Action-Famille in Canada serving the dioceses of that nation, address theological and pastoral implications of NFP.

Monsignor McHugh points out, in reference to the previous chapter, that NFP preserves the inseparable connection between the two meanings, unitive and procreative, of conjugal love and sexual intercourse. That is, even though planning their family, the NFP couple never act against their procreative gift or remove its significance and potential from their conjugal intercourse. He outlines the Magisterial response to NFP as moving from toleration to acceptance to approval and, finally, to advocacy. He strongly urges that NFP be theologically based in the theology of marriage, conjugal love, and responsible parenthood, and that this value orientation always be integrated into the actual teaching of NFP.

Mr. Brunelle continues this reflection, insisting that NFP instruction must follow the pattern of sound pedagogy with clearly delineated content, objectives, strategies, resources, and evaluation. He emphasizes the value orientation accompanying the instruction to achieve affective as well as cognitive objectives. He highlights the critical importance of presenting this affirmative approach to NFP for teenagers, in seminaries and schools training religious educators, and for engaged couples.

Finally, in *Chapter 15,* the five authors of the previous chapters dialogue with the bishops. Father Gallagher responds to numerous practical questions about direct and indirect sterilization, isolation of a pathological uterus without removal, mutilation of the physical wholeness of the body for the psychological good of the person, the refusal to eat, and capital punishment. Dr. Boyle clarifies his discussion of the fourth condition for double effect. He also speculates about the suicidal intent of a person's refusal to eat and the ethical implications of intervention by powerful nations in the crises of Third World nations.

Father Doyle reaffirms the procreative aspect of NFP since the couples have not destroyed the procreative meaning of their action and remain open to parenthood. He emphasizes that the Church faces her greatest challenge today in the crisis of marriage and family life. Monsignor McHugh and Mr. Brunelle extend their theological and pastoral reflections on NFP, noting particularly the need to retain a positive theology of responsible parenthood lest the method become a form of "Catholic contraception." They report on their work in their respective countries and on current techniques and reliability studies of NFP.

The applications of Catholic moral teaching in this Part IV touch on practically all urgent moral questions of this decade. They supply ample opportunity for the conscience formation and education which Cardinal Ratzinger described in Part I. They are also vitally affected by the questions of dissent and proportionalism which he will summarize in the Epilogue.

The Principles of Totality:
Man's Stewardship of His Body

The Reverend John Gallagher, C.S.B., S.T.D.

I. Introduction

Moralists in the last several years have not dealt extensively with the principle of totality, although that principle was relatively prominent in debates on certain medical-moral problems several decades ago. Our present discussion of those problems may be helped if we examine the development of thinking in the Catholic Church concerning this principle.

The expression, "principle of totality," was used by Pope Pius XII in an address to the First International Congress on the Histopathology of the Nervous System in 1952.[1] After this usage by Pope Pius XII the expression became common in Catholic moral theology. However, the reality was discussed long before the expression was coined. St. Thomas Aquinas in the 13th century discussed the reality, although he did not call it the principle of totality.

Put very simply, the principle of totality states that in certain cases, mutilation is allowed when it is necessary for the good of the whole. "Mutilation" here means "any procedure that either temporarily or permanently impairs the natural and complete integrity of the body or its functions."[2] To cut off a finger or an arm is obviously a mutilation, since it impairs the integrity of the body. To cut the optic nerve and to perform a vasectomy are also mutilations, even though nothing is removed from the body. These procedures are mutilations because they impair a bodily function.

II.   St. Thomas Aquinas on Mutilation

We will begin this historical treatment of the principle of totality with St. Thomas Aquinas. In *Summa Theologiae,* II-II, question 65, article 1, Thomas asks whether in some cases it may be licit to mutilate a member of the body.[3] He replies:

Because a member is a part of the whole human body, it is for the sake of the whole, as the imperfect is for the sake of the perfect. Hence a member of the human body is to be dealt with according to what is expedient for the whole. Now a member of the human body is of itself *(per se)* useful to the good of the whole body, yet accidentally *(per accidens)* it may happen to be hurtful, as when a decayed member is corruptive of the whole body. Accordingly so long as a member is healthy and retains its natural disposition, it cannot be cut off without detriment to the whole human being. But as the whole human being is directed, as to his end, to the whole of the community of which he is a part, as has been said above, it may happen that although the removal of a member may be detrimental to the whole body, it may nevertheless be directed to the good of the community, insofar as it is applied to a person as a punishment for the purpose of restraining sin. Hence just as by public authority a person is licitly deprived of life altogether on account of certain more heinous offenses, so is he deprived of a member on account of certain

218

lesser offenses. But this is not lawful for a private individual, even with the consent of the one whose member it is, because this would involve an injury to the community, to whom the man and all his parts belong.

If however, the member be decayed and therefore a source of corruption to the whole body, then it is licit with the consent of the owner of the member to cut away the member for the welfare of the whole body, since each one is entrusted with the care of his own health. The same applies if it be done with the consent of the person whose business it is to care for the welfare of the person who has a decayed member: otherwise it is altogether illicit to mutilate a member.[4]

This article raises several issues:

A. Justifying mutilations by the principle of totality.

    1. on the individual level.
      a) May a diseased member of the body be cut off for the sake of the whole body (or human being)?
      b) Who should make this decision?
    2. on the community level
      a) May a healthy member of the body be cut off as punishment for the good of the community?
      b) Who should make this decision?

B. May mutilations be justified on any basis other than the principle of totality?

We will discuss these different issues in order.

A. Justifying mutilation by the principle of totality

1. *on the individual level*

a) May a diseased member of the body be cut off for the sake of the whole body (or human being)?[5]

May a leg with gangrene be amputated in order to save the person from death? Aquinas's argument here is relatively simple. Since the member is a part of the body, it exists for the sake of the whole body. Since a member is meant to serve the whole body, it should be so dealt with as to serve the body. If it serves the body best by being cut off, then it is licit to cut it off.

Let us examine this supposition that the part is for the sake of the whole. Certain parts do not seem to be for the sake of the whole, at least to the extent envisioned here by Aquinas. This linebacker is part of a football team. It is true that we suppose that he plays, or should play, for the sake of the success of the team. That seems to be implied in the game of football. However, even the most enthusiastic adherent of the Vince Lombardi school of coaching would stop short of supposing that the individual must sacrifice health and even life for the sake of the team simply because he is part of it.

This example illustrates that there are different kinds of wholes and therefore different ways in which a part is for the sake of the whole. This difference is suggested in Aquinas's statement that a member of the human body is *of itself,* or *per se,* for the sake of the whole human body.

The linebacker is part of the football team, but he is more. He has an existence quite apart from belonging to the team, and this existence apart from the team is oriented to goals other than team success. It is only because of one aspect of his being, his membership in the team, that his activity is directed towards team success. This linebacker as human being is not *per se* for the sake of team success.

For a member of the body, however, the case is different. So long as it is a part of my body, my arm has no existence except as a part of my body. An arm does not have its own independent orientation or appetite for perfection apart from the body. Its whole natural tending is integrated into the tendency of the body towards a certain perfection.[6] A pain or a pleasant sensation in my arm is not experienced by my arm. It is experienced by me.[7] Because the member of the body has no perfection which it seeks as its own apart from the body, it exists completely for the body. In sacrificing the member for the body one is not sacrificing any good which is greater than the good of the whole body.[8] The member of the body is *per se* for the sake of the whole body.

b) Who should make this decision?

According to Thomas, the mutilation may be performed only with the consent of the person with the diseased member, or of the one responsible for the welfare of that person.[9]

    2. *on the community level*

      a) May a healthy member of the body be mutilated, as a punishment for the good of the community?

Would it ever be right to punish an offender by mutilating some member of his body? The argument of Aquinas sounds plausible, at least if one accepts the legitimacy of capital punishment. Certain grave offenses are punished by death. The justification is given that this is necessary for the good of the community. To lose a member is a lesser evil than is the loss of one's life. Therefore, Aquinas argues, in certain cases it is right to punish an offender by mutilation, for the good of the community.

Certain twentieth century popes have been unwilling to allow mutilation for the good of any community. We will discuss this issue later.

b) Who should make this decision?

In Thomas's view, any decision to impose mutilation as a punishment must be made by the person who has responsibility for the good of the community. A private citizen may not make this decision. This would be accepted by most people today, who reject lynching or other attempts by individuals or groups to administer their own version of justice in meting out punishment. [10]

B. *May mutilations be justified on any basis other than the principle of totality?*

In the above article, having set forth certain conditions which would justify a mutilation, Aquinas adds: "Otherwise it is altogether illicit to mutilate a member." He seems to be saying that only an appeal to the good of the whole could justify a mutilation, and that there are no other justifying reasons. We must be cautious about our interpretation here, however. In the article Thomas does demonstrate that in some cases a mutilation may be justified by an appeal to the good of the whole. He does not demonstrate that a mutilation could never be justified in any other way. This point, too, will arise in twentieth century discussions of the principle of totality.

III. Mutilation: after Aquinas, to the Early Twentieth Century

A. *Theoretical justification*

On what basis may one allow a mutilation of the body? In

answering this question, Roman Catholic moralists after Aquinas up to the early twentieth century follow the views of Aquinas with few changes or additions. They argue that the members of the body are for the sake of the whole, and therefore mutilations are licit when they are necessary for the good of the whole.[11]

B. *Practical application*

In what situations may mutilation be allowed? In answering this question, moralists after Aquinas expand the application of the principle of totality in several ways.

St. Thomas discussed the amputation of a diseased member for the good of the whole person. Suppose, however, that the member is not diseased. Might it be licitly amputated? A case often considered was that of a man lying on a railroad track with his foot caught under the track. Would it be licit to cut off the healthy foot in order to save the person from being killed by an oncoming train? Roman Catholic moralists in general conclude that, where it is necessary to preserve life, one may mutilate even a healthy member of the body.[12] This is an extension which follows logically from the theoretical justification of the principle of totality. If a member is for the sake of the whole, then logically even a healthy member may be sacrificed to save the life of the whole.

A slightly different question caused some difference of opinion among moralists. Suppose that a tyrant decrees that you must either cut off your hand or be executed. In this situation, may you cut off your hand? Most Roman Catholic moralists who dealt with this question held that it would be licit to mutilate yourself in this situation. They followed the argument that because the part is for the good of the whole, one may sacrifice the part to save the whole.[13] A few moralists,[14] however, including even an author writing in this century,[15] took the opposing view. They argued that self-mutilation in this situation would be illicit because it would be cooperation in the sinful act of the tyrant.

Another kind of case, and one which raises further questions, is castration. In some places a custom arose of castrating boy sopranos in order to preserve their voices. The goods achieved included not only the artistic performance of the singers but also their attainment of an economically comfortable and secure status. Some Roman Catholic moralists allowed such a castration on the grounds that the good achieved justified the harm done. The majority of Roman Catholic moralists, on the other hand, considered the procedure immoral, and their stand was supported by appeal to Church laws opposing mutilation. However, even so notable a moralist as St. Alphonsus Liguori, having presented the arguments on both sides, seems to hold that the opinion allowing such castrations was a probable opinion.[16] Most recent Roman Catholic authors practically all agree that such castrations are not licit.[17]

The position of those who would allow castration to preserve a soprano voice is significant because it allows mutilation for some reason other than to preserve life. In fact, it allows mutilation for a good other than the physical health and well-being of the person. St. Alphonsus seems to be somewhat inconsistent on this point. On the one hand, he seems to hold that mutilation may be allowed only for the sake of saving the life of the whole body.[18] On the other hand, he allows as probable the opinion that castration may be permitted for the purpose of preserving a soprano voice. If nothing else, this shows us that although there was a tendency to want to limit mutilations to those necessary to save life, there was no settled consensus on the matter.

In more recent times the tendency to confine mutilations to those necessary to save life has been abandoned. In 1958, for example, Gerald Kelly stated explicitly that a member may be sacrificed not only to preserve life but also to maintain a reasonable state of well-being.[19] His reasoning is that bodily members do not exist only for the survival but also for the well-being of the person. Accordingly they may be sacrificed to promote that well-being. He requires only that the benefit to total well-being be proportionate to the destruction involved.

Moralists were called upon to consider castration for another purpose. Some people believed that castration might lower sex drive and so help to achieve chastity. May one undergo castration for this purpose? Roman Catholic moralists generally have agreed that one may not.[20] Their position seems to be consistent with that of St. Thomas. Thomas argued that mutilation may not be used to achieve the spiritual good of chastity even though in some cases it may be used to achieve a lesser, bodily, good. Why? In the cases in which it is allowed, mutilation is the only way of achieving the bodily good. Chaste actions may always be achieved without mutilation, however, because such actions are subject to the will.[21] Applying Thomas's argument to castration one can argue thus: it is always possible to preserve chastity by using one's will, without mutilation; therefore one may not use mutilation for this purpose.

Even on this point, however, some twentieth century authors have been willing to make exceptions. If by castration a person could be freed from unusual or morbid concupiscence, then both Vermeersch and Iorio were willing to allow the procedure.[22] Austin O'Malley allowed vasectomy of idiots if this could cure their habit of masturbation.[23] O'Malley believed that masturbation was injurious to health and a source of sin to observers. Apparently O'Malley believed that in certain cases vasectomy was the only way to avoid these evils, and so was willing to allow it.

C. *Dominion over one's body*

Aquinas does not seem to limit in any special way the human person's dominion over his or her own body.[24] He does, however, carefully limit one's dominion over one's own life. While holding that one might sacrifice a member for the good of the whole, Aquinas makes clear, nonetheless that one is never permitted to take one's own life.[25] It is difficult to pinpoint briefly why one's dominion over one's life is limited in a special way for Aquinas. He explains that life is a gift divinely given and is subject to the power of "Him who kills and makes to live." One might reply that not only life but all goods are gifts divinely given and subject to God. However, Aquinas seems to indicate some special way in which dominion over life is reserved to God to account for the fact that whereas other gifts of God may be sacrificed by individual decision, life may not.

Some Roman Catholic moralists after Aquinas seem to want to treat man's dominion over his bodily members as limited in somewhat the same way as is man's dominion over his life. Luis Molina wrote in 1611:

Man is not the master of his own life and members as he is the master of money and of other external goods which pertain to him and which he possesses. The Lord indeed conceded to men dominion over external goods and, after the division of things, each one disposes of those things which belong to him as of things of which he is truly the master; for that reason, by destroying them at his will, he does not sin against justice, since he destroys that which is his own . . . but dominion over life and members, the Author of Nature who created them, reserved to Himself, conceding only the use and administration of them to men. Hence it is that he who deprives himself of life, or who amputates one of his members, when right reason and the health of the body do not prescribe this, he also who unreasonably diminishes his life, or injures a member, or weakens it, sins in a certain way against justice, as a wicked destroyer and dissipator of that which is not his but God's, the care and administration of which has been committed to him.[26]

One might wish to object against Molina that man is not an absolute master but only a steward of any good, whether external property or members of his body, that one has no more right to destroy external goods without good reason than one has to destroy members of one's body. This is not the aspect of the quotation which is most relevant to our topic. What is relevant to our topic is that Molina sees man's dominion over his body as limited in somewhat the same way as is his dominion over his life.

What does this limitation of dominion over one's body mean for Molina? That is difficult to say precisely. Molina would hold that in some cases one may sacrifice a member, but in no case may one take one's own life on one's own authority, so in practice he seems to allow man more dominion over his members than over his life. What we seem to have here is a desire to specially limit man's dominion over his members, but there is only a vague explanation of why this dominion should be specially limited and of what this special limitation means in practice. This vagueness does not prevent this kind of thinking from influencing subsequent ethical thinking. Several later moralists,[27] including some in this century,[28] seem to suppose that just as man's dominion over his life is limited in a special way, so is man's dominion over the members of his body.

IV. Pius XI and Pius XII

The principle of totality becomes prominent in official church teaching in the pontificates of Pius XI and especially of Pius XII. In the context of a condemnation of eugenic sterilization Pius XI stated in *Casti Connubii:*

> Christian doctrine establishes, and the light of human reason makes it most clear, that private individuals have no other power over the members of their bodies than that which pertains to their natural ends; and they are not free to destroy or mutilate their members, or in any other way render themselves unfit for their natural function, except when no other provision can be made for the good of the whole body.[29]

In preceding paragraphs Pius condemned sterilization by public authority, but he so worded his condemnation that it would not apply to sterilizations authorized by state authorities as a punishment for crimes. Pius seems to be dealing with sterilization as a form of mutilation. His treatment generally corresponds with that of Aquinas, but the focus is different. Thomas was concerned mainly to state what kinds of mutilation might be allowed. Pius was concerned to state what kind of sterilization is not allowed. Concerning mutilations done on the responsibility of the individual, Thomas explained that they might be allowed when necessary for the good of the whole body. Pius states that this is the only reason for which they might be allowed. Concerning mutilations decided by public authority, Thomas explains that they may be performed as punishment for a crime. Pius, without ruling on the legitimacy of punitive sterilizations argues that sterilizations may not be done for other reasons. He does not give an analysis to justify precisely why these procedures are not licit.

In 1940 the Holy Office decreed that any direct sterilization, whether permanent or temporary, on either a man or a women, is prohibited by natural law.[30] The use of the term "direct sterilization" perhaps adds a precision to the condemnation of sterilization by Pius XI. A direct sterilization is one in which the purpose of the procedure is to prevent the possibility of conception. The decree does not rule out indirect sterilization, one in which the purpose is something other than preventing the possibility of conception.

226

The principle of totality was of crucial importance in the many statements on medical ethics by Pope Pius XII. He argues, as Thomas did, that because the members of the body are for the sake of the whole, they may be sacrificed when it is necessary for the good of the whole.[31] Some theologians had interpreted the principle of totality to mean that one may never mutilate a healthy organ.[32] Pius XII clarifies that even a healthy organ may be sacrificed when this is necessary for the good of the whole.[33]

May one mutilate a member for the sake of some non-bodily good of the individual, some good such as removal of depression? Some theologians held that one may not do so. They held that one could sacrifice a member only for a bodily good.[34] This, however, does not seem to be the mind of Pius XII. He states that one may destroy or mutilate parts of the body "when and in the measure which is necessary for the good of the being as a whole, to assure his existence, or to avoid or repair grave and lasting damage which cannot in any other way be avoided or repaired."[35] This reference to the good of the being as a whole suggests that not only bodily goods but also other goods of the person can justify mutilation.[36] That this is the proper interpretation of the thought of Pius XII seems to be confirmed by these words from his statement on a later occasion:

> But to the subordination of particular organs to the organism and to its own finality is added the spiritual finality of the individual himself. Physical or psychic medical experiments might, on one side, create some damages on organs or functions but, on the other side, they might be perfectly lawful because they conform to the well-being of the individual and do not transgress the limitations — imposed by the Creator — on man's rights to dispose of himself.[37]

In this passage, Pius states that not only are members subordinated to the good of the body, but the whole person is directed towards a spiritual good. He then strongly implies that not only physical goods, but certain psychological goods, can justify mutilation.[38]

This opens up certain questions which Pius XII does not explore. What kinds of goods of the person would justify mutilation? Would mutilation be justified to cause an increase in intelligence? To fit a person for certain types of employment? To improve one's disposition? Are there general guidelines to separate, among the various personal goods, the legitimate from illegitimate grounds for mutilation?

Another question debated by moralists was this: suppose that there is no present ill health and no present danger to life and health: may one undergo mutilation to forestall a danger which may occur in the future? Some moralists maintained that one may not. [39] Pius in 1952 spoke of mutilation or destruction of a member not only to repair damage, but to prevent it. [40] This can be interpreted as allowing mutilation now to avoid damage in the future.

A pressing concern for Pope Pius XII was the practice by totalitarian regimes of imposing sterilizations and other mutilations on their subjects. To counter these abuses Pius in a well-known passage spells out why the principle of totality does not apply to societies in the same way as it applies to the human body. In the process he gives a clear exposition of the meaning of the principle of totality.

The community is the great means intended by nature and God to regulate the exchange of mutual needs and to aid each man to develop his personality fully according to his individual and social abilities. Considered as a whole the community is not a physical unity subsisting in itself and its individual members are not integral parts of it. Considered as a whole, the physical organism of living beings, of plants, animals or man, has a unity subsisting in itself. Each of the members, for example, the hand, the foot, the heart, the eye, is an integral part destined by all its being to be inserted in the whole organism. Outside the organism it has not, by its very nature, any sense, any finality. It is wholly absorbed by the totality of the organism to which it is attached. In the moral community and in every organism of a purely moral character, it is an entirely different story. Here the whole has no unity subsisting in itself, but a simple unity of finality and action. In the community individuals are merely collaborators and instruments for the realization of the common end.

What results as far as the physical organism is concerned? The master and user of this organism which possesses a subsisting unity, can dispose directly and immediately of integral parts, members and organs within the scope of their natural reality. He can also intervene, as often as and to the extent that the good of the whole demands, to paralyze, destroy, mutilate and separate the members. But, on the contrary, when the whole has only a unity of finality and action, its head — in the present case, the public authority — doubtlessly holds direct authority and the right to make demands upon the activities of the parts, but in no case can it dispose of its physical being. Indeed, every direct attempt upon its essence constitutes an abuse of the power of authority. . .[41]

Here Pius is concerned primarily to rule out certain mutilations done not for the good of the individual but for the good of society. His strong statement, if taken in isolation, could be misleading. For example, he states that in a social group the public authority may not dispose of the physical being of the parts. On the face of it, this would seem to rule out capital punishment or any mutilation imposed by public authority as punishment. We have no convincing reason to suppose that Pius here is ruling out all such punishments.

Pius's strong stand against certain mutilations has implications also for organ transplants from living donors. Transplants of kidneys or other organs normally are not intended to serve the good of the donor. The living donor is undergoing a mutilation for the sake of someone else. If mutilations are allowed only for the good of the individual whose members are mutilated, then these organ transplants seem to be ruled out.[42] (Also ruled out would be any mutilation involved in experimentation not directed to the good of the subject in the experiment.) We will now examine what recent theologians have taught on organ transplants.

V. Organ Transplants from Living Donors

During the 1940's organ transplants became possible. Much of the discussion of the principle of totality since that time has centered on whether transplants from living donors are legitimate.

Some theologians have ruled out all such transplants.[43] Usually their argument involves two points. First, they believe that all mutilations, including transplants from living donors, must be evaluated according to the principle of totality. Second, they believe that the principle of totality allows mutilations only for the sake of the one mutilated, and therefore rules out transplants from living donors.

In arguing that such organ transplants are licit, two alternatives are open. Some have admitted that transplants must be evaluated according to the principle of totality, but they argue that a proper understanding of the principle of totality allows for organ transplants from living donors. Others argue that such organ transplants cannot be justified by appeal to the principle of totality, but they believe that they can be justified on some other basis.[44]

We will limit our discussion here to three authors.

An early defender of the legitimacy of organ transplants from living donors was Bert J. Cunningham in his doctoral dissertation at the Catholic University of America in the early 1940's.[45] This was before the main pronouncements of Pius XII on the principle of totality, but Cunningham had to contend with the negative judgments of Schmitt-Noldin and Iorio (*op. cit.*) and the statement by Pius XI in *Casti Connubii.*

Cunningham points out that it is licit to mutilate oneself in order to save one's own life and also for the sake of certain other benefits to oneself, such as the avoidance of pain or sickness.[46] He then argues that what one is permitted to do for the good of oneself one is permitted to do for the sake of another. He points out that direct mutilation of oneself does not fall into that class of actions which are evil in themselves and therefore never allowed. (If it were evil in itself, it would not be allowed even to save one's own life.) If mutilation is not evil in itself, it may be allowed for a good reason. That good reason may be a good for oneself, but it may also be a good for another.[47]

To support his position that what one may do for oneself one may do for another, Cunningham points out that the members of one's body are directed not only to one's own good but in a certain way to the good of others. Because of the unity of the human species, all men have a natural ordering to the good of others.

230

Because of unity in the mystical body of Christ, men have a supernatural orientation to the good of others. If the individual is ordered to the good of others, then the parts of the individual are ordered to the good of others. Cunningham admits that members in society are not united in the same way as are members of a body. The two kinds of unity are analogous, however. There is sufficient unity of members with others in society to justify a real ordering of individuals and their parts to the good of others.[48]

Cunningham shows how the accepted manuals of moral theology teach that one may, in some cases one should, risk one's life for another, even when the risk is grave. For certain very serious needs of others one should be able to undergo the lesser evil of mutilation.[49] He notes as well that other moralists have allowed blood transfusions, which constitute basically the same kind of action as an organ transplant, the gift of part of one's body for the good of another.[50]

Cunningham places two important restrictions on organ transplantation from living donors. If a transplant will certainly or very probably cause the death of a donor, it is not licit. To undergo such a mutilation would be directly to cause one's death, and this is not legitimate. Also, one may not donate an organ if this will cause sterility in oneself.[51] Cunningham believes that this last restriction is demanded by Magisterial statements.[52]

When he approaches the problem of transplants in the next decade, Gerald Kelly has before him various pronouncements by Pius XII against mutilations for the sake of anyone other than the one mutilated.[53] Kelly does not seem to be trying to break any new ground theologically. His main concern, apparently, is to discern what position should be taken in view of papal pronouncements. He begins by stating the arguments in favor of allowing organ transplants. Here he states little that was not said by Cunningham. According to Kelly, the main reason favoring transplants from living donors is the law of charity, from which arises the principle that "we may do for the neighbor that which in similar circumstances we may do for ourselves."[54]

For Kelly the main argument against transplants is the papal teaching on the principle of totality. Kelly takes seriously the claim that this papal teaching may rule out transplants from living donors. He admits that according to Pius XII one cannot justify such transplants by appeal to the principle of totality. Does Pius also wish to teach that there is no other basis which could justify these transplants? Kelly gives several reasons which suggest that Pius did not want to rule out all such transplants. First he knew about these transplants, and had he wished to declare them illicit he had plenty of opportunity to do so explicitly, but he did not do so. Second, Pius's own teaching regarding medical experimentation seems to allow for some right to dispose of the body for the good of others. [55] Third, by praising blood donors for their charity, Pius obviously approves of this procedure, which is a form of giving a part of one's own body for the good of another. Finally, the strong attack by the Pope against mutilation for the sake of others should be accounted for by his objection to the excesses of totalitarian regimes, and it is not necessary to suppose that they are directed against the possibility of organ transplants.

In summary, Kelly believes that there are good arguments for allowing organ transplants from living donors; the main argument against them is that they might be ruled out by papal teaching. After careful consideration Kelly concludes that they are not ruled out by papal teaching. He concludes tentatively that transplants from living donors may be allowed in certain cases. However, he presents this position as probable rather than as certain. [56]

In the mid 1960's, approximately a decade after Gerald Kelly's writings on the topic, Augustine Regan took up the topic of organ transplants. [57] He believed that if organ transplants from living donors are to be justified, they must be justified by the principle of totality. That is, such transplants can be justified only if they can be shown to be in the interest of the donor. Regan believed that this is the teaching of Pope Pius XII, and that it is required by natural law. To use bodily members for the good of another and not for one's own good is to use them for a purpose for which they are not intended. Before proposing his own solution Regan gives his objections (too numerous to mention here) to all previous arguments in favor of transplants from living donors.

Regan argued that such transplants could be justified by the principle of totality. His argument is based on his notion of what it means to be a person. To act as a person includes a relationship with other persons. Each human being perceives himself to be "incommunicable", to be himself and no other, and he perceives each other person to be "incommunicable". Yet each incommunicable person can enter into a unity with the other in love, living in and by the other. This intersubjectivity enters into the very concept of a human person.

If this is what human beings are, then the gift of an organ for transplantation not only may help another, but may perfect the donor in his intersubjective being. The donor ". . . has become more of a person: deprived of a member, he has received more than he has given, for he has, by communicating to another of his very being, more fully integrated himself into the mysterious unity between person and person."[58] An organ transplant may thereby fulfill the requirement of the principle of totality, serving the good of the donor.[59]

As the debate continued in the 1960's the view began to prevail that transplants from living donors are licit in certain cases. This prevailing view was not based on any consensus as to why such transplants should be allowed. Some tried to justify them by appeal to the principle of totality and some tried to justify them by appeal to some other basis. The statements of Pius XII did not settle the matter. Neither John XXIII nor Paul VI issued any substantive or definitive statement on the issue. Gerald Kelly notes in 1963 that even one of the staunchest opponents of organ transplants from living donors admitted that the opponents' position was solidly probable.[60] A recent writer, while not denying that some opposition to transplants remains, states: "The basic morality of organic transplantation, in practice at least, is established in the teaching of the Church.[61]

VI. Direct Sterilization and the Principle of Totality

A direct sterilization is a procedure whose purpose is to produce sterility, either as an end or as a means to an end. An indirect sterilization is a procedure in which sterility results but such was not the purpose of the procedure. The removal of a cancerous uterus to prevent the spread of the malignancy is an indirect sterilization.

The Church has taught and teaches officially that direct sterilization is never licit. Because of this official teaching,

Catholic theologians in the 1940's and following generally assumed that the principle of totality does not apply to direct sterilization.[62] That is, they did not believe that one can legitimately appeal to the good of the whole to justify direct sterilization. The main argument bolstering this position was as follows: most parts of the body exist principally for the sake of the whole person, and therefore they may be sacrificed, mutilated, when this is required for the good of the whole; the reproductive organs, however, exist principally for the sake of continuing the race, and therefore they may not be directly destroyed or inhibited for the sake of the good of the individual.[63] This argument rules out not only sterilization but any direct contraception.

According to official teaching, is direct sterilization or contraception never allowed? The answer to this question requires some nuances.

In *Casti Connubii* Pius XI holds that one does not sin if one reluctantly engages in sexual relations with one's spouse when the spouse is using contraceptives. Pius requires only that one try to dissuade or deter one's spouse from seeking contraceptive sexual relations.[64] For example, a woman does not sin if she has sexual relations with her husband who insists on having sexual relations and insists on using a condom, provided she seeks to dissuade or deter her husband from this contraceptive act. It seems then that the pope is allowing a close, though passive, role to a spouse in an act of contraceptive sexual intercourse.

The Spanish moral theologian Marcelino Zalba believes that papal teaching would allow a more active role to a person in contraceptive intercourse in the case of rape.[65] Zalba would allow a woman threatened by rape to use a contraceptive to assure that she does not become pregnant. According to Zalba, what is wrong in itself, and never allowed, is contraception or sterilization in order to have voluntary sexual relations without pregnancy. Whenever the sexual relations are voluntary it is possible to avoid pregnancy by refraining from them, and so contraception is not necessary. For Zalba, what is evil about contraception is that in using one's sexual faculty one does two things which are mutually contradictory. One performs an act which by God's own doing and by its very nature is aimed at generation, and at the same time one impedes the natural effect. The woman who takes a contraceptive pill to avoid pregnancy from rape does not fall into this contradiction. She is not co-operating willingly in an act aimed at generation. She is making a correct use of the principle of totality. For the good of the whole she acts to suspend ovulation to avoid a pregnancy which would be wrong.[66]

Zalba would also allow a woman to use a contraceptive to avoid pregnancy when she is unjustly forced into having sexual relations with her husband. For example, if a pregnancy would seriously endanger the life of the wife, and her husband insists on having sexual relations against her will, the wife may use a contraceptive. Zalba sees that as agreeing with papal teaching.

VII. Conclusion

What help does the principle of totality give us in settling practical questions? Moralists generally agree on three points.

First, mutilation is permissible in order to save the life of the person who is mutilated. In such cases the principle of totality by itself provides an adequate, clear and certain norm to settle particular cases. Because members exist for the sake of the whole person, it would be absurd to require that one keep a member at the expense of the death of the person.

Second, a mutilation is permissible for the sake of certain other goods of the person, goods such as improved health or relief from severe and enduring pain. Here the principle of totality provides a partial guidance only. To solve particular cases it is not enough to know that the member is for the sake of the whole. One must also weigh each factor to determine whether the good achieved is proportionate to the damage done by the mutilation. This weighing of factors leaves room for error.

Third, regarding mutilation for any other reason than the good of the person being mutilated, great caution is required lest abuses occur. The parts of a social group are not ordered to the good of the whole in the same way as the parts of a body are ordered to the good of the whole body.

Beyond these points on which there is general agreement, there remain several questions which require further study and clarification. One such question is whether mutilation is allowable *only* for the sake of the person being mutilated. Certain statements of Pius XII considered in isolation seem to rule out mutilations for any other purpose. However, there are several reasons why we should not let the matter rest there.

First, organ transplants from living donors now are allowed by Catholic moralists generally, with no serious objections by the Magisterium. These transplants seem to be justified not for the good of the donor but for the good of the person receiving the transplant.

Second, if Pius XII intended to condemn all mutilations except those performed for the benefit of the person being mutilated, then he is contradicting Aquinas, who allowed mutilation as a punishment, to serve the good of the community. Of course it is certainly possible for a pope to contradict Aquinas. But did Pius XII really intend to do so? Did he intend to accept all of the logical implications of the position that mutilations are justified only by the good of the one mutilated? One implication seems to be that sterilization may not be used as a punishment for a crime.[68] It is clear, however, that Pius deliberately avoided settling the question of sterilization for punitive reasons.[69] Furthermore, if mutilations for the sake of the good of society are ruled out, then surely capital punishment is also ruled out, and Pius does not draw this implication from his position on mutilation.

If it is true that Pius XII did not settle the question concerning mutilations, several further observations should be made.

First, we should be cautious about taking isolated Magisterial statements and making them absolute principles. For one thing, different kinds of Magisterial statements carry different degrees of authority. For example, an address by a pope to a particular audience normally does not carry the same weight as does an encyclical. Furthermore, while it is clear that Pius XII was right to oppose certain abuses going on in his day, this does not mean that all of his formulations of the arguments against them are equally exact and successful. If we absolutize an isolated statement by a pope we may be settling more questions than the pope intended to settle.[70] This can lead to bad moral theology, which both misleads people and brings the Magisterium itself into disrepute. Jesus sharply criticized those who absolutized rules which should have been absolutized.

The unjustified absolutizing of certain moral rules may have good motives. When abuses arise we want to condemn them. We may prefer to condemn them by an appeal to a clear principle which we want to apply everywhere and at all times. The principle declares that a whole, clearly defined class of actions is intrinsically evil, never to be permitted. Such a strict application of a principle seems to be a bulwark against abuse. If we start using proportional arguments, we start making exceptions, and we are in danger of giving in to pressure, allowing the abuse to gain a foothold in practice and an appearance of respectability. However, the fact that it is a bulwark against abuse is not a sufficient reason for absolutizing a moral rule.

Proportionalism and the notion of intrinsic evil are beyond the scope of this paper. They are treated in other chapters in this volume. However, our discussion has some relevance to these topics. Approved Roman Catholic moralists of the past have often used proportionalist arguments to solve many kinds of cases. Certain other kinds of cases were not subject to proportionalist arguments because they were presumed to involve acts which are intrinsically evil. One can ask whether in some cases acts were classed as intrinsically evil, and a rule was made absolute, only because of fear of abuse rather than because the matter was worked out properly in theory. This is said without prejudice to the general question of whether some classes of actions really are intrinsically evil and what the Church should say about proportionalism as an *ism*.

Returning to the principle of totality, if some mutilations may be allowed for the good of others, then we must work on guidelines to indicate what kinds of mutilations are to be permitted. Ethicists are doing that now. However, many of them are doing so with little or no reference to the principle of totality. This is unfortunate. Pius was concerned about the real abuses which easily arise when mutilations are allowed for social purposes, and he was no doubt right in indicating that the principle of totality should be used as a bulwark against such abuses.

Once we admit that *some* mutilations may be permitted for the good of others, we can begin to apply the principle of totality in a nuanced way. The members of society are not parts of a whole in the same way as organs are parts of the living body. Members of society may not be sacrificed for the whole in the same way and to the same extent as members of the body may be sacrificed for the welfare of the body. Nevertheless, members of society can be called upon to make some sacrifices for the good of the whole. What is needed is further work on the different ways in which members are parts of a whole, and the different types of moral obligations which flow from the different types of membership.[7]

Notes

1. *Acta Apostolicae Sedis (AAS)* 44 (1952) 779-89, esp. p. 782. An English translation of this important address is available in *The Linacre Quarterly* 19 (1952) 98-107.

2. This definition is taken from J.J. Lynch, "Mutilation", *New Catholic Encyclopedia,* Vol. X. p. 145.

3. "Mutilate" here for Thomas probably refers to the excision of a part of the body, not to the more general notion contained in our definition of mutilation above. However, his argument applies not only to an excision of a member but also to the destruction of a function.

4. Author's translation, from the Piana Edition, Ottawa, 1953.

5. In this article Thomas seems to use the terms "body" and "human being" *(homo)* interchangeably. At one point he speaks of "the good of the whole body." At another point he refers to "injury to the whole human being." Clearly for him, for the members to be directed to the good of the whole body is for them to be directed to the good of the whole human being.

6. For a more thorough examination of Aquinas's discussion of types of wholes and how they relate to this question, see Martin Nolan, "The Positive Doctrine of Pope Pius XII on the Principle of Totality", *Augustinianum* 3 (1963) 28-44, and John Michael Cox, *A Critical Analysis of the Roman Catholic Medico-Moral Principle of Totality and Its Applicability to Sterilizing Mutilations,* a doctoral dissertation, Claremont Graduate School, 1972, available through University Microfilms International, Ann Arbor, Michigan, pages 11-18.

7. It is worth noting here how one might determine the purpose or goal of any reality. Some writers think of it primarily as a matter of examining the design of a thing (e.g., of an eye or a hand or a heart) and concluding from the design that it has this or that purpose. This is not the principal way Aquinas discovers purpose and end. For him, the end or good of any being is the object of an appetite or tendency of that being. What is naturally good for a being is that for which it has a natural appetite or tendency. For Aquinas, the parts of the body are perceived to be completely for the sake of the whole body because the parts as such do not have any other natural tendency except that which is integrated into the tendency of the whole body to seek its perfection. *Per accidens,* as subject to disease, for example, a member of a body may have some other tendency, but this is not a natural tendency (one coming from its nature) but a tendency dependent on some cause other than its nature. That things are designed in such a way as to accomplish their natural function is, of course, true. Our point here is simply that for Aquinas the good or end is defined as that which a being desires or seeks, not as that for which it has been designed.

8. Of course to sacrifice a member for some minor good of the whole body would be a mistake. However, this is not the kind of case envisioned by Aquinas in this article. He is considering cases in which the health and very life of the whole body is at stake.

9. In the above article Aquinas does not expand on the notion of why one is responsible for one's own health. In the prologue to Part Two of the *Summa Theologiae* he makes clear that a person is constituted as a moral agent by the fact of possessing the power of free choice and thereby having dominion over his actions. It is this which constitutes one as an image of God. If it belongs to the person to direct his or her life and actions to their proper goal, then, logically, dominion over one's own health and members is to be includ-

238

ed in the more general dominion of the person over his life and actions.

10. This matter of authority and responsibility for the welfare of the community raises an interesting question. Often moralists argue that a certain course of action is justified because, although it may be destructive of some particular good, yet it contributes to the welfare of the wider community. Might it be persuasively argued that, not only in the case of punishments, but in any case in which a considerable personal good is sacrificed for the welfare of the community, authorization should be sought from one who is charged with the responsibility for the public welfare?

11. Two American Catholic authors have surveyed a considerable number of major Roman Catholic authors of the past few centuries and have found no significant additions to or differences from the teaching of Aquinas on this point. See Bert J. Cunningham, *The Morality of Organic Transplantation*, Washington, D.C., Catholic University of America Press, 1944, pages 33-39; John Michael Cox, *op. cit.*, (note 6 above) p. 22.

12. See, for example, C.-R. Billuart (1675-1757) *Summa Sancti Thomae Hodiernis Academiarum Moribus Accomodata*, Paris, (1870?), Tom. IV, dissert. X, art IX, n. 1; A. Lehmkuhl (1834-1918) *Theologia Moralis*, 9th Ed., Fribourg i. Bresgau. Herder. 1898, p. 347; Thomas V. Moore, "The Morality of a Sterilizing Operation", *The Ecclesiastical Review* 106 (1942) 444-46.

13. Cunningham, *op. cit.* pp. 38-41, refers to several authors who favor this opinion.

14. Cunningham, *op. cit.* p. 40, cites Fulgentius a Nativitate, *Alphabeticum Quodlibet, seu Moralium Omnium Compendium juxta series Alphabeti*, Naples, 1701, p. 198.

15. See D. Prümmer, *Manuale Theologiae Moralis*, Vol. II, Fribourg i. Br., 1928, n. 116, footnote 96.

16. Cunningham, *op. cit.* pp. 41-42, notes that St. Alphonsus presents the opinions of both sides in *Theologia Moralis*, Rome, ed. P. Leonard Gaude. 1905, Vol. I, n. 373, and in *Homo Apostolicus* Ratisbon, 1842, Vol. I, tr. 8, de quinto praecepto, Cap. I, n. 3.

17. Cunningham, *op. cit.*, p. 42, refers to several authors on this point.

18. Cunningham, *op. cit.*, gives as the position of Alphonsus the view that mutilation is licit only for the conservation of the whole body, and refers to Alphonsus de Liguori, *Theologia Moralis*, Rome, 1905, ed. Nova, ed. P. Leonard Gaude, Vol. I, n. 373, resp. 2.

19. Gerald Kelly, *Medico-Moral Problems* Part I, (St. Louis: The Catholic Hospital Association). 1949, p. 22.

20. Cunningham, *op. cit.*, p. 43, cites one author who seems to think that if it were effective, castration might be used for this purpose. All other authors cited are against it.

21. *Summa Theologiae*, II-II, q. 65, a. 1, ad 3.

22. See Arthur Vermeersch, *Theologia Moralis*, Rome, 1924, Vol. II, n. 323; Thomas Iorio, *Theologia Moralis*, Naples, 1946, Vol. II, n. 167, 3.

23. Austin O'Malley, *The Ethics of Medical Homicide and Mutilation* (New York: The Devin-Adair Company, 1919), p. 263.

24. Of course for Aquinas one's dominion over one's body is limited in that one may sacrifice a member only for a legitimate reason. This is not a special limitation on one's dominion over one's body, however. It means, simply, that one should exercise that dominion according to the moral law, a limitation which applies also to one's dominion over material goods.

25. *Summa Theologiae*, II-II, q. 64, a. 5.

26. Luis Molina, *De justitia et jure*, Venice, 1611, Vol. IV, disp. 1, n. 1, quoted from Cunningham *op. cit.*, p. 20.

27. See, for example, Anacletus Reiffenstuel, *Theologia Moralis*, Munich, 1692, tr. IX, dist. III, quest. I, n. 3, (reference from Cunningham *op. cit.*, p. 24) and Patrick Sporer, *Theologia Moralis*, Paderborn, 1900, edited by I. Bierbaum, Tom. II, n. 396 (reference from Cunningham, *op. cit.*, p. 35).

28. See Austin O'Malley, *The Ethics of Medical Homicide and Mutilation* (New York: The Devin-Adair Company, 1919), p. 26, Dominic Prümmer, *Manuale Theologiae Moralis*, Fribourg, in. Br., 1915, Vol. II, n. 116. Both Cunningham (*op. cit.*, pp. 30-31) and Cox (*op. cit.*, p. 21) appear to adopt this way of thinking as their own.

29. This translation is taken from *The Church and the Reconstruction of the Modern*

World: The Social Encyclicals of Pius XI, edited by Terence McLaughlin, (Garden City, N.Y., Image Books, 1957), paragraph 71. The original Latin text is available in *AAS* 22 (1930) 565.

30. *AAS* 32 (1940) 73.

31. In an address to the *Unione Medico-Biologica "San Luca"* on Nov. 12, 1944, in explaining the limits of the human being's control of his or her members, Pius XII emphasized that members have natural and intrinsic functions, and that one may not arrange one's life and the functions of one's organs according to one's own tastes and contrary to the intrinsic functions assigned to them. See *Discorsi e Radiomessaggi di Sua Santità Pio XII,* Tipografia Poliglotta Vaticana, Vol. 6, 1944-45, pp. 185-86. However, this does not mean that Pius thought one could never mutilate or destroy a member or prevent it from functioning. See *AAS* 44 (1952) 782.

32. Cox, *op. cit.,* p. 41 notes that Alphonsus Bonnar held this position in the second editon of his book, *The Catholic Doctor* (New York: P.J. Kenedy & Sons, 1943), p. 98. (The sixth edition of Fr. Bonnar's book, 1952, does not contain this opinion).

33. See *AAS* 45 (1953) 674-5.

34. This narrower view seems to be the one adopted by Edwin Healy, *Moral Guidance: A Textbook in Principles of Conduct for Colleges and Universities* (Chicago: Loyola University Press, 1942), p. 157.

35. *AAS* 44 (1952) 782 (author's translation).

36. See, for example, the interpretations of John Connery, "Notes on Moral Theology" *Theological Studies* 15 (1954) 602, and Gerald Kelly, "Pope Pius XII and the Principle of Totality" *Theological Studies* 16, (1955) 379.

37. *AAS* 50 (1958) 693-4, translation taken from Cox, *op. cit.,* p. 38.

38. In this context Pius is discussing mutilations in experimentation. It seems, however, that his reasoning would apply to mutilations more generally.

39. Cox, *op. cit.,* p. 43, quotes from Jules Paquin, *Morale et médecine,* 2nd ed., Montreal, Comité des Hôpitaux de Quebéc, 1957, p. 261, giving that author's views in support of such a position.

40. *AAS* 44 (1952) 782.

41. Address to the First International Congress of Histopathologists of the Nervous System, September 13, 1952, *AAS* 14 (1952) 786-7, translation taken from Gerald Kelly, *op. cit.,* pp. 375-6.

42. There are other passages in which Pius XII seems to say that mutilation is licit only for the good of the person who is mutilated. See *AAS* 44 (1952) 782; *AAS* 45 (1953) 747; *AAS* 50 (1958) 693. In another passage, *AAS* 48 (1956) 461-2, Pius argues at length against a use of the principle of totality to justify a transplant from a living person for the good of another.

43. Cox, *op. cit.,* Chapter II, lists the following authors who rule out all organ transplants from living donors: Heribert Jone, *Moral Theology,* (Westminster, Maryland: Newman Press, 1955), p. 135; John P. Kenny, *Principles of Medical Ethics,* (Westminster: Maryland, Newman Press, 1952), pp. 110; 135; Charles McFadden, *Medical Ethics* (Philadelphia: F.A. Davis Co., 1956), 4th ed., pp. 313 + 317; Edwin Healy, *Moral Guidance, a Textbook in Principles, Spiritual Aids and Concise Answers regarding Catholic Personnel, Patients and Problems* (New York: MacMillan Co., 1956), p. 157; M. Zalba, "La mutilación y el transplante de órganos" *Estudios de Deusto* 3 (1955) 295-325; "La mutilación y el transplante de órganos a la luz del magisterio eclesiástico" *Razón y Fé 153 (1956) 523-48.* John Lynch, in his "Notes on Moral Theology" *Theological Studies* 19 (1958) 181, recognizes that in the second edition of his text, *Theologiae Moralis Summa* 2, number 157 + 162, Zalba has softened his opposition to organ transplants to the extent of admitting that the opinion of those who would allow them is a probable opinion. Among earlier writers opposed to transplants from living donors, cf. Noldin, H., *Summa Theologiae Moralis,* ed. by A. Schmitt, Ratisbon, 1938, Vol. II, n. 328; Thomas Iorio, *Theologia Moralis,* Vol. II, Naples, 1939, n. 199. Iorio would allow the gift of parts of one's body which can be replaced (e.g., blood, certain skin or muscular tissue) but not gifts of parts which cannot be regenerated.

44. Because writers on both sides strove to avoid contradicting papal teaching, the debate centered on the proper interpretation of papal teaching. According to some, papal teaching

required that all mutilations be judged according to the principle of totality. These writers could appeal to certain passages from Pius XI: ". . . the individual human being . . . cannot destroy or mutilate them (the members of one's body), or in any other way render himself incapable of his natural functions, except where there is no other way of providing for the welfare of the whole." *Casti Connubii, AAS* 22 (1930) 565; and from Pius XII: ". . . the individual himself has the right to dispose of his existence, of the integrity of his organism, of the particular organs and their capacity to function, only to the extent required by the good of the whole organism" *AAS* 44 (1953) 747. Those authors mentioned in the preceding note as ruling out all transplants from living donors took this interpretation of papal teaching. So did some who allowed transplants from living donors. See, for example: John J. Shinners, *The Morality of Medical Experimentation on Living Human Subjects in the Light of Recent Papal Pronouncements* (Washington, D.C.: Catholic University of America Press, 1958), p. 37-8; Martin Nolan, "The Positive Doctrine of Pope Pius XII on the Principle of Totality" *Augustinianum* 3 (1963) 28-44, 290-324; 5 (1965) 537-59; Augustine Regan, "The Basic Morality of Organic Transplants between Living Humans" *Studia Moralia* 3 (1965) 320-61. These authors believe that one could justify certain organ trasnplants from living donors by appeal to the principle of totality. Other authors argue that transplants from living donors cannot be justified by the principle of totality, but that they can be justified on some other basis. See John Connery, "Notes on Moral Theology" *Theological Studies* 15 (1954) 603 and 17 (1956) 561; Gerald Kelly, "Notes on Moral Theology" *Theological Studies* 24 (1963) 628-9.

45. For this discussion I am dependent on the part of the dissertation which was published as *The Morality of Organic Transplantation* (Washington, D.C.: Catholic University of America Press), 1944.

46. *Op. cit.,* pp. 61-62.

47. *Op. cit.,* pp. 62-71.

48. *Op. cit.,* pp. 71-86.

49. *Op. cit.,* pp. 87-98.

50. *Op. cit.,* pp. 98-99.

51. *Op. cit.,* pp. 100-104.

52. For a treatment of the discussion following the publication of Cunningham's book, see Cox, *op. cit.,* pp. 71-91, and *Theological Studies,* "Notes on Moral Theology", by several authors, *passim,* 1944-1957.

53. Gerald Kelly, "Pius XII and the Principle of Totality" *Theological Studies* 16 (1955) 373-396, esp. 391-396.

54. *Op. cit.,* pp. 392-3.

55. Kelly deals with Pius's statements on experimentation on pp. 385-391 of the article.

56. *Op. cit.,* p. 392.

57. Augustine Regan, "The Basic Morality of Organic Transplants Between Living Human Beings" *Studia Moralia* 3 (1965) 320-361; "Man's Administration of His Bodily Life and Members, the Principle of Totality, and Organic Transplants Between Living Humans" *Studia Moralia* 5 (1967) 179-200.

58. "The Basic Morality. . ." p. 351.

59. All three authors, Cunningham, Kelly and Regan, received criticism for their positions.

60. Gerald Kelly, "Notes on Moral Theology" *Theological Studies* 24 (1963) 630.

61. Cox, *op. cit.,* p. 89.

62. For a discussion of this point, see Cox, *op. cit.,* Chapter IV.

63. See Gerald Kelly, *Medico-Moral Problems* (St. Louis: Catholic Hospital Association, 1958), p. 6 and "Notes on Moral Theology," *Theological Studies* 9 (1948) 94; Nicholas Lohkamp, *The Morality of Hysterectomy Operations,* (Washington, D.C., Catholic University of America Press, 1956), p. 36; Alphonsus Bonnar, *The Catholic Doctor,* 2nd edition, (New York: P.J. Kenedy and Sons, 1943), p. 56; T. Lincoln Bouscaren, *Ethics of Ectopic Operations,* 2nd edition, (Milwaukee: Bruce Publishing Co., 1944), p. 45; Charles McFadden, *Medical Ethics,* 4th edition, (Philadelphia: F.A. Davis Co., 1956), p. 87; Francis J. Connell, "The Pope's Teaching on Organic Transplantation" *American Ecclesiastical Review* 135 (1956) 168; John Ford and Gerald Kelly, *Contemporary Moral Theology II* (Westminster, Maryland:

Newman Press, 1964), p. 316; J. Lynch, "Medical-moral Opinions; Vasectomy and Sterilization" *Linacre Quarterly* 38 (1971) 8.

64. *AAS* 22 (1930) 561.

65. Fr. Zalba's article appeared in *Rassegna di Teologia* 9 (1968) 225-7. For this discussion I am dependent upon an unpublished translation by Fr. Edward J. Bayer, S.T.D. The title of the article is translated as: "The meaning of the principle of totality in the doctrine of Pius XI and Pius XII and its application to cases of sexual violence."

66. See Joseph Farraher, "Notes on Moral Theology" *Theological Studies* 24 (1963) 79-88, for an account of an earlier discussion along similar lines, with reference to an earlier article by Zalba.

67. It is true that some, like Augustine Regan, claim that these transplants are justified by the good done to the donor and therefore by the principle of totality. There are grave difficulties, however, in supposing that this kind of thinking accords with the mind of Pius XII. If Regan is correct, it seems to follow that any voluntary mutilation done for the good of the neighbor can also be for the good of the donor, and the principle of totality can be applied so loosely that it no longer provides the kind of strict limits which Pius XII apparently had in mind. Therefore, whether or not Regan is correct about how transplants can be justified, it is difficult to conclude that his thinking is in accord with that of Pius XII.

68. It might be argued that a punishment is remedial and for the good of the one punished. Usually, however, we suppose that the principal justification for punishment is the common good, and it is difficult to see how the punishment of sterilization would be justified simply as serving the good of the guilty party.

69. See John Ford and Gerald Kelly, "Doctrinal Value and Interpretation of Papal Teaching" in *Readings in Moral Theology No. 3: The Magisterium and Morality,* edited by Charles E. Curran and Richard A. McCormick, (New York: Paulist Press, 1982), pp. 8-9. This article appeared earlier in Ford and Kelly, *Contemporary Moral Theology I,* (Westminister: Maryland, Newman Press, 1958), pp. 19-32.

70. Ford and Kelly make a similar point in the article cited above.

71. Moral theologians might be aided here by work done in other disciplines. See, for example, Jacques Maritain, *The Person and the Common Good* (New York: C. Scribner's Sons, 1947), Chapter IV, and *Man and the State,* (Chicago: University of Chicago Press, 1951), pp. 148-150.

Chapter 12

The Principle of Double Effect:
Good Actions Entangled in Evil

Joseph M. Boyle, Jr., Ph.D.

I. What Double Effect Is
and How It Is Meant to Work

Sometimes moral responsibilities seem to conflict with one another, so that it seems that whatever one does will be wrong. In other cases, it can seem that doing the right thing — for example, refusing an abortion — simply has such tragic or horrible consequences that to do it would be moral fanaticism. Faith tells us that sometimes there is no way out of such moral binds, as the example of Jesus' death and those as the martyrs show. Deliberately doing some kinds of things is always wrong no matter what happens. But the Catholic moral tradition has dealt with some of these cases by developing over the centuries a complex and subtle system of casuistry. The famous principle of double effect is an important element in that system.

243

This principle is meant to resolve certain moral dilemmas, namely, those that arise when one faces a situation in which it seems that one ought to do something, but doing it also involves bringing about a significant harm or evil. The kind of evil in question here is that which can render immoral the human action which brings it about. Thus, these actions which are in some way morally called for but also cause evil need special moral justification. The double effect doctrine provides a way to carry out the process of morally evaluating good actions which also cause evil.

In effect, this procedure distinguishes two quite different ways in which the evil aspect of the action is related to the good one is trying to realize. If the evil one brings about is the means one chooses to realize the good one is trying to do, then the action cannot be justified morally, since one is violating a fundamental principle of Christian morality, formulated by St. Paul in his classic phrase: We may not "do evil that good might come of it" (Rom 3:8). The end does not justify the means. However, if the evil one causes is not the means to one's end, but only a side effect of one's action, one does not violate this principle, and it is possible that the action can be morally justified.

Thus, to take a standard example, faith tells us that direct abortion is always excluded. This is so even if the abortion should be necessary to save the mother's life. This would be choosing an evil means for a good end. However, indirect abortion — for example, if a pregnant woman has a disease which must be treated by a hysterectomy before the child is viable — might be permitted because the death of the child is not the means to saving the mother's life, but only a side effect of an otherwise unquestionably good action.

The principle of double effect is usually formulated as four conditions which must be fulfilled if an action which is morally ambiguous is to be morally permissible. J. P. Gury, S.J., who provided the classical modern formulation of double effect, states these conditions as follows: 1. the agent's end must be morally acceptable (*honestus*); 2. the act itself which brings about the good end and the evil side effect must be compatible with the moral law; 3. the good effect must be brought about immediately, that is not by means of the bad effect; and 4. there must be a proportionately serious reason for actuating the cause — that is, doing the act having the evil effect.

244

The purpose of these conditions is to help a serious person facing a complicated moral situation to determine: first, that the purpose for which the action is being considered is a morally worthy purpose; second, that the act one does is itself morally good; third, that the evil involved in the act is not intended as an end or chosen as a means to the good one seeks; and lastly, that there is a morally sufficient reason for doing what causes evil.

Thus, in the case of indirect abortion already considered, the end is acceptable — saving the mother's life; the act itself is licit — a normal surgical procedure to deal with the malady; the evil effect is a side effect and not the means to saving the mother's life; and saving someone's life is a grave, and can be a morally acceptable, reason for doing what leads to another's death. That would not be so if, for instance, one is unfair to the person killed. But one does not have to be unfair to someone if one accepts his death in saving another's life — for example, if the one thus killed would die together with the one saved if nothing were done.

The doctrine of double effect does not, of course, have application only in abortion cases. It plays a role in distinguishing between withholding extraordinary means and passive euthanasia, and between direct and indirect sterilization. It is part of the justification of military actions in which the death of noncombatants can be foreseen. For St. Thomas, double effect is the possible justification of killing in self-defense. Moreover, double effect is not limited in its application to the life issues, but is used, for example, in the distinction between formal and material cooperation, and in the ethics of deception and causing scandal.

II. Objections to Double Effect

For all its utility as a principle for dealing with difficult cases, however, the double effect doctrine has not been immune to criticism. Pascal's scorn for its use in the hand of laxist moralists in the seventeenth century shows that its lineage is not beyond suspicion.[2] And to many nowadays Pascal's strictures seem altogether too gentle. For double effect appears to many to be a piece of sophistry — a casuistical trick which allows Catholic moralists to avoid some of the unacceptable implications of holding moral absolutes, although it inconsistently and heartlessly requires one to refrain from acting in other cases, however tragic or horrible the consequences may be. "You allow a woman to have her uterus removed even though you know this will lead to her child's death, but you will not allow a doctor to crush the skull of a baby stuck in the birth canal, even though both will probably die unless this is done and the labor allowed to end. This is inconsistent, absurd, and heartless. If one can be permitted, then why not the other?" So the objection goes.

a. Double Effect is a form of moral evasion.

Actually, this kind of objection can be used to express several different lines of criticism of double effect. One of these is that the requirement of double effect that the harm one causes should only be indirectly caused is a form of moral evasion. For we all have to do evil sometimes, and double effect admits this, enjoining only the deviousness of doing it indirectly. This allows us to keep at some distance from the evil — helps us to keep our hands clean, even though in the end we are perfectly willing to do the evil. For example, if a Catholic health care facility were pressed to accept the idea that having some abortions or sterilizations was a necessity, and if its authorities accepted this necessity, but decided that a way should be developed to do these procedures indirectly, it would be difficult to understand their decision except as a form of moral evasion.

This criticism seems to be a devastating objection against any use of double effect simply to keep one's distance from evil that one really accepts. For it is surely a form of moral evasion that any morally serious person will find repellent; it is akin to Pilate's washing his hands of Christ's blood — a transparent form of self deception to which all decent people object. Moreover, Christians especially will recognize this sort of evasion as being a variation on the ritualistic legalism which Jesus and Paul condemned.

But surely any use of double effect in this spirit is an abuse. For double effect is not a way to get what you think you must get, while keeping your distance by way of the indirectness of the causality. It is a way of testing our wills and sorting out our motives to be sure that we are not really setting our hearts on evil in actions where it is not clear precisely what we are doing. What we intend to do is not determined by a sort of speech we make to ourselves after we have resolved to do something; it is the very choice and resolve to do it, and it is what we choose and our choosing it that determines what is direct and what is indirect. So, if we really will the evil, the act cannot be justified by double effect.

b. Double effect is based on distinctions that lack the moral significance double effect gives them — in particular, the distinction between what is intended and what is accepted as a side effect.

When someone objects that there is no real difference between the case allowed by double effect and the case excluded what he may have in mind is that the difference between the cases is not morally important.[3] This objection is absolutely foundational, both theoretically and practically. For the tradition holds that there is a difference in intention between the permitted and the excluded procedure, and that this difference is morally decisive. If the killing is the means chosen to save the mother's life, then it is intended and the procedure is morally excluded. But if the death is a side effect, it need not be intended, even though in some sense it is voluntarily accepted or permitted, and in this case the procedure can be morally justified. But why should differences in intention mark differences between something that is absolutely prohibited and something which under some circumstances one can morally do?

In the face of this objection, it might be tempting to think that double effect is one of those elements of classical moral theology which ought to be jettisoned as part of the renewal of moral theology called for by Vatican II. This suggestion would be ill-conceived if it were based on the supposition that it might be possible to avoid the careful analysis of conflict cases in morality. For dealing with difficult cases — casuistry — is an unavoidable part of moral thinking. Furthermore, one should not suppose that casuistical analysis will always arrive at conclusions that are intuitively plausible or congenial to common sense. For these problems arise precisely when straightforward application of moral principles breaks down. Moreover, under such circumstances, our intuitions and common sense have their own biases. Thus it would be a mistake to try to justify double effect by showing that it gives the "right answers" or that its implications are not sometimes very difficult to accept.

The question remains, however, whether it is necessary to continue to use double effect as part of the methodology for resolving moral dilemmas. The only way to settle this question is to ask whether or not double effect is essentially related to the basic principles of Christian morality. If it is, then it cannot be set aside without compromising these principles. But if not, then it can be put aside as part of classical moral theology which is not essential to Christian morality and can be discarded.

I believe that the double effect doctrine as it comes down to us does suffer in several ways from the shortcomings and limitations of classical moral theology. However, double effect exists to protect central truths of Christian morality. If it should be abandoned in the face of this objection, the Church would, in effect, be admitting that she has been mistaken in thinking that what is morally essential is what we choose, as distinct from the results we foresee but do not choose. Therefore, we cannot simply abandon or radically revise double effect. In the remainder of this chapter I will sketch out the connection between double effect and some basic moral truths taught by the Church. Then I will say a few things about the current reinterpretations of double effect which seem to me to accept the objection and attempt a revision incompatible with Christian moral principles.

III. Double Effect and the Basic Principles of Christian Moral Life: Response to the Second Objection

a. The end to which Christian moral life is directed is the kingdom of Christ.

Perhaps the most basic formulation of the fundamental principle of Christian moral life is the twofold love commandment which prescribes loving God with all our hearts and our neighbor as ourselves. What the love in this commandment directs us towards is the ultimate community of love — the kingdom of Christ in which all things will find their fulfillment. Thus, since the kingdom is something to which we can contribute by our human actions when done out of living faith, and since we can fail voluntarily to do our part in the cooperative effort of building up the kingdom, "Seek first the kingdom of God" is a basic principle of Christian moral life.

The moral significance of the kingdom is strikingly illuminated in a powerful statement of Christian hope in *Gaudium et Spes*, article 39:

> When we have spread on earth the fruits of our nature and our enterprise — human dignity, brotherly communion, and freedom — according to the command of the Lord and his Spirit, we will find them once again, cleansed this time from the stain of sin, illuminated and transfigured, when Christ presents to his Father an eternal kingdom "of truth and life, a kingdom of holiness and grace, a kingdom of justice, love and peace." Here on earth the kingdom is mysteriously present; when the Lord comes it will enter into its perfection.

This statement makes it clear that the morally good actions and enterprises of human beings are parts of the very fabric of the kingdom God is even now mysteriously building up. The good things we do are not merely instrumental to achieving the kingdom but are intrinsic parts — as it were, the very bricks and mortar — of what Jesus will hand over to the Father.

b. We contribute to the kingdom by building up its personal and interpersonal fabric.

What this statement does not make altogether clear is how our actions can contribute to the building up of the kingdom. Some hints are provided earlier in the article where the Council reminds us that it profits a man nothing if he gains the whole world and loses or forfeits himself, and that earthly progress must be distinguished from the increase in Christ's kingdom. Also, article 38 speaks of Christian life in this world as "preparing the material of the heavenly kingdom."

These considerations make it clear that earthly success and good results are not the main things we contribute to the kingdom. *Gaudium et Spes*, article 35 — the article on which *Laborem Exercens* is so plainly dependent[4] — puts this as follows:

Human activity proceeds from man; it is also ordered to him. When he works, not only does he transform matter and society, but he fulfills himself. He learns, he develops his faculties, and he emerges from and transcends himself. Rightly understood, this kind of growth is more precious than any kind of wealth that can be amassed. It is what a man is, rather than what he has, that counts. Technical progress is of less value than advances towards greater justice, wider brotherhood, and a more humane social environment. Technical progress may supply the material for human advance but it is powerless to actualize it.

In other words, the goods which form the fabric of the kingdom are not realized in their most fundamental form by successful projects but by establishing decent human relationships and making ourselves good persons. Human dignity, brotherhood, freedom, justice, truth, holiness, love and peace are not things we can construct and own in the way we can own our material goods and successes. Rather, they are aspects of our moral selves — the selves we constitute by the free choices we make.

c. We build up the fabric of the kingdom by constituting by our free choices selves worthy of the kingdom. Morality is primarily in the heart.

It seems, therefore, that our role in building up the kingdom is primarily a matter of "soul making" or "self making;" it is, less metaphorically, a matter of building up the persons and the interpersonal relationships which are now and forever will be part of the kingdom. This is part of what is meant by the idea that, for the Christian, morality is primarily in the heart. For it is our very selves — both individually and in communion — that are now already, and will be perfectly when the Lord comes, integral parts of the kingdom. And these selves are constituted by our free choices, by what we love and how we set our hearts.[5]

The recognition that morality is primarily in the heart helps us answer the objection that there is no normal significance in the distinction between what is foreseen and what is intended. For what we intend and choose is what we set our hearts on, whereas what we voluntarily accept or "permit" as a side effect has a dif-

250

ferent relationship to our moral selves. Like God, who permits some evils although he wills none, we sometimes may accept evil effects which we could not choose without violating God's image in ourselves and others.

Hence we can understand what St. Thomas had in mind when he said that "moral acts receive their species according to what is intended." He said this in his famous discussion of killing in self-defense, where he argued that the killing of an attacker could be outside the defender's intention, and that then what defined the act morally was not this side effect but the chosen defense which alone was willed.[6]

d. Voluntarily accepting side effects is not self constituting in the way that intending and choosing are. So, the distinction used by double effect is morally significant.

In freely choosing to do something a person determines himself or herself to be a certain kind of person. For example, those who choose, however reluctantly, to end the life of an unborn baby by abortion make themselves killers, set themselves against life. But when the evil one brings about is a side effect only, one's self is not defined by the bringing about of the evil. For in this case one does not act for the sake of the evil but despite it; one does not set one's heart on it as one does when one resolves to do it in order to realize some ulterior state of affairs. Thus, in the case of indirect abortion, the child's death is not anything one seeks to realize but is reluctantly accepted and would be avoided if possible. If the child were to survive the hysterectomy, every effort would be made to save it, and all would rejoice if these efforts succeeded.

The case of Thomas More, as presented in the play *Man for All Seasons*, provides a striking example of how what we intend and choose affects our moral selves differently from what we accept as a side effect.[7] More realized full well that the course he chose to follow would lead to his death. He wanted to stay alive, and knew that he could stay alive if only he would falsely swear an oath. Yet he steadfastly pursued his course because he believed that to do otherwise would be to compromise his very self. Like Jesus, he freely accepted death. But this acceptance was not a choice against life; his choice was to be true to himself — never to swear falsely — and it is this that defined his moral self, not his acceptance of death as a side effect of this choice.

In short, the objection that intending an evil and accepting one as a foreseen side effect are not morally different is based on a view of morality that is much more result-oriented than Christian morality ever can be, because of the latter's concern about the persons and relationships built up in acting faithfully, whether the act gets results or not.

However, this point does not complete the effort to sketch the connection between double effect and Christian moral principles. To do this it is necessary to say something about moral norms, since double effect deals with how moral norms, and in particular, absolute norms, are to be applied in conflict situations.

e. Moral norms and moral absolutes guide our choices so that the selves we constitute will be worthy material for the kingdom.

The role of moral norms in Christian life is easy to understand within the context of our work in building up Christ's kingdom. Moral norms help us to distinguish between earthly progress and the increase in Christ's kingdom; they help us to recognize when we are seeking to gain the world at the expense of ourselves; they show us the way to make our earthly lives and attainments worthy material for the kingdom. In short, moral norms direct our choices so that the selves constituted by them will be good. They exclude those choices which make us persons unable to contribute to and share in Christ's kingdom.

Some moral norms will be absolute if there are some choices a good person should never make. If there are choices which under all circumstances will render any person who makes them unworthy of the kingdom — will constitute a person as one opposed to the human goods which will be part of the kingdom — then there are moral absolutes. And there are such choices. For if we are to serve persons and to reverence what belongs to persons in the way necessary to respect their human dignity and to establish communion with them, then we cannot choose to harm that dignity or to violate that communion.

Thus, for example, to act against human life by the choice to kill an innocent person is to constitute oneself anti-life; the person one kills is not loved; the bonds of communion with that person

252

are broken, no matter how noble or exigent one's ulterior purpose might be. Similarly, the exclusion of adultery is an absolute norm because it protects the fidelity of marriage — an essential part of the existential fabric of the commitment of marriage — from compromise in the face of lust, frustration, and the tragedy of the breakdown of intimate personal relations. Marriage is not a project that can succeed or fail, but a commitment which demands fidelity. Thus, this fidelity must be preserved and protected, especially when marriage fails to be satisfactory. The absolute exclusion of adultery shows what is minimally needed to preserve fidelity, especially when worldly reasons, human hopes and desires, point to another course.

f. Since common sense descriptions of our actions do not always reveal their morally significant features, double effect is needed.

Since moral norms in general and moral absolutes in particular direct our choices toward what is really and lastingly good, it is necessary to be clear about what exactly we are choosing. This necessity is especially important when we face moral dilemmas in which it is not clear exactly what it is that we are choosing. It is in such situations that the clarifications provided by double effect are needed. For as long as human actions are described and thought about in terms other than those that are essential from the point of view of Christian morality, it will be necessary for us to clarify what is really going on from the moral point of view. It will be necessary, in other words, to separate the morally significant features of human actions from common sense descriptions of actions — descriptions which often obscure and fail to reveal what one chooses and intends. Since common sense is based on interests and concerns that are not altogether those of Christ's kingdom, it is likely that the necessity for this kind of clarification will be a permanent one.[8]

Thus, if we describe an action simply as an abortion,we are likely to miss the most central aspects of the act. Likewise, if we talk about "killing in self-defense" or "letting someone die." In this last example the problem arises because the description does not make clear how the person's death is related to the decision to discontinue treatment. Before we can evaluate such a case we need to know whether treatment was discontinued in order to

253

hasten death, or in order to avoid something bad — for example, the waste of useless procedures, pain, or expense. Only then, after exposing the morally relevant features of the decision, can we even begin to arrive at a moral judgment.[9]

In short, since Christian morality is primarily concerned with what is in the human heart — with our use of our self-constituting freedom — a procedure like double effect will be needed as long as common sense descriptions of actions fail to make clear what the intentions and choices involved are.

Of course, there are theories of morality which do not focus on the human heart but rather on the results of our actions. Consequentialism, as it is aptly called, sees morality as an effort to construct a world that is as good as possible.[10] For consequentialists, differences of intention are not important as such; what counts are the predictable results. Therefore, moral absolutes such as that forbidding the killing of the innocent are dismissed. Lenin explained himself as a consequentialist when he said. "You can't make an omelet without breaking eggs," and proceeded to kill all who blocked the success of the revolution.

From a Christian point of view this approach confuses the limited part in providence which we humans have and the divine ordering of the whole of creation to what is good, and it mistakes the building up of this world for the increase of the kingdom. These confusions, quite understandable in post-Christian nonbelievers, lead them to make moral decisions on a basis that only divine knowledge could provide, and, for the sake of the overall good, to choose in ways that compromise their selves and their communion with others. It is not surprising that proponents of this view of morality hold double effect in contempt.

IV. Reinterpretations of Double Effect

In recent years some Catholic moralists have proposed more or less radical reinterpretations of double effect. With the exception of Germain Grisez's work on double effect, most of these efforts have been within the trend of moral thinking which among Catholics has come to be called "proportionalism."

Grisez's version of double effect, to which I have contributed, is based on a criticism of what he regards as the excessively behavioristic view of human action assumed by the manualists. Moreover, Grisez's version does lead to certain practical conclusions at variance with those of the tradition. Nevertheless, it seems to me that Grisez's work on double effect is really a refinement and development which is needed as part of the effort to extricate essential moral doctrine from the limitations of classical moral. This development is compatible with the spirit and basic principles which undergird double effect.[11]

a. Proportionalist reinterpretations of double effect abandon its spirit and specific provisions.

Proportionalist reinterpretations, however, are a different matter. For what they propose as a reinterpretation or replacement of double effect is, in fact, contrary to its spirit and specific provisions. Proportionalism is an approach to moral decision-making according to which one's moral obligation is to choose the greater good, or the lesser evil. The judgments which determine moral obligation are comparative value judgments — that is, they are judgments which state that doing A is the lesser evil rather than doing B. Such judgments suppose that the values at stake can be ascertained and compared or weighed against one another. The application of this method of moral thinking can be, and often is limited in certain ways — for example to conflict situations or moral dilemmas, or, even more narrowly, to conflict cases involving pre-moral goods like life. Sometimes, too, a moral limit, such as the Golden Rule, is accepted by proportionalists, though Catholic proportionalists usually do not make use of this important limit.

It is possible, of course, simply to replace double effect with proportionalism. And I think it is not a falsification of the issue to say that this is what the proportionalist reinterpretations amount to. Various ways of doing this have been proposed. One is, in effect, to redefine the ideas of direct and indirect in terms of proportionate reason or the lesser evil.[12] The most plausible reinterpretation begins by admitting that there is a distinction between direct and indirect action, or between what is intended and what is only accepted as a side effect. This approach also admits that this distinction has some moral significance. What is questioned is the precise moral significance attached to these distinc-

tions in the traditional uses of double effect. Thus, if an innocent •
person's death were not a side effect but a means chosen in a situation where the alternative was horrible, double effect would exclude the choice to kill, but this reinterpretation might permit the
killing as the lesser evil. [13]

This schematic example suggests how different double effect
is from any approach to moral dilemmas based on the proportionalist method. The double effect approach does not compromise the moral absolutes which form the bedrock of Catholic
moral teaching. Rather, it helps us to grasp, and precisely apply
the relevant absolute norm. This contrasts with the proportionalist approach which allows exceptions to traditional moral
absolutes, such as those forbidding adultery and the killing of the
innocent, if making the exception should prove the lesser evil.
Likewise double effect preserves the principle that one must not
do evil that good might come about, by distinguishing between
evil means chosen for the sake of a good end and evil side effects
accepted in the doing of good, whereas proportionalism allows
one to choose an evil — for example killing the innocent or involvement in adultery — for the sake of good if that should be the
lesser evil. So, proportionalism does not deal with moral dilemmas in the same spirit as double effect.

The difference between double effect and proportionalism
might seem to be like the difference between male and female hip-
popotamuses: just as this difference is of interest only to hip-
popotamuses, that between double effect and proportionalism is
of interest only to moralists. But this is not so. The difference is
more like the difference between contraception and NFP, which
Pope John Paul II says is "wider and deeper than is usually
thought," and in the final analysis involves two irreconcilable concepts of the human person (*Familiaris Consortio*, n. 32). This
comparison is especially apt because part of the irreconcilable difference to which the Pope refers is the difference between the
moral outlooks represented by double effect and proportionalism:
if the importance of what people choose is emphasized as in
double effect, contraception and NFP will be seen to be morally
different, since they involve different choices; but, if these differences in choice are overridden by considerations based on the
similarity of results, and of what might be the lesser evil, the difference will be hard to discern. [14]

256

b. "Proportionate reason" is essential to double effect, and needs more analysis, but is not correctly handled by proportionalists.

Of course, the last condition of double effect is usually stated in terms of "proportion." Even if the other conditions are met, if one is not choosing or intending evil but only accepting it as a side effect, one must still have a proportionate reason for doing the action. This means that some consideration of the lesser evil is involved in the procedure prescribed by double effect.

But this consideration is brought into play only after the other conditions by which we have clarified the essential moral nature of the act in question and determined that the intentions involved are not set on evil. Proportionalist reinterpretations, however, swamp the other tests of double effect by beginning with considerations appropriate only after these other tests have been passed.

Furthermore, it is by no means clear that the notion of proportionately grave reason used in the final condition of double effect is the same thing as the proportionalists have in mind when they talk of "lesser evils." For "lesser evil" is one of those terms that has more than a single meaning. For example, lesser evil can refer to the difference between light and grave matter, or to the difference between an unjust and a more unjust state of affairs, or it can be used to refer simply to the morally right but difficult choice as compared to alternatives that are also undesirable (perhaps less so than the morally required option) but not morally required. It was in this sense that Newman spoke of any deliberate sin, even a single venial sin, as a worse evil than the occurrence of any physical evil whatever. None of these uses of lesser evil involves the comparative value judgments presupposed by the proportionalist use of this term.

The proportionalist notion of lesser evil, however, is beset with analytical difficulties. Ever since the time of Jeremy Bentham, philosophers have been asking: where is the scale of values needed to make the comparison of values we must make to determine the greater good or lesser evil? Neither human experience nor philosophical construction have provided one.[15] No doubt, this is one very important reason why many professional

257

moralists, including some of the world's leading Catholic and non-Catholic moral thinkers — have systematically rejected utilitarianism and other consequentialist approaches to moral reasoning. Thus, it seems more proper to say that in proportionalist "reinterpretations" of double effect what swamps the other tests is not simply a kind of consideration appropriate only to the last condition, but a rather dubious interpretation of how that condition works.

This mishandling of the final condition of double effect does not mean that it is not very important. This rather neglected condition of double effect needs more attention than it has received, and one of the merits of the current discussion is to focus on this need. For this condition reminds us that when an action involves evil, it is not sufficient for its moral justification that the evil should be only accepted rather than willed — not intended as an end or chosen as a means. The evil is real and its acceptance is in a real sense voluntary, so further justification is needed. It seems to me that any morally relevant consideration, other than those settled by the prior conditions, is appropriate here. Thus, if one has a special duty to prevent the evil, or if bringing about the evil even indirectly should be unfair, then one should not do the act in question.

Aquinas' discussion of self-defense provides a good example of the kind of considerations that are relevant. Aquinas first establishes that in the lethal self-defense he is analyzing, the death of the attacker is *praeter intentionem*. The death is a side effect of a morally legitimate act of self defense. But other questions immediately arise: what about the force used to repel the attack? And should one forgo the defensive action so as to avoid even an indirect killing? He answers that the force used must be moderate, and that one is not obliged to forgo the self-defense because one is more obliged to provide for one's own life than for the life of another. The first answer seems to be based on a requirement of proportion between what one intends and what one does to realize the intention — that more harm than needed should not be inflicted. This, of course, is not weighing values. The second answer seems to be based on the order of charity — one's obligation to provide for what is within one's area of responsibility. Again it is not that one's life is of greater value than the attacker's,

258

but rather that one's responsibility for it is greater and more immediate. [16]

Finally, the most fundamental issue in the acceptance of proportionalism as a replacement for double effect should be considered: Is proportionalism a way of handling moral dilemmas that comports well with the fundamentals of Christian morality? Does the doctrine of the lesser evil help us to distinguish between earthly progress and the increase of Christ's kingdom? Does it help us to mark the line between what forfeits our selves and what builds up the human fabric of the kingdom? Is it compatible with a morality that focuses on the human heart — on what we make of ourselves by our free choices? It seems to me that the answers to these questions are negative. Proportionalism seems more in line with the result-oriented ethic from which its method, often with restrictions, is taken. In any case, until some plausible affirmative answers to questions like these are forthcoming, proportionalism must be judged a poor substitute for double effect.

Notes

1. See J. P. Gury, S.J. (revised by A. Ballerini, S.J.), *Compendium theologiae moralis*, 2nd ed. (Rome and Turin, 1869), p. 7; these conditions are an explication of Gury's succinct statement of the principle: "It is licit to posit a cause which is either good or indifferent from which follows a twofold effect, one good the other evil, if a proportionately grave reason is present, and if the end of the agent is honorable — that is, if he does not intend the evil effect." See Joseph T. Mangan, S.J., "An Historical Analysis of the Principle of Double Effect," *Theological Studies* 10 (1949), 60-61, for a translation from the fifth German edition of Gury's entire treatment of double effect. Fr. Mangan's classic study provides an account of double effect that goes beyond anything in the manuals. Fr. Mangan's "Making Moral Choices in Conflict Situations," in William E. May, editor, *Principles of Catholic Moral Life* (Chicago: Franciscan Herald Press, 1981), pp. 329-358, provides a readable introduction to double effect; my "Toward Understanding the Principle of Double Effect," *Ethics* 90 (1980), 527-538 provides an introduction in the context of contemporary philosophical objections to double effect.
2. See Pascal, "Letter VII," *Provincial Letters*; see also Stanley Windass, "Double Think and Double Effect," *Blackfriars*, 44 (1963), 257-266.
3. The most influential version of this objection is that of Oxford jurisprudent H.L.A. Hart, "Intention and Punishment," in his *Punishment and Responsibility* (Oxford: Oxford University Press, 1968), pp. 123-124; see also Phillipa Foot, "Abortion and the Doctrine of Double Effect," in J. Rachels, ed., *Moral Problems*, (New York: Harper and Row, 1971), pp. 28-41; my "Double-Effect and a Certain Type of Embryotomy," *The Irish Theological Quarterly*, 44 (1977), 303-318 is a response to Hart's position.
4. See *Laborem Exercens*, n. 26; also John M. Finnis, "The Fundamental Themes of *Laborem Exercens*," in Paul Williams ed., *Catholic Social Thought and the Teaching of John Paul II: Proceedings of the Fifth Convention (1982) of the Fellowship of Catholic Scholars* (Scranton: Northeast Books, 1983), pp. 19-31.
5. It is worth noting that the thinker who has done the most to elucidate the self-constituting character of a person's free choices is Pope John Paul II; see Cardinal Karol

Wojtyla, *The Acting Person*, (Dordrecht, Boston, London: D. Reidel Publishing Co., 1979), pp. 105-186, especially 149-151; this idea is also prominent in his statements as Pope, especially in his emphasis on the "subjective sense" of work in *Laborem Exercens*, n. 6; for an explanation of this teaching, see Finnis, "The Fundamental Themes of *Laborem Exercens*," *op. cit.*

6. See *Summa Theologiae*, I, II, q. 64, a. 7; The relevant sentences are the following: ". . . nothing prevents a single act from having two effects of which only one may be intended while the other indeed may be *praeter intentionem*. Moral acts receive their species from what is intended and not from what is *praeter intentionem* since this is *per accidens*. . .". For an exegesis see my "*Praeter Intentionem* in Aquinas," *The Thomist*, 42 (1978), 657-661.

7. See Robert Bolt, *Man For All Seasons* (New York: Vintage Books, 1962).

8. See Germain Grisez and Joseph M. Boyle Jr., *Life and Death with Liberty and Justice: A Contribution to the Euthanasia Debate* (Notre Dame and London: University of Notre Dame Press, 1979), pp. 381-392, for an attempt to state the basic distinctions of double effect in modern philosophical language; this effort does not, however, remove the necessity for reformulating common sense descriptions of human actions into morally relevant and clear descriptions.

9. See my "On Killing and Letting Die," *The New Scholasticism* 51 (1977) 433-452 for an account of the relevance of intention to the issue of withholding treatment.

10. See Charles Fried, *Right and Wrong* (Cambridge, London: Harvard University Press, 1978), pp. 7-9, for an account of consequentialism.

11. See Germain Grisez, "Toward a Consistent Natural Law Ethics of Killing," *The American Journal of Jurisprudence* 15 (1970), 64-96; and my "Double-Effect and a Certain Type of Embryotomy," *op. cit.*

12. See Peter Knauer, S.J., "The Hermeneutic Function of the Principle of Double Effect," *Natural Law Forum* 12 (1967), 132-162; for a critique see Grisez, "Toward a Consistent Natural Law Ethics of Killing," 79-83.

13. See Richard McCormick, S.J., *Ambiguity in Moral Choice: The 1973 Pere Marquette Theology Lecture* (Milwaukee: Marquette University Press, 1973), especially pp. 70-84.

14. See my "Contraception and Natural Family Plannning," *International Review of Natural Family Planning* 4 (1980) 309-315, for an account of the differences in the choices involved in Contraception and NFP.

15. See Germain Grisez, "Against Consequentialism," *The American Journal of Jurisprudence* 23 (1978) 21-72, for a developed argument that premoral goods must be incommensurable in the way needed for consequentialist weighing of values; for a shorter version of the argument, see *Life and Death with Liberty and Justice*, pp. 346-355.

16. See *Summa Theologiae* I, II, q. 64, a. 7.

Chapter 13

The Moral Inseparability of the Unitive and Procreative Aspects of Human Sexual Intercourse

The Reverend Thomas P. Doyle O.P., J.C.D.

I. The Basic Question and Its Urgency

Sexuality is an essential dimension of every creature, yet for the human person sexuality differs radically from that of any other form of life. There is probably no aspect of humanity that is more influential, powerful and mysterious than sexuality. Just as sexuality itself is mysterious, so is its ultimate form of expression, intercourse. Unlike the sexual joining of the lower animals which is ordered to reproduction, that of the humans has a two-fold finality: it is ordered to the continuation of the species and to communication between persons. Consequently it is really more precise to refer to the sexual joining of the lower animals as "copulation" and to that of humans as "intercourse".

The meaning of "unitive" and "procreative." The reproductive aspect of human sexual intercourse is called "procreative" because it enables persons to participate in God's act of creation. The communicative aspect is called "unitive" because it is a language whereby a man and a woman are able to communicate a commitment to one another and at the same time experience "being one." This commitment is grounded in conjugal *love*, a unique or special kind of love which is rooted in the will and is manifested by the giving of oneself to the other.[1]

In fact people can have sexual intercourse which is neither unitive nor procreative. In spite of this, can these two aspects be *morally separated* without at the same time a) dishonoring God, the Author of life; b) redefining the meaning of sexual intercourse and its place in marriage, and, c) having negative side-effects within culture and society?[2]

It is one thing for couples to choose to have sexual intercourse for non-procreative and/or non-unitive purposes, e.g., for recreational purposes, yet it is quite another matter for a re-direction of the purpose of intercourse to be socially or culturally accepted. Such a re-direction would influence the meaning and stability of marriage, the nurture of children and the role of the family in society. Essentially the moral separation of the unitive and procreative aspects of intercourse can amount to a de-humanization of intercourse. Thus it would become a "thing," subject to exploitation and abuse. Such exploitation not only degrades the very meaning of sexuality but holds a potential for psychic, spiritual or even physical harm to persons.

Searching for the meaning of sexual intercourse. The unitive and procreative aspects of sexual intercourse are ontological realities: they take their meaning from the nature of the human person. Sexual intercourse also serves other ends . . . intercourse can be sought or experienced for other reasons because of its effects on the person. Among these functions are actual reproduction, the actual communication of love and/or affection, the release of tension and the attainment of physical and psychological pleasure.

Pleasure is a powerful function of intercourse and because of this it has much to do with the confusion related to the search for the meaning of intercourse. One way or the other sexual intercourse produces pleasure and this, combined with the fact that intercourse is sub-rational, needing to be under the command of reason, is related to much of the popular definition of what sex is all about.[3]

Sexual intercourse has an intrinsic meaning based on its nature. Nevertheless the meaning of intercourse is influenced by myths, taboos, etc., and by predominant social behavior.

Because of its relationship to human generation, which has an element of mystery about it, as well as the powerful and unique kind of pleasure attached to intercourse, society and culture have repeatedly developed myths, taboos and superstitions which in turn have led to the growth of restrictions and norms surrounding sexual behavior. The sexual urge needs to be under the control of reason and is not completely understandable. Hence the development of the myths etc. which filled the gap of ignorance. These myths, taboos and superstitions with their contingent rules and norms cannot totally define the meaning of sexual intercourse since there is often an arbitrary and therefore distorted dimension in the relationship between the intrinsic nature of human sexuality and the myths.

The other powerful factor in shaping the meaning of intercourse is societal behavior. Sectors of the population tend to define the meaning and purpose of intercourse by what the majority are doing in this regard. Human beings knew about sexual intercourse before they banded together as a society. Therefore it is difficult to see how the meaning of intercourse can be determined from sociological findings. In most, if not all, societies the mores governing behavior are based on what is acceptable and what is unacceptable. This in turn is based to an extent on the myths and taboos etc. As societies become more materialistic and secularistic, or sophisticated in a worldly sense, the myths disappear and behavior patterns are no longer influenced by values no longer considered valid. There must be an authentic value system concerned with sexual behavior which is based on the intrinsic meaning of intercourse.[4] This intrinsic meaning of intercourse rests on the correct understanding of the unitive and procreative aspects and their inseparability. Historically the development of the myths which led to culturally or even legally enunciated standards of behavior was often grounded in a need to protect one or both of these aspects from abuse.

263

Sexual intercourse can take place in a variety of contexts, each of which is related in a different way to the unitive and procreative aspects. Intercourse can take place within marriage, outside of marriage, prior to marriage, within forbidden degrees of blood relationship. The circumstances or context will bear directly upon whether or not the two aspects are fulfilled or separated. Marriage has always been accepted as a context for intercourse. There has always been controversy and conflict as to the social and ethical acceptability of intercourse in extra- or pre-marital contexts. Incestuous intercourse (siblings, parents) is a nearly universal taboo while consanguineous intercourse (cousins, etc.) has been accepted in some cultures. The degree of acceptability of the various non-marital contexts for intercourse has a bearing on the role and development of the concepts of marriage and family within a society.[5]

The Church has long sought a theology of human sexuality that accurately reflects the true nature of man. The moral inseparability of the unitive and procreative aspects of intercourse becomes more than a command when it is grounded in the authentic nature of sexuality. The Church's understanding of sexuality is grounded in the essential goodness of the person. The contemporary teaching, typified in recent Papal and Magisterial pronouncements, is well grounded in historical and scriptural sources.[6]

There is an urgency to this question of the moral inseparability of the unitive and procreative aspects of intercourse. The Church must proclaim this inseparability because the acceptance of the possibility of separating the two aspects can have a profound effect on marriage and family life and respect for human life in general.

II. The Inseparability of the Unitive and Procreative Aspects

The Church teaches, and rightly so, that the unitive and procreative aspects of sexual intercourse are morally inseparable. The nature of this intimate and profound language rules out intercourse solely for pleasure or recreation. Many, however, see the Church's teaching as a dogmatic statement cut off from the reality of contemporary life. If the reasons for the Church's teaching are presented, the entire matter can be seen in a positive light.

The *first* and fundamental reason for the moral inseparability is grounded in the complex nature of human sexuality. *Secondly*, marriage as a natural institution and as a sacrament demands this moral inseparability. *Thirdly*, since human sexuality and sexual activity has a social dimension, the moral separability of the two with the consequent de-personalization of sexual intercourse leads to negative consequences in society.

III. The Nature of Human Sexuality

The human being is unique in that it is the only being created by God for its own sake. The person is good or worthwhile because he is a person. A human being is not simply a highly developed form of animal life with intelligence and rationality. There is a radical difference between the human person and every other form of animal life and this difference lies in the fact that the person is created in the image of God. This unique imaging is expressed in the person's ability to love. This capacity transcends all levels of intelligence, all degrees and kinds of physical appearance and health and every kind of social stratification.

God created man in His own image and likeness: calling him to existence through love, He called him at the same time for love. God is love and in Himself He lives a mystery of personal, loving communion. Creating the human race in His own image and continually keeping it in being, God inscribed in the humanity of man and woman the vocation, and thus the capacity and responsibility, of love and communion. Love is therefore the fundamental and innate vocation of every human being. [7]

Love (self-gift) is meaningless unless it is shared with another person. The person cannot give of himself to a lower animal since the animals cannot, by their very nature, receive this gift. A person may share a kind of affection with an animal such as a pet, but this is not love.

The *Genesis* account of creation explains the extent and nature of human love. The human person is able to love and thus to achieve true self-actualization only with a creature equal to him:

> When God Yahweh says that "it is not good for man to be alone" (Gen 2:18), He affirms that "alone" man does not completely realize this essence. He realizes it only by existing with someone and even more deeply and completely, by existing for someone.[8]

In his "original solitude" man, the human person, was isolated among all of the other creatures, yet he was essentially complete, possessing the ability to love.[9] The *Genesis* account says that it "is not good for man to be alone." A change was needed and this change was directly related to man's uniqueness as a person able to love.

The Holy Father, in his commentary on this passage of *Genesis*, posits that the reference to man's falling into a deep sleep could indicate a return to the moment preceding man's creation " . . . in order that, through God's creative initiative, solitary 'man' may emerge from it again in his double unity as male and female."[10] Upon waking from sleep, the man, now male, discovers the woman . . . the helper fit for him. Man's reaction to the woman points to his realization that she shared a similar nature with him:

> In this way the man (male) manifests for the first time joy and even exaltation, for which he had no reason before, owing to the lack of a being like himself. Joy in the other human being, in the second "self," dominates the words spoken by the man (male) on seeing the woman (female).[11]

The fact that man's original solitude was substantially prior to his companionship with the woman indicates that she is not merely a duplication of the man (male) with incidental anatomical and other differences. Following upon the original solitude there is the "original unity of man and woman." The two share a similar nature yet they are quite separate and different. The human, man, is created in two modes: as male and female. It is vital to understand that man and woman share the same essence yet there is a difference and a complementarity about them that enables man and woman to be something that would be impossible had man not been created in two modes. It is significant that man's potential for love becomes real with the creation of the woman.

The concept of "original unity" is expressed in "giving life to that *communio personarum* that man and woman form . . . " The potential for loving and thus for imaging God is realized in this communion of man and woman.

> . . . we can deduce that man became the image and likeness of God not only through his own humanity, but also through the communion of persons which man and woman form right from the beginning . . . Man becomes the image of God not so much in the moment of solitude as in the moment of communion.[12]

From Adam's sleep emerges "man" yet two different ways of being "man." In these two ways, male and female, we have a key to understanding the human body and its role for accomplishing God's plan for man. The two modes of being human are expressed by means of the body. Male and female bodies are each composed of similar bone and flesh tissues, similar blood types, digestive organs, etc. yet there is an all-pervasive difference that transcends human corporeality and that difference is sexuality.[13] It is no accident that there is an intimate relationship between the *communio personarum* of man and woman that enables man to image God, the fact that the distinguishing factor of the two modes of being human is sexuality and the fact that through sexuality man both expresses love . . . the gift, and shares in the power to generate life.

Since human sexual interaction is not only ordered to generation but to communication, it is called by a special name, "intercourse." The sexual joining of the lower animals is properly referred to as "copulation" which differs from intercourse. Intercourse is not sub-rational but a response of the will. It is not simply the joining of sexual organs but the joining of two persons.

The relationship of the Body to the Person . Personhood is expressed through the body, but the body is not merely a shell or a kind of vehicle which is directed and used by the person. In truth the body is also the person because it is through the body that the person exists and expresses his or her fundamental purpose of imaging the creator. The divider between the two modes of being a person is sexuality, the sexual differences being much more than biological. The reason why man's potential for love as a gift can ever be realized is grounded in sexuality:

> Sexuality is a fundamental component of personality, one of its modes of being, of manifestation, of communication with others, of feeling, of expressing and of living human love.[14]

Through life in the body the person expresses and experiences love in a variety of ways from verbal expression to complete sexual intercourse. Because the human body is distinct from any other kind of body, the expression and reception of love is uniquely human. Sexual behavior and the different ways of sexual expression are evaluated from the context of the meaning of the person: some are acceptable and others are not.[15] Since intercourse is ordered to a twofold aspect of communication and procreation, acceptable modes of sexual expression will conform to these aspects.

The Nuptial Meaning of the Body. The fact that the body expresses the person provides the basis for the theological insight of the nuptial meaning of the body. The capacity to give and receive and to form the *communio personarum* which brings forth the image of God is built upon the sexuality of the male and female. They communicate this self-gift through the language of the body. The body is "nuptial" then because it is designed for communicating love. This nuptial meaning is not confined to the capacity for sexual intercourse. The nuptial meaning permeates the entire person, enabling the person, through the various modes of communication, to express love. Human sexual communication is unique because it takes its significance from the nuptial meaning of the person which is expressed through the body.

Only the human person relates to other persons out of choice and not instinct. He choses whether and how to relate to another person. Communication is always through the body and it may be prompted by intense and total love, lust, emotional neutrality, apathy or deep-seated hatred. Nevertheless, the human body is intended by God to be nuptial or giving in spite of man's capacity for other kinds of bodily communication. The person does not determine when the body will be nuptial since person and body

268

are not separate realities. The person cannot simply use his or her body in a mechanistic way as if person and body did not constitute a natural whole.[16] The intellectual understanding of the nuptial meaning of the person should direct the will in choosing how the body is used in sexual communication.

It is possible to communicate sexually in ways that are clearly not nuptial. Sexual relations can be self-serving, can be ordered only to pleasure or can be loving yet closed to procreation, but *should* they be? The misuse of the body in sexual communication can be a distortion of its nuptial meaning by a disruption of the inner person:

> Concupiscence, in itself, is not capable of promoting union as the communion of persons. By itself, it does not unite, but appropriates. The relationship of the gift is changed into the relationship of appropriation.[17]

Concupiscence has been wrongly interpreted as the sexual urge itself yet this can hardly be true if the twofold aspect of sexual intercourse is good in itself. The Holy Father calls concupiscence a wedge between the body and the person which threatens to rob the body of its donative or nuptial meaning, replacing this meaning with selfish pleasure and possessiveness.[18]

Human sexual intercourse can never be considered merely biological *in se* as is the case with that of the lower animals. Human intercourse is always unique and only analogous to the copulation of the lower animals. Intercourse is a language whereby a man and a woman communicate a special love. Pope Paul VI described the characteristics of this love in *Humanae Vitae*:

> This love is first of all fully human, that is to say, of the senses and the spirit at the same time . . . This love is total . . . it is a very special form of personal friendship . . . Whoever truly loves his marriage partner loves not only for what he receives but for the partner's self, rejoicing that he can enrich his partner with the gift of himself . . . Again this love is faithful and exclusive until death. And finally, this love is fecund for it is not exhausted by the communion between husband and wife but is destined to continue, raising up new lives.[19]

This unique nature of human sexual interaction (intercourse) flows from human nature and is related to the ultimate form of human gift, the cooperation with the Creator in the gift of life to a new person. Intercourse serves more than physical release or pleasure. It is ordered to generation but serves more than fertility.

Reproduction and Procreation. Human fertility and the interaction that leads to conception and birth are inaccurately described as "reproduction." Man and woman are not merely reproducing. They are cooperating with the Creator since God creates the new person in the midst of the sexual intercourse and entrusts the child's nurture to the parents. The proper term for this process is "procreation."

After physical birth the new person is totally helpless, needing complete care. The parents provide physical and psychological nurture for the child, guiding it through the various stages of growth and human development. They also provide emotional and spiritual nurture, the latter being particularly important in view of the child's destiny to share eternity with the Creator.

The child is conceived through the physical act which is the ultimate word in the language of love. After birth, the parents draw the child into their own love relationship, thus nurturing the child's incipient capacity for love. By living out their love for each other the parents bring out the image of God in their child. Procreation, then, involves more than the physical or biological dimension of the sexual relationship. Procreation is a process which is completed by nurture and is dependent on the total union of the man and woman in an on-going love relationship. Human fertility is more than physical cooperation . . . it is a vocation:

> The total physical self-giving would be a lie if it were not the sign and fruit of total personal self-giving, in which the whole person, including the temporal dimension, is present . . . This totality which is required by conjugal love also corresponds to the demands of responsible fertility. This fertility is directed to the generation of a human being, and so by its nature it surpasses the purely biological order and involves a whole series of personal values.[20]

The male and female are not merely reproductive persons. They are procreative persons for two reasons: they have the capacity for bringing other human beings into existence through bodily cooperation, and they are necessary for the proper nurturing of the gift of the ability to love. The man and woman accomplish both of these aspects through their own conjugal love:

Conjugal love reaches that fulness to which it is interiorly ordained, conjugal charity, which is the proper and specific way in which the spouses participate in and are called to live the very charity of Christ who gave Himself on the cross.[21]

These two aspects of the procreational process, physical birth and spiritual nurture, are dependent upon the unitive and procreative aspects of intercourse. As procreative beings, man and woman express the gift of love in sexual communion, possible because of their complementarity. It is only in this union that fertility can be exercised, indicating that God's love is a life-giving love. The love of the parents continues to be expressed and strengthened through the language of intercourse. Thus intercourse as a unitive act promotes the *communio personarum* of the parents in the midst of which the child is raised. Even though individual acts of intercourse do not result in conception they are still procreational acts if they foster the love relationship of the parents.

The finality of intercourse transcends accompanying pleasure. This finality is best explained by the word "procreation" since the *complete* transmission of human life requires an ever-deepening love on the part of the parents.

This unique nature of sexual intercourse becomes even more evident if it is looked at in a three-dimensional context. Intercourse is a language that expresses an already existing love with a view to continuing this love into the future. Intercourse which takes place for pleasure alone, outside of the context of love, is isolated to the present.

If sexual intercourse is to be all that God has intended it to be then there must be a total, mutual acceptance of the man and the woman. As a unitive act intercourse implies a giving and not a taking. The man accepts the woman for who and what she is, not

271

for what he would like her to be or for the pleasure she momentarily provides . . . and vice versa. A man and a woman cannot claim to accept one another unconditionally and at the same time reject the procreative aspect of themselves. This procreative aspect is not merely biological but is grounded in the nuptial meaning of the person. In their original unity man and woman respond to their complementarity in order to realize God's image through love. Man and woman can become "one flesh" precisely because they are procreative beings. This procreative aspect does not depend on the consciousness or will of the person: it is there whether or not the person knows or wants it. Because the person is capable of conjugal love, the gift of self, he is procreative in his very essence. Even sexual intercourse between infertile persons which expresses authentic love and is open to God's will is procreative.

The pleasure that accompanies intercourse as well as the natural tendency to complete a romantic relationship or even a romantic encounter with intercourse lead to the *de facto* separation of the unitive and procreative aspects. People want to have intercourse without the possibility of procreation and often without the added responsibility of an interpersonal relationship. If the parties do not accept each other as procreative beings then the gift of self is limited. Hence even the unitive aspect of intercourse is altered and is a conditioned communication.

Only the *person* bears a responsibility for sexual acts and sexual intercourse since only the person acts from choice and not instinct. The decision to engage in sexual intercourse must be informed by what sexual intercourse *is*, and not simply by the physical or emotional effects that accompany it. Ultimately the choice to engage in intercourse must be shaped by the fact that intercourse is an expression of a special kind of love between two procreative persons.

Some hold that the sexual faculties are essentially biological and become procreative and unitive when this is consciously willed and chosen.[22] Those who follow this understanding also hold that there must be a sense of responsibility in having intercourse: responsibility to the relationship or at least to the experience. This approach focuses on the benefit of sexual relations to the persons. As such it is a pragmatic approach that does not direct their responsibility to the fact that sexual relations are intrinsically personal and procreational.[23] In other words, the responsible choice to have intercourse must be made with the full meaning of intercourse uppermost in mind.

Admittedly it is difficult to argue for an intrinsic meaning to human sexual intercourse while living in a secularist-materialist society. The morality of actions can easily be judged against a pragmatic set of standards since spiritual values are not that acceptable unless they can be rationally demonstrated. "What's wrong with doing it as long as nobody gets hurt?" is a commonplace justification for non-marital intercourse.

Summary. Only human beings are created by God with the capacity to relate in a manner beyond the physical. The gift of self is made on a spiritual level and communicated through the body. Human sexuality is unique because it is the means by which this gift is communicated. At the center of this gift is the power to generate human life and the contingent responsibility to nurture such life. Sexual intercourse is a language which communicates the person. As such it is by nature both unitive and procreative. If one aspect is separated from the other then sexual intercourse can become neither unitive nor procreative.

IV. Human Sexual Intercourse and Marriage

The procreative process demands stability in the man-woman relationship since the *communio personarum* cannot be a series of fleeting encounters with no real commitment. The welfare of society depends on the success of this process. Consequently every society from the most primitive to the most sophisticated has acknowledged God's design for man and woman in the institution of marriage.

The most common definition of marriage is that it is a stable relationship between a man and a woman from which children are born and in which they are given their rudimentary preparation to enter the social group.

When marriage and family life become disrupted from within and when this disruption becomes widespread among families, the society in general is affected. These disruptions are almost always centered around the sexual dimension of the marital relationship. Consequently sexual relations outside of marriage have been proscribed to a greater or lesser degree in most secular and religious societies down through history.[24] Why is sexual intercourse so important that such attention is paid to it? The answer lies in the fact that the male-female relationship, procreative by nature, is the fundamental growth principle for society. Sexual intercourse as a unique human act is grounded in the essence of procreative man and thus reserved to marriage.[25]

The Marriage Community and the "One Flesh." Marriage is defined in contemporary theological language as the "community of the whole of life," a phrase taken from *Gaudium et Spes* and repeated in the Code of Canon Law.[26] Neither of the commonly used Latin phrases (*communitas* — community, or *consortium* — partnership) fully captures the true meaning of the marriage relationship. Marriage is more than a "side-by-side" relationship of two loving people. It is this, a friendship, and more. Marriage is a oneness of two distinct persons which becomes possible because of their sexual complementarity, expressed through the body. This union has a completeness about it which goes beyond itself as it brings new life into existence.

In Gn 2: 23-24 we read that the man leaves his mother and father because he is destined by nature to become "one flesh" with a woman. The preceding phrase in which the man exclaims that the woman is "bone of my bones and flesh of my flesh" describes the kind of union possible because of the male-female complementarity. The term "one flesh" does not refer exclusively to joining in sexual intercourse but to the complete union. Sexual intercourse, as a complete bodily joining, symbolizes and effects the joining of the persons. The spouses become completely "one" not because they are joined in sexual embrace but because of their conjugal covenant.

Exegetes hold that the word pair "bone" and "flesh" is a common Old Testament covenantal formula which refers to strength (bone) and weakness (flesh). It implies the joining together of two distinct persons which together have the capacity to withstand every possible contingency in the relationship:

The statement "this . . . is bone of my bones and flesh of my flesh" occurs again and again in the Bible as an expression of blood relationship, and implies a fully human unity and an attitude of peace which is characteristic of the pattern of life of the clan.[27]

The "one flesh" union of the marriage covenant is not only total but has the same degree of stability as a blood relationship, which can be severed only with death. Thus to be "one flesh" requires nothing short of the total gift of self to one's spouse and the unconditioned acceptance of the other as gift. The sign of this gift is the procreative sexual act whereby the spouses' mutual giving and receiving of each other is open to new life. Perhaps one of the best English-language explanations of the meaning of the one flesh union is found in the traditional marriage vow formula: ". . . for better or for worse, for richer or for poorer, in sickness and in health until death do us part."

Marriage is more than an interpersonal relationship. It is a publicly pronounced, publicly acknowledged and publicly protected commitment. The spouses promise to become "one flesh" and to remain "one flesh" with one another. The man and woman may feel committed to one another and indeed may have expressed this commitment privately, yet it is not a marriage covenant until it is made according to the recognized formula. This public promise is necessary because of the potential for turning away from the relationship.

In spite of the sad reality of divorce, man and woman are basically capable of a permanent relationship. It is for this reason that Christian tradition uses the word "covenant" for the marriage agreement since it denotes a mutual commitment from which there is no turning back. After the covenant is entered into the spouses join in sexual intercourse which both symbolizes the totality of the marital union and continues to renew the covenant.[28]

Sexual intercourse is a profound and powerful language by which to express conjugal love. To be authentic, intercourse must be open to sharing the "one flesh" relationship with God's gift of a child. As a unitive act intercourse communicates the self-gift which the spouses continue to be to each other. As a procreative act intercourse is at once ordered to sharing this gift of love with a child while at the same time it enriches the marital community

. . . the "one flesh" union . . . in which the child will be nurtured.

Marital Consent and Sexual Intercourse. The 1917 Code of Canon Law referred to marital consent as an act of the will whereby the spouses exchanged the *right* to the body for procreative sexual acts (CIC 1081, 2). The 1983 Code has changed this definition and expanded it. It no longer refers to the exchange of a right but to the giving and receiving of persons:

> Matrimonial consent is an act of the will by which a man and a woman by an irrevocable covenant mutually give and accept each other in order to establish marriage.[29]

After the spouses have made the marital covenant with one another they are truly married. If both are baptized, the union is called a "ratified" marriage. When this covenant is consummated by sexual intercourse its stability is strengthened. For ratified marriages, the property of absolute indissolubility is added with consummation. What is it about sexual intercourse that it can have this effect on a marriage covenant? The answer is in the unitive-procreative nature of intercourse.

The above understanding of when marriage came about was more or less fixed with the "consensus-copula" debate between the theologians of the Paris and Bologna schools in the 12-13th centuries. The controversy was over what made a true marriage: the consent of the parties alone or their consent plus sexual consummation? The compromise resolution of the debate held that true marriage exists after consent but that it becomes absolutely indissoluble after consummation.

Gratian, the champion of the Bologna school, argued that sexual consummation transformed the spouses' marital consent into a true marriage. Consent was given to the marital *societas* which included sexual intercourse as an essential element. Gratian's understanding of the essence of marriage is remarkably similar to that of Vatican II. It was, for him, a joining of the man and woman to follow a singular way of life.[30] Gratian also employed an ancient Roman law term but with a new meaning. For the Romans *affectio maritalis* meant simply the will to be married.[31] For Gratian the same words meant much more: the attitude of the will to treat a spouse as a spouse ought to be treated. This was an attitude that was to accompany marital con-

276

sent. It is important for our consideration because of its relationship to the unitive aspect of intercourse. For Gratian the marital society was a "one flesh" union in the complete biblical sense and for this reason he used this metaphor to describe not only the act of sexual consummation but the abiding reality of the marital community which comes about after consummation.[32]

Gratian's overall argument seems to say that the man and the woman are not involved in a true marriage until they are joined in sexual intercourse. They cannot be truly one without experiencing sexual intercourse nor can the purpose of their oneness, procreation, happen without sexual intercourse. Although sexual intercourse in itself does not constitute a marriage, it is the ultimate sign of the fact that a marriage covenant has begun. Perhaps Gratian was saying what the Holy Father so recently said:

> And the coming into being of marriage is distinguished from its consummation to the extent that without this consummation the marriage is not yet constituted to its full reality. The fact that a marriage is juridically constituted but not consummated corresponds to the fact that it has not been fully constitued a marriage.[33]

There is a difference between marriage as a juridical reality, the fulfillment of certain objective legal prescriptions, and the full, human entity of marriage which the legal entity presumes to exist. By their verbal expression of consent, the man-made language of the vows, the spouses create marriage as a juridical reality in the here and now. By this verbal consent they promise to become one . . . they enter into the covenant which exists because of their mutual gift. Somehow sexual intercourse is necessary as a complete expression of the meaning of the marriage covenant:

> The sacramental sign is determined, in a certain sense, by "the language of the body," inasmuch as the man and the woman, who through marriage should become one flesh, express in this sign the reciprocal gift of masculinity and femininity as the basis for the conjugal union of persons.[34]

The language of sexual intercourse is an exclamation of the meaning and purpose of marriage. In order to conform to the full meaning of the "one flesh" it cannot be anything other than unitive and procreative.

The Code of Canon Law refers to sexual consummation *"humano modo"* i.e., in a human fashion. The sexual language of the spouses must be free of violence and coercion or it is not an expression of the conjugal community. To carry the concept of *"humano modo"* one step further, one could argue that the sexual act must also be open to procreation in principle if it is to be fully human. No language quite captures the meaning of marriage or the full reality of the marital commitment like the language of sexual intercourse. To further illustrate this point, there are instances when intercourse alone is considered to be the sole expression of marital consent, sufficient to constitute the juridical reality of marriage.[35]

The very nature of marriage as a union of two giving persons argues that sexual intercourse, as the unique marital communication of two nuptial persons, be unitive and procreative. In fact, these two aspects are almost synonymous with one another so that if one aspect is denied or willed away, the other is also absent. If the procreative aspect of the *person* is rejected can it be said that there has been a mutual giving and receiving of persons? The procreative aspect is intimately bound up with God's image in the person . . . unconditional gift. The key is in the openness to participating in the procreative process and not the actual phenomenon of procreation since many persons may find themselves, through no fault of their own, unable to have children.[36]

Because of what sexual intercourse *is* as a unitive and procreative act, we can draw certain basic moral conclusions. In the first place, sexual intercourse outside of marriage, though it may take place under circumstances of true caring, tenderness or even love, and with a conviction that an interpersonal commitment exists, is not truly *unitive* because there has been no covenant. There has been no real self-gift to communicate through intercourse. The parties, no matter how emotionally and psychologically involved they may be, are still replaceable. They have not taken the risk of making a public commitment of an unconditional and permanent gift of self to each other.

Secondly, sexual intercourse which is habitually contraceptive is a "falsification of the inner truth of conjugal love, which is called upon to give itself in personal totality."[37] Sexual intercourse for personal pleasure alone is unnatural because it does not correspond to the uniquely human meaning of intercourse. . . it does not communicate the nuptial meaning of the body. When lust replaces love as the motivating factor for intercourse, the partners become turned into themselves and intercourse has as its sole purpose the attaining of orgasm. Thus the partners are taking and not giving, and sexual intercourse becomes de-personalized.

Third, there is no room for sexual intercourse with a person other than one's spouse. It is dishonest to become "one flesh" through the language of intercourse with a person with whom one is not committed in the marriage covenant. Sexual intercourse as a language exclusive to the marriage covenant excludes the possibility of any exceptions to the obligations of total fidelity and the consequent prohibition against adultery.

Summary. The permanent man-woman relationship in marriage is possible but depends for its success on the continued giving of the parties one to another. As the natural way for children to be born and nurtured, the marriage relationship needs stability. The stability safeguards the procreative aspect of the relationship and is at once fostered by authentic sexual relations, i.e., those that are both unitive and procreative. If these two aspects are morally separated, then the physical union of the man and woman is not a sign of the biblical "one flesh" union which they became by their covenant.

V. Moral Inseparability and the Social Dimension of Intercourse

Although sexual intercourse is a personal and private act, it has a social dimension. To some extent society and culture have something to say about what sexual intercourse is all about. Conversely, the commonly held sexual mores have an impact on society. Referring to the so-called sexual revolution of the past two decades, a recent Roman document said:

The Church cannot remain indifferent to this confusion of minds and relaxation of morals. It is a question, in fact of a matter which is of the utmost importance both for the personal lives of Christians and for the social life of our time.[38]

Many, of course, would not agree that morals have become bad. They would argue that values have changed and so have standards of sexual behavior. When the parameters of sexual behavior change it involves a widespread acceptance of sexual intercourse for other than unitive and procreative purposes. When the unitive-procreative aspects are separated from sexual intercourse does it follow that there will be certain negative effects in society at large? This is a vitally important question. It is not based on individual acts of sexual intercourse for non-procreative-unitive purposes, but the widespread acceptance of a trivialized and depersonalized theory and practice of sexual intercourse. Recent Roman documents, including *Gaudium et Spes*, do not hesitate to make such a connection referring to widespread disorders of our time.[39]

Those who advocate a non-restrictive morality often base their value system on the belief that sexual intercourse and sexual pleasure is a personal right of the individual. Thus it is in fact divorced from the unitive-procreative aspects which require that sexual intercourse take place within the context of marriage. Sexual intercourse has become a form of recreation and a standardized dating habit for many. Casual sexual encounters, extramarital sexual intercourse and homosexual genital expression are increasingly acceptable and even glamorized to an extent. *Open Marriage*, a book found on many Catholic and secular college campuses in the seventies, attempted to create a philosophy of creative infidelity which redirected the marital commitment from the gift of self for the sake of the other to a commitment to one's growth. At the conclusion the authors write:

> Sexual fidelity is the false god of closed marriage . . .
> Fidelity is then redefined in the open marriage, as commitment to your own growth, equal commitment to your partner's growth, and a sharing of the self-discovery accomplished through such growth.[40]

The authors advocate relationships with members of the opposite sex other than one's spouse. These relationships are supposed to enhance and augment the marital relationship of the open couple. They can include sexual relations:

> These outside relationships may, of course, include sex. That is completely up to the partners involved, If partners . . . do have outside sexual relationships, it is on the basis of their own internal relationships, that is, because they have experienced mature love, have real trust, and are able to expand themselves, to love and enjoy others and to bring that love and pleasure back into their own marriage, without jealousy.[41]

There is no evidence that mutually acceptable adultery has contributed to overall marital stability . . . in fact the O'Neills, authors of *Open Marriage*, are themselves now divorced.

Likewise there is no correlation between living together prior to marriage and marital stability. Sexual intercourse is looked upon as a right to be used if the parties feel comfortable with the relationship and no one is hurt. This same ethic can carry over to married life and becomes the rationale for extra-marital behavior. A more liberalized sexual ethic depends on the premise that extra-marital relations are not necessarily destructive of the person and not restricted to marriage by nature. We find this approach even among Catholic moralists.[42] Some refer to the so-called "pre-ceremonial" Christian couple . . . a man and a woman who "feel" committed to one another and are thus justified in having sexual relations.[43]

It is a fact that most of the barriers restricting sexual intercourse to marriage have fallen. Yet in spite of the technology of artificial contraception there is still a high rate of extra-marital pregnancy, but a disproportionately lower rate of birth due to abortion. Also, the wonders of the "open marriage" have not prevented the divorce rate from reaching new highs every year, leaving behind a trail of scarred former partners and a whole new minority in the general population . . . the child of the single-parent family.[44]

There are other social phenomena that have accompanied the gradual change in sexual morality: the high proportion of sexually transmitted diseases including the new strains of herpes and AIDS and the higher instance of individuals seeking therapy for sexual dysfunction. The basic question is whether there is a cause-effect relationship between a sexual ethic that depends on the separation of the unitive-procreative aspects of intercourse and the aforesaid negative effects which abound in our society. The sexual permissiveness of the "new morality" is a by-product of the trivialization of sexual intercourse into another source of fun.

In positing that the separation of the unitive-procreative aspects of intercourse is at the root of this age's sexually related troubles, we naturally add one more dimension to the overall argument in favor of the moral inseparability of the two aspects or, more accurately, their inseparability from intercourse itself. In this context *Humanae Vitae* was more prophetic than anything else:

> In defending conjugal morals and their integral wholeness, the Church knows that she contributes towards the establishment of a truly human civilization: she engages man not to abdicate from his own responsibility in order to rely on technical means; by that very fact she defends the dignity of man and wife.[45]

Ashley and O'Rourke refer to a "sexual future" which begins with the understanding of sexuality from the viewpoint of the person and extends to its impact on society. Their basic assessment is correct:

> The sexual revolution projects a future in which the Christian vision of human sexuality will appear ridiculous and unrealizable. Yet for Christians human sexuality is governed by norms of hope, a hope on which a truly human future must be built.[46]

The unitive-procreative aspect of intercourse is part of human nature. If man tries to change this meaning to suit a secularist-materialist outlook, then society itself will be changed.[47] The moral inseparability is a statement of what human sexuality is all about, telling us of the uniqueness of the human person and of his proximity to God.

Notes

1. Sacred Congregation for Catholic Eduation, *Educational Guidance For Human Love* (Rome: 1983), n. 32, p. 12: "In synthesis, sexuality is called to express different values to which specific moral exigencies correspond. Oriented towards interpersonal dialogue, it contributes to the integral maturation of people, opening them to the gift of self in love;

furthermore, tied to the order of creation, to fecundity and to the transmission of life, it is called to be faithful to this inner purpose also. Love and fecundity are meanings and values of sexuality which include and summon each other in turn, and cannot therefore be considered as either alternatives or opposites."

2. Alternatives to the traditional monogamous marriage arrangement all involve not simply human relationships but sexual relations. See James and Lynn Smith, *Beyond Monogamy* (Baltimore: Johns Hopkins, 1974); Jesse Bernard, *The Future of Marriage* (New York: World Publishing, 1972); Nena and George O'Neill, *Open Marriage* (New York: Avon Books, 1973).

3. William May, "Sexuality and Fidelity in Marriage," *Communio* 5 (1978), 284: "As a desire, a drive, it is unconscious and instinctual in origin and character, an aspect of our being that helps us to recognize that our life, our being, is not exhausted by consciousness. But it is a serious error to infer from this that the sex drive is something subhuman, subpersonal, merely brute irrationality."

4. This point is well illustrated in any history of marriage. See the classic, E.A. Westermarck, *The History of Human Marriage* 3 vols., 5th edition (New York: 1922). A more recent, though not as thorough, work is B.I. Murstein, *Love, Sex and Marriage Through the Ages* (New York: Springer Publishing Co., 1974). More specialized studies include V. Bullough and J. Brundage, *Sexual Practices and the Medieval Church* (Buffalo: Prometheus Books, 1982) and G. Duby, *Medieval Marriage* (Baltimore: Johns Hopkins, 1978).

5. See Abel Jeanniere, *The Anthropology of Sex* (New York: Harper and Row, 1967).

6. The standard texts: *Casti Connubii* (1930), *Gaudium et Spes* (1965), *Humanae Vitae* (1968), *Declaration on Certain Questions Concerning Sexual Ethics* (1975), *Familiaris Consortio* (1982) and *Educational Guidance in Human Love* (1983). See also John Paul II, *Original Unity of Man and Woman* (Boston: St. Paul Editions, 1981) and *Blessed Are the Pure of Heart* (Boston: St. Paul Editions, 1983).

7. *Familiaris Consortio* , November 22, 1981 (Vatican City: Polyglot Press, 1981), n. 11, p. 19 (Hereinafter referred to as *FC*).

8. John Paul II, audience of Jan. 9, 1980 in *Original Unity*, p. 107.

9. Original solitude was necessary for man to realize his radical difference from every other creature. From this came the need to create another "self" in order that man, as male and female, might be complete and capable of fulfilling his being. See audience of Oct. 10, 1979 in *Original Unity*, p. 43-49.

10. Audience of November 7, 1979 in *Original Unity*, p. 64.

11. *Ibid.*, p. 66.

12. Audience of November 14, 1979, *Original Unity*, p. 73.

13. S.C.D.F., *Declaration on Certain Questions Concerning Sexual Ethics*, Vatican City, December 29, 1975, p. 3: ". . .it is from sex that the human person receives the characteristics which, on the biological, psychological and spiritual levels, make that person a man or a woman and thereby largely condition his or her progress towards maturity and insertion into society."

14. Sacred Congregation for Catholic Education, *Educational Guidance for Human Love* (Rome: 1983), p. 3-4.

15. See William May, *Sex, Marriage and Chastity* (Chicago: Franciscan Herald Press, 1981). p. 10. Dr. May makes the helpful distinction that the human body and human sexuality are goods *of* the person and not goods *for* the person.

16. One's definition of *person* determines many practical conclusions in the area of sexual ethics. See William May, *Sex, Marriage and Chastity*. p. 3-9, especially p. 8: "For the separatist then, a person is a conscious subject of experiences that possesses a body, that is, a human being who happens to be either a male or a female." This definition of the "separatist" seems to describe the meaning of personhood found in A. Kosnik et al., *Human Sexuality: New Directions in Catholic Thought* (New York: Paulist Press, 1977). See p. 83-84: "Within this embodied view of human existence, sexuality is seen as that aspect of our fleshly being-in-the-world whereby we are present and open to that which is not ourselves, to that which is other . . . for us humans, the teleology of the pleasure bond is the intercoursing of subjectivities . . . Subjectivity is embodied in either a male or a female body . . . Our understan-

ding of bodily existence requires that the specific structure of one's body colors the manner in which oneself and the world are experienced . . . Sexuality further serves the development of genuine personhood by calling people to a clearer recognition of their relational nature, of their absolute need to reach out and embrace others to achieve personal fulfillment."

17. Audience of July 23, 1980, in *Blessed Are the Pure of Heart* p. 77.

18. *Ibid.*, p. 76: "Lust in general, and the lust of the body in particular, attacks precisely this sincere giving. It deprives man, it could be said, of the dignity of giving, which is expressed by his body through masculinity and femininity and in a way "de-personalizes" man making him an "object for the other." Instead . . . man becomes an object for man: the female for the male and vice versa . . .The subjectivity of the person gives way in a certain sense, to the objectivity of the body; man becomes an object for man, the female for the male and vice versa."

19. Paul VI, *Humanae Vitae*, July 25, 1968 (Washington, D.C.: USCC), pp. 5-6.

20. *FC*, n. 11, p. 20.

21. *FC*, n. 13, p. 23.

22. Wm. May, *Sex, Marriage and Chastity*, p. 3: "The understanding of human sexuality dominant in our culture can, I believe, be properly described as separatist. By this I mean that the separatist understanding has severed the existential and psychological bond between the life-giving or procreative meaning of human sexuality and its person-uniting, love-giving, unitive meaning. It regards the former as a biological function of sexuality. This biological function can become humanly and personally valuable when it is consciously willed and chosen, but in and of itself it is simply a physiological given."

23. *Ibid.*, p. 6: "When the human significance of sex is seen in this way the principle criterion for evaluating genital sexual activity focuses on the quality of the relationship established and/or expressed by such activity, on the affection, tenderness and fellowship that it both engenders and expresses."

24. Historically it seems that marriage was treated under custom or family law. The public (civil) law only became involved when abuses or problems pressed intervention for the good of the community. Ancient law codes regularly mention penalties for adultery. In the Roman world marriage was under the domestic or family authority until widespread problems related to adultery, exposure of children and childless unions prompted Caesar Augustus to issue the *Lex Iulia de Adulteriis* (18 B.C.) and the *Lex Iulia de Maritandis* (11 B.C.) as civil law attempts to counteract family-related problems.

25. See Wm. May, *Sex, Marriage and Chastity*, p. 97-107. This section on marital chastity discusses the basis for the Church's traditional teaching. May also points out what he sees as the error of those who teach that the proscriptions against adultery are essentially cultural.

26. *Gaudium et Spes*, par. 48, defines the essence of marriage as the *"intima communitas vitae."* Canon 1055 of the *Code of Canon Law* uses the phrase *"totius vitae consortium."* Neither term adequately translates into English the meaning of the marital joining although *consortium* comes closest from an historical perspective.

27. Eduard Schillebeeckx, *Marriage: Human Reality and Saving Mystery* (New York: Sheed and Ward, 1965), p. 18. See also an excellent article by W. Brueggeman, "Of the Same Flesh and Bone," in *Catholic Biblical Quarterly* 32 (1970), pp. 532-542.

28. *Gaudium et Spes*, par. 49: "Hence the acts in marriage by which the intimate and chaste union of the spouses takes place are noble and honorable; the truly human performance of these acts fosters the self-giving they signify and enriches the spouses with joy and gratitude." This same idea is repeated in *Humanae Vitae*, n. 9. See above, note 19.

29. Canon 1057, 2. English translation from *The Code of Canon Law* (Canadian Conference of Catholic Bishops: Collins Liturgical Press, 1983).

30. C. 27, q. 2 in Freidberg, *Corpus Iuris Canonici*, vol. 1, col. "Sunt enim nuptiae sive matrimonium viri mulierisque coniunctio individuae vitae consuetudinem retinens." This is a standard Roman Law definition of marriage. The Romans considered marriage to be radically different from the Christian view, yet Gratian gave new meaning to the older definition by developing other concepts.

31. Adolf Berger, *Encyclopedic Dictionary of Roman Law* (Philadelphia: The American Philosophical Society, 1953), p. 356: '*Affectio maritalis*: Conjugal affection conceived as

284

a continuous (not momentary) state of mind . . . It presumes the intention of living as husband and wife for life and procreating legitimate children." *Affectio* in the Roman Law sense did not mean conjugal love or an attitude of charity between the spouses. For Gratian *affectio* distinguished marriage from concubinage although his interest was more moral than jurdical. Basically the Christian understanding of *affectio* was the will to treat a spouse as a spouse ought to be treated." See also John Noonan, "Marital Affection in the Canonists," in *Studia Gratiana* 12 (1967) p. 482-509.

32. See John Alesandro, *Gratian's Notion of Marital Consummation* (Rome: Officium Libri Catholici, 1971) p. 578.

33. Audience, January 5, 1983 in *Osservatore Romano*.

34. *Ibid.*

35. Certain canonists hold that in those instances when it is necessary to renew marital consent privately, sexual intercourse, performed lovingly between the spouses, suffices as an expression and sign of consent. This situation would occur in cases of marriages invalid due to an undispensed impediment which ceases or is dispensed. It is not always necessary to renew consent according to canonical form. Rather, it may be renewed (canon 1158, 2) even privately and in secret. See James Brennan, *The Simple Convalidation of Marriage* (Washington, D.C.: Catholic University of America Press, 1937).

36. *FC*, n. 14, p. 27: "It must not be forgotten however that, even when procreation is not possible, conjugal life does not for this reason lose its value. Physical sterility in fact can be for spouses the occasion for other important services to the life of the human person, for example adoption, various forms of educational work, and assistance to other families and to poor or handicapped children." In other words, the conjugal love of the spouses prompts them to share this love with others in some way even if they cannot do it with their own child.

37. *FC*, n. 32, p . 61.

38. S.C.D.F., *Declaration on Certain Questions Concerning Sexual Ethics* (Rome: Dec. 29, 1975), p. 4.

39. *GS*, par. 47, *FC*, n. 6, p. 12.

40. Nena and George O'Neill, *Open Marriage* (New York: Avon, 1972), p. 253.

41. *Idem.* Although the O'Neill book is 12 years old, the morality it expresses is still in vogue. For a scientific study of the phenomenon of extra-marital sex, see Gerhard Neubeck, ed., *Extra-Marital Relations* (Englewood Cliffs, NJ: 1969).

42. For example, A. Kosnik et al. *Human Sexuality: New Directions in Cathlic Thought.* After discussing what they call "variant patterns" such as common law marriage (p. 145), swinging (p. 147-148) and adultery (p. 148-49), all of which refer to marriage, the book then gives three approaches to morality. First, the traditional, of which they say "The strength . . . lies in its fidelity to a carefully developed legal understanding of marriage. Its weakness lies in the assumption that such activity is always destructive of human personhood without due regard for any empirical evidence that might support or repudiate such an assumption. This position does not appear convincing to many people of good will today." (p. 149). The *third* approach holds that such variations are largely private matters, depending on the consent of the participants and acceptable as long as nobody gets hurt. (p. 150). The *second* approach, which the authors say is "most compatible with our own" (p. 150) says in part: "Variant marriage patterns depart from one degree or another from the Christian ideal of what marriage ought to be. Therefore they are not tolerated in at least most cases." (p. 150).

43. See "Pre-ceremonial Christian Couples," *Eglise et Theologie* 8 (1977), entire issue. The collection of essays attempts to create a spirituality and theological justification for pre-marital sex by positing that some couples have made a commitment that can justifiably be consummated before it is ratified. (??)

44. According to the National Center for Health Statistics there were the following statistics for 1981: 686,605 illegitimate births (up 20,858 from 1980); 29.6% of every 1000 births were illegitimate and 49.2% of births to girls between the ages of 15-19 were out of wedlock. Also, there were 1,297,606 known abortions in 1980, 76.9% were performed for unwed mothers (763,476 abortions in 1974, 72.6% on unwed mothers). There were 2,495,000 marriages and 1,180,000 estimated divorces in the US in 1982.

45. *Humanae Vitae*, par. 18.

46. Benedict Ashley and Kevin O'Rourke, *Health Care Ethics: A Theological Analysis*, 2nd Ed., (St. Louis: Catholic Health Association, 1982), p. 302-03.

47. See George Gilder, *Sexual Suicide* (New York: Quadrangle, 1973).

Chapter 14

The Bishops and Natural Family Planning: Theological and Pastoral Implications

PART I

The Reverend Monsignor James T. McHugh, S.T.D.

The first half of our chapter intends to provide a theological-pastoral perspective on natur l family planning, with special concern for the pastoral role of the bishop. In *Familiaris Consortio,* the Holy Father states that "the person principally responsible in the diocese for the pastoral care of the family is the bishop," and he urges bishops to exercise "particular pastoral solicitude" by way of personal interest, care, time, personnel and resources, "but above all personal support for the families and for all those who, in the various diocesan structures, assist him in the pastoral care of the family" (no. 73).

It is always valuable to base pastoral initiatives on theological commitments, all the more so in regard to conjugal morality, where "the concrete pedagogy of the Church must always remain linked with her doctrine and never be separated from it" (F.C., 33). In the same document, the Holy Father invites theologians to collaborate with the Magisterium in "illustrating ever more clearly the biblical foundations, the ethical grounds and the personalistic reasons" (F.C., 31) on which the Church's teaching on responsible parenthood rests.

Background

By way of background, the history of natural family planning (or rhythm, as it was originally termed) is usually traced to the work of Drs. Ogino and Knaus in the late 1920s and early 1930s, both of whom independently verified that women have a regular monthly pattern of fertility and non-fertility, and that the time of fertility can be reasonably determined. The immediate result of their findings was the development of calendar rhythm. The temperature method developed in the 1950s and the ovulation method in the 1960s, though the latter received its greatest public visibility through the efforts of Drs. John and Lyn Billings, beginning in the late 1960s and early 1970s.

The development of the Church's teaching roughly paralleled the scientific discoveries. The first phase of this development runs from about 1853 to the early 1930s, in which the Church recognized the new data but made no decision other than the pastoral advice that couples who restricted intercourse to the non-fertile days "were not to be disturbed."[1] The second phase began in the early 1950s, with Pius XII's "Address to the Midwives,"[2] in which the pope affirmed that "observing the non-fertile periods alone can be lawful from the moral point of view," provide there are grave reasons of a medical, eugenic, economic or social nature which exempt a couple from having a child either for a lengthy period or for the entire marriage. The third phase began with Paul VI, who not only recognized the licitness of natural family planning, but also spoke of the positive benefits it could bestow on couples who adopted its use.[3] The present Pontiff has moved further by declaring that it is providential that various methods of natural family planning exist so as to meet the needs of different couples, and that the ecclesial community must take on the task of instilling conviction and offering practical help to those who wish to live out their parenthood in a truly responsible way.[4] In terms of practical help, John Paul II was quite explicit in calling for "a broader, more decisive and more systematic effort to make the natural methods of regulating fertility known, respected and applied" (F.C., 35).

This thumbnail sketch of the Magisterial development shows the movement from toleration, to acceptance, to approval and ultimately to advocacy. In addition to this brief and limited overview of papal teaching, one should not overlook a developing literature in support of natural family planning which consists of statements of recent pontiffs and messages from the Cardinal Secretary of State to NFP Congresses, as well as pastoral letters of various Ordinaries specifically on the values inherent in the commitment to NFP.

Consistent with the overall theme of this volume, my reflections will focus on the theological and pastoral insights pertinent to natural family planning that have emerged during this last phase of approval/advocacy, insights that are found in the documents of the Second Vatican Council, in the writings of Paul VI and John Paul II, and in statements of various American bishops.

The legacy of the Second Vatican Council and the post-Conciliar era in terms of marriage and family life involves three main concepts: (1) the sacramentality of marriage and Christian family life; (2) conjugal love; and (3) responsible parenthood. While very little has been done since the Council to deepen our understanding and increase our appreciation of sacramentality, there seem to be a number of theological themes that provide an enriched understanding of Christian marriage, and expand it somewhat to include the Christian family.

Sacramentality Of Marriage

Nonetheless, it is fundamental to any discussion of natural family planning to place it in the context of the Church's teaching on Christian marriage, which is "the specific source and original means of sanctification for Christian couples and families" (F.C., 56). I believe this was the basic direction of both *Lumen Gentium* and *Gaudium et Spes*, where marriage is spoken of as a special institution created by God (G.S., 48), as a covenant — similar to the covenant between Christ and the Church (G.S., 48), as a source of grace and holiness (L.G., 11, 41), and as a sacrament, that is, a manifestation "of the Savior's living presence in the world, and the genuine nature of the Church" (G.S., 48). It is necessary to highlight the developing theology of marriage so as to give Catholic couples an ecclesial identity, and enable them to realize that the sacrament of marriage confers on them the special graces suitable for their state in life. Moreover, as behavioral scientists remind us, couples' religious and spiritual convictions are a powerful motivation and reenforcement of their commitment to NFP.[5]

Conjugal Love

The primary responsibilities of married couples are described in *Gaudium et Spes* and *Humanae Vitae* in terms of developing conjugal love and pursuing responsible parenthood. Both the Council and the encyclical spoke at length of conjugal love. They described it as "eminently human," that is, interpersonal and mutual. It enriches and ennobles the affectionate exchanges — both psychological and physical — between husband and wife. It is faithful and exclusive, reflecting the unique bond that exists between the two persons. This bond, if nurtured by understanding, tenderness and patience, grows and intensifies in such a way that it is virtually unbreakable. Conjugal love also includes sexual love, that is, it has both a pleasurable and a procreative potential. Sexual pleasure is part of God's plan for married couples to enable them to express their conjugal love and to deepen their intimacy and unity. But conjugal love is more encompassing — it includes affectivity, the heart and the will, the emotions and the body.[6]

The procreative potential of sexual love, while upheld by the Church as inseparable from the unifying aspect, has been largely rejected as a complementary dimension in contemporary society. Demographic reports and predictions give evidence of the success in restricting childbearing and denigrating the life-giving potential. On the other hand, Eric Erikson postulates a generativity stage in the life cycle, and laments the fact that at a time when so many couples have become expert in the use of birth control, they "may need enlightenment in regard to what they are *not* doing."[7]

Responsible Parenthood

It is precisely to balance the tendency towards overemphasizing the genital aspect of sex that the Church also insists on responsible parenthood. Unfortunately, for some this concept is a subterfuge for the avoidance of procreation. However, as described by the Council and recent popes, responsible parenthood involves the following elements:

- a free, informed, mutual decision by the couple

- regarding the frequency of births and size of the family

- based on their conscientious assessment of their responsibilities

- to God, themselves, their children and family and the society of which they are a part

- and enlightened by the authentic teaching of the Church's Magisterium regarding the objective moral order and the licit methods of spacing or limiting pregnancies.

Decisions regarding childbearing and childrearing are certainly in the forefront of the fundamental choices that couples make in marriage. But it is a mistake to think that such decisions are fraught with tension, lacking in mutual agreement, or threatening to conjugal love and family well-being. More realistically and more commonly, such decisions reflect the couple's values and attitudes, and are reached in relative calm.

Nonetheless, efforts to formulate and carry out decisions regarding childbearing and childrearing should begin in courtship and should be characterized by positive anticipation. In other words, a man and woman plan to marry *and* to have a family. "Family planning" in its broadest sense should be a positive concept that gives primary attention to *building a family*, to fostering basic human relationships that exist therein, to appropriate enjoyment of the spiritual, cultural and material advantages of modern society, and to fulfilling the mission of the Christian family — "manifesting to all Christ's living presence in the world and the genuine nature of the Church" (G.S., 48). For Christian spouses, responsible parenthood is based on and rooted in their appreciation of their role as co-creators, as participants with God in the on-going work of creation.

Accordingly, conjugal love and responsible parenthood derive their greatest strength from an understanding of God's creative love, his willingness to share his life and eternity with each person and his sending of his Son to redeem the human family. Efforts to understand the divine plan of creation/redemption also lead to a deeper appreciation of the natural world and the powers and capacities of human nature. This leads to a respect for human sexuality, for procreation, and for the harmony and integrity of the process of human reproduction. It points to the wisdom of working with human nature and preserving the unbreakable connection between the unitive and procreative aspects of sexual intercourse described above in chapter 13.

It is in light of these understandings that John Paul II has called for a deeper study of the difference, both anthropological and moral, between contraception and reliance on natural family planning. The difference, according to the Holy Father, is much deeper than usually thought, and one that reflects, in the final analysis, one's fundamental conviction regarding the dignity of the human person and of human sexuality.

In the pertinent section of *Familiaris Consortio*, John Paul II further explains the moral and anthropological aspects of the difference. The moral perspective focuses primarily on the Church's moral teaching, the reasons for that teaching and the consistency of the moral principles with a Christian understanding of marriage, sexuality and parenthood. The anthropological perspective focuses on the human person, his or her physical, psychological and spiritual capacities and the choices and decisions that are called for to live a moral life. For John Paul II, the unifying element is the dignity of the person which is based on God's creative love and redemption by Christ. The presentations in *Familiaris Consortio*, and in the September 24, 1983, *ad limina* address to a group of American Bishops are predominantly pastoral and find resonance in the experience of many in the NFP movement. However, a theological and pastoral reflection should also draw on supportive data from the physical and behavioral sciences, and be properly sensitive to data that signals caution.

The Anthropological Perspective

Couples who make the fundamental choice in favor of childbearing and childrearing are still faced with determining the spacing of births and the ultimate size of the family. In carrying out these decisions, couples should respect the natural cycle of fertility and infertility and should limit sexual intercourse to those times when pregnancy will not occur. For the record, this involves abstinence for about eight days a month. This choice of natural family planning, in the words of John Paul II,

> involves accepting the cycle of the woman, and thereby accepting dialogue, reciprocal respect, shared responsibility and self-control (F.C., 32).

These four criteria would be readily agreed to on the grounds of common sense. However, a review of some psychological and sociological studies over the past fifteen years provides further confirmation of their relevance.

1. *Dialogue*. The choice of NFP requires communication directed toward setting priorities, pursuing agreed-upon goals and maintaining an openness to the future. Sociologist Thomasina Borkman writes that NFP is value-oriented behavior, at least to the extent that the couple perceive NFP as more desirable or less problematical than other methods.[8] Mutual consistency in behavior requires mutual understanding and commitment. Social scientists stress the need for motivation and for confidence in all family planning decisions, and this is especially applicable to NFP.[9] Some motivational factors originate outside the couple, such as religious teaching, health considerations, and contemporary feminist perspectives. But the mutual internalization of these factors and experiential verification of their value requires communication. Borkman claims that "satisfied, experienced NFP users are positive about NFP because they have constructed positive ideas and values about NFP that feed back constructively on their behavioral experience."[10] Furthermore, Borkman, supported by others, argues that "an explicitly positive value-oriented model of NFP needs to be taught to potential users of NFP."[11] This

293

teaching experience in turn needs to be reinforced by mutual dialogue, and by small support groups. In a survey of NFP users, couples indicated that the choice of NFP not only required communication, but actually generated it. The communication revolved around the method chosen, the identification and charting of the signs of fertility, sexual feelings and, for some, other aspects of the marriage relationship. In the overwhelming majority of cases, the communication provided positive motivation.[12]

2. *Reciprocal Behavior*. Integral to sexual activity in marriage is respect for one another as individual persons and as partners.[13] As Borkman indicates, NFP is interpersonal behavior, not behavior of unrelated individuals. Thus it requires not only reciprocity, but intimacy, that is, sensitivity to the other person's needs and difficulties, a certain confidentiality or privacy, and development of a wide variety of ways to manifest appreciation, understanding and empathy. Scholars tell us that intimacy is an indispensable quality for a healthy marriage, but also difficult for couples to achieve.[14] Borkman, in her survey of NFP couples, found that they spoke spontaneously of their sexual relationship in terms of intimacy, both in regard to ways other than intercourse of deepening intimacy, or feeling the absence of intimacy during the time of abstinence.

In 1979, a group of scholars met regularly at the invitation of the NCCB Committee on Pastoral Research and Practices to discuss marital intimacy. At the 1980 World Synod of Bishops, utilizing their research, Cardinal Bernardin stated that "intimacy is not synonymous with genital sex. It is a much broader and more inclusive reality; its spiritual dimension is paramount. The climactic expression of sexuality in the conjugal act is, however, a highly important element in marital intimacy. This also embodies an important spiritual dimension. It is important, therefore, that the Church offer positive encouragement to husbands and wives in their quest for growth through sexual intimacy; a growth which, according to research done in the United States, contributes both to the religious devotion and development of the husband and wife relationship and to the effectiveness of their efforts to transmit their religious values and tradition to their children.[15]

3. *Shared Responsibility*. Decisions regarding the spacing of

294

births and the size of the family must be mutual decisions, and responsibility for carrying out such decisions should be borne equally by both partners. Scholars agree that for a couple to achieve confidence, competence, and commitment in NFP, a modification of sexual behavior must be mutually agreed on. Bardwick and Marshall point to the possibility of manipulation or domination if both partners do not see NFP as a mutual responsibility.[16] Twerski warns that couples should not deny the deprivation involved in periodic abstinence, but should accept the sacrifice as mutually shared.[17] Bardwick notes that NFP requires "the cooperation of the couple" notably in regard to understanding the parameters and accepting the periodic abstinence.[18] Borkman and Shivanandan, in their study of couples, found that 93 percent of those with overall positive abstinence experience were also positive in regard to the joint responsibility in using NFP, while only 50 percent of those who were negative or mixed in regard to abstinence had positive attitudes toward joint responsibility.[19]

It should be remembered that NFP involves only one aspect of family life and that sharing responsibility also involves sharing other tasks and obligations — care of existing children, regard and care for grandparents, assuming and meeting financial obligations.

4. *Self Control.* Spouses must recognize the value of sex in their marriage, as well as each one's own need for self-discipline and self-mastery. In a highly charged sexual environment such as we live in today, self-mastery calls for continual efforts to relate sex to marriage, and to avoid attitudes or patterns of behavior that tend to trivialize sex.

Yet, especially in a healthy marriage relationship, we recognize the unifying and rewarding aspects of sexual intercourse, and it is unwise and possibly psychologically disorienting to ignore or explain away the sacrifice involved. Experienced teacher-couples as well as NFP users profit from facing the fact of abstinence, keeping it in proportion and seeing it as an integral part of their marriage relationship and a value for their psychological and spiritual growth. But self-control is essentially a learned experience, and the rules for experiential learning can be helpful to NFP users. It is also important that periodic abstinence not be looked upon simply as deprivation, but also in terms of sublimation. Twerski emphasizes that periodic abstinence should not be seen as rejection or denial of sexual pleasure, but as postponement of gratification. He argues that postponement of gratification should be practiced in other areas of life as well, otherwise it will be extremely difficult to single out the area of sex and demand tolerance of frustration or sacrifice therein. In terms of positive benefits, Twerski notes, " the mutual adherence to that which one believes to be right, and tolerance of deprivation without external coercion, can draw a husband and wife together in a union even stronger than that based on affection alone."[20]

The Moral Difference

In *Familiaris Consortio* John Paul II explains the moral difference between contraception and natural family planning in terms of the inseparable connection between the two meanings of conjugal love and sexual intercourse, that is, the unitive and procreative dimensions.

He also cites the Council and *Humanae Vitae* to the effect that the moral propriety of any method of birth control is based not simply on sincere intentions or an evaluation of motives, but on objective standards which in turn are founded on the nature of the human person and his or her acts. Perhaps the phrase would be better rendered as the dignity and nature of the human person and his/her acts. I say this because truly human actions should be understood as actions of persons, that is, as acts proceeding from a free and informed decision. At the same time, human acts have their own inherent purposes and limitations and this is one of the considerations in the process of deciding whether to do or avoid an action. Circumstances influence the decision as does the basic intent of the actor. But regardless of the circumstances or of the underlying intent of the person, one cannot give moral approval to an act that denies or violates his or her dignity or that of another person. That is why blasphemy, rape, and direct killing of the innocent are morally as well as socially unacceptable. It is also the nature of the human person to act knowingly and to respect the inherent purposes and potentialities of the actions he or she performs, that is, how these actions conform or fail to conform to God's overall plan. In Christian marriage, a couple accepts the vocation to love one another, to share their lives together and with their offspring, and to grow in holiness. Part of their married life involves sexual love, including sexual intercourse, which enriches them and generates new life. Their sexual love must always be directed to the fulfillment of their vocation, and their sexual activity, if it is to maintain its integrity and inner dynamism, cannot consistently deny or frustrate either the unitive or procreative dimensions of sexual intercourse.

Summary And Conclusions

The following points provide a summary and some pastoral implications:

1. The successful practice of natural family planning is dependent on quality instruction, plus continued encouragement and support. This points to the need for an objective presentation of NFP in premarriage instruction, and ready access to good instructional programs throughout the diocese.

2. The understanding and practice of natural family planning fosters a more Christian understanding of human sexuality. Accordingly, positive attitudes toward NFP should be created in family life and sex education courses, and couples practicing NFP should be invited to assist in the establishment and conduct of such courses.

3. The role of priests is to motivate, encourage and support couples in their commitment to natural family planning. Accordingly, they should develop ways to show couples how NFP is based on and consistent with the Church's teaching on marriage and family life.

4. The role of bishops and priests is to promote positive attitudes toward natural family planning and create a supportive atmosphere for couples to carry on this ministry or apostolate. This can be accomplished by a pastoral letter or statement by the bishop, support from the priests' council, active involvement by some priests who serve as chaplains to NFP leadership, and the provision of basic organizational resources for the leaders and

teaching couples. It would also include encouragement of Catholic hospitals, physicians and nurses to be part of a systematic diocesan program.

In his September 1983 *ad limina* address to a group of American Bishops, John Paul II stated that "a special and important part of your ministry to families has to do with natural family planning." His comments seem to summarize the ideal pastoral attitude, and make a fitting conclusion to this part of our chapter.

> Those couples who choose the natural methods perceive the profound difference — both anthropological and moral — between contraception and natural family planning. Yet they may experience difficulties. Indeed they often go through a certain conversion in becoming committed to the use of the natural methods, and they stand in need of competent instruction, encouragement and pastoral counseling and support. We must be sensitive to their struggles and have a feeling for the needs that they experience. We must encourage them to continue their efforts with generosity, confidence and hope. As bishops we have the charism and the pastoral responsibility to make our people aware of the unique influence that the grace of the sacrament of marriage has on every aspect of married life, including sexuality (cf. *Familiaris Consortio*, 33). The teaching of Christ's Church is not only light and strength for God's people, but it uplifts their hearts in gladness and hope.

> Your episcopal conference has established a special program to expand and coordinate efforts in the various dioceses. But the success of such an effort requires the abiding pastoral interest and support of each bishop in his own diocese, and I am deeply grateful to you for what you do in this important apostolate.

Notes

1. Responses of the Sacred Penitentiary to the Bishop of Amiens, France, March 2, 1853 and to Father Le Compte, June 16, 1880. Cited in Griese, O., *The Morality of Periodic Continence*, 1942, Catholic University of America Press.

2. Pius XII to the Italian Catholic Union of Midwives, October 29, 1951, in *Moral Questions Affecting Married Life* (Nos. 29-37), 1951, Washington, D.C., National Catholic Welfare Conference.

3. Paul VI, Encyclical Letter *On the Regulation of Birth (Humanae Vitae)* (No. 21), 1968, Washington, D.C., USCC Publications.

4. See John Paul II, Apostolic Exhortation *Familiaris Consortio* (No. 35), and Address To a Study Group at the Catholic University of the Sacred Heart, Rome, July 3, 1982 (No. 3).

5. See Max Levin, M.D., "Sexual Fulfillment in the Couple Practicing Rhythm", in *Proceedings of the Second International Symposium on Rhythm*, ed. McHugh, J., 1968 Washington, D.C., USCC Family Life Bureau; Thomasina Borkman, Ph.D., "Experiential Learning and the Professional in *Natural Family Planning." Natural Family Planning: Development of National Programs*, Claude A. Lanctot, M.D., et al, International Federation for Family Life Promotion, (IFFLP), Washington, D.C.; Conrad Baars, M.D., "Rhythm — An Expression of Marital Love", in *Proceedings of the Second International Symposium on Rhythm, op. cit.* Also, for the overall relationship of religion to fertility decisions, see: Chamie, Jos., *Religion and Fertility* (New York: Cambridge University Press; 1981); Johnson, N., "Religous Differentials in Reproduction: The Effects of Sectarian Education", *Demography*, Vol. 19, No. 4; Janssen, S., and Hauser, R., "Religion Socialization and Fertility", *Demography*, Vol. 18, No. 4.

6. John Paul II to Two International Research Groups in Rome, November 3, 1979, in *L'Osservatore Romano* (English edition) December 3, 1979.

7. Erik Erikson, "On the Generational Cycle — An Address", *The International Journal of Psycho-Analysis*, Vol. 61, 1980.

8. Thomasina Borkman, Ph.D., "A Social Science Perspective of Research Issues for Natural Family Planning", paper presented at the *Research Workshop on NFP: Reality and Potential*, Bethesda, MD., June 27-29, 1979.

9. See for example: Borkman, T., (1979), *op. cit.*; Bardwick, J., "Psychological Aspects of Implementing Natural Family Planning Programs", in *International Seminar on Natural Family Planning*, (1979), Ireland, Department of Health; Yahraes, H., "Improving Communication in Marriage", in *Families Today* (NIMH Science Monographs), (1979), Washington, D.C., U.S. Government Printing Office.

10. See Borkman, T., (1979), *op. cit.*

11. Borkman, T., (1979), *op. cit.*; Twerski, A., "Psychosocial Aspects of Natural Family Planning", *International Journal of Natural Family Planning*, (Winter, 1979), Bardwick, J., (1979) *op. cit.*; Robertson, M.E., "Social Factors in Family Planning", in Uricchio-Williams (eds.), *Natural Family Planning* (Washington, D.C.: Human Life Foundation, 1973).

12. Borkman, T. and Shivanandan, M., "The Impact of NFP on Selected Aspects of the Couple Relationship", paper presented at *Second International Symposium on Natural Family Planning*, Pittsburgh, Pa., May 22-25, 1983.

13. Fishman, R. & B., "Enriched Marriage as a Reciprocally Resonant Relationship"; in Mace, D., (ed.), *Prevention in Family Services: Approaches to Family Wellness* (1983), Beverly Hills, Sage Publications.

14. Durkin, M., "Intimacy and Marriage: Continuing the Mystery of Christ and the Church"; Shea, J., "A Theological Perspective on Human Relations Skills and Family Intimacy"; Kilgallen, J., "Intimacy and the New Testament", in Greeley, A.,*The Family in Crisis or in Transition* (New York: Seabury Press, 1979).

15. Bernardin, J., "Toward a Spirituality of Marital Intimacy", in *Origins*, October, 1980.

16. Bardwick, J., "Psychodynamics of Contraception with Particular Reference to Rhythm", in Uricchio-Williams (eds.), *op. cit.*; Marshall, J., "Psychologic Aspects of the Basal Body Temperature Method of Regulating Births", in Uricchio-Williams, *op. cit.*

17. Twerski, A., *op. cit.*

18. Bardwick, J. (1979) *op. cit.*

19. Borkman, T. and Shivanandan, M., *op. cit.*

20. Twerski, A., *op. cit.*

PART II

Mr. Gerard E. Brunelle

Introduction

In so short a presentation on such a vast subject, I would like to take three precautions:

1) I shall not be addressing all the suggestions I should like to make in this sensitive area of conjugal and family ministry.

2) In taking a somewhat critical view of the present situation, I am not implying that nothing is being done. I acknowledge that many efforts have to be commended and many results recognized.

3) Although I am addressing the matters to bishops, I view them in a perspective of shared ministry, otherwise I would obviously not have accepted this responsibility.

1. Ministering within an Educational Frame-Work

As an educator, I should like to offer this reflection on family ministry implementation within the working structure of one current educational perspective: the behavioral objectives approach to teaching-learning situations. Such an approach views education, on the one hand, as an attempt to raise the level of consciousness through the gaining of new knowledge and, on the other hand, as an attempt to motivate learners into modifying or reinforcing their behavior in keeping with the newly acquired knowledge. In other terms, knowledge tends to become a part of one's values and thus to be adopted into one's lifestyle.

In keeping with these broad educational goals, various integrated or systemic components are involved:[1]

1. Knowledge or contents are chosen;

2. Objectives are written;

3. Strategies are selected and implemented;

4. Resource persons are selected and educational materials are set aside;

5. Finally, after an experimenting phase has been completed, a period is determined to evaluate all components of the system.

Evaluating is an essential step in behavioral approaches to education and I believe it is too readily overlooked in ministerial circles. Without proper assessment from time to time, any form of educational approach will lose its vigor, stagnate and become inefficient.

2. The Contents

In ministry involving sexuality, marriage and family, three elements of contents are to be presented:

— *the first content deals with theology:*

First of all, we are referring to the biblical vision of person, sexuality and marriage. Translating that vision into educational language, we can say that: God the Creator has endowed sexual body-spirit persons with a vitally essential tension between the love-sharing dynamics and the life-transmitting dynamics of their sexualness which attains its full meaning in the whole of conjugal love and life as specifically signified in genital intercourse between spouses.[2]

Let us note immediately that this integrative pattern of the unitive aspect (love-sharing dynamics) and the pro-creative aspect (life-transmitting dynamics) of human sexuality implies that the God-given power to transmit life is a reality of personhood which goes much further and much deeper than the mere spacing of children. This power is an intrinsic component of our sexual selves. This reality is to be brought to consciousness by the acquiring of knowledge about God, His views on sexuality (as revealed in Scripture and in Church tradition) as a means to reach Him through body-spirit personhood, my own and that of others. When fertility (life-transmitting power) is put in that perspective, such a power has better chances of being appreciated as a life-growing value which, through sexual mastery (chastity), is to be

301

respectfully managed. No matter what a person's marital status is, he or she must take into account the gift of life-transmitting empowerment.[3] Natural family planning is but one means of achieving respectful fertility management as applied in the context of the community of love and life which is marriage.

— the second content deals with spirituality:

Within the love-life community of marriage, conjugality draws its spiritual meaning from the Paschal Mystery. The giving-receiving event of Jesus' suffering, death and resurrection is the fountainhead from which as spouses, we are resourced and motivated in order to live out our lives as signs (sacraments) of what we are called to be: love-sharing and life-transmitting.[4]

This vision of marriage as a spiritual enrichment process growing out of the Paschal Mystery has helped to gain deeper insight in the qualities of conjugal love described in *Humanae Vitae*: fully human, total, faithful and exclusive as well as life-transmitting (fecund).

Briefly, each of these qualities or characteristics can be described in the following manner:

— *fully human*: exercised in genuine freedom, without coercion;

— *total*: as it was with Jesus for His Father, each spouse, as a male body-spirit person or a female body-spirit person is to be completely available and vulnerable to the other in the totality of his or her whole being;

— *faithful and exclusive*: each to the other in all manner of relational and personal gestures regardless of difficulties, drawbacks, disappointments and sufferings;

— *open to creativeness*: i.e. attuned to God's final say on life; accepting that love and life reach far beyond even the most genuine, integrated, body-spirit love-making since the giving-receiving of one to the other sparks new life. Such "new life" was given to us through, in, and by the meaningful enfleshed event of the suffering, death and resurrection of Jesus.

302

None of these characteristics is to be omitted if the spouses as persons and indeed the marriage covenant itself are to grow in spiritual wholesomeness.[5]

It follows that theology and spirituality rather than moral norms of "dos and don'ts" are the proper setting in which the sacrament of matrimony should be presented if we are to give it its authentic meaning and its prophetic role in our present-day context.

— the third element of content deals with present-day values:

If I were a bishop's confessor, I think I would give him as penance that he watch TV for 5 week-day afternoons in a row. This would serve to help him make concrete evangelical discernment of our times. For what would he be forced to watch?

— Soap Operas![6]

Over three hours of "romance", infatuation and sexual activity which demean young people, husbands, wives by valuing them not as whole persons, but only by presenting them for their material usefulness or their sexual gratification. Very few situations do not overtly convey that marriage is a hassle, that parents and spouses are a burden to be delivered from in any manner possible. Low self-esteem and despair are the common fare.

In their busy, sheltered lives our bishops perhaps have not yet come to realize fully that these influences are shaping the attitudes of most people around us. We too often fail to perceive the amount of suffering and fear which permeates our lives from these programs through their projecting of a negative view of persons. The characters in these shows are constantly inflicting hurt on themselves and on others. This suffering comes from, and, at the same time, leads to the rejection of self and others and even sometimes to the destruction of self and of others. As viewers, we are projected into a context of exploitation, sexual exploitation being but a mere symptom of the unbridled urge to dominate.

From a Christian standpoint it can be read into this that the fear of self and of others resulting from original sin has not been graced with the acceptance of self resulting from the redeeming event of the Paschal Mystery.

— Soap operas laced with commercials . . .

Have we come to the awareness of what attitudes are being pounded into the hearts and minds of so many for financial gain?

— Easy living: There are car batteries that you get and forget. Everything has to be worry free. *— Synthetics:* Through substitutes we can get the pleasure of taste without any negative consequences. This, of course, is better than the "real thing". Sometimes even the "real thing" contains nothing genuine. *— Reaching goals without the responsible behavior of self-restraint:* There are products allowing you to lose weight and still go on eating! Taste, chew and enjoy! *— Appearances:* there is toothpaste that will take the ugly yellow nicotine and tar stains off your teeth while you can go on smoking and gradually commit suicide with a nice bright smile.

Clearly, these are practical applications of proportionalism whereby the greater good to be chosen is some form of sensual pleasure geared to personal gratification.

Through constant repetition from all forms of media, attitudes are being shaped by directing us in our choices as consumers. However, by viewing ourselves merely as consumers we tend to apply to our intimate selves and to our relationship with others the same criteria as we do for choosing any consumer product. Choosing a sexual lifestyle "suitable for me" tends to become the same type of procedure as selecting which kind of shampoo will make my hair "squeaky clean." And if ever unfortunate side-effects have to be dealt with, allegedly minor items such as unplanned pregnancy, venereal disease or emotional breakdown, or disruption of another person's life, these may be suppressed or side-tracked by using the proper gadgets or drugs, or again by the ridding of one's guilt or the disposing of one's partner. It is not sufficient to condemn however. As Church educators we must learn to use these realities as a starting point in raising people's consciousness of their own value and that of their environment. This is good ground for planting the seed of God's redeeming grace. But we have to learn to know that ground, or else we shall not be planting properly.

When our convictions change on the deep-rooted influences involved, perhaps then we shall draw up pastoral objectives in keeping with real-life situations. What should some of these objectives be?

3. Two Sets of Objectives

There are two sets of educational objectives:

1) *cognitive objectives*

These are directed towards acquiring knowledge *per se*. Concerning the God-given power to transmit life, choosing cognitive objectives should concern itself with the knowledge young people and/or couples are to acquire as regards the vision of Scripture and Church on matters linked to conjugal intimacy presented as a living sign of the Paschal Mystery. Cognitive objectives should address themselves to the following questions: How is the recognition of ourselves as body-spirit life-transmitting persons associated with growth in our intimacy and in our relationships? What makes respectful fertility appreciation and respectful management so important to the whole of marriage viewed as the community of love and life?

2) *affective objectives*

This set of objectives aims at behavior modification or reinforcement.

In the domain of marital theology and spirituality, the knowledge and appreciation of fertility as a gift is expected to be followed by respectful management of the power to transmit life.

Outside marriage, this means abstention from genital intercourse. Within marriage, it means that the spouses will integrate periodic continence into their genital relationships, i.e. take into account the fertile and infertile phases of the wife's ovarian cycle.

Affective objectives are akin to the evangelical reality of metanoia or conversion.[7]

4. Evaluating Educational Strategies and Resources

To suggest strategies and resources capable of pursuing these objectives, I have selected three specific groups of persons who, in my opinion, should be awarded privileged consideration among the concerns of bishops. They are:

1) Teenagers 2) Seminarians 3) Pre-married couples.

1) *Teenagers*

Whether it be in schools, parish religion classes, or youth groups, strategies involving sex and/or family-life education should carry a whole and wholesome view of sexuality. This entails that neither one of the two meaningful dynamics of sexual expression should be left out or belittled. Sometimes the break between these two dynamics is suggested under the very subtle and reassuring pretext of better communication through "caring, sharing and loving". However caring, sharing and loving in sexual encounter such as is often overtly or covertly promoted are incomplete and can be easily turned into addiction to genital activity or result in sexual exploitation of others if not appreciated and assessed in the light of the gift of transmitting life. Truly caring means fully respecting every intimate dynamism of one's self and of the other. Truly sharing means opening up all aspects of my total self to the other. And loving in faithful exclusiveness means a giving-receiving relationship truly possible only in the permanency of the marriage relationship. Any other type of arrangement runs a high risk of becoming demeaning for persons (easily set aside like objects) and trivializing for the "sacramental" relationship (not being fully committal).

Such a genuine commitment to self and deep communion with the other is not arrived at instantly or without effort, and thus should be presented as a challenge to which young people are capable of rising in faith. Educators should be challengers!

As a wedge into the acquiring of such appreciation and with the intention of arriving at such behavior, every sex education program addressing itself to teenagers should include, for both young men and young women, precise information on the processes of the female ovarian cycle and the facts of male anatomy and physiology. This should be followed up with charting instructions for young women, taking into account the various parameters leading to precise ovulation detection.[8] The sooner positive knowledge is acquired and suitable behavior actuated, the sooner young women will appreciate the delicate and awesome reality of being a female body-spirit person and, by the same token, the sooner they will be able to impart this reality to their male peers and thus command respect for that reality as a component of their whole and wholesome selves.

306

Ignorance creates fear, prejudice, internal isolation, and tends to seek transient security measures and too often leads to destructive behavior. Knowledge, on the other hand, engenders peace of mind, appreciation of self and of others, leads to self empowerment and consequently to contructive relationships. We should make it a point to evaluate sex-education programs according to the two integrated dynamics of sexuality and to overview very carefully the criteria which are followed in selecting teachers, educators and counselors of young persons whose task it is to transmit human values from a faith perspective.[9]

The dilemma of parents

As ministry persons we must also live in the awareness that, although parents stand to be the primary educators of their children, not a few of them are faced with the following profound dilemma. How can they feel comfortable and be motivated in encouraging their teenagers to consider fertility as a positive power in their growth as sexual body-spirit persons, when they themselves are not dealing with that power through respectful management? Young persons detect only too quickly whether values are given mere lip service or whether they are suggested from a living-witness experience.[10]

2) Seminarians

Concerning this group, we must first of all face the fact that most men entering the seminary have received the same basic education as their high school and college peers. Older men often come from lifestyles wherein few theological and spiritual values on sexuality have ever been viewed at all, either because of sheltering or because of negative sexual behavior from which they have only recently converted. On matters of sexuality, they have been exposed over and over again to the idea that their life-transmitting power is not too important and that their sex drives can be catered to if they do not engender guilt or if they are actuated in a "non-hurting situation among consenting adults." There is a lot of "metanoia" to be reckoned with here, if these men are to be led into a lifestyle that views complete abstention from genital activity (the vow of chastity) as 1) the genuine form of respectful fertility management in their own lives, and 2) as a means to answer the call to make their ministerial selves fruitful for the Church by advocating the vision of its teachings on matters of sexuality, marriage and family.

At the risk of sounding like some square conservative inquisitor type, I should suggest that we take a good hard look at the curricula on sexuality and marriage in the institutions where our seminarians or other ministry oriented persons are being trained. Are you positive that they are being presented with a vision of sexuality that encourages mastery of their sexual instincts and body drives as a means of acquiring mastery of self? Is Church teaching on sexual behavior being belittled as Vatican propaganda, not in keeping with "more modern views of sexual lifestyles," or again as a betrayal of the spirit of Vatican II? Or, on the grounds of conserving tradition, is there a tendency in some instances to revert to forms of Puritanism negating enfleshed realities?[11]

Whether it be through the oppressive denial of sexuality or the glorification of feelings, either of these approaches is extreme and hardly conducive to a genuinely balanced view of the God-given reality of enfleshed sexual body-spirit personhood. It is through this personhood that the Incarnate Word is revealed to each one of us. What these persons being trained for ministry have been acquainted with during their formative years they shall propose and be a witness to. Their attitudes towards sexuality are bound to influence the attitudes of others regarding their own intimacy, their relationships, and the spiritual worthiness of the marriage commitment.

3. Pre-married couples

After many years of involvement in marriage preparation programs and after visiting half of the dioceses in Canada over the last eighteen months, I would like to insist on the urgent necessity for re-evaluating the whole pastoral sector of marriage preparation.

This is a good place to start immediately, if we are really going to develop educational strategies in keeping with the dynamics of conjugal love-life, while considering the real-world value system in which the couples are daily living out their lives.

This is a privileged sector where, as Church, we will show whether we wish our pastoral energies to be channelled into a world permeated with God-absent lifestyles, especially regarding marriage, or whether we are going to carry on in the land of make-believe Christianity wishing that the world had not gone sour on Christian tradition.

Many couples committed to marriage preparation ministry of one form or another are dissatisfied with their situation for a number of reasons of which I shall cite three:

1) The time-frame is too short:

A few hours of skimming over the basics of marriage commitment are not sufficient even to suggest, let alone integrate, sorely needed resourcing. If ministry persons can be found to provide eight week reconstruction programs for the separated and divorced, how can such human resources not be found to propose marriage preparation sessions extending into six or seven evenings or three or four weekends? I hesitate to suggest the opinion that perhaps we do not deem such efforts worthwhile.

2) The power to transmit life is being negatively presented:

When dealing with sexuality and intimacy, the gift of the life-transmitting power is not included as a component of that intimacy. Rather, fertility is presented as a drag on improving conjugal growth or an impediment to spousal reciprocity. Sometimes it is even viewed as preventing couples from being fully intimate. This, of course, is hardly a positive manner of introducing the Catholic vision of marriage as the community of both love and life.

Fertility is usually associated with child preventing rather than with respectful conjugal living. Furthermore, the power to transmit life is too often viewed as something to be feared, to be avoided and/or to be treated, since it is associated with diseases such as Herpes II. It is always by evaluating strategies that real objectives reveal themselves.

3) Natural family planning is being misrepresented:

NFP is being called "rhythm" or "calendar", and presented as a non-effective method compared to "more modern means of birth control." This is clearly language coming from perspectives promoted by such organizations as Planned Parenthood. In some programs willful childlessness is being suggested as an accepted option in Catholic marriages.

If NFP couples are being invited in by marriage preparation facilitators, they are often being warned "not to come on too strong and not to disturb these fine young persons' lifestyles by laying all this guilt on them with negative views of contraception." They must present all types of contraceptive methods both artificial and "natural". (Even the misnomer "natural contraceptive methods" indicates to what dimension of "fertility awareness" young couples are being introduced). Contraceptive behavior tends to become a "non-value" question. Subjective choice is the solution and feeling comfortable with one's decisions is the way to go. Objective content is given little room, if any, and the negative physiological, psychological and spiritual side-effects experienced over twenty years of generalized contraception are hardly mentioned.

I would suggest that NFP user and teacher couples be systematically invited by Church leadership to share in drawing up and developing marriage preparation programs. Integrating such strong baptismal forces into curricula-implementing could serve one or more of the following purposes in this very sensitive area of family ministry:

— *First,* it would help to choose leadership among persons who are knowledgeable in and witness to a vision of marriage respectful of the full dynamics of conjugal love-life.
— *Secondly,* it would show support for the efforts which NFP groups are so courageously contributing under the strain of opposition from sometimes unexpected quarters.
— *Thirdly,* it might give rise to cooperative action among the groups and organizations proposing various respectful fertility monitoring parameters.

Being mandated to serve the Church by responding to an essential and timely need in family ministry could prove a unifying factor for these groups and might help them become aware of how unconstructive bickering among themselves can be. This would not dispossess each of its identity but rather contribute to show the values of each's particular approach.

However, they too need to be trained as educators, and having recourse to their expertise does not imply that NFP user and

310

teacher couples should not be given the opportunity to be enriched with training in adult education. They must acquire ability to implement educational strategies which lead pre-marrieds to integrate positive knowledge and behavior into their lives. Church teaching should never be used as some sort of spiritual club with which to knock potential learners over the head. Faithfulness to truth is challenging when it proposes a response to the capability of living according to God's grace.

As was suggested for teens, confidence must be built up both in leadership and in young couples.

5. Conclusion

The knowledge, appreciation and respectful management of our life-transmitting power is a means to self growth because it is a response to God's original intention that we respectfully exercise stewardship over all of Creation. It is the original ecological design beginning with ourselves as a vital link in the life-respecting chain.

Through our baptism we have been given the mission to proclaim and to witness the fact that in the Paschal Mystery our body and our spirit have been reconciled. This redeeming reconciliation is a call to grow deeper and deeper in the respectful vision of all the creative forces dwelling in us.

Our shared responsibilities in ministry, whether they be baptismal, diaconal, presbyteral or episcopal should direct us in choosing our educational strategies in keeping with the enrichment of the mystery of an enfleshed Jesus and in response to our calling to live as genuine proclaimers of that mystery.

The choice of each and every content, objective, strategy, resource and their evaluation should be directed to that mystery, in response to that calling.

Notes

1. Since this paper has no pretense to be a scholarly development of the behavioral objective approach to education, no reference to one specific school shall be given. The original concept proposed by such persons as Maslow, Burns *et alii* has been considerably added upon and modified over the years following a number of teaching-learning experiences. What is important to focus on is the "systemic concept", i.e. each component is intrinsically connected to the organic whole, therefore, none is expandable if the goals and objectives are to be attained and, if, following valid evaluation procedures, further experiencing is to be pursued significantly.

2. The interpretation of the "original meaning" of marriage was given by Jesus in Matthew 19:5. It refers to the creation narrations of Genesis 1:26-29 and 2:18-24. Respectful stewardship of the whole of creation must take into account all the dynamics of all creatures. For a love-sharing couple the power to transmit life constitutes one of these dynamics. Cf. John Paul II, *Original Unity of Man and Woman* (Boston: Daughters of St. Paul, 1981), pp. 1-84.

3. Cf. William E. May; *Sex, Marriage and Chastity*, Reflections of a Catholic layman, spouse and parent (Chicago: Franciscan Herald Press, 1981), pp. i-xi, 1-170. As positive comments on the meaning of sexuality and marriage, this book as well as others like it by Professor May certainly deserve to be considered as educational material for ministry training programs.

4. The spiritual insight of the conjugality of the cross is developed by the French theologian, Gustave Martelet, S.J., in his book *Oser croire en l'Eglise* (Paris: Seuil, 1978), in Chapter IX: "L'Eglise de l'amour conjugal et du sacrement de mariage." pp. 166-179.

5. It is usually agreed upon that no part of our bodies is distinct from the whole body. Medication always affects not only that organic matter being treated but the whole body-person as well; *I* have a headache, *I* am being treated for an ulcer, etc. This is true also of the psychic and/or spiritual dynamics of persons and of their marriage relationship. Cultivating one quality of conjugal life enhances all of the others. Neglecting one of the aspects of marriage such as the power to transmit life tends to stunt the growth of all other characteristics and hence of the whole marriage. Cf. Brunelle, G.-E; *Genital Encounter and Contraception — A Faith Perspective*, Ottawa, Family Action Publications, 1983, pp. 1-24.

6. The outline proposed here concerning U.S. afternoon TV, and some evening programs, applies as well to shows telecast in French on both Radio-Canada and TVA.

7. An interesting connection could be further pursued between the concept of "behavior modification" and the invitation to "change our hearts" as revealed in Judeo-Christian tradition. Perhaps the possibility of investigating how to translate the Gospel teachings of "metanoia" into contemporary terms would be worthwhile. As Christians we are called upon to "reveal in faith" the full value of human intuition.

8. There are basically three parameters or signs observed in the detection of fertility-infertility phases of the ovarian cycle: 1) fluctuations in basal body temperature; 2) presence, absence and quality modification of cervical mucus; 3) shift of the cervix in the vaginal cavity. Varous NFP groups have recourse to one of or a combination of these body changes to observe ovulation. Through the learning process, women and couples develop abilities capable of observing other secondary signs associated with the basic ones, so that in a vast majority of marriages ovulation can be pinpointed with great accuracy.

9. The FAMILY ACTION project in Canada is implementing programs for teens and the pre-married in cooperation with diocesan core-groups who are putting together strategies in their own regions. Hopefully, these groups from various parts of our country will develop educational materials which, in a positive way, will transmit the views of the Magisterium on sexuality and marriage. As educators, it is our responsibility to translate these teachings into coherent, relevant and significant educational language (Cf. *Humanae Vitae*. nos. 22, 25, 26, 28-29, 30. Also *Familiaris Consortio*, part 4, sections I-III).

10. This difficult and very sensitive situation concerning parents, and adult teen counselors as well, is adequately addressed by Martin, Mary Catherine, Ph.D., in *Fertility Acceptance and Natural Family Planning*, Respect Life Series, Washington D.C., USCCB, 1981, pp. 1-16.

11. Sound criteria in assessing what is being delivered on these issues in ministry training institutions would be the consideration and the interpretation, if any, which certain official documents are or are not receiving within their curricula: *Gaudium et Spes*, 47-52; *Humanae Vitae*; *Persona Humana*; *Familiaris Consortio*. And more recently, *The Educational Guidance in Human Love* or the *Charter of the Rights of the Family*.

Chapter 15

Pastoral Concerns
Regarding Applied
Moral Theology

Part I — Discussion With Father Gallagher and Doctor Boyle

Bishop: Would Pope Pius XII extend the principle of totality beyond the physical organism to the psychological or other aspects of the human person, and thereby justify certain acts which might be called mutilation? If I understood the principle correctly in the past, you could not extend it into the psychological realm, it had to be confined within the limits of the physical organism.

Father Gallagher: I think it's clear enough in Pope Pius XII that he doesn't intend to confine the principle to the organism as body or as physical. He does intend to extend it to other goods of the human person, but he would still see grave problems about extending it beyond the individual human person to the

313

social whole. The reason he gives is that the parts of the social whole are not only parts but they have their own individual goals. The point that he's making is that as soon as you move beyond the parts of an individual to the parts of a social whole, you have a competing set of goals, one against the other, and you are necessarily into a proportional argument. Because there's no competition between the members and the whole of the body, that's not a problem. As soon as you're in a proportionalist argument, you're into a problem of making that judgment without being subjective and without allowing a particular interest to dominate.

The real problem that I have with proportionalism is that you have to ask the question, who makes the exceptions? In the whole discussion of exceptions, the impersonal form is always used. But the impersonal form can mean an objective, all-knowing judge, or it can mean us human beings. As soon as you say, we human beings make the judgments, then you have self-interest, bias, and rationalization, therefore, subjectivism. So the whole problem is to raise the question in such a way that it may be subject to public verification, that is the only way we have of trying to guard against this subjectivism.

In order to guard against subjectivism, we raised totality to the level of principle and intrinsic evil, and some people are happy to do that. But if you push intellectually for logic in Pius XII you can't mean intrinsic evil, because he does allow it in certain cases. So the solution, it seems to me, is to try to determine what kind of social goals would allow you to justify mutilation. We must discover how we can raise exceptions to a level of public scrutiny and public discussion, rather than have individuals who make their own biased judgment. But I don't think that there's any problem in principle in moving totality beyond the individual. There is a problem of how you do that objectively.

Bishop: There are questions regarding transplants which raise issues in need of attention today, although they may not specifically be related to the principle of totality. One question that we have in mind is, since the number of available organs is limited and the need great, how do we determine who should receive these organs: on the basis of who can pay for them, on the basis of first come, first served, or whatever? Our second question is, what would be considered a just expenditure of funds to make transplants available in society, when the cost will eventually have to be absorbed by insurance and thus make insurance premiums so costly that the poor may be unable to afford them?

Father Gallagher: The question is the limitation of the number of available organs. The prevailing thought is that you start off with the medical indications of which transplants are most likely to be medically successful and medically useful. Once you have made that kind of judgment, most ethicists would say that beyond that medical indication you should go to a lottery as the only fair way. I would agree with that opinion, because as soon as you use any indication beyond the medical, you are always giving advantage to a particular interest group. For example, the clergy might get the transplants if you're in a Catholic area!

I would also say that if, in fact, donations are good, especially donations not from living donors but from people leaving their organs at death, then it is probably incumbent upon the teachers of the Christian Churches to make that clear to their people to alleviate the shortage.

As for expenditure, what would be a good percentage of the gross national product to put into this, that is a question that cannot be answered on the level of medical ethics alone. When you talk about expenditure, you may talk about it in isolation and say, for example, how much your life is worth. But it's never really in isolation, it's always with reference to alternative uses of that money. If the alternative is recreation or the alternative is smoking, that's one question. If the alternative is feeding starving people, it is another. If the alternative is building nuclear weapons, that is still another. The question of what would be a just percentage of the gross national product to go into transplants cannot be answered as a medical ethical question. It has to be answered in terms of certain priorities within the total social fabric.

Bishop: Father Gallagher spoke about permanent sterilization as mutilation, what about temporary sterilization in the case of certain contraceptives?

Father Gallagher: Certainly Father Zalba looks upon even temporary sterilization as a form of mutilation. I think if he were pressed on that point, it might be questionable, although it is a temporary disruption of a function. If you try to justify that by the principle of totality you are obviously going to have to call upon a justification beyond the good of the individual. I think it's perfectly persuasive that our procreative faculties do not exist for our own good. Therefore, temporary sterilization cannot be justified simply by an appeal to the good of the individual, it would have to be justified by an appeal to the good of the family and the good of society as a whole. But, as soon as you make the goods to be considered that wide, I think that you fall into the whole area that Dr. Boyle described, of needing a knowledge which only God could have. As soon as you start making proportional judgments when the good to be sought and the evils which might result are so vast, the judgments become purely arbitrary. The goods that appeal to you are going to be the ones that come to the forefront. Because in that kind of case the use of proportional arguments would be almost inevitably subjective, although I might not want to call the acts intrinsic evil, I would be willing to say that, *de facto*, we have an exceptionless norm.

Bishop: In the case of diabetes where insulin is very necessary to the health of the woman, and yet there are secretions from the placenta in the case of pregnancy that interfere with the effectiveness of the insulin and therefore affect very seriously the life of the woman, can you justify suppression of ovarian function? Is that analogous to such allowed precedures as suppression of ovarian function when the hormonal secretions would contribute to the spread of cancer? A second question would advert to the whole case that goes back to the sixties of the nuns in the Congo and the use of a diaphragm in the case of threatened rape. How about the case of sterilizing an adolescent girl, unmarried and mentally deficient, for her protection because any sexual intercourse would be a form of violence and rape?

Father Gallagher: With regard to the first question, I would suggest using the direct-indirect distinction. Where the intention is directly to sterilize, it seems to me that the act comes under

316

the general restrictions against sterilization. When your purpose is something else, namely to prevent some other thing happening, then the indirect sterilization doesn't come under the general restrictions.

Now, as to the case of the adolescent retarded girl, I think that it can first be safely said that, as in the case of the nuns in the Congo, the basis for saying that contraception can be used is that what is wrong is to sterilize oneself with the intention of positing an act which is of itself procreative while denying the procreative action. Therefore, in the case of rape, it is justified to use contraception, you are not contradicting anything. Now can that be applied to the retarded girl? I think in some cases it could, but there would have to be extreme caution here, because there are many degrees of retardation.

There is a temptation to take the retarded and lump them all together and say they are all more or less pre-human and not responsible. But some retarded persons can be responsible for their actions, some mildly retarded people can function as parents. Still others can be treated with simple custodial care so that sex is not likely to be imposed upon them violently. This would cover most cases of the retarded. In the extreme case, where the inevitable result of the girl's fertility is going to be an abortion, then I can see that the same reasoning from the example of the nuns in the Congo would be applicable. In this case there seems to be no other way out, because any sexual activity is going to take a form equivalent to violence because the girl is incapable of consent.

Bishop: I would like to use an example and have you comment on it. The isolation of the uterus seems to be both a medical and moral solution when it is in a pathological condition. In this pathological condition a hysterectomy would be approved if a woman cannot bring a child to term. From a medical point of view the isolation of the uterus through tying of the tubes is much better for the woman and the total person than a hysterectomy and it certainly does not do violence to the person or the person's body. Could not the principle of totality be used in this case?

Father Gallagher: In the case which you give, where a hysterectomy could be medically indicated because of an inability to carry a child to term, there it seems to me that you are starting with a case in which meaningful procreative activity is already precluded. It is excluded because becoming pregnant and dying is not meaningful procreative activity. The hysterectomy could be justified on that grounds because one has nothing to protect. There you are saying the principle of totality cannot be used to remove the uterus as long as meaningful procreative activity is possible. When it ceases to be possible it is a little bit artificial to continue to make the uterus dominant in the moral consideration. So I think from that point of view the isolating of the uterus could be justified by the principle of totality.

Bishop: Dr. Boyle, would you comment further on your statement that proportionate reason is essential to double effect and needs more analysis, but is not correctly handled by proportionalists?

Doctor Boyle: The fourth condition for using the double effect principle is usually stated in terms of "proportionately grave reason" or something of that sort. My problem is that I don't think that the kind of weighing and balancing of pre-moral goods that the proportionalists want to do can be used for this condition. I don't think that there is any objective way to weigh different kinds of values and to arrive at the judgment that A is a lesser evil than B. "Lesser evil" is one of those phrases that has lots of different meanings, and when the lesser evil in question is based on comparing the value of pre-moral goods and evils, I do not think it is possible to be objective.

So the question is: what does the fourth condition mean? It's very important, and I think a lot more depends on that fourth condition than we have thought. Even if you satisfy the first three conditions for double effect you still have an act that involves something bad. There is a voluntary acceptance or permission or toleration of the evil foreseen in the voluntary act. So even if the first three conditions are met, you're still doing something that has a harmful or evil side effect which is something that, other things being equal, we ought to try to prevent.

Now the question is, what exactly does the last criterion mean, and does it mean that we should use proportionalism as understood by the proportionalists? I think a lot of people would say, yes, that's where proportionalism has its role. My opinion is that proportionalism must be limited to that if it's to be used at all, but I have trouble even with that use of proportionalism. But then what is to be considered here? It seems to me that the answer to that question is: any morally relevant considerations that are appropriate that would constrain you from doing something otherwise good, good in itself and having a good purpose, but having a bad effect. You should consider anything that would require you not to bring about that bad effect. I think the clearest example might be bad effects in violation of the golden rule or of justice and such things as that. But in other words it's bringing in the other morally relevant considerations. The tradition talked loosely about this sort of thing, when dealing with proportionate reasons, because the importance of that last clause was not sufficiently realized.

An example of this fourth condition for double effect is found in St. Thomas' discussion of killing in self-defense. In my opinion, although scholars dispute this, that discussion of self-defense in the *Secunda Secundae*, q. 64 a. 7, is where the double effect discussion starts. The first thing St. Thomas does is to settle the question of intention. He makes it clear that killing is involved, the killing of an attacker by a private person, but he shows that the death of the attacker is *praeter intentionem,* it's outside your intention, it's indirect in other words.

Then he raises some other questions, saying that, nevertheless, it can be that a certain act proceeding from a good intention can be rendered illicit, if it's not proportioned to the end. Thus if someone in defending his own life uses more force than is necessary, this is illicit. So the proportion there is between the means you're using to defend yourself and the end. That is not proportionalism in the modern sense.

St. Thomas also says it is not necessary for salvation that someone forego the act of moderate self-defense to avoid the death of the other, because a man is more bound to provide for his own life than for the life of another. In other words, under proportionate reason he's bringing in another consideration: even if it is indirect, you're killing somebody. Don't we as Christians have an obligation to look out for the other person's life rather than our own? St. Augustine, facing that same question, not as analytically as St. Thomas did, said no, you can't kill in self-defense. St. Thomas, however, appeals to his understanding of the order of charity in which you are more obliged to take care of yourself than somebody else. So under proportionate reason St. Thomas considers that what you do must be proportioned as a means to an end and that the other morally relevant consideration in this situation, namely, bringing about somebody's death even if you're not intending to kill them, must be examined. He asks if such killing would be a violation of our concern for our neighbor and he says no. I would argue yes.

Bishop: Could either or both of you reflect from your work with the principle of totality and the principle of double effect on the newly emerging situations of people refusing to eat and the use of forced feeding, as in the case of Mrs. Bouvia in California?

Doctor Boyle: It seems to me from reading the newspaper accounts of Mrs. Bouvia, that what she really is doing is committing suicide passively. She has come very close to saying that in the published interviews that she has had. I think that this is a case where the moral question is fundamentally a question of suicide. It seems to me that you can commit suicide, and in fact do almost any sin, by not doing something as well as by doing something. Her refusal to eat under the circumstances seems to me to be a means of ending her life because she doesn't want to live anymore and her life at the present time is miserable. She obviously has a very miserable life and it's a shame that something can't be done to make her life more livable as far as she sees it.

But I think the problem is much more a legal problem than a straight moral problem because in the law no one is permitted to treat someone against their will. So if someone wants to refuse treatment, even if that should be suicidal in terms of passive suicide, it seems to me that there is a legal and moral obligation to respect the decision of that person. You could try to talk them out of it, but the right to refuse treatment is very strong. In the law, and I think morally too, we have an obligation to respect people's right to refuse treatment. That is essential to having any kind of due order in this area.

What is perplexing is the question, is feeding medical treatment? That's the same kind of question that has a lot of us perplexed about nasogastric feeding of people who are in comas. The law is not clear about that. Her plainly suicidal intention is part of what is making the courts perplexed about it. But, morally speaking, I think that what she's doing is a decision to end her life, and it is not behaviors that are important morally, but choices. The choice she is making is to end her life. Therefore I don't think the distinction of ordinary or extraordinary means can be brought in.

Father Gallagher: I'm not going to try and talk about the facts of this particular case. But it is possible for a medical condition to arise in which the taking of food is no longer required, when a person, for example, is gagging almost uncontrollably or when stuffing a pipe down an almost unconscious person's throat causes severe discomfort or forced feeding of various kinds causes severe problems. In these cases artificial nourishment may become "extraordinary means."

The other question is, suppose you think that in this case it is suicidal if the person doesn't eat, that there isn't a sufficiently grave reason for them not to eat, in that case, you must first discover whether that person is competent. If the person is competent, then it seems to me that the person has a right to refuse treatment, even when they're wrong. In other words, we have no moral obligation to override somebody's refusal of treatment. If they're not competent, then I think one would override their judgment.

Bishop: Father Gallagher, when you spoke of sterilization, you said it could not be allowed because in this case it's not really the good of the body which is involved, but the good of the human race. What is the good of the human race for a family which already has several children or for a country which is already over-populated?

Father Gallagher: What I tried to say was that sterilization brings in not simply the good of the individual but the good of the race. That's what causes the problem, that doesn't solve the problem. Precisely what is good of the human race? One might say that from one point of view there are certain goods of the human race that are not served by procreation in a particular instance, that's one point of view, one part of the good. Another part of the good is the impact of allowing sterilization on the very meaning of sexuality as it exists in a culture. You cannot have sterilization allowed without it imperceptibly changing the whole way that people view procreation. That's another factor. I'm saying all of those factors become very, very hard to calculate. It becomes, to my mind, almost impossible to calculate what is for the good of the human race in that case.

An isolated case was brought up earlier in which meaningful procreative activity is no longer possible. Then it seems to me that this consideration changes our judgment, and the isolation of the uterus in that case can be done because there is no more reference to the good of the human race in that particular procreative system.

Bishop: Father Gallagher, what do you think about the death penalty, its morality or immorality? May it clearly be included in the principle of totality?

Father Gallagher: That's a huge question, and what I can say is going to be only a little bit of help. Certainly in St. Thomas you have a justification for capital punishment in the principle of totality. For the good of the whole, you may sacrifice individual members. The problem with that is precisely that it is always going to be imposed by particular people with particular biases. We have a just war theory based on the same principle of totality which never seems to have stopped any war. In the history of Christianity we have Christians going to war with each side justifying themselves by the just war theory. It's an excellent theory, at least in the hands of Augustine it was an excellent theory. But one has to ask about the reality of a theory which never stops wars. The just war theory should stop all wars, because no two sides can ever be justified. No war should ever happen because there would be a side in the right and a side in the wrong and the side in the wrong would not go to war, they would surrender.

We have to say in theory that the death penalty can be justified, but in practice it always has this tremendous problem that it is always administered by people who have a bias. That is about as far as I could go. That is as close as I would come to consistent pacifism. I'm not going to be a consistent pacifist, but I would come fairly close to it. I would say one could justify the death penalty if one could be assured of a magistrate who was objective.

Bishop: May the intervention of the super-power nations in the Third World countries be considered in the light of the double effect principle?

Doctor Boyle: I don't see how it would apply. In any intervention you must be doing something when you are choosing to intervene. Perhaps some of the things which are related to double effect that come up in discussions of just war doctrine might be applied, but we have to get down to specific acts. But when we get to specific acts, especially when they are in the political arena, it's enormously difficult to try to figure out what they are. If it is hard to tell what exactly the human act is when we call it abortion, trying to figure out exactly what is going on in terms of human action when it's a corporate human action of a very complex sort, becomes far more difficult.

Bishop: Sometimes the countries of the Third World ask for help, and then the super-power nations commercialize the war. Is that the double effect?

Doctor Boyle: It seems to me that double effect does not shed any particular light on commercializing a situation and taking advantage of it. It seems to me that the question of commercialization and various kinds of cultural interchange have to be sorted out in terms of the moral principles that are involved. And if, in fact, there is a kind of clear exploitation, then it's wrong, just straight out. I don't see how double effect is going to be too much help in that area, but for specific cases it might come to bear. I don't think double effect is going to be able to get people off the hook to allow them to do things that are shady. By and large that applies whether we're talking about our individual choices or our corporate choices.

Bishop: Doctor Boyle, in your judgment, may a diocesan bishop permit the moral theology professor in the diocesan seminary to teach proportionalism, in addition to double effect or even to the exclusion of double effect?

Doctor Boyle: My hunch is no, if he's proclaiming it as a Catholic position.

Bishop: Father Gallagher, in some parts of our country, judges have offered convicted rapists the option of a long prison sentence or castration. Is there a moral justification for this form of mutilation?

Father Gallagher: It has never been condemned by the Church. Perhaps it should have been, but it has never been, and in theory it could be a justified sentence. I haven't really studied it enough to know whether in practice it's effective and so on.

Bishop: It seems to be a developing thing among some judges in parts of our country.

Father Gallagher: Well, it's cheaper than keeping people in prison. I'm afraid that that might be the motivation rather than that there has been a study of the effectiveness of castration as a penalty.

Bishop: May an individual choose to donate an organ of his body without which he cannot live, so that he may save the life of another? Can we use the example of Maximilian Kolbe who offered his life to save the life of another?

Father Gallagher: I tend to think not. It was certainly legitimate for Maximilian Kolbe to offer his life, to undergo death for the sake of another. But I do not think it would be legitimate to kill oneself. I think there is a difference between undergoing death and actually taking one's life. I think that self mutilation which would lead to death would be much closer to killing oneself than undergoing death from somebody else. That's my initial reaction to the question.

Bishop: Doctor Boyle, in the light of our discussions about the principle of double effect, could you just briefly outline the perceived weaknesses or difficulties with the principle of double effect that are giving rise to the proportionalists' theories? In other words, why doesn't it seem to be adequate, and in what areas doesn't it seem to be adequate?

Doctor Boyle: I think the main difficulties are the ones I already presented. A lot of people today don't see the importance of the distinction between what's intended and what's tolerated as a side effect. I think, theoretically, that is the most important thing. Because I think that, I spend most of my professional time working on this, trying to deal with just that issue. I also think the principle falls under the shadow of the criticism

324

that this is a bad sort of casuistry, just a way of getting people off the hook whereby you can get them off on some things but not on others. This arises out of some abuses. I think there are certain abuses plus a real theoretical difficulty with the distinction between what is intended and what is tolerated that are really at the heart of the objections. It seems to me that to give an honest presentation you ought to start with the objections as Aquinas does all the time in his articles in the *Summa*. That is what I was doing.

Part II — Discussion With Monsignor McHugh, Father Doyle and Mr. Brunelle

Bishop: If a couple are practicing NFP, how are they practicing the procreative aspect of their marriage contract?

Father Doyle: I believe it would be in their intentionality because the procreative dimension is a freely chosen dimension. The exercise of sexual intercourse can be procreative if it's within the context of NFP when it's done with a sense of responsibility to the relationship and to the children they already have. I would make the distinction between every act of intercourse actually tending toward reproduction and every act of intercourse being procreative in the sense that it expresses at least an openness to procreation. If the couple practice NFP and if the timing is wrong and a pregnancy occurs, they are open to life. They have not closed out the procreative meaning of their act and relationship.

Bishop: How do we educate and convince our people concerning the beautiful philosophy and theology of marriage which the Church has, as expressed by our speakers?

Father Doyle: I believe that one of the best ways of applying this theology would be in the teaching of the people in general from the pulpit and in schools where they are taught the Church's teaching. If we believe this doctrine, we should also have the courage to present it and not back down. Secondly, I would never underestimate the power of marriage preparation and discernment programs in dioceses.

I think that the crisis facing Catholic family life and marriage is the greatest single one that the Church has to deal with in this country, because of our materialism and so on. We are in a position perhaps not unlike that of St. Augustine and others when the early Church faced a culture that was completely alien with regard to marriage and family life as presented to us by the Gospels. At the time that Christianity came into existence, abortion was rampant in Rome, divorce was accepted, concubinage was accepted, prostitution, etc. Against these customs, our Church was able to succeed to a certain extent in inculcating our values of marriage and family life. The best example is the fact that the Church was able to bring about a realization that both man and woman had to be faithful to the marriage relationship, prior to that the man was not bound by fidelity. The man could go to a prostitute, as long as it wasn't someone else's wife. So today I would say marriage preparation programs and the presentation of our theology in an integral and a positive manner is a beautiful thing which can bring a tremendous amount of happiness down the road and even now, if it's accepted and worked at.

Mr. Brunelle: I would like to add that very concretely, the first step that we have to take is to raise the level of awareness with people in search of themselves. A great number of us are living at a very low level of self-awareness. Consumerism brought it about that we hardly know who we are anymore. Young people do not realize what is being impressed upon them as human beings; how they are being manipulated through everything they hear and see in the media. In raising their level of awareness, some of them come to realize that perhaps there is more to life than the vision of themselves as commodities. For example, a few years ago, Datsun had a commercial that claimed "You are driven." The educator's role is to take that slogan and say "Why can't we be in the driver's seat?" Do we have to be driven? The idea is to start with small examples which people encounter every day and, as pastoral agents, become convinced that people are coming from this type of culture and go on to raise the level of awareness of self and of the environment. In a marriage preparation structure, young people should be invited to discover even more the enriching reality of themselves, in order to view marriage as an enrichment process for the persons they are and the couple they desire to become.

Father Doyle: I was for a number of years in Tribunal work in Chicago and this changed my attitude toward marriage and the theology of marriage. I appreciated more than ever the insight that the greatest gift parents offer their children is loving each other. I came from parents who did, and I learned from their example. If you have a tribunal in your diocese there's a lot of information in that tribunal with regard to broken marriages, the autopsies that were done on defunct relationships and why they ended. Some of the insights which people have learned through the annulment process could be looked at practically and tied in with marriage preparation or discernment programs. Thus the program can be very realistic, not just pie in the sky with a lot of poetry. It must be realistic because the marriage commitment and what's going to happen after the wedding is profoundly important for the healthy life of the Church.

Monsignor McHugh: One of the things that should be done is the provision of positive presentations of the theology of marriage, conjugal love, and responsible parenthood in continuing education for priests. Since *Humanae Vitae,* the overwhelming amount of discussion has centered on pastoral approaches to meet particular needs of individual persons. But the positive presentation of the grand panorama, the total mosaic in which these concepts fit, has been largely neglected, overlooked, or set aside for the time being. That is the specific plea that John Paul II makes in *Familiaris Consortio,* urging that there be positive presentations of the total picture of the Church's teaching. We can rely upon priests to find ways to deal with hard cases, but if our whole pedagogy to priests is steeped in meeting the hard cases, then the more positive, the more ennobling, the more dignified approach to Christian marriage gets lost in the shuffle.

Bishop: Presuming that the process of in vitro fertilization is done with proper respect for a fertilized egg, and presuming the sperm has been acquired in the proper way and so forth, and, presuming this married couple have done all they can to give birth to a baby, does in vitro fertilization violate the moral inseparability of the unitive from the procreative aspects of marital relations? Is in vitro fertilization objectively sinful? If so, why, and how would you explain to someone like a television interviewer?

Monsignor McHugh: First of all, the Church opposes in vitro fertilization or test tube reproduction precisely because it separates the unitive from the procreative dimensions of the act. This is a problem for many Catholics because Catholic families and Catholic couples have been schooled to place so high a value on having children that, unfortunately, perhaps more than the rest of the population, they feel themselves deficient in their marital relationship if they do not procreate. We have never taught that, but that's the way people intuit our high value on childbearing. However, what we have to remember and recall to our couples or families is that the couple is to remain open to be co-creators with God. We as human beings don't have total dominance over procreation, it is a cooperative effort between the couple and God. Not simply between the couple themselves, but between the couple and God. If God in His providence does not deign to send children into a marriage or a family, that is not a sign of deficiency in the marital relationship, nor is it a negative judgment on a couple. Rather, it is part of God's overall design.

Just as some couples struggle with the tendency toward too frequent childbearing and the difficulty in establishing some order in their childbearing, so other couples struggle with the absence of childbearing. But if they have a solid understanding of the marital relationship and of the fact that Christ is present in their lives and in their marriage, regardless of the number of their children, then they can progress in holiness in that sacrament quite without childbearing. That does not minimize the hurt, but I think that, at the same time, if we school our people to a more enriched view of God's providence, they will be able to cope with the problem of no children just as others cope with the problem of possibly too frequent reproduction. We're just not in control of all these things. I know that television interviewers are not happy with that answer, and many of the viewers may not be either, but I don't think it's a harsh answer. We have to learn the way to phrase it in a positive way so that we don't come across as being heartless in our rendering of the answer.

Mr. Brunelle: Couples who have been told they cannot have children ought to get a second and even a third medical opinion on this matter. They should also be invited to get in touch with and to get help from an NFP Teacher Couple. I say this out of experience, having met medical doctors, one of whom is a specialist on infertility in a very large clinic, who knew nothing, for instance, about cervical mucus as a pre-ovulation indicator. Secondly, I would like to note that our society bears this contradiction, that on the one hand, the use of all kinds of contraceptives is being encouraged which often induces sterility, and, on the other hand, couples who have no children feel guilty about their situation. Contraception takes life away from love while in vitro techniques take love away from life. They are the two sides of the same anti-life coin of the contraceptive mentality. Just because there is an in vitro clinic in the block does not mean that you have to use its resources and that their manipulative technology is an enhancement of the person. Availability does not make technology ethical. Life transmission powers are a gift of God to be managed respectfully, not a right to be exercised according to one's choosing.

Bishop: There is a new procedure called low tubal ovum transfer (LTOT) in which the ova are transferred around the blockages in the fallopian tubes and fertilized through natural sexual intercourse. The main practitioner of this procedure seems to be in Dayton, OH. He is a doctor who was involved with in vitro fertilization some time ago, but came onto the staff of one of our Catholic hospitals and wanted to do in vitro. Through the help of the staff of the Pope John Center, he and the hospital personnel were informed about this new process which he is now pioneering. He believes that this process would take care of about 95% of the problems that are now dealt with through in vitro fertilization. Other information can be had from the Pope John Center.

Bishop: I had the privilege of being at a conference by the two Doctors Billings in London, Ontario, a few months ago. Dr. John Billings gave us an example of a couple who had been trying to have a baby for years and gone to all kinds of clinics. He maintained that the observation of the mucus discharge was very valid in this particular case, that the woman in question was only fertile for a few hours in each of her cycles. He told the woman that as soon as she felt the slippery mucus she should call her husband, no matter where he was, and have marital relations. She became pregnant! From that meeting too I received the greatest encouragement that I think I have had since I'm a Bishop in the joy of the 120 couples who were there, and in the positive approach to life and to the spiritual life of the two Doctors Billings. It was as good as a retreat to me, and I told them so. Despite that, I would like to raise the question whether many times in the presentation of natural family planning there is the impression given that the Church is joining forces with the anti-conception people?

Monsignor McHugh: I think that we all recognize the real inherent danger of couples being expert at natural family planning and thereby failing in their major responsibilities to their marriage and their family, that is, for selfish reasons or for non-substantial reasons choosing the path of avoiding childbearing or putting an end to their childbearing at a time in which under a more Christian investigation, they might go forward with another child. NFP couples are not in any way immune to the dangerous influences in our culture which denigrate childbearing. For practical purposes, in the United States and Canada the limit is two children per family. Cultural attitudes are pretty firmly set now, and there are few couples who think very much about going beyond having two children. In most of western Europe the effort is to stimulate people to have two children because the birth rate is so low. In any case, that is the reason for the emphasis on the Church's teaching on conjugal love and responsible parenthood.

It is the consideration of a commitment to these two values, conjugal love and responsible parenthood, that provides the balance and enables couples to make decisions in regard to childbearing, relatively free of the selfishness that would otherwise be forced upon them by the cultural attitudes in which we are all caught. This helps them to be generous in their childbearing and to go beyond two or maybe go beyond three children and, at the same time, it helps them face the real problems of having to delay or forestall a child for some months, some years, or perhaps even permanently. My point is that you can become technologically expert in the use of NFP, as you might in the use of a pill or any other artificial method of contraception, and be lacking the value orientation. It is precisely the challenge to this movement and to the Church to put natural family planning in the context of value commitments so as to raise the vision of married couples, to give them motivation and to help them see their childbearing, whether it is rapid or somewhat delayed at times, in the context of their responsibilities to God, to themselves, to their family and the society of which they are a part.

Mr. Brunelle: NFP is not merely a technique, a suppressor of our life-transmitting powers. We, as human beings, have the God-given capacity to transmit new life. This value orientation of a call to stewardship has to start early on in life. As an example, let me mention a Family Life Program being prepared for use in elementary schools and eventually up through high school in Edmonton, Alberta. How do you convey this positive vision of life-transmission to second graders? What is attempted in the awareness education to sexuality is to make youngsters proud of the fact that, as boys and girls, they are called to grow up to be men and women, and, as men and women, to become Mommies and Daddies. What an eight-year-old boy or girl is grasping is that parenthood is valued as an enhancing life-calling and life-style. As they grow up and become more aware of their growth in personhood, that vision is developed through various educational strategies.

However, if parenthood is hardly mentioned or if it is demeaned, then as couples' needs arise for family planning, they will readily downgrade their fertility powers and suppress their ability to transmit life. If later on they are made aware of the enrichment value of their life-transmitting powers, then their whole behavior patterns and attitudes have to be modified and that is very difficult. In this context deep modification is deemed impossible and even suggesting it is considered oppresive, not in keeping with today's situations. That is why educating to the vision should start very young. In our family, when our daughters had their first menstruation, the best gift we could think of for them was an ovulation chart along with an explanation of how to use it. This, we think, is a gesture that conveys our positive vision and the intrinsic value of our own life-transmitting powers.

Bishop: Monsignor McHugh, could you tell us how many dioceses are affiliated with your office of NFP here in the United States? Could you also tell us what are the most recent developments in NFP technique or method? Thirdly, what is the success rate of NFP, and how would that compare with artificial means?

Monsignor McHugh: There are 154 dioceses in the United States who have appointed someone as a diocesan coordinator for NFP programs. That's the preponderant number of dioceses in the United States. The only problem with that is that very often the person appointed already has ten jobs and this is the eleventh hat. I met with a number of couples from the Texas dioceses at lunch today. One of the things that they wanted me to tell the bishops was that to expand the programs also expands the need for resources.

With regard to new developments in techniques or methods, from reading the scientific literature I believe we know as much as we can reasonably expect to know about the methods of NFP right now. That does not mean there is no chance of future development or scientific breakthrough, but from all the research that has been done, and it is significant, we've learned about as much as we can about these two methods. There are a variety of methods, but they all boil down to either the ovulation or mucus method, on the one hand, and the symptothermal method, on the other hand. There isn't any significant scientific work going on right now. My own personal suspicion is that there is going to be a breakthrough from some other area of science that we haven't even thought about, that's the way medical breakthroughs generally come.

With regard to reliability, this is a little bit more nebulous and difficult to answer. First of all, it's very difficult to compare natural family planning which is essentially an educative technique and motivational effort, with a technological instrument like a condom or a pill or an IUD. However, the critical analysts of reliability find that natural family planning is as successful as the modern artificial methods of contraception if, first, it is well taught, and second, the people are motivated to stay with it. The underlying, non-negotiable, indispensable element is that it is well taught. This means that a couple has to go through a series of instructions, learn the techniques, test them out, have them checked a little bit over a period of about 6 months, 6 menstrual cycles. Generally they have it mastered at that point.

The second thing that we have found from our experiences in the dioceses is that, after the couples have mastered the techniques, at some future point they flag a little in their determination or their motivation and they look for a little extra support. We have come to understand that what they're looking for is not simply another rehash of the methods, but a supportive community that provides encouragement for the commitment that they have made. The NFP couples look for other couples of like mind, not only in terms of methods, but of their vision of marriage and family life. If those two elements come together, good teaching at the outset and supportive encouragement along the way, then we can expect couples using NFP to be as successful as couples using modern artificial methods of contraception.

Mr. Brunelle: FAMILY ACTION in Canada has correspondents in 42 of the 72 dioceses and I have visited 37 of them in the last year and a half. I agree with what Msgr. McHugh said regarding techniques, we have good ones, reliable ones. Of course, it is not only a question of techniques, but of couples getting to know themselves as couples and women getting to know their bodies and, thus, to know themselves as well. Male persons can learn about the dignity, intensity and significance of the ovarian cycle and its intrinsic value to female persons only if women know it well and have integrated it into their own lives. We have an on-going slogan which we use in our family. As humor changes occur and tempers flair due to a progesterone surge three or four days before menstruation, we all declare: "Here comes the progesterone!" This is an example of the sort of observations of our behavior in our relationships that are possible and very helpful when the ovarian cycle is observed and integrated into our lifestyles as a couple and even as a family.

I wish to add an observation with reference to surveys and statistics. We have to pay very close attention to the results of surveys and studies. We must be very attentive to phrases like "Certain studies say," and "Surveys tell us that" as they are often found in Planned Parenthood type material or in mass media comments. When the survey or the study is not identified or no details are given, then references are too often just pure claims. When we read statistics, and especially their interpretation, we have to inquire very carefully as to the objectives of the survey or study. Regarding the NFP field, we have to know whether the research was for mere efficiency. If the objective is pure birth control efficiency, the survey might be counting all pregnancies as failures, so that whether the couple wanted to have a child or not is irrelevant to that type of survey. This is how a lower efficiency rate or reliability rate is often attributed to NFP techniques, since in that type of research, any pregnancy is considered a birth control failure. As one of my friends says: "You know what statistics remind me of? They remind me of political prisoners; if you work them over properly, they will admit to just about anything!"

Bishop: The inclination in gatherings like this is to focus on negative aspects and problems with Church teaching. Monsignor McHugh, what are the hopeful signs about marriage and family life in the Christian era ahead of us?

Monsignor McHugh: My comments reflect predominantly my experience in the U.S., but not exclusively because I attended the 1980 Synod of Bishops and could see there a great deal of positive growth, both among the bishops and in the family movements in various parts of the world. In the last two years in which I have traveled around the U.S., I have been positively edified by the commitments and sacrifices that married couples have made in the NFP apostolate. They are largely a volunteer army, they are out there doing their teaching and encouraging others to practice NFP from a sense of dedication, a sense of understanding of Christian marriage and family life, a dedication to those ideals, a self-mastery of their own sexual drives and an ability to communicate that to others.

I have found that in many, many dioceses the leading people in the NFP movement, as indeed frequently in the family life movement, are lay couples. Those in the NFP movement are extremely well-trained and highly committed. Those dioceses who already have very strong family life movements have done well immediately in implementing the program for

334

NFP. They have almost intuitively sensed the importance and necessity of it.

In terms of an appetite or a desire for a better understanding of the Church's teaching on marriage and family life, that appears also in seminaries and among some theologians. I don't mean to characterize some theologians as good and some as bad; but for too long now some have been worried primarily about handling difficult problems. I now see a resurgence of interest in trying to address marriage and family life in a larger spectrum.

Last year we ran a meeting for NFP people from around the country in Washington. We were amazed at the number of people that came and spent four days there, and we never talked about the NFP methods. We talked about Christian marriage and family life, the dynamics of the family cycle, the inseparability of the two meanings of marital intercourse that Fr. Doyle addressed, and about *Familiaris Consortio* of Pope John Paul II.

I find among married couples a real interest in the Church's teaching and in the articulations of Pope John Paul II, not only in *Familiaris Consortio,* but in all his utterances about marriage and family life. Married couples seem to think, and I fully agree, that they have a champion in the present Pontiff. Not that they didn't have champions in previous Pontiffs, but this one is highly articulate, strongly convinced, and determined that he is going to speak in behalf of the values of Christian marriage and family life. To have that kind of leadership at the very top is a highly encouraging and motivational factor for those who want to follow.

EPILOGUE

His Eminence Joseph Cardinal Ratzinger

When I recall my reaction last September to the kind invitation of Archbishop Pilarczyk to attend this Bishops' workshop on moral theology, I can think of a number of reasons why I thought I should not come. Rome is not around the corner. I have plenty to do as it is. I have spent my academic life teaching dogmatic theology. There are others who could go instead of me. But the over-riding reason why I *did* come, and the real reason why all of you came, is to do what we can, together, to understand more clearly what bishops can and should do in this important field. I said in my opening talk that the critical question facing us, not only as Church, but even as a human society, is our moral response to the pressing problem of moral evil in its legion forms.

I spoke of the bishop as a witness to the moral life of the Church. He teaches, not what he himself has discovered, but what

337

the *Ecclesia catholica* continues to proclaim as the moral life of all who wish to follow Christ Jesus and acknowledge Him as Lord.

And what is a Lord? We say "Our Lord" so quickly that we forget that it is a title with a meaning, and not just a vestige of a passé medieval piety. To acknowledge Jesus as Lord, accepting His lordship over us, is to say, not only to Him, but to everyone we meet, that it is *He* and not we, who is guiding our lives, making the ultimate decisions which count, calling the shots. And when the Master returns, we should say to Him, "We have done no more than our duty."

Because we believe that the Church has her origins in the Lord, we believe that He, her living Lord, will never abandon her. He will never abandon her because He is not the hired hand. If He were, one might rightly guess that such a time as ours would be just the time for Him to leave. No, He is the Good Shepherd. This image, which the gospels love to use, is also an image which we can, in deep humility, apply to ourselves. We are, by the office of Bishop received at our episcopal ordination, called by the Lord Himself to be pastors for His flock.

The word "pastor," with biblical roots well into the Old Testament, is not simply the one who guides the sheep, or defends them from wolves, or finds them when they get lost: fundamentally, from the Latin word *pastor,* he is the one who nourishes his flock. He leads them to the place where they can be fed, and where their thirst can be quenched. For us, it is essential that we see ourselves as ministers of the Church specifically sent to nourish those entrusted to our care. In the area of moral teaching, what we teach must nourish our people. They must be able to consume, to take in what we teach. And so we have a real commitment to teach clearly, in words, and by our very lives, which the people will hear and see and understand. But most of all, what we teach must be good for them. The shepherd, the pastor, knows what is bad for his flock, where the food is that will help them grow, and where the weeds and the desert areas are which cannot nourish them. If he leads them there, they will not eat, they will not grow, they will not live. And the shepherd must do this constantly. If he is willing to do it only occasionally, say once or twice a month, by the time he returns, the sheep will have died of starvation.

But he must, *we* must, feed the sheep. It is not an option. It is an obligation. I might go so far as to say that, for us, it is an *exceptionless moral norm.* If we fail to do it, we are not pastors, we are not bishops. Feeding the sheep is our very identity.

As I was listening to the talks these past few days, the number of thoughts and reactions I have are too many for the short space of time I have tonight. I want to thank all of the speakers for their work. Every talk was clearly well prepared. On Tuesday, I thought it might be possible to say a few words about each talk, noting where I thought them helpful or where some more work needs to be done. But summarizing not only so *much* work, but so much *good* work, would surely not do justice to any of the talks. I was consoled by the fact that each of you have been taking notes all along, and probably have plenty to think about for a long time. But what is equally clear is that two underlying questions concern us all. The first is *dissent,* its various kinds and the question of whether, if ever, it can be justified. The second is the issue of *proportionalism,* and how, if at all, it is helpful to articulate the Church's teaching on moral issues. I decided to spend my time only on these two issues.

On Dissent

First of all, it seems to me that what has to be recognized is that *dissent* is a *decision.* It is the decision reached at the end of the process of human knowing. I stress this not only because dissent is the conclusion of a reflection, but also because we are, or should be, aware that all of our decisions have effects. I do not mean to focus on any reactions of the teaching authority which could be construed as punitive against the dissenter. I do want to focus on the fact that dissent is a free act of the person which involves him in the taking of an intellectual stand, with no claimable support from the enlightening Spirit of truth, but which nevertheless puts distance between the one who dissents and the ones who do not. Dissent is not a parlor game, it is serious business and should be recognized as such, not only by the Church, but also by the person who decides to take the dissenting position. Isolation of anyone in a community is a problem.

Personal Dissent

I would distinguish between the forms of dissent. The first is what we might call *personal dissent*. It occurs when the individual believer, for whatever motive, chooses not to agree with the teaching of the Church. It obviously needs to be noted that the seriousness of the dissent, and the degree of alienation which it causes, depends directly on the importance of the Magisterial position being disagreed *with*. If I deny the presence of the Lord in the Eucharist, I am more alienated from the Church than, say, if I think that the Church's solemn liturgical feast days should be different. Clearly, that does not *eo ipso* make the Church's solemn feasts unimportant or optional, but it does identify the difference between a basic tenet of faith and those decisions of a more prudential character.

Personal dissent is also qualified by the fact that the person who dissents may do so for any number of reasons, not all of them substantial. He may not have understood the statement. He may have misunderstood *another* statement which affects his understanding of *this* one. The causes of dissent in a person can even be of an entirely sentimental kind. He may, after all, not like his bishop!

But important for us is the fact that private, personal dissent is to be distinguished from the dissent of a teacher, or the dissent of a theological specialist. Alienation from the community, even in the private, personal form, has grave implications for the spiritual life of the individual. On the other hand, because it is an individual, it is limited. Such is not the case for the *teacher*. A person who teaches in the name of the Church is taking what is basically a personal dissent and exaggerating its importance and its damage by propagating it. But the particular grave damage here is not simply that he teaches his dissent, but that he teaches it in the name of the Church. It is odd that people who have grave misgivings about the right of the Church to exist in any institutional form, seem to have no problem with the contradiction implicit in teaching in a Catholic school, which, after all, is an institution. Integrity seems to me to require that the person who dissents *should not*, precisely because he *cannot*, teach in the name of the Church, or even give that impression.

Dissent of the Researcher

I would distinguish further, between the dissent of the *teacher* and the "dissent" of the *researcher*. Properly speaking, the researcher who is involved in a study which yields results which are in opposition, or appear to be, to the teaching of the Church, is making an assertion which even he maintains is tentative. If the scholar is dedicated to truth, he cannot on one hand, deny he thinks what he thinks; but on the other hand he will never claim to *know* what he merely *thinks.* Since dissent is always a decision, and is not just personal confusion, the apparent dissent of the researcher is not really dissent at all. There exist in the Church various forums for discussion and development of new positions. But discussion and development do *not,* of themselves, imply departure. An obvious dogmatic example would be the manner of how the Pope teaches. We have an obligation to discuss and deepen our understanding of the papal office. As the Spirit guides, we can improve. But we can not depart from the teaching.

To return to my point about the dissent of teachers, it is clear that when one teaches one is doing something different from research. If the teacher does not recognize that, there are many more than *one* reason why he should not be teaching in the first place.

The Council and Assent

As I said in my opening talk, the teaching of the Council on the levels of assent is very important for us here. *Lumen Gentium,* paragraph twenty-five, gives *three* criteria for deciding: the *character* of the document, the *frequency* of repetition of the teaching, and the *manner* of speaking. It is clear that the Church teaches in various form of seriousness. The decrees of a legitimate Council, papal definitions and encyclicals all differ and have a clear history· of development which must be considered if they are to be interpreted correctly. When the Church teaches something continually, that is more important than something she has taught only occasionally, or has ceased to emphasize at all. Finally, the document itself will reveal diverse manners of speaking within the same composition. Not every concept in a papal document of definition is being defined infallibly. It seems to me that this distinction will help a great deal. If I say that the position of the Church against artificial contraception has had a continuous history for the last fifty years, it simply *cannot* be maintained that it is a position of no consequence and less importance. Further, to make the observation that a particular statement is not infallible is not all that helpful, especially if the statement itself never pretended to be so. Just because a statement is not in the most solemn form possible, it is not rendered theologically insignificant to serious Catholic theological study.

Perhaps a word about the *sensus fidelium* would be in order here. I would distinguish between the *sensus fidei* and the *sensus fidelium*. The *fideles,* the faithful, are those who maintain the *sensus fidei.* The single most salient characteristic of the *sensus fidei* is its *catholicity.* Catholicity does not simply imply a *universality* of place and time, but also a *continuity* in the community of faith, which links the contemporary Church to the Apostolic Church, the community of the believers in Jesus of Nazareth. This continuity is a sign which is always clear: if, as St. Vincent of Lerins said in his famous dictum, a belief has been held *semper, ubique et ab omnibus,* then as we can see in light of *Lumen Gentium,* paragraph twenty-five, that teaching makes a compelling claim on my belief. What can be misunderstood by the *sensus fidelium* is that if a particular group of Catholics can be shown to dissent from the official teaching of the Church, some have said that this would then constitute a *locus theologicus* and justify a change in the teaching. This widespread dissent is usually shown today by means of statistics. Theologians cite percentages of people who disagree with *Humanae Vitae.* But what such percentages cannot show, and which they would *have* to show to be the real *sensus fidelium,* is that the faithful of *all* times and places have shared the same or a similar belief. Statistics cannot be used to take the vote of those who have already preceded us, marked with the sign of faith.

What I find all the more odd about this method of polling people who dissent, is that it is often used by those very theologians who organized the dissent in the first place. If a theologian succeeds in getting his opinion across to even a considerable number of people who happen to be Catholics, it does not yet follow that the argument which preceded the dissent is justified by that subsequent dissent. The widespread dissent is not a *proof* for the dissenting theologian, but it *may* be his *fault.*

On Proportionalism

One very general observation can be made at the outset to put this issue into context. The attempt to assess the proportion of the good or bad likely to proceed from a proposed action, is really a common-sense judgment we all make rather routinely. Even the principle of totality and the whole tradition of examining the circumstances of an act imply a notion of proportionality and, I think, with some effect. Proportionality, then, is not a *bad* thing to consider, but neither is it the *only* thing we must consider if we are sincere in our efforts to discern the goodness or badness of our actions. The problem with *Proportionalism* as a moral theological method seems to me to lie principally in its exclusivity. We must ask whether this is the *only* helpful tool at our disposal to arrive at a moral judgment.

When used exclusively, proportionalism ultimately rests upon a presupposition which we cannot accept. Proportionalism implies that what is *good* is not really good in *itself,* but is merely better. If masturbation and contraception were *only* physical or ontic or premoral acts, that is to say, without necessary involvement of the spiritual dimension of the agent, I doubt very much whether anyone would perform them. It is because the body and the soul of the person interpenetrate one another that the hypothesis of a purely physical act represents a false distinction. It is precisely because of the personal involvement, with its personal goals, and its personal effects, that masturbation and contraception cannot be seen as devoid of moral content in and of themselves.

There is, not surprisingly, broad consensus here: I know of no one who would not resent being treated like a thing. Things are things, and persons are different from things. To treat a person like a thing is as unjust as it is unrealistic. Since all moral questions have to do with persons, all moral theories should take the inseparability of the soul from the body into account. They should also take into account the fact that because it is only *people* who do actions describable as moral or immoral, all actions are automatically and immediately inseparable from the person who performs them. They cannot therefore be adequately described as merely ontic, since they always involve the person who performs them.

For a correct assessment of the morality of a human act, the person's three fundamental relationships in life must *all* be taken into account. He has a relationship with God, his neighbor and himself. The last relationship, with himself, is the mysterious fact that man develops and achieves self-realization and actuation only

343

insofar as he relates to the first two relationships with God and neighbor. Consequently, to exclude from our moral consideration the effects an action will have on *all three* relations, is *not* to recognize man in his fullness.

What any authentic Christian moral theology needs is a context in which it can be seen what the moral life is to which the Christian is called, not simply what the *immoral* life forbidden to him is. This context, I think, can best be described by the Biblical insight that morality for the Christian is conformity to Jesus. Entering into a relationship with Him, so as better to conform to Him, reconciles us to God and forgives our sins. To impede that relationship is to prevent that reconciliation.

Conclusion

A final general remark: One observation which I think is a fairly clear one and which can be honestly made with no implication of rancor, is that the theological community and the college of bishops itself has, since the Council, been subject to a considerable amount of polarization. This polarization, in fact, is implicit in the need we all felt to come to this special moral theology workshop in the first place. While it may *not* be accurately described as a *crisis,* it should be a cause of concern. Of course a certain amount of difference of opinion is not only a permanent quality of the theological enterprise, it can be a stimulating and productive thing. But if this polarization can be measured in degrees depending on how far from the Magisterium one side departs, then it is in danger of becoming a very unproductive, and in fact, corrosive thing.

The image of the pastor returns here and continues to be of help. The first epistle of Peter says, ". . . shepherd the flock of God among you, exercising your supervision not under compulsion but voluntarily, according to the will of God, not for sordid gain but eagerly, not lording it over those allotted to your care, but proving to be examples to the flock. And when the chief Shepherd appears, you will receive the unfading crown of glory." Here we have combined two notions — that of pastor and that of example. What the bishop does, and in fact how he does it, either nourishes and builds *up* the flock, or deprives it and scatters it.

344

The notion of unity is a key one here. A flock *is* a flock precisely because it is unified, not everyone wandering all over the countryside on his own. No, the shepherd clearly must be a cause of unity and an instrument to maintain that unity once it is achieved. Practically speaking, we must strive to moderate the polarization which can drive some members of the Church away. I do not mean to suggest some policy of sheer compromise which establishes some extrinsic and temporary unity, such as might be found in the negotiations of labor contracts.

The mind of the Church, the true *sensus fidei,* is epitomized in the prayer of Jesus Himself in the long discourse at the end of John's gospel: "Father, that they may be one, just as we are one. That they may be perfected in unity. That the world may know that it is you who sent me. That the love, with which you loved me, may be in them." I find it compelling that we can find broad consensus for ecumenical unity, that is, unity between the various denominations into which Christianity has been split. We can see the scandal, the evil involved in the fact that the Body of Christ has been divided. But should not that same fervent desire for unity between the Churches also result in a renewed appreciation for unity within the Catholic Church herself? This desire for unity is not simply a matter of intellectual agreement. It involves the unified desire of mind and heart, soul and body, which will not only result in a love for unity, but practical, concrete actions to bring it about.

It might be helpful to see the importance of the unity of the Church in an area different from the field of moral teaching, something less sensational, and if so, perhaps more enlightening. I am referring to the liturgy and the whole question of liturgical renewal. It seems to me to be obvious that the Church-wide reform of the Church's liturgical life would *never* have happened, *could* never have happened, were it not for the unified approach to this ecclesial need which was produced by the Council. The college of bishops in unity with the Pope, and with his wholehearted support, were able to reform and renew the liturgy *only* because of the prior ecclesial unity which is what we mean by *communio.*

It must be recognized as contradictory that one cannot seriously desire something for which one does not will the *means.* Ecumenical unity is doomed if, while seeking it, the Catholic Church becomes further divided. If we applaud the progress made in liturgical reform, we contradict ourselves if we do not simultaneously promote the unity which made it possible in the first place. I would like to conclude these partial remarks with the words again of First Peter: "Even if you should suffer for the sake of righteousness, you are blessed. Do not fear their intimidation and do not be troubled. Sanctify Christ as Lord in your hearts, always being ready to make a defense to everyone who asks you to give an account for the hope that is in you." It is the hope that is in us that has brought us all here. If we recognize this hope as the immense gift of the Spirit which it is, we will also realize that, having so much in common, nothing will seriously threaten the flock of Christ, whose pastors we are, by His grace and will. To Him, with the Father and Spirit, be glory now and forever. Amen.

Index

347

351

Quantification, 129; see: Calculation, Calculus
Quantitative, 7

Ramsey, Paul, 138, 144, 150-57, 161
Rape, 123, 158, 185, 234-35, 296, 312, 326
Ratified marriage, 276
Rationalism, 76, 108
Reason, 16, 19, 43, 142, 207, 263, see: Right reason, 186, 188
Reconciliation, 36-41, 101-02, 311, 349
Redemption, 33, 42, 98, 146, 148, 292
Reductionism, 70, 187
Reformation, 47-48, 138, 142, 146
Reformation of Church, 87
Reformation period, 158
Reformers, 48, 50, 53
Regan, Augustine, 232-33
Relativity, 73
Religion, 89, 91, 110, 177
Religious education, 99
Religious experience, 69-70, 73-74
Religious values, 294
Researcher, 340-41
Responsibility, 295, 311
Responsible family planning, 128, see: Responsible parenthood, 288-89, 291-92, 330
Revelation, 8-11, 32, 42-43, 107, 144, 146, 149, 209
Revisionism, 101, 125-27, 133, 193-94, 197
Rhythm, see: Calendar rhythm, Natural Family Planning
Roman Catholic Church, 68, 77, 112, see: Catholic Church
Roman Curia, 72
Romans, 34, 170, 203, 244
Rome, 66, 89, 337

Sacraments, 208, 290, 303
Sacred Congregation for the Doctrine of the Faith, 96, 108
St. Alphonsus Liguori, 109, 205, 223
St. Augustine, 9, 50, 54, 56, 149, 156, 319, 322, 326
St. John, 345
St. John the Baptist, 36
St. Matthew, 175
St. Nicholas of Flue, 92-93
St. Paul, 34, 38-39, 41, 50-51, 65, 98, 147, 160, 166-79, 202, 244, 246
St. Peter, 65, 344, 346
St. Thomas Aquinas, 91-92, 98, 112, 128-29, 146, 156, 196, 200, 217-27, 236, 245, 251, 258, 319-20, 322

St. Thomas More, 251
St. Vincent of Lerins, 342
Saints, 11, 19, 111, 140
Salaverri, J., 85
Salvation, 38-39, 98, 137, 155, 168-69, 319
Scandal, 109
Schleiermacher, F., 146
Schmitt-Noldin, 230
Scholastic manualists, 84
Scholastic period, 66
Scholastic point of view, 101
Scholastic theology, 47
Scholastics, 49-51, 143
Schüller, Bruno, 125
Science, 6, 106
Scientific theology, 22
Scriptural exegesis, 104
Scriptures, 41, 46-48, 53, 56, 73, 112, 147, 154, 171, 301; see: Bible
Secular humanism, 74-75
Self-control, 295
Self-defense, 185, 189, 245, 251, 253, 258, 319
Self-discipline, 295
Self-giving, 265, 270, 273, 275, 278
Self-mastery, 295, 334
Self-mutilation, 222, 324
Self-righteousness, 71-72, 153
Seminary, Seminaries, 102-03, 208, 307, 323, 335
Sensus fidei, 342, 345
Sensus fidelium, 342
Sermon on the Mount, 37, 39-41, 49, 55, 145, 147
Sex education, 297, 306
Sexism, 71, 137
Sexual act, 96-97
Sexual behavior, 168, 295, 307
Sexual differences, 268
Sexual ethics, 70, 96, 198, 281
Sexual intercourse, 124, 131, 133, 158, 184, 188, 190, 194-95, 234, 261-82, 294, 296-97, 325
Sexual love, 290
Sexual morality, 173, 202
Sexual politics, 71
Sexuality, 54, 96, 261-82, 287-311
Sheep, 338-39
Shepherd, 338, 344-45
Shivanandan, M., 295
Side effect, 245-58, 262, 304
Sin, 31-36, 51-52, 97-98, 100, 139, 142, 148-49, 154, 157, 159-60, 165, 234, 320; Sin against Holy spirit, 100-01; Serious sin, 98; see: Mortal sin, Venial sin

353

Situation ethics, 121, 145, 172, 196, 204
Sixth commandment, 96-97
Slavery, 10, 14
Sobriety, 43
Social behavior, 263, 280
Social injustice, 101
Social justice, 77
Social order, 77, 101, 147
Society, 262-63, 265, 273-74, 279, 291, 316, 329, 337
Soteriology, 35, 40, 159, 177
Spaemann, R., 14-15
Specialist, 5, 19
Specialization, 20
Spirit, see: Holy Spirit
Spiritual direction, 69-70, 108
Stanton, Elizabeth K., 108
Statistics, 342
Sterilization, 108, 185, 226, 233, 245-46, 315-17, 321-22
Stoics, 17
Straub, A., 85
Suarez, Francis, 48
Subject, 8
Subjective morality, 55, 64, 113
Subjective value, 177
Subjectivism, 314
Subjectivist, 133-34
Subjectivity, 8, 13, 207
Sublimation, 296
Suicide, 145, 320
Sullivan, F.A., 85
Summa Theologica of Aquinas, 91, 200, 218, 317
Summum bonum, 129-30, 133
Super-ego, 14
Support community for NFP, 333
Symptothermal, 332
Synod of Bishops, 1980, 294, 334

Tautological norms, 123-24
Teacher, 340
Teenagers, 306, 311
Teleologists, 184, 188, 191-92, 202, 204, 207-08; see: Proportionalists
Teleology, 128-29, 132
Telos, 128-29, 139
Temptation, 33, 89, 317
Theologians, 5, 13, 20-21, 48, 52, 66, 92, 103-04, 108, 112, 133, 146, 183, 191, 203, 209, 227, 340
Theology, 35-36, 71
Thielicke, Helmut, 143
Thing, 342
Thomas Aquinas, see: St. Thomas Aquinas
Thomas, G.F., 138, 146

Thomas More, see: St. Thomas More
Torah, 49-50
Totality, principle, 217-38, 314-22
Tradition, 11-12, 20, 32, 43, 46, 53, 74, 106, 125, 166, 169, 171, 243, 247, 255, 294, 319, 343
Transcendentalism, 108
Transplants, 229-33, 236, 314-15
Trent, Council of, 66
Tribunal, 327
Trinity, 51
Truman, Harry, 198-99
Truth, 54, 71, 75, 83, 88-89, 105, 112, 169-70, 172-73, 248, 250, 267, 341
Twerski, A., 295-96
Two Ways, 46

Unborn, 22, 250
Unitive aspects of intercourse, 261-82
Universality, 126
Urs von Balthasar, Hans, 88
Utilitarianism, 126, 128-30, 154, 159, 196-99, 258

Value, 43, 56, 75-76, 109, 113-14, 123, 125, 127, 130-32, 172, 193, 195-96, 201, 203, 255, 257-58, 263, 273, 293-95, 307
Vasectomy, 218, 224
Vatican I, Council of, 66
Vatican II, Council of, 22-23, 42, 48, 50, 66, 82-84, 87-88, 99, 102, 112-13, 209, 247, 249, 276, 289, 296, 308, 341, 344-45
Venial sin, 53, 55-56, 95-97, 142, 158, 257; see: Sin
Verantwortungsethik, 40, 100
Vermeersch, A., 224
Vincent of Lerins, see: St. Vincent of Lerins
Voluntarism, 101

Walzer, Michael, 153
War, 146, 150-151, 153, 190, 198, 201, 322
Well-being, 223
Will of God, 8-10, 12, 42, 47, 68, 70, 72, 139, 144, 171, 272, 344
William of Ockham, 47
Wisdom, 19, 48, 50, 54, 106, 156
Witness, 19-20, 22-23, 37, 50, 54, 105-06, 109, 111-12, 337
Woman, 266, 271-76, 279, 281, 326
Word of God, 51, 308

Yoder, J.H., 138, 146-47

Zalba, M., 109, 234-35, 316

354

Pope John Center Publications

The Pope John XXIII Medical-Moral Research and Education Center has dedicated itself to approaching current and emerging medical-moral issues from the perspective of Catholic teaching and the Judeo-Christian heritage. Previous publications of the Pope John Center include:

SEX AND GENDER, A Theological and Scientific Inquiry, edited by Mark F. Schwartz, Sc.D., Albert S. Moraczewski, O.P., Ph.D., James A. Monteleone, M.D., 1983, 420 pp., $19.95.

TECHNOLOGICAL POWERS AND THE PERSON, Nuclear Energy and Reproductive Technologies, (Proceedings of the Bishops' Workshop for 1983, Dallas), 520 pp., $15.95.

HANDBOOK ON CRITICAL SEXUAL ISSUES, edited by Donald G. McCarthy, Ph.D., and Edward J. Bayer, S.T.D., 1983, 230 pp., $9.95.

HANDBOOK ON CRITICAL LIFE ISSUES, edited by Donald G. McCarthy, Ph.D., and Edward J. Bayer, S.T.D., 1982, 230 pp., $9.95.

MORAL RESPONSIBILITY IN PROLONGING LIFE DECISIONS, edited by Donald G. McCarthy and Albert S. Moraczewski, O.P., 1982, 316 pp., $9.95.

HUMAN SEXUALITY AND PERSONHOOD, Proceedings of the Bishops' Workshop in Dallas, February, 1981, 254 pp., $9.95.

GENETIC COUNSELING, THE CHURCH AND THE LAW, edited by Albert S. Moraczewski, O.P., and Gary Atkinson, 1980, 259 pp., $9.95.

NEW TECHNOLOGIES OF BIRTH AND DEATH: Medical, Legal, and Moral Dimensions. A volume containing lectures presented by 9 scholars at the Workshop for Bishops in Dallas, January, 1980, 196 pp., $8.95.

A MORAL EVALUATION OF CONTRACEPTION AND STERILIZATION, A Dialogical Study, by Gary Atkinson and Albert S. Moraczewski, O.P., 1980, 115 pp., $4.95.

ARTFUL CHILDMAKING, Artificial Insemination in Catholic Teaching, by John C. Wakefield, 1978, 205 pp., $8.95.

AN ETHICAL EVALUATION OF FETAL EXPERIMENTATION, edited by Donald McCarthy and Albert S. Moraczewski, O.P., 1976, 137 pp., $8.95.

These books may be ordered from: The Pope John Center, 4455 Woodson Road, St. Louis, Missouri 63134. Telephone (314) 428-2424. Prepayment is encouraged. Please add $1.00 for shipping and handling for the first book ordered and 25¢ for each additional book.

Subscriptions to the Pope John Center monthly newsletter *Fthics and Medics,* may be sent to the same address, annual subscriptions are $12.00.